Jazz Musicians, 1945 to the Present

Jazz Musicians, 1945 to the Present

DAVID DICAIRE

McFarland & Company, Inc., Publishers

Jefferson, North Carolina, and London

Library of Congress Cataloguing-in-Publication Data

Dicaire, David, 1963–
    Jazz musicians, 1945 to the present / David Dicaire.
        p.   cm.
    Includes bibliographical references and index.

    ISBN 0-7864-2097-9 (softcover : 50# alkaline paper) ∞

    1. Jazz musicians—United States—Biography.   2. Jazz
singers—United States—Biography.   3. Jazz—History and
criticism.   I. Title.
ML394.D53   2006
781.65'5092273—dc22   2006003226

British Library cataloguing data are available

Cover photograph ©2005 Digital Vision

Manufactured in the United States of America

McFarland & Company, Inc., Publishers
    Box 611, Jefferson, North Carolina 28640
        www.mcfarlandpub.com

To Diz and Bird,
for their contributions
to modern music

Table of Contents

Introduction

From its very beginning, the nature of jazz has been to reinvent itself. Well before jazz's conception the various elements that would eventually serve as its foundation—blues, European music, voodoo ceremonies, the dances at Congo Square, and the brass bands that played at funerals, parades and celebrations—were constantly evolving. Even after the style had solidified into one coherent sound, changes continued.

The earliest form—the sassy brass band—eventually gave way to a more cosmopolitan jazz during the Roaring Twenties as the music was transported from New Orleans to the larger cities of Chicago, New York, Detroit, St. Louis and Los Angeles. By the end of the decade the emergence of soloists and more complex arrangements from the simple, blues oriented pieces of the past paved the way for the big band sound. The emphasis on swing brought the genre unprecedented popularity. But, during the Second World War, the shifting tides in jazz began to build once again.

It is difficult to measure the impact that the Second World War had on jazz. Before the advent of the war the genre was internationally known, but once the war ended, the music, like the country, was in disarray. Many jazz fans and artists had been drafted and some, like Glenn Miller, never returned. The recording ban between 1942 and 1944 also hurt the industry. New taxes on cabarets and dance halls forced owners to do business in a different way. The larger ensembles were scaled down into smaller combos.

The new style of jazz that would rise and eclipse all others had begun even as the big band stomp provided the soundtrack for the war generation. The radical departure would forever change not only traditional jazz, but the entire spectrum of modern music. Bebop, or bop as it became known, was a revolution of titanic proportions. By the end of the 1940s the camps were clearly divided between the traditionalists and the modernists.

The bop revolution, spearheaded by Charlie Parker, Dizzy Gillespie,

1

Bud Powell, Max Roach, Charlie Mingus, Miles Davis, Kenny Clarke and others, would take jazz to uncharted territories. The creation of cool jazz, hard bop, soul jazz, Latin jazz, free jazz, avant-garde, jazz-rock fusion, world fusion, contemporary funk, new age, third stream, and universalism were all direct or indirect outgrowths of the bop pool. That the music has continued to develop and evolve is a tribute to the power and individual creativity of its practitioners.

The groundwork for bebop was established before the Second World War. The big band style didn't suit the tastes of the young artists who craved a new direction. Many players began to explore and push the boundaries that bop pioneers Lester Young, Art Tatum, Coleman Hawkins, Jo Jones, Charlie Christian, and Jimmy Blanton had set down during the swing years. A new school of thought emerged that emphasized advanced harmonies, altered chords, and chord substitution. The recording ban from 1942 to 1944 allowed the inventors of bebop the time to refine their alternative ideas into a mature, cohesive sound.

Bebop, which sounded totally disconnected to many longtime jazz fans, was truly a reflection of the emerging face of crowded, noisy urban centers that were soon to dominate the country. The fractured sounds conveyed the emotions of a cross-section of the populace in the thriving metropolises, the affluent neighborhoods, the rising middle class suburbs, and especially the plight of the poor, inner-city African American.

Although bebop seemed like a radical departure from the big band sound, it wasn't that far removed. In each style the musical ideas were tossed back and forth among the players, except in bebop it was usually done in a smaller group that underlined greater improvisational techniques. This smaller setting encouraged the soloist to explore new musical territory.

Undoubtedly the major difference between the two styles was the rhythm section. In bop, the drummers—the heartbeat of any jazz group—concentrated on a quicker attack by riding the cymbals, freeing them from essential timekeeping duties to a position of challenging the soloists in the band. Bop moved much faster than swing or any type of jazz that had preceded it. The frantic pace seemed disjointed and cacophonous to the ears of big band and swing enthusiasts.

Another difference between the old school and the new school was the underlying fact that the masses could not dance to bop, unlike the earlier styles—particularly swing—which unseated jazz from its high perch among genres of popular music. Bebop and the newer styles of jazz were an acquired taste, and the public turned its attention to rhythm and blues, which would evolve a decade later into rock and roll.

Bop required an expansive mind. The music of Charlie Parker, Dizzy

Gillespie, Bud Powell, Thelonious Monk, Charles Mingus, Clifford Brown, Kenny Clarke, Max Roach, Fats Navarro and all of the other practitioners was not meant for mass audiences. It was a specific language with a specific code that alienated traditionalists and drew in music lovers who were curious, most of them young, a decade before the rock and roll explosion.

The bop revolution was an exciting time in jazz despite the many detractors who criticized the music. Legendary performers such as Charlie Parker and Dizzy Gillespie were the acknowledged leaders of the new movement. Almost fifty years after his death, Charlie "Yardbird" Parker is still immortalized. The jazz modernists and the new styles of music that they introduced became part of daily American life, and to this day they and their music remain an integral part of the culture.

Eventually, the new ideas of bop evolved and divided into two different camps: cool jazz and hard bop. Cool jazz was primarily a West Coast style that emphasized the swinging rhythms and bright melodies of the swing era coupled with bop's rushing harmonies. Hard bop was a harsher, bluesier version of bebop that keyed on darker, moodier themes. Many of the best cool jazz and hard bop players were graduates of the bop school—Miles Davis, Max Roach, Clifford Brown, Art Blakey, Dexter Gordon, J. J. Johnson, Charles Mingus and Thelonious Monk, among others.

In the 1950s, a new subculture emerged, dubbed "beatniks" by the press. They were antithetical to the mainstream during the bland, conformist Eisenhower years, when middle-class America established itself as the dominant cultural force in the country. The beatniks, with their dark clothing, love of poetry, bongo drums, bohemian lifestyle, and "anti-stance" to traditional values, embraced the new styles of jazz as the soundtrack of their generation. It was this group that heralded Charlie Parker as the new musical messiah and adopted the Gillespie look complete with goatee, French beret, horn-rimmed glasses, and cool, finger snapping attitude.

Throughout the 1950s jazz continued to reinvent itself, using bop as its point of departure, but also incorporating ideas that stretched as far back as the nineteenth century. The genre took on more fractured forms as musicians continued to push the boundaries that bebop had first challenged. The desire for freedom in improvisation sparked new styles that matured in the 1960s, including avant-garde and free jazz.

Although they shared some of the same qualities, including experimentation and improvisation, the two new styles also differed radically. Avant-garde jazz clung tenaciously to a sense of structure while at the same time exploring futuristic ideas. In free jazz, the only boundary was the limit of the musician's emotional depth and skill. It was the music of the present, a musical expression of the artist's personality, and personal struggle for total freedom.

There were two main geographic hubs for practitioners of free and avant-garde jazz. Interestingly, the same two cities that had helped spread the voice of jazz in the 1920s—Chicago and New York—served as the headquarters for the new sounds forty years later. In Chicago, the Association for the Advancement of Creative Musicians (AACM) was formed by Muhal Richard Abrams and included the Art Ensemble of Chicago. The main goal of the organization was to promote the experimental and free nature of musical expression—particularly jazz. In the 1980s, the Knitting Factory became New York's equivalent to the AACM and also promoted the self-expression of artists. The Knitting Factory eventually grew into a record label and recorded many of the avant-garde and free jazz players.

Fusion was another stream of experimental jazz that grew from the roots of bop. Like other styles, including blues, country, folk, R&B, and rock, jazz expanded its parameters to include different styles of music. The welding of jazz with electric instruments was a revolution that produced some of the most breathtaking music ever heard in the genre's long history. Miles Davis, a bop, hard bop, and cool jazz artist, sparked the style that produced an entire school of fusioneers.

Fusion demanded highly skilled players schooled not only in the history of jazz, but also in blues, rock, country and classical music. Because of the need for a wider range of thoughts and ideas, artists became scholars, many emerging from accredited institutions with degrees in musical theory. Comprising the new breed of jazz musicians were educated individuals who combined theory and practice in their music. Although the free form and avant-garde players were often better educated than musicians of previous generations, they did not sacrifice for musical theory the invaluable experiences of jamming in clubs, dressing rooms, street corners, halls, and basements.

Jazz fusion was interesting for many reasons. While it borrowed from other genres, it also influenced the very types of music that it incorporated into its style. Rock bands such as Chicago and Blood, Sweat & Tears added these elements to their basic sound. The Rolling Stones would add a horn section on their 1972 tour as a direct result of the popularity of the new trend. Blues bands featured more saxophones, trombones, and trumpets in their lineups. Groups like George Clinton's Funkadelic and Sly and the Family Stone—boasted driving horns with their funky rhythms.

By incorporating rock, blues and other musical styles into its form, jazz fusion brought itself more mainstream attention. The style possessed such an eclectic persona that it had a wider appreciation throughout the record buying market. The music was for everyone who liked rock, blues, jazz, and soul. In the past, where jazz musicians remained heroes within that realm, the newer artists became household names because of their ability to appeal to a cross-section of the record buying public.

Jazz fusion also introduced the music of distinct cultural flavors attracting a different set of players. Miroslav Vitous, Michael Gibbs, Billy Cobham, Philip Catherine, John McLaughlin, Brian Auger, Flora Purim, Jan Hammer, Joe Zawinul, Airto Moreira, Jean-Luc Ponty, and Gato Barbieri were all born outside of the United States. Although jazz had long boasted practitioners from every corner of the globe, the magnetism of jazz fusion seemed to draw an even greater number from the international community.

Jazz fusion also brought about the necessary changes of different instruments and the use of electric bass and keyboards in order to create the new sound. Jean-Luc Ponty, the violinist, wasn't the first to play the instrument in jazz, but he was the first to plug in. Ron Carter, Stanley Clarke and other bassists went electric, adding entirely different textures of sound. Keyboard players Herbie Hancock, Joe Zawinul, Chick Corea, and Keith Jarrett created new dimensions with their experimental flair.

Today, the term contemporary jazz comprises a diversity of styles: acid jazz, neo-traditionalism, third stream, and universal, as well as older variants like Dixieland, fusion, swing, big band, cool, bop, and bebop. The various styles reflect a fractured world in which the genre requires many faces to satisfy the needs of a multi-cultural population. While some fans of new traditional aren't impressed with acid jazz, each form has its supporters.

This book is dedicated to the jazz artists of the modern era and is divided into five different categories. The Bop Revolution traces the development and radical changes that occurred in the 1940s. The Hard Bop and Cool Jazz School section is a logical extension of the first part. The third section celebrates the avant-garde free jazz players who created their own musical universe. The fourth category champions the jazz fusion artists who proved that jazz could effectively be integrated and expanded with other styles. The fifth category is dedicated to the young lions, the new breed of musicians who carry on the tradition of more than a century.

It has been over a hundred years since Buddy Bolden ushered in the jazz age with his blaring trumpet. The metamorphosis that has occurred in the genre mirrors the many changes that have taken place in America and the world. But no matter what angle the music is perceived from, in the end it remains jazz.

PART ONE

The Bop Revolution

By the end of World War II the big band sound was waning. The war, the recording ban, and new taxes that forced the large outfits to pare down all spelled the end of an era. But even before the demise of the style, the seeds of change had already been planted and the jazz wind was blowing a different tune.

The major talents of the swing era had advanced far beyond the rigid boundaries of that style and inadvertently laid the foundation for a group of young, brash instrumentalists to reinvent the traditional jazz sounds of the day. The practical theory of advanced harmonies, altered chords, and chord substitutions sparked the imagination of the new breed.

At the beginning of the 1940s musicians in clubs, backrooms, and apartments all over New York City were experimenting with a different sense of melody and improvisation as well as a unique approach to rhythm. The emergence of bop would shock the purists and divide the jazz community into two opposing camps.

Overnight, an army of like-minded musicians bought into the ideas of bop and revolutionized jazz. The saxophone, which was considered nothing more than a novelty instrument at the turn of the century, was at the forefront of this musical revolution. While Charlie Parker was the definite leader, he blazed the path that Pepper Adams, Earl Bostic, Sonny Criss, Dexter Gordon, Wardell Gray, Johnny Griffin, Gigi Gryce, Sonny Rollins and Sonny Stitt all followed. Each was a very talented artist in their own right and added an individual element to bop that they created with burning passions.

Although Parker was heralded as the messiah of the modern jazz movement, the true theoretical genius of bop was Dizzy Gillespie. He was always quick to explain the theories of this new thing with a definite patience and enthusiasm to anyone who cared to listen. Although a great trumpeter, he wasn't the only one. Fats Navarro, Clifford Brown, Howard McGhee, and Miles Davis all made their mark with the instrument. In some ways, Davis surpassed Gillespie and Parker, his two mentors.

The furious tempo of jazz changed the method of every instrumentalist, as well as each singer. In an effort to keep up to the rapid pace of the music, vocalists began to scat sing. Although not a new technique— Louis Armstrong had utilized it in the 1920s—the style suited bop perfectly. But not all bebop singers were scatters. Because of her abundant talents, Sarah Vaughan could work in any medium. Other important singers of the period include Eddie Jefferson and King Pleasure. Frank Sinatra, who began his career with the big bands would also incorporate bop elements into his style. Ella Fitzgerald also started out in the big band/swing era but was a converted bebopper who took scat singing into an entirely new dimension. Unfortunately, many of the female singers of the big band era never did make the necessary adjustments and faded into nostalgia, like the style itself.

The piano, one of the cornerstones of any jazz style, was also approached differently. Bud Powell and Thelonious Monk, in an effort to keep up with Parker and Gillespie, made the piano go bop. Barry Harris, Hampton Hawes, Marian McPartland, Dodo Marmarosa, Red Garland, Tadd Dameron, and John Lewis were also noted pianists dedicated to the new style. Others like Oscar Peterson took the basic rudiments of bop and headed in an entirely different direction.

But of all the instruments, it was the approach to drums that underwent the greatest change. The shift from concentrating on the bass drum to riding the cymbals enabled Kenny Clarke, Max Roach and Art Blakey to revolutionize how people listened to jazz. Roach and Blakey would make their biggest impact in hard bop. Philly Joe Jones was another important bop drummer.

The emergence of Jimmy Blanton hinted at greater possibilities on the bass. Oscar Pettiford picked up on the nuances to become the first important bop player. Charles Mingus, Ray Brown, Cecil McBee and Red Mitchell followed suit. Of the foursome, it was Mingus who would emerge as the single most influential bassist of the modern era.

Although the guitar was not one of the key instruments in the bop revolution, it did play a solid role. Barney Kessel stands out as the leader, but Kenny Burrell, Bill DeArango and Herb Ellis all made invaluable contributions. Wes Montgomery began with bop and went on to carve out his own musical universe.

Some of the brass and reeds did not fit into the bop scheme. With the exception of Joe Marsala and Jimmy Hamilton, there were no prominent clarinetists that made a major impact. While the flute was never dominant in any era, it remained silent for some time, but made a strong comeback during the cool period. In modern jazz, on the trombone one name stands out above all others: J. J. Johnson. Not only could Johnson keep up with Diz, Bird and the rest, he reinvented how the instrument could be played, breaking from the tailgate method, and in the process wrote his own chapter in jazz history.

From the ashes of the big band/swing era rose a different kind of outfit, the bop band. Usually they consisted of small combos, but three leaders, Woody Herman, Stank Kenton and Claude Thornhill, all took a different path. Each played bop style jazz with a larger group and made it work. Of note, Dizzy Gillespie also led his own bop big band, proving to all detractors that his theories were valid and functional.

The following individuals are those who advanced the theories of bop, the instrumental pioneers in changing the shape of the music forever.

Kenny Clarke was the chief timekeeper of the bebop sessions that included Gillespie and Parker. He was also an innovator, taking his cue from Papa Jo Jones in shifting the emphasis from the bass drum to the high cymbals. Klook took it one step further and paved the way for every drummer that has come along in the past sixty years.

Dizzy Gillespie is one of the true giants of jazz. He boasts an extensive catalog, but more than any other player he shaped the way bebop players dressed, talked, walked, and acted.

Thelonious Monk combined a dark sense of humor with a wild imagination to create his own distinct sound. He was misunderstood but is a standout on the piano.

Charlie Parker, along with Dizzy Gillespie, was one of the key figures in bebop. His unmatched genius cast a shadow over the music scene for the next fifty years. He is considered the unquestionable messiah of the modern jazz movement.

Oscar Pettiford was the logical extension of the territory explored by Jimmy Blanton. He set the tone for all bass players that followed.

Barney Kessel was bop's main guitarist who jammed with Parker and Gillespie and had a long, distinguished career.

J. J. Johnson was the main exponent of the bop trombone and changed how the instrument was played after forty years of the same style.

Bud Powell was one of the prime architects of the bebop revolution and his ability to improvise on the fly allowed him to keep pace with Dizzy and Bird.

Sarah Vaughan's roots are in bebop. Although she would forge a long, illustrious career exploring other musical styles, she never totally moved away from bop.

Oscar Peterson's style defies true categorization. Bop was only part of his sound; he demonstrated what a talented musician could do with the basic elements.

Sonny Rollins was one of the many artists who embraced hard bop in the 1950s and 1960s, developing his own distinct sound on the tenor saxophone.

KENNY CLARKE (1914–1985)
Klook's Blues

With the advent of bop the entire musical structure of jazz as it had been played for the last sixty years was destined to change dramatically and forever. A different rhythm path was needed as a launching pad for the solo flights of Charlie "Bird" Parker, Dizzy Gillespie and others. The drummer now provided the key to freedom and the first stickman to recognize this duty gave the world his Klook's blues. His name was Kenny Clarke.

Kenny Clarke was born Kenneth Spearman Clarke on January 9, 1914, in Pittsburgh, Pennsylvania. Like so many other jazz artists he was from a musical family. His father was a trombonist and his brothers played a variety of instruments, including drums and bass. Clarke was surrounded by music from his earliest days and developed a keen interest in honing his skills on the vibes, piano, trombone, and drums while a schoolboy. Although Baby Dodds and Zutty Singleton were the biggest name drummers in jazz during his teenage years, Clarke adopted Jo Jones as his main hero. While Clarke was growing up in Pittsburgh, not far away another future bop percussionist who would attain much fame in jazz circles was making his way in the music business. His name was Art Blakey.

In his teens, Clarke gigged with Leroy Bradley's outfit in Pittsburgh. His first professional name band was with Roy Eldridge and it also included his brother Joe. Kenny furthered his musical education by joining the Jeter-Pillars outfit, in which he performed outside his hometown for the first time in his blossoming career. In 1935, he joined Lonnie Simmons's group and traveled to New York, where he first experimented with a new sound on drums.

Clarke continued his apprenticeship with the Edgar Hayes Big Band and stayed with it for a full year. It was during this period that he made his recording debut. Although he would eventually be a prime mover in the bop revolution, he was firmly a swing drummer at this point in his career. As a member of the Hayes band, Clarke was also able to tour England. He loved Europe, its people, and the culture. Years later after his legend had long been established in America, he would move permanently across the Atlantic. While overseas, he led his first recording session play-ing with a small combo.

Although he was an accomplished drummer, Clarke had not com-pleted his full musical education. He left the Hayes band and joined the Claude Hopkins Orchestra for short time before playing in Teddy Hill's Big Band from 1939 to 1941. It was in Hill's band that he befriended a young trumpeter named Dizzy Gillespie who shared Clarke's idea of playing a new kind of jazz. However, the leader of the group was unhappy with Klook's radical style and fired him.

In 1940, before Clarke found himself the leader of the house band at Minton's Playhouse in New York, he performed with Roy Eldridge and in Sidney Bechet's quartet. At Minton's, he was able to jam alongside the misunderstood genius pianist Thelonious Monk. While the band played swing and popular arrangements of the day, the music created after hours was something revolutionary. His old pal Dizzy and a young alto saxophon-ist from Kansas City named Charlie Parker often dropped by to jam. Monk would stick around and Clarke was the designated drummer for these all-night sessions.

Soon word spread around as other young musicians with radical ideas came by to investigate and sit in. They included two trumpeters, one from Illinois whose father was a dentist, and another from Key West, Florida. As well, there was the pianist right from New York City who could keep up with the wild alto player. After jamming for hours the musicians grew closer together. They all shared a new vision for a new kind of jazz; they felt like revolutionaries.

Dizzy Gillespie and Charlie Parker were the acknowledged leaders of the movement that would be dubbed bop, and later on bebop. But the trumpeter from Florida, Fats Navarro, the trumpeter from Illinois, Miles Davis, and the fire-wagon pianist from New York City, Bud Powell, would also be instrumental in the development of the new style.

In order to jam and keep up with all of these young musicians with fast-tempo ideas, Clarke was forced to change his style. Taking his cue from his idol, Jo Jones, Clarke rode the cymbal so the music could flow freely. Although his official stay at Minton's was short lived, he continued to drop by when it didn't conflict with his schedule. For the next couple of years he was often on the road with a variety of bands, including the outfits of Louis Armstrong, Benny Carter, Ella Fitzgerald (which included Dizzy Gillespie and from which they were both simultaneously fired) and with Red Allen in Chicago for an extended period.

After he left Red Allen, he formed his own group that included Ike Quebec and Coleman Hawkins. They played at various clubs including Kelley's Stable. A born leader, Clarke by this time had developed his bop style, although he hadn't reached his full maturity. A three-year military tour of duty interrupted his progress, but once he was discharged, he decided to throw his hat into the bebop ring full time. At this juncture the lines had clearly been drawn between the old school of jazz (the swing masters) and the new school of jazz (the bop generation).

Upon his return, Clarke joined Gillespie's big band, which played full-blown bop to interested audiences despite dissension from the old guard. Klook put a group together for a recording session, then joined pianist Tadd Dameron for a brief stint. The drummer returned to Gillespie's band in 1947 and joined the group on a tour overseas. While the others returned to America, he extended his stay and grew more enchanted with the European lifestyle. Clarke returned to the United States and worked with Dameron again, augmenting the latter's sextet. By this time the change in recording techniques allowed for the complete Clarke style to be captured. His extensive use of the cymbal was now prevalent both on the records he made with other groups and those he made leading his own outfit. Clarke's group included Milt Jackson, Kenny Durham, Billy Mitchell, Julius Watkins, and Joe Harris. He also played on Miles Davis's seminal *Birth of the Cool* album that signaled the beginning of the cool style of jazz, a form that blossomed in California during the 1950s. In 1952, seeking a more permanent working environment, Clarke helped found the Modern Jazz Quartet.

The Modern Jazz Quartet's pianist was John Lewis, whose roots ran deep with bebop pioneers Parker (who he recorded with) and Gillespie (who he arranged for). Member Milt "Bags" Jackson, the foremost exponent of the vibraphone (outside of Lionel Hampton), also had roots in bebop, playing in Dizzy's small combos and later recording with Thelonious Monk. Percy Heath, a bass player who had jammed with Parker, Gillespie, Navarro, and Monk, rounded out the group.

During Clarke's tenure in the Modern Jazz Quartet (1951–1955), the group, under the guidance of Lewis, attempted to meld swing with European musical forms. An experimental outfit, they endured much criticism because of their desire to play unconventional music. Their fusion of jazz with other musical styles was ahead of their time. The band's initial efforts paved the way for the jazz fusion of the 1970s.

Perhaps because he was not accustomed to the harsh criticism the band received or because the music the Modern Jazz Quartet was making did not suit his tastes, Clarke moved on to freelance work for a couple of years. He accumulated a long list of credits, including a stint as house drummer for the Savoy label and several albums under his own name. His musical talents were always very much in demand. Along with Max Roach, he had become one of the premier stylists. Hundreds of young, aspiring stickmen copied him. Clarke was of the generation infatuated with Europe, and with France in particular. He moved to France in 1956 and remained there for the rest of his life.

Once in France, it didn't take long for Clarke to find work. He was immediately invited to do studio sessions; he toured exclusively with some of the visiting American jazz giants and formed a group with two of his bop cohorts, Bud Powell and bass player Oscar Pettiford. They called themselves The Three Bosses and though the trio was short-lived (1959–1960), they played to enthusiastic crowds.

In 1961, Clarke found a steadier gig when he formed a group with Belgian pianist Francy Boland. It was called the Kenny Clarke–Francy Boland Big Band and it also included the tenor saxmen Johnny Griffin and Sahib Shihab, and trumpeter Idrees Sulieman. They recorded frequently and backed touring American jazzmen such as Louis Armstrong, Benny Carter, Sidney Bechet, and Coleman Hawkins, among others. When the group broke up in 1973, Clarke found plenty of work on the bandstand and as a teacher. He returned to the United States that same year to participate in a Duke Ellington fellowship program at Yale University.

Clarke, who had tasted European life on the few tours he had made while still living in America, adjusted very easily to life in Paris. He earned a very good living in Europe and even married a Dutch woman. He was an honored member of the French arts scene. Of all the jazz expatriates, he was the most successful.

He worked with the cream of European soloists and boasted a full touring schedule far into the 1970s, making a serious impact on jazz overseas. He also recorded on a regular basis, proving that he had not lost his edge. Eventually, in the 1980s, Clarke began to slow down because of age, but he could still drop explosive bombs on the snare drum that continued to amaze the audience and his fellow band mates. He hadn't abandoned the style that had helped revolutionize jazz.

Kenny Clarke, one of the genuine pioneers of the bop revolution, died on January 26, 1985, in Paris. He was 71 years old.

Kenny Clarke was more than just an innovator of bebop. He was also one of the most important drummers in the history of jazz. His stature in the genre's history is highly regarded even to this day. To keep up with the manic drive of Parker and Gillespie, the percussionist in those jam sessions had to change the style that had confined rhythm keepers for the last fifty years. Clarke did just that.

He was the bridge between the innovations of Papa Jo Jones and Max Roach. He took the use of the cymbals and high hat introduced by Jones one step further. Like all highly skilled drummers, he was forced to keep a solid rhythmic foundation with the other members of the rhythm section, but was also responsible for filling in the gaps created by the front line horn players. He managed to do all that and much more.

His flexibility was the key to his fame. He could propel the music along at reckless speed, matching the rest of the rhythm section note for note, or he could play cat and mouse with the soloists in the band, creating an opposite voice by providing blasts from his cymbals and snare drums. He was always more interested in making the music flow than counting beats. He added accents where he felt they were needed and his timing instincts were impeccable.

Like all other important jazz musicians, Clarke had a strong influence on a large contingent of the drumming fraternity. He paved the way for many of the later stylists who would make an impact in cool, free jazz, and avant-garde. A partial list of those whose sound he helped shape includes Beaver Harris, Louis Hayes, Elvin Jones, John Lewis, Max Roach, John Stevens, Ron Jefferson, Albert "Tootie" Heath, Larance Marable, Paul Motian, and Art Blakey. His sphere of influence also included rock drummers Ginger Baker, John Densmore, Carl Palmer, John Bonham, Charlie Watts, and Mitch Mitchell, to name a few.

Kenny Clarke was an ambassador of jazz and spent the last thirty years of his life in France. A spokesman for the bebop revolution, he was always keen on joining in any jam session and his participation in those late night musical adventures at Milton's Playhouse is the stuff of legend. He was an architect of the bop style along with Gillespie, Parker, Monk, Powell, Navarro, Davis, and others. His life story is that of a man who was at the right place at the right time with the right product. The quick stickman who could drive the music along at a frenetic pace will be forever remembered for his Klook's blues.

Discography

Bohemia after Dark, Savoy 0107.
Plays Andre Hodeir, POLYG 8345422.
Telefunken Blues, COLUM COCB-50314.
1946–1948, Melodie Jazz Classic B00005OW5Q.
The Golden Eight, Blue Note 4092.
Jazz Piano, MGM E-205.
Kenny Clarke All-Stars, Savoy 12006.
Kenny Clarke, Vol. 1, Savoy MG-15001.
Kenny Clarke, Vol. 2, Savoy MG-15003.
Telefunken Blues, Savoy 106.
Plenty for Kenny, Savoy MG-12007.
Septet, Savoy 12008.
The Trio, Savoy MG-12023.
Klook's Clique, Savoy 12083.
Kenny Clarke Meets the Detroit Jazzmen, Savoy 243.

When Lights Are Low, Philips 71312.
Kenny Clarke in Paris, Vol. 1, Disques Swing SW-8411.
Jazz Is Universal, Atlantic 1401.

WITH KENNY CLARKE–FRANCY BOLAND BAND

Handle with Care, Atlantic 1404.
Now Hear Our Meanin, CBS 62567.
Sax No End, Saba SB 15138.
Flirt and Dream, SABA SB15071.
All Smiles, SABA K.133, 453.
Faces, MPS 15218.
More Smiles, MPS BASFCRM 746.
All Blues, Saba MPS15288.
All Blues/Sax No End, Polygram 523525.
Fellini 712, SABA 15.220.
Three Latin Adventures: Latin Kaleidoscope/Fellini 712.
Live at Ronnie's, SES 12006.
Blue Flame, SABA 22910 6.
Red Hot, DC 22911.
White Heat, MPS 0068189.
Clarke-Boland Big Band en concert avec Europe 1,
Trema/Distrisound 6.
Clarke-Boland Big Band, Koch 2275990.
Calypso Blues in Sextet with Kenny Clarke, RW101.
Our Kind of Strauss, RW 106.

═══════════════

DIZZY GILLESPIE (1917–1993)
The Bop Catalyst

There were many important figures in the development of bop, including Charlie Parker, Thelonious Monk, Kenny Clarke, J. J. Johnson, Oscar Pettiford, Bud Powell, Fats Navarro and Clifford Brown. But in order for the new style to properly challenge the established sound and to gain respect, it needed a leader, someone able to explain the advanced musical theories of bop in a clear, concise manner. The responsibility rested on the shoulders of the man known as the bop catalyst: Dizzy Gillespie.

Dizzy Gillespie was born John Birks Gillespie on October 21, 1917, in Cheraw, South Carolina. He was the youngest of nine children and grew up poor. But one day Gillespie discovered the ticket out of his impoverished conditions when he caught "the Fever." Music offered one of the few opportunities and escapes from a lifetime of economic struggle.

Since there were no funds for lessons or new instruments, Gillespie taught himself how to play the trombone at the age of ten and then switched to trumpet when he was twelve. This streak of independence would serve him well throughout his career. Although he aspired to be a successful musician, he spent some time pursuing an education at Laurinburg Institute in North Carolina. An agricultural school, Laurinburg was not able to boast Gillespie as one of its graduated alumni. With the burning desire to blow his horn and follow in the footsteps of his idol, Roy Eldridge, Dizzy quit school and took his first step towards being a successful jazz artist.

By this time he had become proficient enough on the trumpet to earn a spot in Frankie Fairfax's band stationed in Philadelphia. A year later, after acquiring some much needed experience, he joined Teddy Hill's Orchestra. It was about this time in his career that he earned the nickname Dizzy—because of his infectious laughter and distinct personality—which would stick with him for the rest of his career. Jazz, which has contributed some of the most colorful characters to the history of music, counts Dizzy Gillespie as one of its most eccentric and unique individuals.

It was with the Teddy Hill Orchestra that Gillespie made his first recordings, most notably one called "King Porter Stomp." Although the song was light-years from the style of music that would make him famous, Dizzy had announced to the world that he was ready to conquer it. He also toured Europe with the band and the exposure gave him a taste for globetrotting.

Dizzy eventually left Teddy Hill's orchestra and drifted for a while, working as a hired trumpeter. Then in 1939, he secured a spot in Cab Calloway's Orchestra and remained there until 1941. This stint was important in his development as a musician and his growth can be traced to the many songs he cut with the famed bandleader, including "Pickin' the Cabbage." Gillespie, who had gained a reputation for clowning around, went a too far and as a result was fired from the band.

The following two years marked one of the darkest periods in Gillespie's career, lacking direction and focus. He drifted through a variety of bands led by Ella Fitzgerald, Coleman Hawkins, Benny Carter, Charlie Barnet, Fess Williams, Les Hite, Claude Hopkins, Lucky Millinder, and Duke Ellington for a brief spell. He recorded with Lucky Millinder. He also contributed arrangements to the bands of Benny Carter, Jimmy Dorsey and Woody Herman that were a blueprint for his ideas of a new jazz. Still, he remained frustrated with the progress of his musical career until he met a young saxophone genius from Kansas City named Charlie Parker.

Perhaps it was more than fate that Parker and Gillespie would meet and exchange musical ideas, since they both craved a more exciting direction as well as a sympathetic ear to validate their creative ideas. The two future legends began to jam together after hours at Minton's Playhouse and Monroe's Uptown House. Like chemists in a lab concocting a new substance, the two worked on their vision for a different kind of jazz that would challenge the established school.

The pair was given a chance to give their new music a dry run when they joined Earl Hines's big band. With Parker on tenor saxophone and Dizzy on trumpet, they planted the seeds for the bop revolution. Although their ideas didn't make the immediate and powerful impact they had hoped it would, they knew they were on the right track. Some time later the pair joined Billy Eckstine's new bop big band. The ensemble also featured a young vocalist named Sarah Vaughan. Dizzy recorded a few songs with Eckstine, but it was the sessions with Coleman Hawkins that really fueled the bop revolution.

In 1945, it all came together beautifully. Once the two-year strike by the musicians' union was over, freedom rang throughout the jazz world again. Dizzy and Parker took full advantage of the situation by teaming up to deliver their musical ideas through recordings. The debut of such numbers as "Salt Peanuts," "Shaw 'Nuff," "Groovin' High," and "Hot House" made many jazz fans stand up and take notice. The music was frantic and exciting. The old big band style sounded stale and outdated in comparison. The momentum for the new music was building.

After an unsuccessful attempt at forming his own big band, Gillespie, along with Parker, traveled to the West Coast to plant the seeds of bebop there. They found work rather quickly and spent a long time at Billy Berg's club in Los Angeles. But the City of Angels was not as receptive to the new music as Dizzy had hoped it would be and he returned to New York. Parker remained behind.

A year later Dizzy once again attempted to form a big band to play bebop, something that everyone thought impossible. This time the results were quite different. For the next four years, his group was the breeding ground for the new music. Gillespie's group featured many of the most important young musicians to nurture the bop style, including Milt Jackson, John Lewis, Ray Brown, Kenny Clarke, James Moody, J.J. Johnson, Yusef Lateef and a young John Coltrane.

It was during this period—the late 1940s and early 1950s—that the Gillespie legend was born. His music was the coolest sound around and emulated by all the young hip cats aspiring to be big names in jazz. He also cut a recognizable figure with his colorful berets, trimmed goatee, and bop glasses. The beatniks that claimed bop as the soundtrack of their generation adopted the Dizzy look.

In 1950, Gillespie broke up his trendsetting orchestra, but remained very active in music. Anytime he and Parker reunited it was an event, including the concert at Massey Hall in 1953. By this point in his career Dizzy could dictate his performance schedule. He participated in worthwhile projects like the Jazz at the Philharmonic tour. He also led all-star recording sessions that included Stan Getz, Sonny Rollins, and Sonny Stitt on various dates.

Gillespie's star status in the music world was such that in 1956 the State Department asked him to form a big band to spread the gospel of jazz all over the world. The tour took him and his aggregation to the Far East, Europe, and South America. During the two-year tenure of the group a variety of sidemen passed through, including Lee Morgan, Joe Gordon, Melba Liston, Al Grey, Billy Mitchell, Benny Golson, Ernie Henry and Wynton Kelly. They grooved on arrangements provided by Golson, Liston, and Quincy Jones, as well as Dizzy's first-rate material.

In 1958, Gillespie returned to leading small groups that featured some of the best young talent in jazz. Junior Mance, Leo Wright, Lalo Schifrin, James Moody and Kenny Barron are just a few that learned from the master. Despite the evolution of bop into different fragmented styles, Dizzy remained in the spotlight. He cut a recognizable figure with his bent trumpet, puffed cheeks that made him look like a bullfrog, and colorful beret. He was one of jazz's biggest stars and by this time was acknowledged as one of the elder statesman of the music that he played with such pride and distinction.

Throughout the 1960s he could be found either in the recording studio adding to his lengthy discography, heading an assembled all-star big band, and jamming at some jazz festival with anyone who dared share the stage with him. At many of these festivals Gillespie was the main drawing card; people flocked to the venues to witness the legend. Unlike other bop pioneers whose popularity waned, Dizzy remained relevant.

As the decade of the 1970s unfolded, Gillespie had spent more than half of his life in music. Now in his 50s, his sharp, frenetic playing sadly began to deteriorate. For the rest of his career he continued to record and perform around the world but his work was erratic. Despite the erosion of his musical skills, he was still regarded by all the young players as a fountainhead of jazz. Perhaps his last great adventure was as leader of the United Nations Orchestra that featured Paquito D'Rivera and Arturo Sandoval.

On Jan. 6, 1993, jazz fans and the entire music world were saddened with the passing of Dizzy Gillespie in Englewood, New Jersey. He was seventy-five years old.

Dizzy Gillespie was one of the most vital jazz musicians throughout the genre's long and colorful history. He made many, many contributions to the genre. He excelled in every facet, as a musician, bandleader, arranger, songwriter, architect of new musical directions, assimilator of different textures to his jazz structure, and ambassador for the music he loved so much. He covered an enormous amount of territory during his long, distinguished career.

Arguably, he was one of the greatest trumpet players, if not the greatest of all time. His understanding of complex jazz chords, harmony, and rhythmic textures had a breadth and depth all its own. He was blessed with incredible technique. He was nearly impossible to imitate. Many of the young trumpeters eager to play the new bop music found it very difficult to adapt to Gillespie's style. Instead they copied Fats Navarro or Miles Davis.

Perhaps it was the blinding speed or imaginative improvisations that intimidated all those eager to emulate him. Or, perhaps it was his ability to slide from the highest note to the lowest and make it all fit together in one neat package like a very intricate puzzle. Surely, his facility in mixing recognizable notes with slurred ones proved too challenging for many Gillespie wannabes. Also, the ease with which he could spontaneously create new, intricate chords baffled many listeners, including his partner, Charlie Parker.

But it was his ability to make the strange notes and chords sound fresh and exciting that remained his true calling card. He coaxed unique music from his trumpet that sounded as if he was on a different planet playing alien compositions tuned to please earthlings. Undoubtedly, Gillespie changed the manner of playing the trumpet forever.

He also used rich and varied rhythmic textures, most notably those of Afro-Cuban and Latin origins. The inclusion of the noted Cuban percussionist Chano Pozo in his band in 1947 revolutionized the basic rhythmic structures of jazz. Although there had been a longtime Cuban and Latin influence in jazz, Gillespie was the first one to truly tap into this rich vein. His ability to fuse his new ideas with the advanced polyrhythms laid down the foundation for the jazz fusion that would occur in the 1960s and 1970s.

Although the old guard initially rejected his new ideas, Gillespie eventually shifted everyone to his point of view. After all, the essence of jazz had always been improvisation and Dizzy simply put a new spin on tired phrases. Jimmy Dorsey and Woody Herman were just two of the many bandleaders who bought some of Dizzy's arrangements.

There is another aspect of Gillespie's career that must never be overlooked, and that is his musical union with Yardbird Parker. The combination of the two turned the jazz world upside down. No one had ever heard of two horn players creating the dimension of sound that they were able to coax from their individual instruments. Although the partnership did not last for a long time, its impact reverberates even today.

But despite the camaraderie between the two, there were stark differences. Whereas Parker was surly, unapproachable, and moody, Gillespie was friendly and enthusiastic with a sunny disposition. They were both brilliant musicians—Bird the master of the alto saxophone and Dizzy the master of the trumpet—but the latter's understanding of the new music went deeper than that of his good friend. As well, Dizzy wrote down all of his arrangements and was constantly eager to show the new generation how to bop. Bird never wrote anything down and, therefore, unlike Dizzy, was not responsible for making sure the tradition was carried on in a scholarly way.

Gillespie was a formidable bandleader. Although his group broke up in 1945, he reassembled it and proved to all detractors that one could play bebop within a big band setup. A well-respected individual, he gave many musicians their first big break, including a young John Coltrane. His ability to draw different players of various backgrounds into one cohesive unit ranks him with the best of the bandmasters: Duke Ellington, Count Basie, Benny Goodman, Jimmie Lunceford, Artie Shaw, Harry James, Chick Webb, Lionel Hampton, Miles Davis, Stan Getz, Woody Herman, Glenn Miller and the Dorsey brothers.

It was Gillespie more than any bop architect who not only championed the new music, but also defined the image with his goatee, horn-rim glasses, and beret. It became the uniform of rebellion that was adopted by all the hip cats. The image of Dizzy's puffed cheeks and bent trumpet are as synonymous with jazz as Louis Armstrong's round, moon shaped face.

Gillespie was one of the great ambassadors of jazz; he was always eager to pose for a picture, shake hands, and take time out to explain the new music. He was known throughout the music world as a genius, someone who was friendly and transcended the lines of different styles. He also delivered the blues to many different countries around the world, including Asia, Europe, Latin America, South America and Australia.

Like all other jazz giants Dizzy Gillespie was a pure individual, and it was this individualism that allowed him to stretch the boundaries of jazz beyond the imagination of anyone before him. He is remembered for many reasons, particularly his originality, but perhaps most important was his ability to overcome all obstacles and to remain the bop catalyst.

Discography

Vol. 1, 1937–1940, Masters of Jazz 31.
Vol. 2, 1940–1941, Masters of Jazz 41.
Vol. 3, 1941–1942, Masters of Jazz 45.
Vol. 4, 1943–1944, Masters of Jazz 86.
Vol. 5, 1945, Masters of Jazz 110.

Vol. 9, 1946–1947, Masters of Jazz 149.
Shaw 'Nuff 1945–1946, DSR 53.
Dizzy In Paris 1952, EMBR 841.
1945, Classics 888.
1945–1946, Classics 935.
1946–1947, Classics 986.
1947–1949, Classics 1102.
His Best Recordings 1937–1947, Best of Jazz 4064.
The Complete RCA Victor Recordings 1947–1949, Bluebird 66528.
1940–1946, EPM 158812.
Birk's Works: The Verve Big-Band Sessions 1956–1957, Verve 527900.
Dizzy Gillespie & His Orchestra 1946–1948, EPM 159552.
Dizzy Gillespie & The Legendary Big Band Live 1946, BSTA 1534.
Gillespie/Rollins/Stitt, Sonny Side Up—Verve Master Edition 1957, Verve 521426.
The Bop Sessions, Gazell 1005.
The Complete RCA Victor Recordings 1937–1949, RCA Records 66528.
Compact Discs 1937–1947, Best Of Jazz 4064.
A Dizzy Retrospective, Caroline 840.
Absolutely the Best, Fuel 2000 Records 061 086.
An Electrifying, Verve 557 544.
At Newport, Verve 513 754.
Bahiana, Pablo Records 2625–708.
Battle of the Horn, SOMET TOCJ-8013.
Be Bop, Laserlight 17126.
Bebop Enters Sweden 1947–49, Dragon 318.
Best of Dizzy Gillespie, Pablo Records 2405–411.
Bird Songs: The Final Recordings, Telarc Jazz Zone 83421.
Blue Moon, Columbia River Entertainment Group 120000.
Champ, Columbia COCB-50296.
Closer to the Source, Atlantic 7567807762.
Digital at Montreux, 1980, Original Jazz Classics 882.
Dizzier and Dizzier, VICTOR JAZZ/RCA VICTOR 68517.
Dizzy Atmosphere, Drive Archive 42011.
Dizzy Gillespie & Modern Trumpets, DIAL TOCJ-6207.
Dizzy Gillespie 1946–49, RCA ND89763
Dizzy for President, KnitClassics 3001.
Dizzy Gillespie and His Big Band, GNP/Crescendo 23.
Dizzy Gillespie Story, Savoy 0177.
Dizzy Gillespie: Jazz Collection, Laserlight 36011.
Dizzy in Paris, Ember 841.
Dizzy in South America, 1956, Vol. 1, Consolidated Artists Productions 933.
Dizzy in South America, 1956, Vol. 2, Consolidated Artists Productions 934.
Dizzy's Diamonds: The Best of Verve Years, Verve 513875.
Dizzy's Party, Original Jazz Classics 823.
Free Ride, Original Jazz Classics 784.
Giants/Portrait of Jenny, Collectables 5616.
Gillespiana/Carnegie Hall Concert, Verve 519 809.
Greatest Hits, VICTOR JAZZ/RCA VICTOR 68499.
Groovin' High, Band Stand 1513.
Groovin' High, Drive Archive 41018.

Groovin' High, Indigo (UK) 2068.
Groovin' High, Jazz Hour 73550.
Groovin' High, Prism Entertainment 514.
Groovin' High, Savoy 78814.
Groovin' High, Savoy 0152.
Jambo Caribe, Verve 557 492.
Jazz After Dark: Great Songs, Public Music 8009.
Jazz From Paris/Diz & Strings, VERVE POCJ-2646.
Le Jazz De A–Z, BMG 74321247532.
Les Incontournables, TELDE 630158402.
Live 1946, BandStand 1534.
Live at the Royal, BBC Music 7002.
Live, Chester, Pennsylvania, June 14, 1957, Storyville 2040.
Manteca, POLY POCJ-2772.
Melody Lingers On, POLYG PHCE-6014.
Musician-Composer-Raconteur, Pablo Records 116.
Night and Day, Collector's Edition 22.
Night and Day, Magnum Collectors 9.
Night in Tunisia, Early Bird 1007.
Night in Tunisia 1945–1950, Giants of Jazz Recordings 53314.
Oo Bop, Tradition/Rykodisc 1027.
Paris Jazz Concert, Malaco 1201.
Paris Jazz Concert 1960, Malaco 1205.
Perceptions, Verve 537 748.
Planet Jazz, BMG 74321520692.
Plays in Paris, BMG 74321409402.
Plays in Paris, RCA Victor 40940.
Pleyel Jazz Concert 1953, RCA Victor 40939.
Professor Bop, Le Jazz 25.
School Days, Savoy 0157.
Shaw 'Nuff, Musicraft 53.
Something Old, Something New, Verve 558 079.
Soul Time, Jazz Time Records 8153.
Sweet Soul Live, Master Tone Records 8991.
Swing Low, Sweet Cadillac, Impulse! 178.
Talkin' Verve, Verve 533 846.
The Bop Sessions, Gazell 1005.
The Champ, Savoy 78815.
The Champ, Savoy 0170.
The Complete RCA Victor Recordings 1937–1949, RCA Records 66528.
The Cool World/Dizzy Goes Hollywood, Verve 531 230.
The Quintessence: New York–Chicago 1940–1947, Fremeaux 224.
The Rhythm Man, Magnum 022.
To Bird with Love, Telarc 83316.
To Diz with Love: The Diamond Jubilee, Telarc 83307.
Triple Play: Dizzy, Telarc Jazz Zone 83451.
Ultimate Dizzy Gillespie, Verve 557 535.

THELONIOUS MONK (1917–1982)
Epistrophy Blues

Many of the modern jazz artists were able to forge a new sound by combining elements of the past with their own brilliant ideas. In the process they expanded the parameters of traditional jazz and paved the way for future experiments. One of these figures was able to harness the energy of the bebop revolutionists with the swing of the traditionalists to create his distinct epistrophy blues. His name was Thelonious Monk.

Thelonious Sphere Monk was born October 10, 1917, in Rocky Mount, North Carolina. He moved to New York City when a youngster and started his musical career playing the piano before his tenth birthday. Although initially influenced by James P. Johnson, almost from the very beginning Monk was not interested in the music that surrounded him but more in creating his own universe with its own logic, rules, and fun.

He played at various local gigs but was constantly evolving his style and because of his different approach to the piano, it was hard for him to find steady work. He played music that made perfect sense to him, but was often thought of as weird and chaotic by other musicians; that is, until he met Kenny Clarke. The drummer from Pittsburgh and Monk became part of the house band at Minton's Playhouse in New York. While they played standards during their time on the bandstand, it was the late night jams that proved to be more interesting. They met other young kindred spirits like Dizzy Gillespie, Charlie Parker, and Bud Powell, who were keen on reinventing traditional jazz ideas.

After leaving Minton's Playhouse, Monk worked with Lucky Millinder and Cootie Williams. As a sideman in these bands he received very little positive attention. But with Coleman Hawkins, Monk seemed to hit his stride, as the elder statesman was one of the few ears sympathetic to the musical universe that the pianist was trying to create. He made his recording debut with Hawkins and the few sides demonstrated a genius that was somewhere between Ludwig van Beethoven and Art Tatum.

However, the ensuing years were lean ones for Monk; it was simply a case of him being ahead of his time. His creative pieces that were shunned by critics and audiences foreshadowed the future movements of hard bop and free jazz. In the next few years, he recorded sporadically and scarcely performed live. Few understood Monk, a genuine original who was labeled by many as too spaced out to work with. As a result he was forced to find employment outside the music business in order to survive.

His career received an important boost in 1955 when he was signed to the Riverside label and recorded an album that instead of alienating fans and critics, captured their imaginations. But more importantly, by this time his musical style didn't sound so revolutionary. Other artists that had emerged from the bebop talent pool were now expected to do their own thing, a formula Monk had been following all along. Suddenly he was praised for his originality instead of scorned for his distinct sound.

Monk, who had once found it extremely difficult to secure the odd gig, was booked at the famous Five Spot club. This performance was much different from others because his quartet featured a young tenor saxophonist named John Coltrane. After the death of Charlie Parker, the jazz world had been looking for the *next one*. Coltrane ended that search.

Although the Monk-Coltrane relationship didn't last long, it was enough to propel the moody pianist into the forefront of the jazz world. Monk took full advantage of the situation and began to spin his magic. He replaced Coltrane with Johnny Griffin and soon developed the grand reputation of someone with a keen eye for young talent. It only enhanced his increasing popularity.

Suddenly he was much in demand and he traveled with his group all over the country playing his own thing. One of his best performances was at Town Hall. Monk, with his personalized code of dress, his totally unique piano style, and dynamic group, was a huge hit. At one time during the lean years it seemed that no one wanted to work with him because of his idiosyncrasies; then overnight everyone wanted to share in his creativity.

Throughout the latter part of the 1950s and all of the 1960s, he was one of the major forces in jazz. Although the personnel in his group would change (he added tenorman Charlie Rouse to replace the departed Griffin), Monk rolled on. He received a handsome record deal from Columbia, and constantly toured the country as well as Europe. He was creating dynamic music and each successive album was greatly anticipated by jazz fans and critics.

As the 1970s beckoned, he could look back on his previous decade with great satisfaction, as he had emerged as one of the true leaders in contemporary jazz. In the process he had become a living legend. He augmented his stature by participating in the *Giants of Jazz* recording in the early seventies. But Monk, always an unpredictable character who lived in his own universe, quit the music business in 1973.

It was reported that the great piano genius had suffered a mental breakdown. Never again would he tour or record on a regular basis. Although he did make a few well-received appearances, he lived like a recluse for the remainder of his life. He refused all visitors and retreated further into his own dark realm. Despite his departure from the real world, he remained an idol to a generation of jazz musicians.

After almost a decade of near constant seclusion, Thelonious Monk, the introverted piano genius, died on February 17, 1982, in Weehawken, New Jersey.

Thelonious Monk was a unique jazz artist in a genre that breeds originality. He developed his own piano style that was misunderstood by all for many years because it so deviated from the norm. But once he was accepted, he recorded an enormous wealth of material that has since been dissected, discussed, and admired for over twenty years. To this day his influence continues to be felt and his work revered.

Monk was his own piano player. He sought the other side of the instrument's capabilities and wasn't interested in following the established paths of Art Tatum, Earl Hines or any of the stride and boogie-woogie pianists. Although Duke Ellington and Teddy Wilson influenced him, one can argue that those two pianists developed their own style to suit their own musical visions. If there is one completely original piano player in jazz, it was Monk. He even differed greatly from Bud Powell, his fellow bop pianist.

Monk incorporated killer fractured chord combinations and perverse melodies into his playing. His fertile imagination and obscure humorous side gave his music an unearthly feeling. He achieved more with less. He left open spaces in his playing and could create a complete mood with a few sparse notes. His style was uncluttered and he used the other accompanying instruments to create musical dots that required the audience to connect them to complete the song in their minds.

Perhaps the most incredible fact about Monk's music was its multiplicity. Although he was an original bop artist, his music was so rich that it has appealed to different generations of stylists for obvious reasons. The hard boppers believed his music was that of a messiah. The free jazz/avant-garde movement embraced him like a long lost brother. The contemporary school heralded him as one of its godfathers.

Monk's creations stretched the borders of the genre to such extremes that more than twenty years after his death the debate of whether or not his music is jazz continues. He gave the world a number of compositions to puzzle over, including "'Round Midnight," "Straight No Chaser," "52nd Street Theme," "Blue Monk," "Ruby My Dear," "Well You Needn't," "Off Minor," "In Walked Bud," "Misterioso," "Epistrophy," "I Mean You," "Four in One," "Criss Cross," "Ask Me Now," "Little Rootie Tootie," "Monk's Dream," "Bemsha Swing," "Think of One," "Friday the 13th," "Hackensack," "Nutty," "Brilliant Corners," "Crepuscule with Nellie," "Evidence," and "Rhythm-a-Ning." Many of his songs became standards and countless musicians adopted them into their repertoires.

Despite his eccentricity, Monk made a huge impact on a number of artists who recognized him for what he was: a true genius. A partial list includes Ran Blake, Ted Curson, Andrew Hill, Elmo Hope, Rahsaan Roland Kirk, Michel Legrand, Orange Then Blue, Jean-Luc Ponty, Cecil Taylor, Mal Waldron, Cedar Walton, Mike Westbrook, Michael White, Hugh Lawson, Alan Skidmore, Dick Wellstood, Mary Lou Williams, Randy Weston, Stan Tracey, McCoy Tyner, Ornette Coleman, and Chick Corea. Another jazz artist who has carried on the tradition is T. S. Monk, the son of the famous pianist-composer. Although the young Monk, a drummer, has not made quite the same dent in jazz, he is probably a late bloomer like his father.

If the list of artists that cherish Monk's music indicate his large sphere of influence, the list of musicians that he performed alongside also sheds some light on his stature in the jazz world. The sidemen who supported and learned from the immortal Monk include Art Blakey, Milt Jackson, Lou Donaldson, Lucky Thompson, Max Roach, Julius Watkins, Sonny Rollins, Clark Terry, Gerry Mulligan, John Coltrane, Wilbur Ware, Shadow Wilson, Johnny Griffin, Donald Byrd, Phil Woods, Thad Jones and Charlie Rouse. Of particular note is John Coltrane, who was the leader of the free jazz movement and took one step further Monk's firm desire to be different and successful.

Since his death, the legend of Thelonious Monk has continued to grow and reach new heights. Many have tried to continue the legacy, including his son, Marcus Roberts, and Tommy Flanagan. The Thelonious Monk Institute encourages young players to take the fresh sounds in their heads and share them with the world, reinforcing the fact that the attitude and spirit of the man who gave us his Epistrophy Blues will never die.

Discography

1944/1948, Jazz Archives 159502.
1947–1948, Classics 1118.
5 By Monk By 5, Original Jazz Classics 362.
Alone in San Francisco, Original Jazz Classics 231.
At Town Hall (Limited Edition)(+2 Bonus Tracks), JVC VICJ-60511.
Bemsha Swing, ATJCD 5966.
Best of Thelonious Monk, BLUEN TOCJ-66032.
Blue Monk, BCD JTM8111.
Best of the Blue Note Years, Blue Note Records 95636.
Big Band and Quartet in Concert, Legacy Records 57636.
Blue Monk, Band Stand 1505.
Blue Sphere, Black Lion BLM 51051.
Brilliant Corners, Original Jazz Classics 026.
Criss-Cross, Legacy Records 48823.
The Early Thelonious Monk (Live At Minton's) 1941, Moon CD 086-2.
Epistrophy, Affinity 26.
Epistrophy Vol. 2, Jazz Hour 73546.

Genius of Modern Music Vol. 1, Blue Note Records 81510.
Genius of Modern Music Vol. 2, Blue Note Records 81511.
Genius of Modern Music Vol. 3, Blue Note Records 81512.
Greatest Hits, Legacy Records 65422.
Immortal Concerts, Giants of Jazz Recordings 53112.
In Italy, Original Jazz Classics 488.
In Japan (1963), Early Bird 1012.
It's Monk's Time, SONY COL4684052.
Jazz Profile, Blue Note Records 23518.
Live at The It Club—Complete, Legacy Records 65288.
Live at the Five Spot, Discovery 799786.
Live at Newport, SBPG 62389.
Live at Newport, C2K 53585.
Live at Monterey '63 Vol. 2, Mobile Fidelity Sound Lab 686.
Misterioso, Original Jazz Classics 206.
Monk in Tokyo, Legacy Records 65480.
Monk Alone: Complete Columbia Solo Recordings, Columbia 65495.
Monk in France, Original Jazz Classics 670.
Monk's Blues, Legacy Records 53581.
Monk's Dream, Columbia 40786.
Monk's Miracles, Columbia DS338.
Monkism, Laserlight 17179.
Monk's Music (+2 Bonus Tracks), RIVER VICJ-60309.
More Genius of Thelonious Monk, EMI TOCJ-1604.
Paris Jazz Concert Vol. 1, Malaco 1200.
Paris Jazz Concert Vol. 2, Malaco 1211.
Piano Solo, RCA Victor 40936.
Piano Solo, BMG 74321409362.
Plays Duke Ellington, Original Jazz Classics 024.
'Round Midnight, Prism Entertainment 509.
San Francisco Holiday, Milestone Records 9199.
Solo Monk, Legacy Records 47854.
Something in Blue, Black Lion BL 152.
Spastic & Personal, Alto 725.
Sphere, Affinity 1529.
Standards, Legacy Records 45148.
Standard Monk, Bandstand 1529.
Straight, No Chaser, Columbia 64886.
Sweet & Lovely, Moon Records 79.
Thelonious in Action, Original Jazz Classics 103.
The Art of the Ballad, Prestige Records 11012.
The Complete Blue Note Recordings, Blue Note Records 30363.
The Complete Prestige Recordings, Prestige Records 4428.
The Complete Riverside Recordings, Riverside Records 022.
The Composer, Legacy Records 44297.
The Essence of Thelonious Monk, Legacy Records 47930.
The Genius, Giants of Jazz Recordings 53327.
The London Collection Vol. 1, 1201 Music 9005.
The London Collection Vol. 1, Black Lion 760101.
The Man I Love, Black Lion BL 197.
The Nonet: Live!, Le Jazz 007.
The Paris Concert, Le Jazz 33.

The Riverside Tenor Sessions, Analogue Productions 37.
The Thelonious Monk Memorial Album, Milestone Records 47064.
The Unique Thelonious Monk, Original Jazz Classics 064.
Thelonious Himself, Original Jazz Classics 254.
Thelonious Himself, JVC XRCD 60170.
Thelonious Monk Trio, Prestige Records 7027.
Thelonious Monk and the Jazz Giants, Riverside Records 60–018.
Thelonious Monk Quartet in Japan, 1963. 2172.
Thelonious Monk Quartet, Evidence FCD 105.
Thelonious Monk Quartet, Live in Paris, 1964 FCD 132/2.
Thelonious Monk Quartet, Live in Paris, Alhambra, 1964 Vol. 1, FCD 135.
Thelonious Monk Quintets, FCD 32–109.
This Is Jazz #5, Legacy Records 64625.
Underground, Legacy Records 40785.
Thelonious in Action, JVC VICJ-60491.
Thelonious Monk, PREST VICJ-60463.
Thelonious Monk Vol. 2, VOGUE BVCJ-37021.
Unique, JVC VICJ-60351.
Thelonious Monk, 1944–1948, EPM 159502.
Who's Afraid of the Big Bad Monk?, KG 32892.

CHARLIE PARKER (1920–1955)

Bird's Blues

In every generation there are imitators who revere the past perform-ers and attempt to duplicate the sound of their idols. In every generation there are also innovators, those individuals who hold respect for past accom-plishments, but are adventurous and desire to explore uncharted territory. In order for bop to gain the respect it sought, a hero was needed, a larger than life figure able to fuel interest in the new music. One man cast his shadow over the modern movement with his Bird's blues. His name was Charlie Parker.

Charlie Parker was born Charles Parker, Jr., on August 29, 1920, in Kansas City, Missouri. Tragedy would enter Parker's life quickly; his father left the family when little Charlie was still a young boy. The elder Parker, a minor vaudeville performer who played piano and sang, would find him-self on the wrong end of a knife while Charlie was still a teenager. Parker's mother raised him alone and encouraged his musical curiosity. Parker's first instrument was the tuba, but he switched to the alto saxophone while still in high school. As a young boy, Parker's imagination was a like a V-12 engine waiting for the magical key to start it up. The key that triggered the ignition was music; sadly, Parker never found a way to shut the motor off. The running engine was supplemented by heroin, a drug that Parker began experimenting with in his early teens.

He was fascinated with the music that he could hear in his head but could not reproduce on the sax, causing much frustration. Parker would have to pay some hard dues before he could successfully translate the strange blues sounds that dominated his thoughts into concrete music. So enamored with a career as a musician and obsessed with coaxing the obscure sounds from the rich vein of his imagination was Parker that he quit school when he was fourteen.

After honing his skills enough to find work in some of the territory bands around Kansas City, Parker joined Lawrence Keyes' Deans of Swing. The band included saxophonist Freddie Culliver and singer Walter Brown, two musicians that Parker would later join in Jay McShann's Orchestra. Charlie Parker was 17 years old and the idealistic youth was ready to take on the world.

But before he could tell everyone his story with his dynamic interpretation of the blues, he had some tough lessons to learn. The vicious cutting contests that were such an integral part of the jazz scene in the 1930s found Parker, one of the most brilliant musicians of the twentieth century, ridiculed by older, more experienced musicians. No one was prepared to listen to his unique take on the blues. The negative response forged his resolve and he began to seriously master the blues in every key by practicing upwards of eighteen hours a day. He lived, ate and breathed music. The engine was now running on all cylinders and impossible to turn off.

In the summer of 1937, he joined George E. Lee's band and traveled to a resort in the Ozarks with the bandleader. During this era Lester Young was quickly being acknowledged as the greatest saxophone player in the world and one of his most fervent disciples was the impressionable kid Charlie Parker, who memorized every one of the Prez's solos note for note. It was a season of transformation, as Bird matured into something special on the alto saxophone. He had completely mastered chord progressions and explored every dimension connected to them.

Parker's musical education was furthered by the all night jams at the local park with some of the area's younger musicians. Later he would be in Buster Smith's group. Smith tutored his young protégé, allowing him time in the spotlight. Eventually, Parker left Smith's band and joined Jay McShann's outfit, but left three months later to satisfy his traveling itch. He rode the rails to Chicago where he jammed with King Kolax's band before disappearing once again. He would embrace this vagabond lifestyle throughout his career.

His whereabouts for the next few months are still a mystery. Some accounts report that he ventured to the Big Apple in early 1939 seeking his fame and fortune. It is believed that he was denied a working union card and took a job as a dishwasher at a diner in Harlem in order to hear the great Art Tatum, who was the featured entertainer at the venue. Others claimed Parker spent time in Baltimore, while another version has him back in Kansas City playing for a local group. Wherever he went, one thing was certain: Parker was evolving quickly, constantly shedding his musical skin as he strived for his ultimate level. When he emerged from his woodshedding time, he had left behind the Lester Young influence and had forged his own distinguished sound.

In 1940, he rejoined McShann's group in Kansas City. The time he spent with the territorial outfit was a finishing school. He reached his full maturity, as evidenced on the recording "Confessing the Blues." The early 1940s proved to be a period of relative calmness in his often turbulent life and as a result he enjoyed a very creative period where he began to properly write down his first songs. It was about this time that he met a young trumpet player from South Carolina who understood the frustration of introducing new musical ideas into a rigid format. The trumpeter's name was Dizzy Gillespie.

Parker's luck began to change. His nearly nonstop practicing started to pay dividends when selected writers brought attention to his inspired solos and fresh ideas. It was also at this point that he gained the nickname Yardbird, or Bird for short. The moniker gave him an instant identity that separated him from the dozens of other sax players on the scene.

When McShann took his group to New York for a residency at Savoy's, Parker discovered Monroe's Uptown House and the after hours jams that were taking place there. When the bandleader left New York to return to Kansas City, Parker stayed behind. He played with Noble Sissle's band for a brief period before joining pianist Earl Hines's orchestra, which included his pal Dizzy, in 1942. During this period Parker played the tenor saxophone.

While they performed regularly with Hines, it was the after hours jam sessions at Minton's Playhouse with other like-minded young jazz cats that gave them the spark to continue evolving the new ideas and style. Bud Powell, Chubby Jackson, Big Sid Catlett, Don Byas, Vic Coulsen, George Treadwell, Kenny Clarke, Thelonious Monk, and Max Roach all joined Parker and Gillespie in the groundbreaking late night musical gatherings.

After leaving Hines, Parker played with Cootie Williams and Andy Kirk before finding a spot with Billy Eckstine's band. Eckstine, who had been in Hines' band, was excited by the possibilities of the new thing and wanted to feature as many of the new revolutionists as possible. Gillespie, Parker, and Sarah Vaughan were just three of the big names that played together in the group.

After leaving Eckstine a few months after joining him, Parker formed his first group with Joe Albany on piano and Stan Levey on drums. A recording session with Tiny Grimes in 1944 was a dry run for his later collaboration with Dizzy Gillespie. It took Parker and Gillespie some time to find the right complementary players, but eventually Miles Davis, Argonne Thornton, Curly Russell and, most importantly, drummer Max Roach joined them. On later recordings Bud Powell added his genius touch on piano. Although the new music recorded on the Savoy label infuriated the purists, Parker and his bandmates had no intentions of giving up their chosen musical path.

Gillespie and Parker took their musical partnership one step further when they appeared together with pianist Al Haig, bassist Curly Russell, and Stan Levey on drums at the Three Deuces on 52nd Street, the heartbeat of the new bebop music. It was this quintet that would record the classics "Shaw 'Nuff" and "Salt Peanuts" with Catlett instead of Levey on drums. In a later session that included more traditional jazz players like Teddy Wilson, Red Norvo and Slam Stewart, Gillespie and Parker stood out, indicating the true future path of jazz.

When he wasn't jamming on stage or cutting records with Gillespie, Parker appeared as a sideman for the Continental label on sessions with Sarah Vaughan, among others. Bird also led his own group that included Sir Charles Thompson, Buck Clayton and Dexter Gordon. They played a residency at the Spotlite before he rejoined Dizzy at the end of 1945.

In 1946, Parker accompanied Dizzy's sextet to California, and a year later when everyone returned to New York, Bird remained in sunny Los Angeles. On the West Coast he jammed with a whole new group of bop enthusiasts, including Chet Baker, Howard McGhee, Wardell Gray, and Charles Mingus, among others.

Unfortunately, despite the change in scenery he continued his self-destructive habits, but since heroin was much harder to obtain he had to settle on alcohol and other stupefying drugs. By the end of 1947, Parker was in a very bad way, but he still took part in the famous Dial sessions, which include some of the most important recordings of his career. He joined Norman Granz's Jazz at the Philharmonic concerts, some of which were recorded and released at a later date. It was after a Dial session in July that Bird was placed in Camarillo State Mental Hospital for six months after setting the mattress in his motel room on fire while drinking.

Upon his release, Parker returned to New York and entered one of the most creative periods in his life. He formed a quintet with trumpeter Miles Davis, pianist Duke Jordan, bassist Tommy Porter and drummer Max Roach. Bird, a musical genius, had surrounded himself with musicians who complemented and at the same time challenged him. They laid down the perfect format for his extended solos of seemingly disorganized rushes of cascading notes. Although the personnel in the band would change (Kenny Durham replaced Miles Davis and Al Haig replaced Duke Jordan), it was this group that Bird toured with extensively throughout the United States and Europe. They played clubs like the Three Deuces on 52nd Street.

A year later, Parker traveled to Sweden and shocked the Scandinavians into submission with his hard blowing, complex sound. Upon his return he was able to record with his idol, Lester Young, as well as Coleman Hawkins. The sessions produced the *Jazz at the Philharmonic* set. Later on, he would jam with Johnny Hodges and Benny Carter, a collaboration that was captured on the album *Funky Blues*.

It was around this time that Parker began a contracted association with Norman Granz and his Jazz at the Philharmonic. Granz was one of the most important figures behind the scenes and recorded Parker in a variety of musical environments: strings; Afro-Cuban; a variety of instruments such as the oboe, flute, bassoon, and French Horn; and with vocal groups. Although they didn't always provide the best rhythm patterns for Parker, he always managed to record a couple of classics on each album to add to his musical canon.

Parker began to feel the ill effects of his living-on-the-edge lifestyle in 1951 when he was diagnosed with a peptic ulcer; he also suffered liver and heart troubles that would plague him the rest of his life. Although many believe that his best playing days were behind him, he managed to exude moments of his former brilliance, such as the Massey Hall concert in 1953 with his old pal Dizzy. On that night Bird proved to all in attendance that he was among the greatest blues players in the history of the genre.

Despite this triumph, problems persisted. His cabaret license was revoked, preventing him from playing clubs in New York—including Birdland, the joint that had been named for him. His heavy drug addiction and unpredictable actions made him unreliable and undesirable to work with. In 1954, he spent some time in Bellevue hospital after two failed suicide attempts.

On March 12, 1955, Charlie Parker, the alto saxophonist with the wild-eyed licks that had helped reinvent jazz, died in the apartment of Baroness Nica de Koenigswarter in New York City. The young genius left us when he was 34 years old, prematurely worn out by drugs and alcohol.

Charlie Parker was one of jazz's most pathetic figures, and probably its greatest genius. His contributions to the genre are immeasurable, as long after his death his legend continues to confound and amaze new generations. His depth of popularity is so astounding that individuals who don't even like jazz know his name. His credentials as the most innovative alto saxophonist have never been truly challenged.

Parker, who always claimed that he was simply trying to play the sounds he heard in his head, revolutionized how the alto sax was played. To achieve his vision he concentrated on chromatic progressions to create the new harmonies that were essential to his style. His uncanny sense of rhythm allowed him to fall on different accents on the line, but he was still able to make it swing. He wreaked havoc on conventional divisions of beats in order to play the music that he heard. He combined his superb technical dexterity with an emotional edge that has never been equaled. His style on alto saxophone is instantly recognizable.

Parker combined complex chord changes in every blues key with a machine gun–like attack, spraying notes delivered at lightning speed. His ability to instantly improvise the most intricate passages and weird phrases has influenced every saxophonist for the past sixty years. In the modern era, perhaps only John Coltrane was able to equal Parker in imagination, originality, technique and sheer fuel.

Although a complete list would surely fill a book, the following are just some of the musicians who were influenced by the Parker magic: Buddy Collette, Art Farmer, Don Friedman, Wardell Gray, Eric Kloss, Oliver Nelson, Julian Priester, Heiner Stadler, Sonny Stitt, Rene Thomas, Bob Wilber, Gerd Dudek, Luis Gasca, Alex Foster, Yusef Lateef, Jeff Coffin, Leo Parker, Serge Chaloff, Cecil Payne, Norman Connors, J. R. Monterose, Toots Thielemans, and David Bixler. But the reverberations of his legend have spilled beyond the borders of jazz and throughout the music world into rock, blues, country, rap, and soul.

Along with Dizzy Gillespie, he was one of the prime architects of bebop, although he cast a different shadow than his musical soul mate. Parker was aloof, a tortured genius who was thought by many to be suicidal and crazy. He did indeed try to take his life near the end. In truth, Parker was misunderstood because of the personal demons that he was never able to conquer.

He gave the world a treasure trove of classics that have been pillaged and plundered by two generations of alto saxophonists. An early list includes "Dizzy Atmosphere," "Groovin' High," "Salt Peanuts," and "Shaw 'Nuff," and others, many of which he recorded with Gillespie. Later he added "Now's the Time," "Ko Ko," "Billie's Bounce," "Cheryl," "Buzzy," "Bird Gets the Worm," "Blue Bird," "Another Hairdo," "Barbados," "Parker's Mood," "Constellation," "Ornithology," "Mouse the Mooche," "Yardbird Suite," and "A Night in Tunisia."

After his release from Camarillo State Mental Hospital he was still able to deliver classics. A partial list includes "Dark Shadows," "This Is Always," "Cool Blues," "Bird's Nest," "Relaxin' At Camarillo," "Cheers," "Carvin' the Bird," "Stupendous," "Home Cooking," "Dexterity," "Bongo

Bop," "Dewey Square," "The Hymn," "Bird of Paradise," "Embraceable You," "Drifting on a Reed," "Quasimodo," "Charlie's Wig," "Bongo Beep," "Crazoology," "How Deep Is the Ocean," "Bird Feathers," "Klactoveesed-stene," "Scrapple From the Apple," "My Old Flame," "Out of Nowhere," and "Don't Blame Me."

There have always been two sides to the Charlie Parker story: that of the brilliant musician and that of the lurid tales of his drug abuse and wild ways. Sometimes the two intertwined; many accounts claim Bird was drunk or high on something and played greater than anyone had ever heard him play before. In an even account of the aspects of his life, both must be presented because they are equally important to the Charlie Parker story.

In 34 years, about half of that as a professional musician, Parker changed the face and course of jazz as well as popular music forever. He is on par with 20th Century musical giants like Robert Johnson, Jimi Hendrix, Muddy Waters, Duke Ellington, Louis Armstrong, and Hank Williams. Although he might not be rated as the greatest jazzman in the history of the genre, there was only one Charlie "Yardbird" Parker and he gave the world his bird's blues that will live on forever.

Discography

Charlie Parker Vol. 1 & 2—Young Bird 1940–1944, Masters of Jazz, 78.
Vol. 3, Masters of Jazz 104.
Vol. 4 1945, Masters of Jazz 113.
Young Bird, Vol. 6, 1947, Masters of Jazz 142.
Jazz at Tiffany's 1950–1954, DRSK 372.
The Best of Bird—Vol. 2, Legends 490.
At Birdland Vol. 2 1950–1951, EMBR 504.
At the Open Door, EMBR 508.
The World of Charlie Parker, EMBR 817.
1945–1947, Classic 980.
1947, Classic 1000.
1947–1949, Classic 1103.
Jazz at the Philharmonic 1949, Indigo 2087.
The Complete Live Performances on Savoy, Savoy 17021.
Phonodor Original Sound Recordings from 1944-1948, SPVR 31112.
BeBop & Bird Vol. 1, 1946–1952, Rhino 70197.
BeBop & Bird Vol. 2, 1946–1952, Rhino 70198.
Yardbird Suite: The Ultimate Charlie Parker Collection 1945–1952, Rhino 72260.
The Complete Savoy & Dial Studio Recordings, 1944-1948, Savoy 92911.
Bird at the Hi-Hat 1953–1954, Blue Note 99787.
Early Bird 1940–1945, EPM 158572.
1944–1946, EPM 158802.
Cool Blues 1947, EPM 159512.
Essential, PLG 517173.
Jazz at the Philharmonic 1949, PLG 519803.
Charlie Parker, Verve Jazz Masters 15, PLG 519827.

Bird & Diz—Verve Master Edition 1950, PLG 521436.
Verve Jazz Masters 28: Plays Standards, PLG 521854.
The Master Takes, PLG 523984.
Bird's Best Bop on Verve, Verve 527452.
South Of the Border 1948–1952, Verve 527779.
Confirmation: Best of the Verve Years, 527815.
Charlie Parker, Verve Master Edition, 539757.
Ultimate Charlie Parker, Verve 559708.
Cole Porter Songbook, 823250.
Compact Jazz, PLG 833288.
Charlie Parker Sides (Jam Sessions), 833564.
Bird: The Complete Charlie Parker, PLG 837176.
Jazz 'Round Midnight—Ballads, PLG 847911.
Charlie Parker with Miles Davis: Cool Bird 1947, MAGC 20.

OSCAR PETTIFORD (1922–1960)

Deep Passion

The exploits of Jimmy Blanton changed the role of the bass player in jazz forever. It was this young genius who took the instrument into the modern era, and established the platform from which all future string players would derive their inspiration. Although there were a few good bassists that dared to make it go bop, only one possessed the necessary talent and the deep passion. His name was Oscar Pettiford.

Oscar Pettiford was born on September 30, 1922, in Okmulgee, Oklahoma, on a reservation, and came from musical stock. His father, of half Cherokee blood, was originally a veterinarian who was bitten by the music bug. His mother was of Choctaw blood and served as the music teacher to the eleven children in the family. When Oscar was three, they moved to Minneapolis and it served as the Pettiford band's base of operations. Many of Oscar's sisters and brothers were musically talented. Alonzo, a trumpet player, was a member of Lionel Hampton's band at one time. Another brother, Ira, played trumpet, guitar and bass, and performed with the great piano player Earl Hines. As a youngster Oscar learned the ropes of the entertainment industry while performing in the family group.

Despite his love of music, Oscar quit for a few months in 1942 and worked in a plant producing material for the war. He was a frustrated musician because of the limited opportunities in Minnesota at the time. Upon his return to the music scene, he was coaxed to move to New York by passing musicians who admired his unquestionable talent on the bass. Pettiford, aside from minimal instruction by his sister, was self-taught.

Pettiford arrived in New York in 1943 and like many young, penniless musicians, he was armed with a dream, talent, determination and not much else. But he immediately discovered the jazz scene at Minton's Playhouse and worked with Thelonious Monk for four months. He also made his first recordings in an all-star session that included Coleman Hawkins and Art Tatum. After a brief stint with Roy Eldridge, Pettiford joined forces with Dizzy Gillespie. The union lasted for a few months before they parted company. From that point on, Oscar led his own outfit; it played in many of the jazz spots on 52nd Street that other bop artists frequented. He joined Boyd Raeburn's group and recorded with them before moving on.

He resettled in California and played clubs in Los Angeles, San Diego, and San Francisco. After his West Coast period Pettiford joined Duke Ellington's orchestra, fulfilling a childhood dream of playing with the Duke. He stayed with Ellington almost three years before striking out on his own once again.

He returned to New York, formed a combo with pianist Erroll Garner, and later worked with George Shearing. Pettiford augmented his outfit to include Lucky Thompson, Bill Harris, Red Rodney, and Shelly Manne. Sometime later he joined Woody Herman's orchestra, which was experimenting with bop in a large band setting. Zoot Sims, Stan Getz, Ernie Royal, Serge Chaloff, Terry Gibbs and Red Rodney were some of the others in the group.

As a member of Herman's big band, Pettiford was allowed to stretch out musically and he really began to tap into his deep reservoir of talent. While a member of the group, he broke his arm during a baseball game, which knocked him out of action for eighteen months. But there was something positive derived from the injury. He was forced to change his style and substitute sound for speed; he also picked up the cello for the first time. The ability to play the cello came to him naturally, much the same way the bass did.

After debuting with his new instrumental skill, Pettiford moved on to the Louis Bellson–Charlie Shavers unit before forming his own group for a USO tour of the Pacific Islands. His all-star outfit included J. J. Johnson, Howard McGhee, Charlie Rice, Skeeter Best, and Rudy Williams. However, due to an altercation between Pettiford and Best, the tour wasn't as successful as it could have been.

Pettiford returned to New York in 1952 and for the next six years led his own combo, adding different players to augment the lineup. He played at the Café Bohemia, a prime jazz joint, that served as a crossroads for all musicians arriving and departing the Big Apple during that era. As a result, he jammed with a great number of musicians and astounded many with his abilities on the bass and cello. These sessions sharpened his skills and added a new dimension to his playing.

During this period of his career, he played mostly in a four-piece unit that consisted of himself, Gigi Gryce, Art Farmer, and Kenny Clarke. The rhythm section of Clarke and Pettiford was pure musical sound poetry. They steamrolled through their songbook with a definite finesse, but also with a definite power. Stan Katz, Horace Silver, and Jerome Richardson were just some of the players that passed through the band over the years.

In 1958, Pettiford left America and never returned. He settled in Europe and played with Jazz at Carnegie Hall, an all-star outfit that toured all over England and the continent. He worked in France, Germany, and Austria before settling in Copenhagen. He spent a year with Stan Getz before leading his own aggregation of Danish jazz enthusiasts.

In September of 1960, Pettiford became ill with strep throat. It led to complications and on the eighth of that month he died in a Copenhagen hospital. He was thirty-eight years old.

Oscar Pettiford was a talented player who was a logical musical extension of Jimmy Blanton. But he was more than just a Blanton imitator—he carried on the work that the young genius had begun but never finished. He added the cello to his musical arsenal and played it with the same grace, technique and mastery as he did the bass. Pettiford was also in the thick of the bop revolution and stands out as the best bebop bassist of the era.

Pettiford's theory of playing the bass was similar to Charlie Christian's in that they both tried to imitate horns. Oscar, with his incredibly powerful, nimble fingers, coupled with his skillful touch, could very easily make his bass sound like a horn. He had the facility to create spheres of sounds by gliding his fingers along the strings. To put his style in proper perspective, Pettiford was the exact opposite of the slap-bass players like Pops Foster; he didn't attack the bass, he conjured sounds out of it like a magician pulling a neat trick.

Although firmly entrenched in the bop style, he laid down the foundation for the future direction of all bassists. The hard bop, cool, avant-garde, free jazz, fusion and contemporary players derived their practical playing from the theories of Pettiford's innovations. In a musical period that featured such solid virtuosos as Chubby Jackson, Slam Stewart, Eddie Safranski, Curly Russell, Tommy Potter, Al McKibbon, Nelson Boyd and Ray Brown, Oscar stood above them and helped shape their mature sound.

Pettiford influenced all those that followed him, including Mark Dresser, Sam Jones, Cecil McBee, Pierre Michelot, Charles Mingus, Sirone Aaron Bell, Stafford James, Tommy Potter, Nabil Totah, Gerald Veasley, Paul Chambers, Stanley Clarke, Erik Friedlander, Milt Hinton, Buell Neidlinger, Andy Simpkins, Gene Taylor, Leroy Vinnegar, Buster Williams, Red Mitchell, Charlie Haden, Niels-Henning Orsted Pedersen, Gary Peacock, Ron Carter, Jaco Pastorius, Charles Duvivier, Percy Heath, Charles

Fambrough and Christian McBride. His reach stretched into the realm of rock, blues, and pop.

Pettiford was also a first-rate composer. He played on a number of classic songs, as part of a group or as a leader. The list he gave to the world includes "Tricotism," "Laverne Walk," "Bohemia After Dark," "Swingin' Till the Girls Come Home," "Honeysuckle Rose," "Something for You," "The Man I Love," "Interlude," "March of the Boyds," "Stuffy," "Hollywood Stampede," "Swamp Fire," "Chasin' the Blues," "The Pendulum at Falcon's Lair," "Now See How You Are," and "Blues in the Closet." Many of them became staples in the musical vocabulary of several bassists.

He was an architect of the bebop revolution. He was in the thick of the creation of the new sound and bridged the gap between Blanton's achievements and everything that followed. Like many of the other bebop practitioners, anecdotes of his actions made him a legend. He indulged happily into the jazz lifestyle; he was a heavy drinker with a fiery temper who loved to stay up all night jamming with like-minded musicians. But no matter the stories that contradict the talent, Oscar Pettiford will always be remembered for the deep passion he brought to jazz.

Discography

First Bass, IAJRC Records 1010.
Oscar Pettiford Sextet, Vogue BMG 40945.
The New Oscar Pettiford Sextet, Orig. Jazz Classics B00002SWKS.
Oscar Pettiford Modern Quintet, Bethlehem BCP 1003.
Another One, Rhino Records B00004R5ZZ.
Jazz Mainstream, Bethlehem B00005HTLU.
Complete Oscar Pettiford in Hi-Fi, Phantom B0000565ZN.
Blue Brothers, Phantom B0000565ZM.
Deep Passion, Impulse B0000CD7Z5.
Montmartre Blues, Black Lion B00005NT30.
Bass by Pettiford and Burke, Rhino Records B00002MZ3N.
Vienna Blues: The Complete Sessions, Black Lion 760104.
Bass Hits, Pearl 1071.

BARNEY KESSEL (1923–2004)

Guitar Goes Bop

The jam sessions on 52nd Street in New York in the early 1940s are of seminal importance for a variety of reasons. It was at these late-night rendezvous that the young practitioners came together to forge a new sound that would irrevocably change the course of modern music. Dizzy, Bird, Monk, Oscar Pettiford, J. J. Johnson, Kenny Clarke, and Fats Navarro were all-important figures in making history. When Bird and Dizzy took their bop jazz to the West Coast in 1946, they converted a whole group of interested musicians, including the man who made the guitar go bop. His name was Barney Kessel.

Barney Kessel was born on October 17, 1923, in Muskogee, Oklahoma. He was drawn to the musical limelight at an early age, but it wasn't until his early teens that he began to seriously study the guitar. His curiosity was piqued when he saw his first electric guitarist in Muskogee. An avid fan of the radio, Kessel had heard an electric guitar played on the air by a member of the country band Bob Wills and the Texas Playboys. But the visual experience convinced him that he really needed to have one, and he received a National guitar with a pickup.

One of his first gigs was as part of Ellis Ezell's band; Kessel was the only white musician amongst them. In the heart of the Deep South, he was already breaking with tradition by playing with African Americans. Like many practitioners of the bop style, he was color blind regarding race. It would prove good training for his later jam sessions with the great black bop mainstays Charlie Parker, Dexter Gordon, Dizzy Gillespie, Bud Powell and Thelonious Monk, among others.

Kessel was a fan of all types of music, a natural occurrence since Oklahoma was such a hotbed of the blues, country, jazz, Mexican, and mountain music. Although he developed a taste for a variety of styles, his favorite was jazz. However, during his youth, jazz guitarists, with the exception of Eddie Lang and Lonnie Johnson, were regarded as background rhythm makers. But all of that changed forever with the emergence of Charlie Christian in the late 1930s.

Christian was the messiah for many guitarists in the era between the two world wars. Although his career was tragically cut short by his early death, he influenced innumerable guitarists with his slick, emotional solos and intricate, chunky chord patterns. One of the first guitarists to explore the many possibilities of the electric sound, he opened the door for countless future players, including Kessel, with his innovative ideas and desire to play guitar like a horn. Eventually, Barney met his idol and it proved to be a life-changing experience for the developing guitarist.

Although Oklahoma presented solid opportunities for aspiring musicians, Kessel decided he needed a change of scenery and moved to the West Coast in the 1940s. Because of his roots, he was open to new adventures and when bop came calling he was an immediate convert. With his solid musical background, his dexterity, and his taste for jazz, he started to jam on Central Avenue in Los Angeles—the West Coast's answer to New York's 52nd Street. He supported himself with a series of low-paying jobs. He found some work with the big bands of Chico Marx, Charlie Barnet, and Artie Shaw. He also recorded with an offshoot of Shaw's band. Despite his skill and musical diversity, there was a shortage of work. Kessel possessed all the tools to be the fastest trigger in the West but remained a struggling musician.

His luck began to change in the middle of the decade. In 1944, he appeared with the Prez in the short film *Jammin' with Lester*. It was one of the first serious attempts to present jazz on the big screen, but the racial convention at the time shunned the visual portrayal of the two races working together on equal terms. As a result, Kessel was kept to the far background and appeared as a silhouette throughout the movie.

But in many ways, 1947 was the breakthrough year for Barney Kessel. He jammed with Charlie Parker during the latter's visit to Los Angeles and was included on the Dial session that produced the classic "Relaxin' at Camarillo." He also made his first recordings, including his own composition, "Swedish Pastry," with clarinetist Stan Hasselgard. He topped off the successful year with his first Esquire Silver Award. It would not be his last.

In the 1950s, his star rose significantly, as he divided his time between several projects. In 1953, he took the plunge and joined Oscar Peterson's Trio, which included bassist Ray Brown. Kessel toured and recorded extensively with the great pianist, and the exposure to national and international audiences was priceless. When he left after only one year to pursue other interests, his star status was sealed.

Because of his versatility, Kessel was much in demand as a studio musician. One of these sessions included his fine guitar work on Julie London's 1955 major hit, "Cry Me A River." He also became a studio ace, but the most satisfying part of his rising career was his recordings for the Contemporary label. The release of *To Swing or Not to Swing; Let's Cook* and *Some Like It Hot* catapulted him to the top of the jazz guitar heap and made him a mentor to all aspiring six-stringers.

It seemed that he was everywhere in the 1960s. He entered the decade with a solid reputation but didn't rest on his laurels. He enhanced his popularity with more strong albums for the Contemporary label, often accompanied by Ray Brown and Shelly Manne. The trio called themselves the Poll Winners and their time together proved to be a very successful phase in the guitarist's long and impressive career.

He also continued his prolific studio work and could be heard on the theme songs of several television shows, including *I Spy, The Man from UNCLE,* and *The Odd Couple,* among others. He also added his distinct guitar sound to four Elvis Presley movies. He provided the music for the movie *Cool Hand Luke.* He passed on his guitar knowledge with a series of teaching manuals those aspiring musicians seriously coveted.

One of those guitar protégés particularly touched by the Kessel magic was a young Phil Spector. One of the most enigmatic figures in rock history, he would go on to become the "wall of sound" producer, working with many different acts, including the Beatles. Barney participated on the sessions of Spector-led bands.

He played with several rock artists, including Buffalo Springfield, sat in with Sonny and Cher on their big hit "The Beat Goes On," and worked with the ultimate California surfer band, The Beach Boys. It was Kessel who turned Brian Wilson on to the possibilities of the theramin an instrument that the leader of the group would use on the *Pet Sounds* session, including the international hit "Good Vibrations."

In 1969, Kessel decided that he needed a change of scenery and moved to Europe. During his sabbatical he worked with George Wein's Newport All-Stars. He resettled in California in the fall of 1970, and returned to the lucrative world of studio sessions.

The year 1973 was a very satisfying one for Kessel. He began an association with a group called the Great Guitars, which included Herb Ellis and Charlie Byrd. It was an interesting mixture of styles. Byrd, who studied classical guitar under the tutelage of the revered Andres Segovia, added his charming flamenco inflected licks to the hard, smooth bop and swing of his two partners. Ellis, an important guitarist in his own right, had also played with Oscar Peterson. The group toured and recorded together to enthusiastic audiences.

It was also during this year that Kessel appeared at the Montreux Jazz Festival with a British rhythm section comprised of Brian Lemon on piano, Kenny Baldock on bass, and Johnny Richardson on drums. Their set was captured in the documentary film *Summertime in Montreux.* Kessel played some of his standards, including a mind-blowing rendition of "Laura," and the Beatles' staple "Yesterday." His ingenious inclusion of a modern rock piece from the Fab Four, who were still immensely popular despite their breakup three years before, not only satisfied the younger portion of the crowd, but also illustrated his versatility.

Throughout the years he recorded many important albums with various musicians such as tenor saxman George Auld and Harry "Sweets" Edison, among others. He also recorded with the legendary Stephane Grappelli. Their collaboration included the touching "I Remember Django," a tribute to the late, great Django Reinhardt. Grappelli and Reinhardt had been partners for years in Europe. Like all other jazz guitarists who began their careers in the 1940s, it was impossible not to be influenced by the gypsy guitar ace. There was a mutual admiration between Kessel and Reinhardt, although they never had a chance to play together.

In 1981, Kessel recorded the album *Solo*, his only unaccompanied album; it clearly demonstrated the sheer beauty of his guitar genius. He continued to tour and record with a variety of jazz artists, his skills still sharp despite his advancing age. Although the reign of bop had come and gone, he was still revered among many in jazz circles for his legendary contributions to the style.

In 1992, he suffered a stroke that ended his career. However, his legacy lived on; his catalog was an incredible body of material, much of which is quite excellent. Twelve years later, on May 6, 2004, Barney Kessel—the man who made the guitar go bop—passed away. He was eighty years old.

Barney Kessel was one of the most diverse jazz artists in the history of the genre. A prolific recording artist, he possessed broad tastes and recorded not only jazz records, but blues and pop as well. His immense talent, his dexterity, and his ability to wrap himself around one of his originals or a song from some other artist made him a standout. He had a certain touch no matter what style he played in.

Charlie Christian was the greatest single influence on Kessel, as his ability to solo with such grace and power that was so enthralling. Although Barney enjoyed a much longer career than his idol, he always remained enchanted by the magic that Christian created. Arguably, the student moved jazz guitar beyond the contributions of his mentor. Django Reinhardt's prowess also made a strong impact on Kessel, but to a lesser extent.

Although he never received the same credit as Charlie Parker or Dizzy Gillespie for the creation of bop, Kessel was in the thick of the emergent music. He was the single most important bop guitarist. While Parker created new worlds with his alto sax, and Gillespie expanded the possibilities of the trumpet, Kessel made the guitar sing bop. While Charlie Christian is clearly identified as the forefather of bop guitar, Kessel was an important son who would have made the father figure proud.

A list of the many guitarists that professor Kessel influenced only proves his importance. Bola Sete, John Abercrombie, Larry Carlton, Jim Hall, John McLaughlin, Wes Montgomery, Rene Gustafsson, Bill Harris, Joe Puma, and Tommy Tede are just a handful of the jazz artists that owe a debt to him. Two of the outstanding students of the school were Wes Montgomery and John McLaughlin, who have greatly shaped the sound of jazz in the past forty years. Barney made an impact on every future stylist in the cool, hard bop, free, avant-garde, jazz fusion, universalism, and the new thing fold.

But Kessel's sphere of sway extends beyond the borders of jazz. It includes folk artists such as Bob Dylan, who has recorded blues, gospel, rock and pop. Rock artists such as John Mellancamp, Robbie Krieger of the Doors, and some of the new blues artists such as Keb Mo', Alvin Young-blood Hart, Corey Harris and Ben Harper were all touched by his magic. Although the mainstream popularity of some of these artists has overshadowed Kessel's own achievements, they remain linked to his groundbreaking style.

He worked with some of the biggest as well as lesser known names in jazz, including Red Callender, Billie Holiday, Jimmy Rowles, Shelly Manne, Roy Eldridge, Ella Fitzgerald, Red Mitchell, Charlie Parker, Larry Bunker, Paul Smith, Lester Young, Don Lamond, Charlie Shavers, and Bud Shank. Unfortunately, Kessel was never able to record with his idol, Charlie Christian. The pure joy of hearing the two together would have proven to be one of the genuine golden moments in jazz.

Barney Kessel remains a vital part of jazz history. His guitar legacy will no doubt continue to have a direct effect on new artists for many years. His sweeping repertoire has found its way into the stage performances and recordings of many different artists. He will forever be remembered as the man who made the guitar go bop, and stretched the creative boundaries of the instrument.

Discography

Just Jazz Concert, Decca DL7013.
Julie Is Her Name, EMI CD 7–99804–2.
A Slow Burn, Polydor LP 2307 011.
Swinging Easy, Black Lion 760 112.
I Got Rhythm, Black Lion 3139 7613–2.
Kessel's Kit, RCA SF 8098.
Great Guitars, Concord CD 6004.
Great Guitars II, Concord 4023.
Great Guitars—Straight Tracks, Concord 4421.
Great Guitars—At the Winery, Concord 4131.
Great Guitars at Charlie's, Georgetown, Concord 4209.
Four!—Hampton Hawes, Contemporary 7553.
Swinging Party, Contemporary LP S 7613.
Guitar Workshop, MPS LP 545 113.
Just Friends, Sonet LP SNTF 685.
Easy Like, Vol. 1, Original Jazz 153–2.
Kessel Plays Standards, Original Jazz 238–2.
Barney Kessel, Vol. 3: To Swing or Not to Swing, Original Jazz 317–2.
Music to Listen to: Barney Kessel, Original Jazz 7–99804–2.
Let's Cook, Contemporary 12318.
Barney Kessel Plays "Carmen," Original Jazz 269.
Some Like It Hot, Original Jazz 168.
Guitar Workshop, Saba 545 113.
Feeling Free, Original Jazz 179.
Reflections in Rome, RCA LISP 34013.

Two Way Conversation, SONET SLP-2547.
Barney Plays Kessel, Concord 4009.
Soaring, Concord Jazz 6033.
Poor Butterfly, Concord Jazz 4034.
Jellybeans, Concord Jazz 4164.
Solo, Concord Jazz 4221.
Spontaneous Combustion, Contemporary 14033.
Red Hot and Blues, Contemporary 14044.
The Poll Winners with Ray Brown and Shelly Manne, Contemporary S7535.
The Poll Winners Ride Again, Original Jazz 607.
Poll Winners Three!, Original Jazz 7565.
The Poll Winners/Exploring the Scene, Contemporary 7581.
Workin' Out, Contemporary S 7585.
The Poll Winners Straight Ahead, Original Jazz 409–2.

———

J. J. JOHNSON (1924–2001)
Trombone Goes Bop

The trombone, like other instruments in jazz, has enjoyed different stages of development in the hands of various innovators. The trombonist of the Dixieland and swing eras produced mostly growls and slurs. However, it was thought that the trombone was too slow for the frenetic new bebop music. That was, until one individual reinvented the use of the instrument and made the trombone go bop. His name was J. J. Johnson.

James Louis Johnson was born on January 22, 1924, in Indianapolis, Indiana. It was in his native state that the music bug bit him hard. He toyed with a few instruments, including the piano, when he was about eleven, but settled on the trombone. In his teens his musical heroes were Dickie Wells and Trummy Young, two of the finest trombonists in the big band period. As a youngster, Johnson dreamed of playing on par with his two idols.

Although he had always showed an appreciation for music, it was in high school that he developed a strong taste for jazz. As a teenager Johnson's musical style was firmly rooted in swing. He and his friends listened to Duke Ellington, Jimmie Lunceford, and Count Basie. His parents encouraged his musical interests; Johnson senior bought his son his first trombone.

His parents wanted him to go to college after he graduated from high school, but Johnson opted instead for a career as a jazz musician and left home at eighteen to pursue his dreams. In 1942, he joined Snookum Russell's band and took in much of the country while on tour with the group.

While on the road he encountered different musicians that helped shape his mature sound. He met a trumpeter named Fats Navarro who was already hinting at new musical ideas that baffled Johnson since they appeared so radical. Another important influence was Fred Beckett, a member of Lionel Hampton's band who played the trombone differently than everyone else at that time by substituting slurs and slides for linear improvisation. Others that captured J. J.'s imagination at the time were Roy "Little Jazz" Eldridge and Lester Young, the Prez.

Johnson returned to Indianapolis after a stint with Russell and found work as a dishwasher in a restaurant, restricting his musical activities to the weekends. At this point, despite the positive but limited experiences he had enjoyed, J. J. was discouraged and unconvinced that his musical dreams would ever be realized. He was waiting for his big break and it came when he joined Benny Carter's band.

It was with Carter that Johnson made his first recording that hinted at his greatness, especially on the cut "Love for Sale." The three years he spent with the group was a continuous musical education as he was surrounded by quality personnel that included Carter, Max Roach, Curly Russell, Freddie Webster, Karl George, and Porter Kilbert, among others.

In 1945, after playing in the initial Jazz at the Philharmonic concert, Johnson joined Count Basie's ensemble for a year. Already at a young age his resume boasted tenure in two of the best-known bands in the land. He could have easily carved a solid name for himself playing big band music, but he elected to follow a different musical path.

In 1946, he was swept away by the bop revolution. By this time the ideas that Navarro had talked about many years before had materialized into concrete sounds. Although the trombone was considered too cumbersome to produce the speedy, hard-driving bop lines, Johnson had different ideas. He became one of the young enthusiasts around 52nd Street jamming with Gillespie, Parker, Navarro, Bud Powell, Thelonious Monk, et al. The young trombonist amazed his bebop cohorts with his agility on the instrument. He often sat in with Gillespie at the Spotlite and began to carve out a name for himself in jazz circles.

The late-night jam sessions eventually turned into recording dates and the fastest trombonist in jazz became an invaluable sideman on some of Parker's cuts, as well as with Gillespie's big band and with Illinois Jacquet's outfit. He made noteworthy contributions to Sonny Stitt's *Genesis* album. But perhaps his most famous appearance during this period was on the groundbreaking *Birth of the Cool* recording with Miles Davis. With each successive new adventure, Johnson was handsomely padding his resume.

In 1946, he also began to lead his own recording dates for the Savoy label with a backup group that included the incomparable Bud Powell on piano and Cecil Payne on alto saxophone. It was these sessions that turned him from promising trombonist into a real star. Many refused to believe that he was capable of playing a valve trombone with such speed and dexterity. It was because of this disbelief that many sought to see him live, which only enhanced his blossoming career.

Johnson would lead further recording sessions that included an all-star lineup of Kenny Clarke, trumpeter Clifford Brown, pianists Horace Silver and Wynton Kelly, bassists Charles Mingus and Paul Chambers, and tenor sax man Hank Mobley. The result was *The Eminent J. J. Johnson,* Volumes, 1 & 2, on the Blue Note label—the definitive bop trombone albums. With this release he had proven to all detractors that it was very possible to make the sliding brass instrument go bop.

In between his solo adventures, Johnson was a member of the Illinois Jacquet band and remained with the group for two years. When he left Jacquet's group in 1949, Johnson gigged around the New York area where there was never a shortage of work, including residencies with Stan Getz and Fats Navarro. He also played with Dizzy Gillespie and Woody Herman on several occasions. In the fall of 1951 he joined bassist Oscar Pettiford's band for tours of Japan, Korea and some Pacific Islands.

Upon his return from touring with Pettiford, Johnson joined Jazz Inc. for a series of concerts. The group included Miles Davis, Zoot Sims, Milt Jackson, Percy Heath and Kenny Clarke. Although they boasted a talented lineup, the group found little work. Johnson would freelance some more around the New York area but became disenchanted with the music business and took a job with an electronics company.

He gigged occasionally, but it wasn't until 1954 that he returned to the music scene in full force when he teamed up with another trombonist named Kai Winding. The interesting pairing of the two top bop trombonists produced the album *Jay and Kai.* A mildly successful experiment, it showcased J. J. Johnson the writer more than the possible exciting combinations of the two fine musicians. Although Winding would receive credit as a solid trombonist, he played second fiddle to Johnson's superiority.

Kai Winding was born in Denmark in 1922 and moved to the United States with his parents when he was twelve. Winding learned how to play the trombone and became proficient enough to join the Benny Goodman and Stan Kenton bands for brief spells. Winding recorded with several different combinations and formed a group with Tadd Dameron, Allen Eager, and Fats Navarro that played at a club called the Royal Roost for a brief time. While Winding and Johnson had crossed paths over the years, the pairing of the two was an interesting one.

They were a contrast in styles. While Winding was louder and brasher than Johnson, the latter was the more inventive of the two. They recorded on various occasions and played a number of concerts before breaking up in 1956. Although they would reunite for occasional concerts (including a European tour in 1958), and recorded together a few times, they mostly pursued their own individual careers.

Although Johnson made the smooth transition from bop to hard bop, it seemed that he was always ahead of his time. No one, with the sole exception of Kai Winding, was capable of doing the same things on the trombone and therefore J. J. was an anomaly in jazz. His domination of the instrument from the early 1950s on proved to be a double-edged sword. While he greatly advanced its popularity, he also relegated it to a more defined role. Any other trombone player at the time was lost in the shadow of Johnson's impressive sphere of power.

For the rest of the 1950s he was spurred on by the new musical ideas that were reinventing jazz every few months. He began to compose some of the most complex music ever heard. He formed a quintet that included at various times Bobby Jaspar, Freddie Hubbard on trumpet, Clifford Jordan on tenor saxophone, Cedar Walton on piano, Arthur Harper on bass and Al Heath or Kenny Clarke on drums. He always surrounded himself with talented sidemen who not only understood his musical ideas but were also capable of executing them on record and live on stage. Despite the promise his outfit demonstrated, Johnson broke it up in 1960.

He retreated to his home in New Jersey to spend more time with his wife and two sons. For much of the decade he led a double life, one as family man the other as the greatest trombone player of the day. He toured with the legendary Miles Davis for a year, but the pressures and loneliness of the road contrasted too sharply with the comforts of home. He found a compromise between the two clashing worlds by pursuing the lucrative life of arranger and writer. Already a noted creator of some of modern jazz's best songs, he pursued this side of the music business.

His writing skills became much in demand. John Lewis, who at the time was musical director of the Monterey Jazz Festival, was impressed enough with Johnson to ask the talented composer to write extended movements for his forty-piece orchestra. The result was *Rondeau for Quartet and Orchestra*, two long-running pieces. An ambitious musician with unlimited creativity, Johnson was also writing music that blended jazz with classical strains. He wrote a six-part composition for Gunther Schuller's orchestra called *Perceptions*. In order to execute the work properly, he enlisted the sharp skills of John Lewis and Jimmy Giuffre, who welded their individual sounds to Schuller's musical visions. Word of Johnson's creative talents spread quickly; Dizzy Gillespie, was intrigued by Johnson's work with Schuller, and in 1961 Diz released his own recording of *Perceptions.* The album featured the orchestral group that Dizzy had been playing with at the time, and Schuller stepped in to conduct the Johnson arrangement.

Throughout the rest of the 1960s Johnson split his time between writing for his own outfits as well as for others, and touring and recording with his various combos. Although he had received credit for changing the role of the trombone in jazz, he also had a keen eye for talent. He always ensured that all personnel in his ensembles complemented his skills. Despite his undisputed genius, it was around this time that his popularity began to decline from the golden years of the previous two decades. His style had been put aside in favor of a new brass band expressionism that was the current wave among trombonists.

But Johnson remained an important name in Jazz circles because of his previous seminal work. A proven artist with an abundance of talent, he turned away from the trend of the day to write movie and television scores, as well as appearing in lucrative studio sessions. He wrote the theme song of *Starsky and Hutch,* the very popular police drama in the 1970s.

Although throughout most of the 1970s he shunned live performances in order to concentrate on his studio and television work, Johnson played a concert in Japan in 1977. From that point on he assumed a more regular touring schedule, often leading his own quintet. Despite nearly a decade of no live appearances, he returned to the stage with relative ease. He was a dynamic performer who always gave the audience its money's worth.

In 1987, he returned to Indianapolis, his hometown, where he resumed recording, touring and playing. An annual *Downbeat* Poll winner, he was delighted with all the awards he received, especially an honorary doctor of music degree from Indiana University and the Indiana Governor's Arts Award in 1989.

In the 1990s he continued to add to his legend. The new generation of jazz fans that were unfamiliar with his name quickly learned that J. J. Johnson was a force to be reckoned with. Although he would never rediscover the immense popularity that he enjoyed in the 1940s and 1950s, he was still renowned in jazz circles.

In the mid–1990s, Johnson began to slow down. On February 4, 2001, Johnson, who had been in declining health, died of a self-inflicted gunshot wound. He was 77 years old.

J. J. Johnson is the greatest trombone player of all time. While many debates have raged over which Jazz musician is better than the other for almost all instruments, there is no questioning Johnson's supremacy. While Jack Teagarden and Kid Ory stand out as excellent players of their era, neither had as far-reaching an influence on modern jazz as did Johnson.

While Ory produced the tailgate effect and Teagarden amazed all with his growls and slurs, Johnson reinvented how to play the instrument. He ignored the growls and slurs that were the trademark of all swing and Dixieland players, and concentrated on other possibilities. He dreamed of playing the fast, agile lines of bebop and did just that.

As the new-sound master of the trombone, he has never been equaled. His work was technically perfect, as he possessed an immense amount of talent and imagination. Many of the leading trombonists who followed Johnson took a page from his book. A partial list includes Bob Brookmeyer, Jimmy Cleveland, Bruce Fowler, Curtis Fuller, Herbie Harper, Jimmy Knepper, Tom "Bones" Malone, Albert Mangelsdorff, Ray Anderson, Benny Powell, George Lewis, Grachan Moncure III, Roswell Rudd, Slide Hampton, Wayne Henderson, Delfeayo Marsalis, Bill Watrous, Robin Eubanks, Julian Priester, Raul DeSouza, Matthew Gee, Frank Rosolino, Steve Turre, Kai Winding, and Jerry Tilitz.

But not only was Johnson a superior trombonist, he also was a masterful composer. He created a wealth of music that inspired comparisons with major artists. A few examples of his unique songwriting talents include "Blue Mood," "Teapot," "Elora," "Get Happy," "Yesterdays," "I Waited for You," "El Camino Real, "Sketch for Trombone and Orchestra," "Perceptions," "Poem for Brass," "Cannon for Bela," "Time After Time," "Old Devil Moon," and "Capri."

He worked with a variety of jazz personalities including Ernie Royal, Stan Getz, Percy Heath, Sonny Rollins, Jerome Richardson, Rudy Van Gelder, Joe Newman, Paul Chambers, Milt Jackson, Ella Fitzgerald, Count Basie, Kai Winding, Benny Carter, Robin Eubanks, Steve Turre, Clifford Brown, Sonny Stitt, John Lewis, Kenny Clarke, Chet Baker, Jimmy Giuffre, and Gunther Schuller. All who shared the stage or a recording studio with Johnson were amazed at his ability to take the trombone down avenues that were thought to be impossible.

J. J. Johnson was a dedicated jazzman who envisioned new duties for the trombone and turned his ideas into reality. He remains one of the most eminent jazz figures for his many contributions as a bop, hard bop, avant-garde, and free jazz musician. Although there are many good trombonists, none have ever matched the creativity, fire and imagination of the man who made the trombone go bop.

Discography

Amazing Grace, Phantom B0000564L3.
At the Opera House (live), Polygram Records 831272.
Be-Bop Legends Live 1964–65.
The Best of J. J. Johnson: My Destination Is Love, Hot Productions 67.

Birdlanders, Dis3 351455.
Blue Trombone, Columbia Tristar B00008FX73.
The Brass Orchestra, Verve 537 321.
Cape Verdean Blues, Blue Note Records 84220.
Cleopatra Jones, Wea B00005B471.
Concepts in Blue, Original Jazz Classics 735.
Dial J.J., Legacy Records 65475,
The Eminent J. J. Johnson, Vol. 1, Blue Note Records 81505.
The Eminent J. J. Johnson, Vol. 2, Blue Note Records 81506.
The Eminent J. J. Johnson, Vol. 3, Blue Note Records 81507.
The Finest of J. J. Johnson, Bethlehem.
The Four Trombones: The Debut Recordings, Prestige 24097.
Heroes, Verve 528 864.
Jay and Kai, Savoy Jazz 163.
Jay and Kai Octet, Collectables 5677.
J. J. Inc., Columbia 65296.
J. J.!, DMG 7432125727.
J. J.'s Broadway, Verve B0000ACAO7.
J. J. Johnson's Jazz Quintets, Savoy 0151.
Jazz Quintets, Savoy 78813.
Let's Hang Out, Verve 514 454.
Live at Cafe Bohemia 1957, FRESH FSRCD143.
Live in London, Harkit B00007GOVG.
Nuf Said, Charly/Snapper B000024QM3.
Origins: Savoy Sessions, Savoy B0000695R4.
Pinnacles, Original Jazz Classics 1006.
Planet Jazz, RCA 21599742.
Proof Positive, GRP Records 145.
Quintergy Live, Polygram Records 48214.
Savoy, Prestige & Sensation: Complete Early Recordings, Definitive 11161.
Say When, RCA B000008BEZ.
Standards: Live at the Village Vanguard, Verve 510 059.
Tangence, Polygram Records 26588.
The Total J. J. Johnson, BMG 74321477912.
The Trombone Master, Columbia 44443.
Vivian, Concord Jazz 4523.
We'll Be Together Again, Orig. Jazz Classics 909.
Yokohama Concert (Live), Pablo 2620109.

BUD POWELL (1924–1966)

Hot House Blues

The bebop revolution featured some of the greatest names in jazz history and each "bopper" starred on a particular instrument. Charlie Parker took the alto sax to dimensions never heard before; Dizzy Gillespie brought

the bent trumpet to the forefront; Oscar Pettiford brought bop sophistication to the bass; Kenny Clarke created different rhythm paths that
enabled others to explore different solo territory. The foremost bebop
pianist on the scene was a man who gave the world his hot house blues.
His name was Bud Powell.

Earl "Bud" Powell was born on September 27, 1924, in New York City
into a musical family. His grandfather was a musician, as well as his older
brother William, who played trumpet and violin. But it was William Sr.,
Bud's father, who was the biggest influence on his youngest son's early
development. William Sr. played the piano and taught the rudiments to
Bud when the latter was six. This musical education consisted of closely
studying the classics, including Beethoven, Liszt, Chopin, Debussy, and
Schumann.

Later, Bud would gain an interest in jazz and listen intently to the
work of Billy Kyle, pianist in the John Kirby group. He would later discover Earl Hines, Art Tatum, and Teddy Wilson. But the boogie-woogie
kings of the 1930s, Pete Johnson, Albert Ammons, and Meade "Lux" Lewis,
also had an influence on him. Amid these myriad unique styles were the
elements that Powell would incorporate to create his own individual sound.

In his teenage years Powell was a musical gypsy, wandering from one
place to another absorbing all the hot sounds that were going down. At
fifteen, he quit school to work in his brother's band, but soon drifted to
Coney Island and found work in the clubs there. He played in many
different bands, including an outfit called the Sunset Royals, and performed
in various Harlem spots and all over the village. Always ready to jam with
anybody that was interested, Powell eventually found his way to Minton's
Playhouse. It was here that he met the shy and retiring pianist Thelonious
Monk, one of the young cats playing the new music.

He made his recording debut in 1942 on the Duke label, but he had
yet to fully develop his distinct touch. However, his later recording sessions with the Cootie Williams Big Band (he joined in 1943) demonstrated
a more mature style on the piano. The intricate double-timing that would
become his trademark surfaced on the cut "I Don't Know." In his two-year
stint with Williams, he greatly developed his powerful skills.

He then immersed himself in the 52nd Street scene that included John
Kirby, Dizzy Gillespie, J. J. Johnson, Dexter Gordon, Kenny Clarke, Miles
Davis, Charlie Parker, and Thelonious Monk, among others. Powell often
backed Johnson, Gordon and Sonny Stitt in the recording studio, as well
as cutting records with a loosely formed all-star outfit called the Bebop
Boys. He also added his personal piano touch in a recording date with the
great Charlie Parker, but their volatile personalities barred them from
working together often; the mix of the two proved to be too explosive.

Powell also cut albums with Miles Davis, Fats Navarro, Lucky Thompson, Dexter Gordon, Kai Winding, Milt Jackson, Oscar Pettiford, Max Roach, Curly Russell, and Kenny Clarke. Like his bebop cohorts, he performed at many of the hip jazz clubs in New York, including the Birdland. There was never a shortage of studio or live work; however, despite the numerous recording sessions and all-star jams, Powell was never involved in any long-lasting project due mainly to his frequent visits to mental hospitals.

His instability was a result of a career-changing incident that had occurred during his tenure with Williams. In an altercation with racial overtones, Powell was severely beaten by the police and as a result suffered health problems for the rest of his life. In those days, the term "police brutality" had not been coined nor used to describe treatment of a person of African American descent. Powell carried on, despite the severe headaches that plagued him, and he still managed to become instrumental in the creation and rise of bop.

The years between 1947 and 1951 were filled with good and bad times. On the positive side, in 1949, Powell began an association with the Blue Note label that produced some of his greatest efforts, including the classic "Dance of the Infidels." Sonny Rollins and Fats Navarro backed him on the first session. On later recording dates, Tommy Porter and Roy Haynes accompanied him.

On the negative side, he had a breakdown in late 1947 that resulted in a long stay at Creedmore Mental Institution. He was given electroshock treatment that further knocked him off balance. Released after almost a year, he returned to the institution within three months. An unstable individual with a volatile personality, he did not help himself with his bouts of heavy drinking.

In the spring of 1949, Powell emerged from the hospital and enjoyed a long period of tranquility. In 1951, however, the darkness returned and he was committed once again and wasn't released until 1953. During his stay he had been subjected to more electroshock treatment. For the remainder of the decade he cut many sides for Victor, Verve and Blue Note. Flashes of his feverish piano playing that had electrified audiences and his bandmates would occasionally surface. But, sadly, with each successive recording, his deteriorating health illustrated a loss of his previous supreme command of the keyboard.

One of the highlights of the decade was his participation at the Massey Hall concert in 1953 that included the unbeatable lineup of Charlie Parker, Dizzy Gillespie, Charles Mingus, and Max Roach. On that evening, Powell proved to everyone that he was the greatest bop pianist and that he could still reach those dizzying heights of his earlier career. Unfortunately, the good times would not last.

He continued to record when he wasn't institutionalized, but he had lost much of his ability. Powell, who had grown tired of New York, sought refuge in Paris in 1959. By this time he was married with children and moved his entire family to Europe, where he remained for five years. Despite the change in scenery, he still experienced periodical breakdowns and spent some time in mental hospitals while in the French capital.

In Paris, Powell recorded with a visiting Dizzy Gillespie and Dexter Gordon on separate occasions. But the same demons that had haunted him in New York resurfaced across the Atlantic. With one single drink Powell could go from stable human being to dangerous and deranged. In 1963, his health problems were further complicated by a battle with tuberculosis. But he regained his forces and resumed his fleeting jazz career.

He returned to New York in the summer of 1964 to pick up the pieces of his life in the United States. One of his first gigs was at Birdland, where for one night he was triumphant. Although he was unable to create the magic of the old days, he still played with inspiration and shades of his former dynamic self. He did a little recording during his residency at Birdland. But by the fall of the same year he resumed his erratic behavior, disappearing for long stretches of time and failing to show up for concert dates.

In 1965, in a concert tribute to the late, great Charlie Parker, Powell appeared on stage at Carnegie Hall looking in ill health and playing poorly. To those who had been amazed by his skills there was great disappointment, since it was apparent that he had returned to New York to die. He did participate in a couple of recording dates with the avant-garde that showed him in better form than the Carnegie Hall fiasco, but he never could regain his old touch.

The dark side now shadowed his everyday existence and he faded from the music world. Two years later, his former bandmates and everyone else were reading about his sad and untimely death on July 31, 1966, in New York City. He was only forty-one years old, another jazz great who left us much too early.

Bud Powell was a bop jewel. Although there were other bebop piano players, including Thelonious Monk, Tadd Dameron, Barry Harris, Hampton Hawes, Al Haig, Dodo Marmarosa and John Lewis, none possessed Powell's furious drive. He played the piano with the same ferocity that Charlie Parker played the alto saxophone. Although his career was tragically altered by that incident back in the mid–1940s, the pianist still made a significant impact on the world of jazz.

His style was a study in contrast, his playing a counterpoint in tension derived from the ability that he could muster with both hands. He was able to generate immense horsepower, he played incredible runs of melodic lines with his right hand while his left hand played rhythm. He juxtaposed the two worlds to create pure excitement. His style was a step forward from the stride piano players that he had admired in his youth.

He also incorporated the vast imagination and rhythmic variety trademarks of the great Art Tatum. Like Earl Hines, he was also able to blast his way through a brick wall like a thundering stampede of horses. But Powell was a bop artist and explored hidden nuances within the music that none of his early influences had discovered. There was an eerie edge to his music that separated it from the work of his contemporaries and those who came before him.

Undoubtedly, because of his superior technical skills, Powell is considered a giant of modern piano. Although few ever matched his emotional fervor, many attempted to follow the path he blazed. His influence on Toshiko Akiyoshi, Richie Beirach, Teddy Charles, Eddie Costa, Kenny Drew, Harold Land, Walter Norris, Hazel Scott, Charlie Shoemake, Art Taylor, Mal Waldron, Hugh Lawson, Lou Levy, Matthew Shipp, Sir Charles Thompson, Ramsey Lewis, McCoy Tyner, Hampton Hawes, Junior Mance, and Hod O'Brien is apparent. All of these artists were able to incorporate one or several aspects of Powell's style into their own.

Despite his erratic career as a recording artist and performer, he still managed to give the world a bouquet of musical gifts. They include "Hot House Blues," "Bud's Bubble," "Indiana," "Glass Enclosure," "I Want to Be Happy," "Polka Dots and Moonbeams," "Somewhere Over the Rainbow," "Dance of the Infidels," "52nd Street Theme," "Wall," "Bouncing with Bud," "Straight, No Chaser," "Little Willie Leaps," "Blues for Bouffemont," "Hallucinations," "Un Poco Loco," and "Tempus Fugit."

Powell was one of the prime architects of the bop revolution and paved the way for later styles of jazz, including hard bop and avant-garde. He meshed together nicely with Dizzy Gillespie, Kenny Clarke, Charles Mingus, Barney Kessel, Dexter Gordon, J. J. Johnson, Max Roach, and, at times, even Charlie Parker, despite their discomfort with one another. If he hadn't suffered his career-changing injury he might have been the greatest bebop artist of them all—including Parker and Gillespie.

Like Hines, Fats Waller, and Art Tatum, Powell has his place as an important connection between eras. He is, with Thelonious Monk, the link between the swing/big band era and the later contemporary sound. Bud's importance in the history of the piano cannot be overstated; he was one of the true giants who overcame seemingly insurmountable obstacles to achieve his status.

The Bud Powell story is one of jazz's most engaging yet saddest tales. What if he had never suffered that blow to the head? How many more treasures would he have given us? How many more incredible performances would he have left etched in our memories? The brutal beating robbed him of a long career. Many felt that he had just tapped the immense wealth of his undeniable talent.

In many ways Powell was Charlie Parker's alter ego. They both played their instruments fast and furiously with great dexterity and were arguably the quickest of all the bebop performers. They both possessed an incredible wealth of talent that many felt was never totally exercised. But more than anything, they lived on the edge. Factoids in the press about them were commonplace and it wasn't surprising that they went over with the public, regardless of their accuracy. They both suffered many skirmishes with the law, some racially motivated, others brought on by their erratic behavior.

There remains a Bud Powell cult following. Although many are intimidated by his incredible power, there is firm confirmation around jazz circles that he was a unique individual whose memory deserves to be respected. While others might have surpassed his achievements, no one has ever matched the pure emotional impact of the man who gave us his hot house blues.

Discography

Bouncing with Bud, Delmark 406.
Bouncing with Bud, Mobile Fidelity Sound Lab 703.
Jazz at Massey Hall, Volume 2, Original Jazz Classics 111.
Round About Midnight at the Blue Note, Dreyfus Records 36500.
1945–1947, Classics (import) 1003.
Best of Bud Powell, Blue Note Records 93204.
Bud Plays Bird, Blue Note Records 37137.
Bud's Bubble 1944–1947, EPM 159742.
Early Buds, Topaz Jazz Records 1059.
In Paris, Warner Archives 45817.
Jazz Giant, Verve 543 832.
Lausanne 1962, Naked City 5.
New York All Star Sessions, Band Stand 1507.
Vol. 4 At the Golden Circle, Steeplechase B000027T4L.
Piano Interpretations by Bud Powell, Universal/Verve B000034CFG.
Pianology (1961–64), Moon 55.
Strictly Powell, RCA Records 51423.
The Amazing Bud Powell Vol. 1, Blue Note Records 81503.
The Amazing Bud Powell, Vol. 2, Blue Note Records 81504.
Amazing Bud Powell Vol. 3, BLUEN TOCJ-1571.
Amazing Bud Powell Vol. 4, BLUEN TOCJ-9123.
The Complete 1946–1949 Roost/Blue Note/Verve, Definitive 11145.
The Essen Jazz Festival Concert, 1201 Music 9009.
The Genius of Bud Powell, Verve 827 901.
Time Waits, Blue Note Records 21227.
Tribute to Cannonball, Legacy Records 65186.

Ultimate Bud Powell, Verve 539 788.
Young Bud, Indigo (UK) 2106.
Complete Bud Powell on Verve, Verve 521 669.
Best of Bud Powell, BLUEN TOCJ-66033.
Blues In the Closet, VERVE POCJ-2744.
Genius of Bud Powell, VERVE POCJ-9232.
Jazz Original, VERVE POCJ-2741.
Lonely One, VERVE POCJ-2742.
Moods, VERVE POCJ-2740.
Piano Interpretations by Bud Powell, VERVE POCJ-2743.
Planet Jazz, BMG 74321520642.
Time Waits: The Amazing Bud Powell, BLUEN TOCJ-1598.
Bud Powell 1945–1947, Classic 1003.
Bud Powell, Early Buds, Pearl 1059.
Complete Blue Note & Roost Recordings 1947–1958, Blue Note 30083.
Bud Powell: The Scene Changes, 1958, Blue Note, 46529.
The Amazing Bud Powell Vol. 1, 1949–1951, Blue Note 81503.
The Amazing Bud Powell Vol. 2, 1951–1953, Blue Note 81504.
Best of Bud Powell on Verve 1950s, PLG 523392.
Ultimate Bud Powell, PLG 539788.
Genius of Bud Powell 1949–1951, PLG 827901.

SARAH VAUGHAN (1924–1990)

The Divine Miss V

The graceful presence of the female jazz singer adds dimensions to music that males are unable to provide. The sultry, liquid quality of the feminine voice is a trademark of not only jazz, but of all popular music. One of the most recognizable styles from the middle part of the twentieth century and for the next forty years belonged to the Divine Miss V. Her name was Sarah Vaughan.

Sarah Lois Vaughan was born on March 27, 1924, in Newark, New Jersey. Like so many other blues, rock and jazz singers, her first musical connection was with the church. She sang in the choir as a child and studied the piano for eight years, developing a fine touch on the ivories. But her strength was her rich, sensuous voice that contained many facets, allowing her to stretch beyond gospel music.

She paid her dues and honed her skills singing in many dives. Even back then, when she was making little money to keep body and soul together, anyone who heard her knew she was something special and with a bit of luck would someday be a huge star. Her big break came when she won a talent contest at the Apollo Theatre. Earl Hines, the great jazz pianist, hired her to front his band, its lineup consisting of bop visionaries Dizzy Gillespie and Charlie Parker. Unfortunately, due to the recording ban, she was unable to make any records for two years.

She was a savvy singer who made connections easily, building a system of networks that would serve her well during her long, illustrious career. In 1944, she joined Billy Eckstine's big band. Eckstine, who gave many bop artists their first break, was a longtime friend of Vaughan's. She found herself in a band that once again included the demonic Charlie Parker and Dizzy Gillespie. Because of her association with the two most important founders of bop, she was categorized firmly in that revolutionary camp.

Parker and Gillespie played bop, and Vaughan, whose longevity was directly linked to her ability to adapt to any kind of material, was forced to develop an individualist bop phrasing that became part of her vocal arsenal. Later Ella Fitzgerald would also create her own distinct bop voice. In fact, many singers would make the necessary adjustments in order to record with the musicians playing the new music.

After leaving Eckstine's band, Vaughan worked for a few months with John Kirby. But she was a truly gifted singer who didn't need to belong to a group to make it. From 1946 until her death over forty years later, she became the epitome of the solo star. Although she suffered a rough start, the experiences toughened her up and enabled her to endure the many pitfalls of the music business. Her early records for the Continental label showcased a young singer who had not reached her prime, but could take any song and turn it into something special with her incredible talent. All the trademarks that would make her a household name were present on those first, unpolished recordings.

It didn't hurt that for the first sessions she had talented sidemen like Charlie Parker and Dizzy Gillespie. Both musicians were important pieces in her rise to stardom, but they weren't the only ones. After a successful set of songs cut for the Musicraft label that only enhanced her reputation, the Jimmy Jones band, which included the cool one, Miles Davis, backed her. Although she proved that she could handle any type of material and was one of the great vocal talents in jazz, in any assessment of her career, especially in the beginning of it, one must take note that it was the bop musicians who supported her musically.

In the 1950s she began to spread her creative wings. Although she had proven without a doubt her mastery of the new jazz idiom, she ventured into popular music with winning results. One of the most versatile singers in the history of jazz, she was also capable of singing blues, pop, and rhythm and blues with equal class and distinction. She was simply a gem of a singer with an uncanny sense of rhythm and timing.

She recorded for a number of different labels and many of the songs became treasured classics. Vaughan was able to separate her jazz performances from her pop sessions. For example, the collaboration with the noted trumpeter Clifford Brown in 1958 was a jazz outing, while the EmArcy recordings contained more pop oriented material. Interestingly, it was the 1945 recording session that produced "Lover Man," during which Gillespie and Parker provided back up, that forever established her jazz credentials.

Although she had accomplished much at this point in her career, the 1960s and 1970s were truly her golden years. She performed often with a trio of piano, double bass and drums that formed her backup band, but also appeared on stage with a big band or symphony orchestra. During this period she recorded for the Roulette, Mercury and Columbia labels. Even a five year absence from the studio didn't hurt her career.

Vaughan was a true road warrior, crisscrossing the entire country and the world, entertaining everyone with her classic show. Because of her flexibility she was not restricted to any single venue. For instance, she could kill in a jazz club one night and wow the crowds the next evening at a rock and roll palace like The Fillmore. The exposure to a different type of audience enlarged her fan base and allowed greater crossover appeal.

In 1977, she signed on Norman Granz's Pablo label. Granz was ecstatic to have the great Sarah Vaughan in his stable of stars. Her trio (which had over the years featured jazz greats Jimmy Jones, Roy Haynes, Richard Davis, Roland Hanna, Bob James, Jan Hammer, Jimmy Cobb, Andy Simpkins and Harold Jones) became a quartet under the direction of her husband, Waymon Reed, from 1978 to 1980.

By the 1980s, Vaughan could look back at a lengthy career with many, many triumphs. She had recorded an extensive catalog of hits and pure classics on a variety of labels, followed by a number of greatest hits packages available to a public who could never get enough of that magical voice. She was an enduring entertainer whose forty-year career was filled with many achievements and few disappointments.

On April 3, 1990, in Los Angeles, California, Sarah Vaughan, one of the greatest singers in the history of modern music, passed away. She was 66 years old.

Sarah Vaughan was a genuine jazz jewel. With the possible exception of Billie Holiday and Ella Fitzgerald, Vaughan was the greatest female jazz singer in the history of the genre. But she was a diamond who could not be confined to one style of music. Her catalog is filled with a variety of styles that includes pop, blues, and soul numbers. Her thousands of live performances helped spread the gospel of jazz and jazz-tinged material. She was one of the first performers to incorporate different elements in her essentially jazz-based sound.

While Charlie Parker will always be identified as the supreme alto saxophonist, Dizzy Gillespie one of the main trumpeters, J. J. Johnson the prime trombonist, Vaughan's instrument was her voice. Like the saxophone, trumpet, and trombone, she could play any style with her individual instrument and often her singing sounded like a finely tuned trumpet, wailing saxophone, chiming piano or ringing guitar.

Her voice possessed a phenomenal edge and an emotional power that enabled her to bring even the most inferior song to life. There were many layers to her vocal style, each timbre capable of creating a spark of magic. With a four-octave range, she rivaled many opera singers. Several singers who have gained immense stardom have never been capable of covering the same spectrum.

One of her greatest assets as a singer was her improvisational skill. She could take any song and shape it differently every time she performed it, adding unusual dimensions to the number. She was a master at accenting the rhythms and syllables in a word that could completely change the meaning and course of a song. Her scat singing was excellent and only Ella Fitzgerald and Louis Armstrong could be said to be on the same level.

Her use of dynamics and space that formed the cornerstones of her unique style were two more elements that made her a legend. As a vocalist she possessed every weapon any singer could ever hope to have; however, Vaughan boasted more than her fair share of these skills in an embarrassment of riches. She was able to execute all of her musical gifts into one package of professional power.

Another characteristic that made Vaughan so remarkable was her ability to blend her voice with each individual instrument that backed her up. She could get down low and gritty with the saxophone or reach the higher end of the flute's sound. She could rumble with the bass, hop with the single run notes of the guitar and piano, as well as blare aloud like the feistiest trumpet.

It is almost impossible to list all of the songs that Vaughan touched with her special magic. A few of her many masterpieces include "Embraceable You," "April in Paris," "Body and Soul," "Tenderly," "Ain't Misbehavin'," "Black Coffee," "My Man's Gone Now," "Everything I Have Is Yours," "Lullaby of Birdland," "I'm Glad There Is You," "Shulie A Bop," "Interlude," "If You Could See Me Now," "Tenderly" and "It's Magic." Her extensive catalog is beyond remarkable.

There is scarcely a singer over the last sixty years who has not been touched by the Vaughan magic. A short list includes Nina Simone, Anita Baker, Aretha Franklin, Rickie Lee Jones, Betty Carter, Fionna Duncan, Karin Krog, Patty Richards, Nnenna Freelon, Lula Reed, Carmen McRae,

Joe Lee Wilson, Rebecca Kilgore, Claire Martin, Suzanne Pittson, Eboni Foster, and Loston Harris.

Sarah Vaughan was one of the true great jazz vocalists and her fame reached titanic proportions. She was admired not only by her legion of fans, but also by contemporary artists of every musical style, including blues great B. B. King. Although she has been gone since 1990, her voice still echoes throughout the music world, proving there is no silencing the Divine Miss V.

Discography

All Time Greats [4/3], Stardust Records 1026.
At Mister Kelly's Complete Sessions, POLYG UCCM-9034.
In the Land of Hi-Fi, POLYG UCCM-9035.
No Count Sarah, POLYG UCCM-9039.
Sarah Vaughan's Finest Hour, Verve 543 597.
Viva! Vaughan, Verve 549 374.
16 Most Requested Songs, Legacy Records 53783.
1946–1947, Classics 989.
1947–1949, Classics 1101.
1950–1954, Giants of Jazz Recordings 53165.
1960–1964, Giants of Jazz Recordings 53176.
A Portrait of Sarah Vaughan, Gallerie 454.
A Touch of Class, Disky 865232.
After Hours, Blue Note Records 55468.
Brazilian Romance, CBS Masterworks 42519.
Cocktail Hour, Cocktail Hour Records 218008.
Compact Jazz, Verve 830 699.
Copacabana, Pablo Records 2312–125.
Crazy & Mixed Up, Pablo Records 2312–137.
Diva of Jazz: Great Moments, Classic World Productions, Inc. 9946.
Duke Ellington Songbook One, Pablo Records 2312–111.
Duke Ellington Songbook Two, Pablo Records 2312–116.
Embraceable You, Laserlight 17110.
Everything I Have Is Yours, Drive Archive 42035.
Favorites, Sony Music Special Products 13517.
Forever Gold, St. Clair 5719.
Gershwin Live!, CBS Masterworks 37277.
Golden Hits, Mercury 824 891.
How Long Has This Been Going On?, Pablo Records 2310
I Love Brazil!, Pablo Records 2312–101.
In Hi-Fi, Columbia 65117.
In the City of Lights, Justin Time 8474.
Jazz Fest Masters, Volcano Entertainment 32086.
Jazz Profile, Blue Note Records 23517.
Jazz Round Midnight, Verve 512 379.
Jazz Sessions 1944–50, Blue Moon 7801.
Love Me Or Leave Me: The Best Sarah Vaughan, Recall 161.
Lover Man, Meteor 31.

Many Moods of Sarah Vaughan, Ember 3333.
Quiet Now: Dreamsville, Verve 543 252.
Rodgers & Hart Songbook, EmArcy 824 864.
Sarah Sings Soulfully, Blue Note Records 98445.
Sarah Vaughan, Timeless Treasures 107.
Sarah Vaughan 1944–1946, Classics 958.
Sarah Vaughan Sings Broadway: Great Songs From, Verve 526 464.
Sarah Vaughan with Clifford Brown, Verve 543 305.
Sarah's Blues, JMY 1002.
Sassy Sings & Swings, EMI-Capitol Special Markets 57591.
Sassy Swings the Tivoli, EmArcy 832 788.
Send in the Clowns, Legacy Records 64610.
Sings George Gershwin, Verve 557 567.
Sings the Mancini Songbook, Verve 558 401.
Slow & Sassy, Pearl Flapper 7809.
Snowbound/The Lonely Hours, EMI 109.
Soft & Sassy, Hindsight 601.
Songs of the Beatles, Rhino Records 16037.
Sophisticated Cissy, Drive 3533.
The Best of Sarah Vaughan, Pablo Records 2405–416.
The Complete Sarah Vaughan ... Vol. 1, Mercury 826 320.
The Complete Sarah Vaughan ... Vol. 2, Mercury 826 327.
The Complete Sarah Vaughan ... Vol. 3, Mercury 826 333.
The Divine ... The Columbia Years (1949–1953), Columbia 44165.
The Essential Sarah Vaughan, Verve 512 904.
The Man I Love, Giants of Jazz Recordings 53326.
The Masters, Eagle Rock 485.
The Quintessence: New York (1944–48), Fremeaux 228.
The Revue Collection, Revue Collection 423.
The Roulette Years (1960–1963), Blue Note Records 94983.
The Very Best of Sarah Vaughan, Collectables 5903.
Time After Time, Drive Archive 41021.
Ultimate Sarah Vaughan, Verve 539 052.
Verve Jazz Masters 18, Verve 518 199.
Verve Jazz Masters 42: The Jazz Sides, Verve 526 817.
You're Mine You, Blue Note Records 57157.
The Best of Sarah Vaughan, Pablo Records 2405–416.
I Get A Kick Out Of You, MASTE 503362.
Live At Newport & More, JVC VICJ-60556.
O Som Brasileiro de Sarah Vaughan, BMG M10027.
Portrait of Sarah Vaughan, MCI GALE454.
September Song, HALLM 304082.
Thou Swell, BCD JTM8124.
Touch of Class, EMI TC865232.
What More Can A Woman Do Vol. 2, ABM ABMMCD1156.
Wonderful Music of Sarah Vaughan, BCD WMO90316.
The Divine Sarah Vaughan: The Columbia Years 1949-1953, SONY 44165.
Swinging Easy 1954, PLG 514072.
Rodgers & Hart Songbook 1954–1958, PLG 824864.
Golden Hits 1958, PLG 824891.
Misty/Vaughan & Voices 1958, PLG 846488.

OSCAR PETERSON (1925–)

Canadian Suite

An illustrious chain of Jazz pianists runs throughout the history of the genre. Many have been major contributors to the realm of symphonic blues and have rightfully earned their position in the gallery of jazz giants. Although they played the same instrument, each pianist had their own individual sound. One performer who ranks as one of the most brilliant gave the world his "Canadian Suite." His name is Oscar Peterson.

Oscar Emmanuel Peterson was born on August 15, 1925, in Montreal, Quebec. Peterson came from a musical family; his sister was a fine pianist who won many competitions. Oscar himself was no slouch; eight years after he began his study of the piano, he won a talent show that began his rapid acceleration towards a professional career. It was his weekly spot on a radio show in his native Montreal that brought him one step closer to his ultimate goal. His stint in Johnny Holmes's Orchestra was also a valuable learning experience. His early influence was the great Art Tatum.

In 1945, he made his recording debut with the Victor label, and after more than thirty-two sides he was beginning to get noticed outside of Montreal. He boasted an overwhelming command of ballads, intricate blues patterns and pop. His talent spread over the breadth and depth of the spectrum of jazz. However, he would often be categorized as a swing and bop player, since it was as close to any handle that could be attached to his very personalized brand of the genre.

In 1949, he began an important partnership with Norman Granz, who would serve as his manager and fuel Oscar's immense popularity. As a guest at the Jazz at the Philharmonic concert, Peterson astonished everyone with his remarkable technique, showmanship, and class. It would be the first of thousands of JATP concerts for him over his long, distinguished career.

As a result of his professional relationship with Granz, Peterson became one of the most prolific recording artists in the genre. Granz was a strong believer in saturating the market with product and there was always fresh material to release from Peterson. In 1950, Oscar teamed with Ray Brown. The two recorded "Tenderly," which did much to infuse the pianist's name in the minds of the record buying public.

In 1952, Peterson and Brown teamed up with Barney Kessel, who could not maintain the incredible performance pace that the trio was setting. Herb Ellis replaced Kessel and the three of them—Peterson, Brown, and Ellis—became so musically close that their sound was seamless. They developed into one of the best-loved jazz combos, touring and recording on a regular basis.

The chemistry between the trio was what set the jazz world on fire. They swung hard and their music was at the cutting edge of bebop. Their competitive nature only enhanced the band's reputation and the spirit was carried onto the stage as well as the recording studio. As a power group they were able to generate a wall of sound that many full orchestras containing a dozen or more musicians had a difficult time matching.

After five solid years as one of the top combos in jazz, Ellis left the fold. Instead of trying to find a replacement, Peterson, Granz, and Brown decided to change the dynamics of the band. They hired drummer Ed Thigpen. Although they were still a very competitive trio, the change in format shifted the emphasis to Peterson. He became the dominant figure in the group that remained together for seven years, recording a large number of albums and performing hundreds of concerts. They were one of the most popular combos in jazz.

The departure of Thigpen in 1965 prompted a search for a new drummer. Louis Hayes came in for a year, then was replaced by Bobby Durham, who stayed for three years. Ray Price lasted one year. Bass player Brown, who had been with Peterson for thirteen years, quit the band in 1966. Sam Jones replaced Brown and left in 1970. George Mraz briefly took over Jones' seat. The revolving door of sidemen didn't slow Oscar down.

In an effort to give back to the community, he opened up the Advanced School of Contemporary Music in Toronto, where he was living. Although it was a noble idea, the venture lasted only three years. Peterson, who was always on the road or in the recording studio, was never able to give the project the attention it needed to be a success.

In 1968, Peterson began a series of unaccompanied piano solos while doing double duty with his trio. In 1972, still under Granz's management, he signed on the Pablo label. Although he continued to make solo albums, guitarist Joe Pass and bassist Niels Pedersen often accompanied him on these sessions. Because of his vast talents, he also appeared on many collaborations with different artists, among them Count Basie, Dizzy Gillespie, Roy Eldridge, Harry "Sweets" Edison, Clark Terry and Jon Faddis.

Throughout the 1970s and 1980s Peterson only added to his legendary status. A man with a fantastic array of musical weapons at his disposal, he remained at the top of the heap of jazz pianists, playing his bop-enriched style amid the various changes that swept through the genre. He always provided a counter balance to the disjointed sounds of the new thing in jazz. His sound was reliable, solid and dependable, but never boring. He had also long ago assumed the distinction of being the best Canadian jazz export.

In 1990, Peterson was reunited with old bandmates Herb Ellis and Ray Brown; they recorded four CDs together that proved to be a joyous occasion. In 1993, Peterson suffered a stroke that seriously limited his playing. After two years of rest and recovery, he returned but with diminished power in his left hand. Since then he has continued to record and perform at a much slower pace than in his heyday.

Oscar Peterson is one of the wizards of the piano. He has proven over his long, colorful career that his command of the instrument was first rate. With the exception of Art Tatum, he is probably the greatest piano player in the history of jazz. In some circles, he is thought to have surpassed his idol Tatum.

Because of his versatility, it has always been very difficult to categorize Peterson. The swing camp claims him as one of their own but the bop crowd makes the same statement. In many ways Peterson's music has never been about specific musical styles. The essence of his work has always been about substance over style. If he sounded like he was intentionally playing bop or swing, it was almost by accident.

Like all other jazz artists, Peterson is a blues player who has taken the genre to frontiers it had never been to before. He is capable of playing in any style; there is even an element of stride piano in his work. He experimented with the rhythms of the stride pianists and gave it a modern twist. His playing contains a rich texture of complex chords and speedy runs of notes.

He has always explored new sounds and his technique allowed him to be adventurous. His style was one of two hands doing many things at once to create the illusion of a roomful of pianists instead of a solo act. With his powerful right hand he played incredible runs up and down the keyboard with frightening speed, while his left hand pumped out his diverse rhythms. In many ways, Peterson, like Bud Powell, imitated on the piano what bop artists Charlie Parker and Dizzy Gillespie did on their respective instruments.

As one of the founders of modern jazz, Peterson has influenced many. They include Patrice Rushen, Toshiko Akiyoshi, Monty Alexander, Dorothy Ashby, Michel Legrand, Adam Makowicz, Paul Smith, Cecil Taylor, Ronnell Bright, Joe Bushkin, Marty Napoleon, Phil Nimmons, Mickey Tucker, Phil Wilson, Ramsey Lewis, Kevin Eubanks, Paul Keller, Jay Leonhart, Junior Mance, and Loston Harris. He has touched everyone who has fallen under his magical spell.

He is one of the most prolific recording artists in the history of jazz and has collaborated with a number of other musicians, including his bandmates, Herb Ellis, Ray Brown, Niels Pederson, Ed Thigpen, and Barney Kessel. He has also recorded with Ella Fitzgerald, Roy Eldridge, Ben Webster, Louie Bellson, Alvin Stoller, Clark Terry, Dizzy Gillespie, Stan Getz, Harry "Sweets" Edison, Benny Carter, Buddy Rich, Count Basie, Freddie Green, and Coleman Hawkins.

He gave the world "Tenderly," "C-Jam Blues," "I'm In the Mood for Love," "Satin Doll," "At Long Last Love," "Perdido," "Just Friends," "Indiana," "Sweet Georgia Brown," "Canadian Suite," "Take the A-Train," and "Honeysuckle Rose." Many of the songs that he recorded were covers of classics given his special touch and a complete list would fill several volumes. His body of work is amongst the most expansive of any Canadian artist.

Among bop pianists he holds a special place. He was a powerhouse like Bud Powell, but veered in a different direction. His music and style were more accessible than Thelonious Monk's efforts. While he may never be credited with being an important architect of bop, Peterson added a texture to the style that none of the other pianists could ever produce. But unlike Powell and Monk, he stretched well beyond the style's confined structure.

Oscar Peterson remains one of the best loved jazz figures in the history of the genre. He is a polite individual, with a well-known sense of humor and majestic touch on the piano. Arguably the greatest jazz artist to emerge from the Great White North, he will forever be remembered as the man who took the piano into the modern era. His sound is instantly recognizable and the legend of the man who gave the world his "Canadian Suite" lives on.

Discography

At the Concertebouw, Verve 521 649.
At the Stratford Shakespearean Festival, Verve 513 752.
Encore At the Blue Note, Telarc 83356.
I Got Rhythm, Giants of Jazz Recordings 53340.
Immortal Concerts Part One, Giants of Jazz Recordings 53203.
Immortal Concerts Part Two, Giants of Jazz Recordings 53204.
Last Call at the Blue Note, Telarc 83314.
Live at CBC Studios, 1960, Just A Memory Records 9507.
Live at the Blue Note, Telarc 83304.
Nigerian Marketplace, Pablo Records 2308–231.
Night Train, Verve 521 440.
On the Town with the Oscar Peterson Trio, Verve 543 834.
Saturday Night at the Blue Note, Telarc 83306.
Sound of the Trio, Verve 543 321.
We Get Requests, Verve 521 442.
West Side Story, Verve 539 753.
West Side Story, DCC Jazz 1068.
Oscar Peterson Trio Plays, VERVE POCJ-9222.
Trio, VERVE POCJ-9214.
A Summer Night in Munich, Telarc Jazz Zone 83450.
1945–1947, Classics 1084.
1951, Just A Memory Records 9501.

A Royal Wedding Suite, Original Jazz Classics 973.
A Tribute to Oscar Peterson: Live, Telarc Jazz Zone 83401.
An Oscar Peterson Christmas, Telarc 83372.
At Zardi's, Pablo Records 2620–118.
Blues Etudes, Verve 818 844.
Cole Porter Songbook, Verve 821 987.
Compact Jazz, Verve 830 698.
Essential Oscar Peterson—The Swinger, Verve 517 174.
Essential Oscar Peterson—The Swinger, Verve 517 174.
Exclusively For My Friends, Verve 513 830.
Exclusively For My Friends: The Lost Tapes, Verve 529 096.
First Recordings, Indigo 2070.
Jazz 'Round Midnight, Verve 513 460.
Jazz Portrait of Frank Sinatra, Verve 825 769.
Jazz Soul of Oscar Peterson/Affinity, Verve 533 100.
Live, Pablo Records 2310–940.
Live at the Barbican, BBC Music 7001.
Live at the Northsea Festival 1980, Pablo Records 2620115.
My Favorite Instrument, Verve 821 843.
Oscar in Paris ... Live at the Salle Pleyel, Telarc 83414.
Oscar Peterson in Russia, Pablo Records 2625–711.
Oscar Peterson Meets Roy Hargrove and, Telarc 3399.
Oscar Peterson's Finest Hour, Verve 543 599.
Oscar's Boogie, Jazz Hour 73596.
Paris Jazz Concert, Malaco 1208.
Plays Broadway—Verve Jazz, Verve 516 893.
Plays Duke Ellington, Pablo Records 2310 966.
Plays the Duke Ellington Songbook, Verve 559 785.
Quiet Now: Time and Again, Verve 543 250.
Song Is You: The Best of the Verve Songbooks, Verve 531 558.
The Complete Young Oscar Peterson (1945–1949), RCA Records 66609.
The Gershwin Songbooks, Verve 529 698.
The History of an Artist, Pablo Records 2625–702.
The London Concert, Pablo Records 2620–111.
The More I See You, Telarc 83370.
The Paris Concert, Pablo Records 2620–112.
The Personal Touch, Pablo Records 2312–135.
The Vienna Concert, Philology 34.
The Will to Swing: At His Very Best, Verve 847 203.
Time After Time, Pablo Records 2310–947.
Tracks, Verve 523 498.
Trio Live in Chicago, Verve 539 063.
Triple Play, Telarc 83447.
Ultimate Oscar Peterson, Verve 539 786.
Verve Jazz Masters 16, Verve 516 320.
With Respect to Nat, Verve 557 486.
75 Birthday Celebration, EMI 3145439022.
Action, POLYG UCCM-9001.
Best of Jazz Piano, MERCU PHCY-3039.
Duke Ellington Songbook, VERVE POCJ-2745.
First Recordings, INDIG IGOCD2070.
Girl Talk, POLYG UCCM-9003.

Hello Herbie, POLY 8218462.
In a Romantic Mood (+5 Bonus Tracks), VERVE POCJ-2642.
Mellow Mood, POLYG UCCM-9004.
Most Famous Hits, ARCAD 6516.
Reunion Blues, POLYG UCCM-9010.
Soft Suns, POLYG POCJ-2575.
Tenderly, VERVE POCJ-2571.
Travelin On, POLYG UCCM-9005.
Tristeza on Piano, POLYG UCCM-9008.
Way I Really Play, POLYG UCCM-9006.
Oscar Peterson Trio & The Buddy De Franco Quartet, Live, JZBA 2111.

SONNY ROLLINS (1930–)
The Cutting Edge

The 1940s and 1950s were a great period of change in jazz. In the span of a few years the music shed the swing/big band image and rushed through bop, later on bebop, and then split into two camps of hard bop and cool jazz. Many of the bop pioneers moved on to later versions of the style. The innovators that fueled the rapid development of each form were always searching for ways to take the music down a different path. One of these figures always seemed to be on the cutting edge of the new thing. His name is Sonny Rollins.

Sonny Rollins was born Theodore Walter Rollins on September 7, 1930, in New York City. Before he adopted the tenor saxophone as his prime instrument of choice, he played the piano and the alto. In his teens he was drawn to the fury and excitement of bebop, jamming with J. J. Johnson and Bud Powell. Rollins loudly broadcasted with his emotional playing that there was a new tenor saxophone on the scene and it was going to shake the jazz world.

He made his recording debut with Babs Gonzales in 1949 on the album *Strictly Bebop*. More importantly was his participation in the *Amazing Bud Powell* session, where Rollins proved he could play with the major bop artists of the time although his style had not yet reached its full maturity. But Sonny, who was playing alongside Charlie Parker and Dizzy Gillespie when he was still too young to be drafted into the army or drink legally in a bar, was already years ahead of his time.

In the early days of the emerging sound of bop, Rollins was one of the creators and lived on 52nd Street, the heartbeat of the new music. Although he played with some of the biggest names on the scene, including Diz, Bird and Miles Davis, it was his record *Moving Out* that really brought him the prominence he was seeking. The technical consistency that he had been lacking was present in abundance on his breakout recording. Rollins added to his impressive credentials, serving time as a member of the Max Roach–Clifford Brown unit.

After the tragic death of Brown in 1956, Rollins and Roach continued to play together and it was the great bop drummer who provided the drive to the tenor's masterpiece recording *Saxophone Colossus*. On this album more than any other Rollins truly came into his own and proved that he was more than a just another saxophonist blowing fast, hard notes. With the untimely death of Charlie Parker, Rollins quietly filled the position as the top sax player in jazz.

From this point on Rollins continued to record important work with a variety of partners. On *Way out West*, bassist Ray Brown and drummer Shelly Manne accompanied him. He teamed up with Philly Jo Jones on the album *Newk's Time* and paid homage to one of his early idols, Coleman Hawkins, by redoing "Body and Soul." He collaborated with Thelonious Monk on *Brilliance* and *Sonny Rollins, Volume 2*. Later on, he jammed in live sessions with the great Elvin Jones, as the duo challenged each other and produced two hot records: *Live at the Village Vanguard* and *More from the Vanguard*.

In the late 1950s, Rollins recorded "The Freedom Suite," a nineteen-minute piece dedicated to the struggle of the common African American. He was a decade ahead of his time with this recording that made a bold radical and racial statement. The record was eventually released as *The Shadow Waltz* in watered-down form. The original was considered too controversial for a nation struggling with the civil rights issue. On this album, Max Roach and Oscar Pettiford backed him.

From 1959 to 1961, Rollins went on a sabbatical. He contemplated the sweeping changes that were taking place in jazz at the time with free players Ornette Coleman, Cecil Taylor, and John Coltrane bursting on the scene. During this period of self-reflection Rollins meditated on a bridge, practicing his tenor so he could fit in the new style.

Upon his return he teamed up with Jim Hall on the album *What's New*. Although there was a noted change in his playing, much of the fire and passion of his pre-sabbatical days was still intact. A couple of years later he finally was able to test his mettle with the new thing players, including Don Cherry, Bob Cranshaw, and Billy Higgins. The album *Our Man in Jazz* was a success and proved that his time off to rethink his musical position had paid off handsomely. Although he no longer occupied the position as the number one saxophone player in the world (the title was a contest between Ornette Coleman and John Coltrane), Rollins was still a dominant force in jazz.

He remained one of the most important saxophonists during much of the 1960s despite the emergence of others that were part of the free jazz/avant-garde talent pool. He continued to roll out quality albums that demonstrated he had not lost any of his magic touch. Although a bop player at heart, Rollins managed to expand his saxophone vocabulary in order to fit in the new music without losing any of his original brilliancy. This ability to adapt so readily indicated his wide range of musical tools.

After a good run throughout most of the 1960s, Rollins retired again for a couple of years. He reemerged in 1971 and once again showed that the long layoff had not affected his playing, although the burning intensity, the trademark of his sound, had somewhat diminished. But he continued to make good records, including *Next Album, Horn Culture, The Cutting Edge, Nucleus, The Way I Feel* and others. He worked with bagpipe player Rufus Harley on the albums *Next Album* and *The Cutting Edge*.

Rollins seemed to run out of steam through much of the 1970s and 1980s. He recorded sporadically and his live appearances were irregular. His records and performances were received with mixed results. Although he still could deliver the goods, his best days were clearly behind him. However, his high level of skill, his ability to change with the times, and his freedom to explore various styles allowed Rollins to carry on into the 1990s. His vast body of work speaks volumes of his accomplishments throughout his long career.

Today he is a one of the few grand masters of jazz, a living legend and an inspiration to the young lions.

Sonny Rollins is a jazz troubadour. He was in the forefront of the scene for three decades before slowing down. In his prime his horn always remained sharp and ready. He added an incredible wealth of material to the archives and played with just about every big name of the past seven decades. While other figures of the bop revolution—Charlie Parker, Bud Powell, Fats Navarro and Clifford Brown—died young, Rollins managed to forge a long, prosperous career.

Rollins is one of the most brilliant tenor saxophone players in the history of the genre. His daring, driving sound, the tonal distortions, the freedom from harmonic restrictions, and his expressive forces are all cornerstones of his style. He played wide with an aggressiveness and imagination that rivaled Lester Young, John Coltrane and his idol, Coleman Hawkins. Rollins was never afraid to venture outside the norm and because of his curiosity he always managed to sound fresh.

He gave the world a number of classic songs that have passed the test of time: "Vierd Blues," "Swinging For Bumsy," "Solid," "Valse Hot," "Blue 7," "St. Thomas," "Come Gone," "Wagon Wheels," "I'm An Old Cowhand," "The Surrey with the Fringe On Top," "Body and Soul," "Sonnymoon for

Two," "The Freedom Suite," "Don't Stop the Carnival," "Brownskin Girl," "Jungoso," "Olea," "Three Little Words," "Four," "Blessing in Disguise," "East Broadway Rundown," "To A Wild Rose," "Skylark," "Poinciana," and "Playin' in the Yard." Although not all are his own compositions, Rollins could always take a song from another performer and put a special spin on it. His ability to reinvent without tampering with the basic framework allowed him the luxury of repeating a classic that had been done a hundred times over without making it sound stale.

He has had a large influence on a number of jazz artists, some of them saxophonists, and others playing different instruments. A partial list includes Monty Alexander, Albert Ayler, Tubby Hayes, Buck Hill, Jean-Luc Ponty, David Schnitter, Charlie Shoemake, Wayne Shorter, Jack Walrath, Fred Anderson, Zbigniew Namyslowski, Pat La Barbera, Ray Pizzi, and Pharoah Sanders.

Rollins is one of the architects of bop music along with Parker, Gillespie and others that hung around the 52nd Street scene creating history. The most remarkable fact about Sonny's inclusion in the bop revolution was his tender age. At seventeen, when most saxophonists were still trying to sort themselves out musically, he was challenging musicians twice his age.

Although firmly entrenched in the bop camp, Rollins was one of the many artists who ventured down different avenues and was responsible for the rapid change of styles in the genre. He possessed enough flexibility to emerge out of the confinements of bop to provide jazz with a new direction. Although not the only musician to start out in bop and to explore a different style, Rollins did it as well as anyone else and better than most.

Despite an erratic career that has seen its share of sabbaticals, there is no denying Rollins's many contributions. He has added his own individual chapter to the long history of jazz. He remains one of the elder statesmen and his cutting edge performances are the stuff of legends.

Discography

Bebop Professors, Capitol CR-8812.
J. J. Johnson's Jazz Quintets, Savoy Jazz SV-0151.
Mad Bebop, Savoy Jazz SLJ 2232.
Trombone by Three, Fantasy/OJC OJCCD-091-2.
The Amazing Bud Powell, Vol. 1, Blue Note B21Y-81503.
Miles Davis and Horns, Prestige PRLP 7025.
Sonny Rollins with MJQ, Prestige PRLP 7029.
Dig, Fantasy/OJC-005.
Conception, Prestige 7013.
Monk, Fantasy/OJC-016.
Thelonious Monk and Sonny Rollins, Fantasy/OJC-059.

Early Art, New Jazz 82158.
Bags Groove, Fantasy/OJC-245.
Movin' Out, Fantasy/OJC OJC-058.
Worktime, Fantasy/OJC-007.
Raw Genius, Vol. 1, Victor SMJ 6185.
Raw Genius, Vol. 2, Victor SMJ 6196.
More Study in Brown, EmArcy 841637-2.
Perfection Collection on EmArcy, EmArcy Ph 19JD-10201-10.
Pure Genius, Vol. 1, Elektra Musician EL-60026.
Clifford Brown and Max Roach at Basin Street, EmArcy 814648-2.
Sonny Rollins Plus 4, Fantasy/OJC OJC-243.
Tenor Madness, Fantasy/OJC 124.
Saxophone Colossus, Fantasy/OJC 291.
Sonny Rollins Plays for Bird, Fantasy/OJC 214.
Sonny Boy, Fantasy/OJC 348.
Max Roach + 4, EmArcy MG-36098.
Jazz in 3-4 Time, EmArcy MG-36108.
Tour de Force, Fantasy/OJC 095.
Sonny Rollins Vol. 1, Blue Note B21Y-81542.
Brilliant Corners, Fantasy/OJC 026.
First Recordings, Musicdisc 550142.
Way Out West, Fantasy/OJC 337.
Max Roach + 4 and More, EmArcy 82673-2
Sonny Rollins, Vol. 2, Blue Note B21Y-81558
Jazz Contrasts, Fantasy/OJC-028.
The Sound of Sonny, Fantasy/OJC OJC-029.
That's Him, Fantasy/OJC 085.
A Night at the Village Vanguard, Vol. 1, Blue Note B21K-46517.
A Night at the Village Vanguard, Vol. 2, Blue Note B21Y-46518.
Duets, Verve 835253-2.
Sonny Side Up, Verve MGV8262.
Alternate Takes, Contemporary C-7651/5C-7651.
The Freedom Suite Plus, Fantasy/OJC 067.
Brass and Trio, Metro Jazz 1002.
The Modern Jazz Quartet at Music Inn, Vol. 2, Ultradisc 632.
At Music Inn, Metro Jazz 1011.
Newk's Time, Blue Note B21Y-84001.
Sonny Rollins and Contemporary Leaders, Fantasy/OJC 340.
The Bridge, Bluebird 07863-61061-2.
What's New, Bluebird 07863-52572-2.
Out Man in Jazz, RCA Victor, 2612.
Alternatives, Bluebird 07863-61124-2.
In Jazz, RCA Victor 2725.
Sonny Meets Hawk, RCA Victor 2712.
All the Things You Are, Bluebird 2179-2.
Sonny Rollins and Company, RCA 66530.
How's the Time, RCA Victor 2927.
The Standard Sonny Rollins, RCA Victor 3355.
There Will Never Be Another You, Impulse IA9349.
Sonny Rollins: On Impulse, Impulse 5655.
Alfie, Impulse 39107.
East Broadway Run Down, Impulse 161.

Sonny Rollins's Next Album, Fantasy/OJC 312.
Horn Culture, Fantasy/OJC 314.
Sonny Rollins in Japan, Victor SMJ 6030.
The Cutting Edge, Fantasy/OJC 468.
Nucleus, Fantasy/OJC 620.
The Way I Feel, Fantasy/OJC OJCCD-666-2.
Easy Living, Milestone M-9080.
Don't Stop the Carnival, Milestone MCD-55005-2.
Milestone Jazz Stars, Milestone M55006.
Rolling Stones, Virgin V21Q-39502.
Love at First Sight, Fantasy/OJC 753-2.
No Problem, Milestone M-9104.
Reel Life, Milestone M-9108.
Sonny Days Starry Nights, Milestone M-9122.
The Solo Album, Milestone M-9137.
Sonny Rollins Play-man, Milestone M-9150.
The Essential Sonny Rollins, Riverside FCD-60-020.
Dancing in the Dark, Milestone M-9155.
Falling in Love with Jazz, Milestone M-9179.
The Best of Sonny Rollins, Blue Note B21Y-93203.
Here's to the People, Milestone MCD-9194-2.
The Complete Prestige Recordings, Prestige 7-7PCD-4407-2
Old Flames, Milestone MCD-9215-2.
Plus 3, Milestone MCD-9250-2.
Silver City, Milestone 2MCD-2501-2.
Global Warming, Milestone MCD-9280-2.

PART TWO

Hard Bop and Cool Jazz

Hard bop and cool jazz were outgrowths of bop, incorporating some of its elements but also following their own individual paths. Hard Bop was a hard-driving, dark, brooding style that stripped bop to its bare essentials. There was urgency in hard bop, the blues of country players transplanted into the jungle, dirt and noise of the big city. In fact, hard bop was a reflection of urban existence, the pent up frustrations, the fast paced lifestyle, and the sea of restless humanity.

Cool jazz was opposite to hard bop in many ways. It was a more laid-back, sunnier style that added positive shades to bop's somewhat darker themes and had more of a swing feel to it. The mellow and melodic phrases reflected the fact that cool jazz emerged on the West Coast. It imitated the lush California sunsets, the beauty of the boundless dreamy Pacific Ocean and the tanned, healthy appeal of the average Californian.

The beginning of the East Coast hard bop style can be traced to the formation of the Jazz Messengers. Although New York was the hub of hard bop, other major urban centers, mainly Detroit and Philadelphia, supplied a number of enthusiastic soldiers to the primarily African American cause. The improvisational quality of hard bop reflected the necessary life skills required by the inner city dweller in order to deal with the daily struggles they faced.

The beginning of the West Coast Cool School can be traced to the release of Miles Davis's *The Birth of the Cool*. California was the center of the cool jazz wave that featured predominantly white artists. The sweeter, more romantic cool jazz phrases reflected the less frenetic pace of life on the left coast.

Hard bop roots were traced almost directly to bop's harsher tones. The roots of cool jazz could be found in the works of twentieth-century classical composers such as Maurice Ravel and Claude Debussy. Hard bop was more spontaneous while cool jazz was more concise and devised. Hard bop was suited to stormy, overcast days of hard rain and harsh winds. Cool jazz created an atmosphere of hot, bright days on breezy, sandy coastlines.

73

A hard bop saxophonist could be found playing on a noisy street corner with his tin cup, while a cool jazz saxophonist could be found playing to the ocean sunset on a wind-swept beach.

Despite the differences, the practitioners of each style developed warmth and respect for one another since most of them played together during the bop revolution. Of course, the lines were blurred and many of the jazz artists played both styles. Miles Davis, credited with ushering in the cool jazz era, was often on the East Coast playing hard bop. To stereotype and regulate either style would be to undercut their breadth and depth.

Some of the main proponents of hard bop were Gene Ammons, Art Blakey, Clifford Brown, Max Roach, Miles Davis, Dexter Gordon, J. J. Johnson, Clifford Jordan, Jackie McLean, Charles Mingus, Hank Mobley, Cannonball Adderley, Thelonious Monk, Lee Morgan, Sonny Rollins, Horace Silver, Sonny Stitt, and Kai Winding.

Some of the important students of the cool school of jazz were Chet Baker, Dave Brubeck, Miles Davis, Paul Desmond, Gil Evans, Jimmy Giuffre, Shelly Manne, John Lewis, Milt Jackson, Gerry Mulligan, Shorty Rogers, Howard Rumsey, Hampton Hawes, Claude Williamson, Buddy Collette, Wes Montgomery, Herbie Mann, Lennie Tristano, Lee Konitz, and Warne Marsh.

The artists featured in this section provide a broad section of both the hard bop and cool jazz styles.

Art Blakey is generally considered the godfather of hard bop, and long after musicians heading in other directions considered the style passé, he was still pounding out hard bop on his drum kit.

Dave Brubeck was a genuine cool jazz practitioner whose famous quartet enjoyed international success. He incorporated classical elements into his unique sound. Although chided for his inability to swing, he was an instrumental figure in 1950s and 1960s jazz.

Charles Mingus, an intimidating bass player and genius of musical composition, cut a path through the jazz world that is still discussed to this day. The controversial, innovative musician was firmly in the hard bop camp.

Dexter Gordon, a West Coast giant of the saxophone, was also a hard bop warrior. A large man, he had his roots in bop; he was a convert immediately after witnessing Gillespie and Parker roar through town.

Wes Montgomery was the epitome of cool jazz guitar. His career took a long time to get on track, and only a premature death stopped him from becoming the greatest six-string slinger in the genre's history.

Max Roach was an effective drummer who, like Clarke, forsook the bass drum and concentrated on the high cymbals. He went on to be a force in hard bop.

Jimmy Smith was the acknowledged king of the organ. His laid-back cool and sophisticated style defined how the instrument has been played in the past forty years.

Miles Davis is an example of someone who crossed over the line and played both cool jazz and hard bop. Later, he would initiate jazz fusion that would dominate the scene for over a decade.

Horace Silver, along with Art Blakey, is considered one of the grand-daddies of hard bop. His harsh blues style on the piano set the standard for all others to follow.

Herbie Mann was the coolest flute player on the planet for much of the 1950s and 1960s. His attire, attitude and attraction helped propel the popularity of the flute in jazz circles.

Jackie McLean was a dedicated hard-bopping alto saxophone player with one of the grittiest sounds in the 1950s. His work with Art Blakey is the stuff of legends.

ART BLAKEY (1919–1990)

Freedom Rider

The innovations that Kenny Clarke and Max Roach introduced to rhythm within a jazz group setting fueled the next generation of drummers, dubbed the hard boppers. Although many learned from the great bop stickmen, one student was able to extend the complicated work of the two professors in order to create his own supreme style. In the process he became known as the freedom rider. His name was Art Blakey.

Art Blakey was born Abdullah Buhaina on October 11, 1919, in Pittsburgh, Pennsylvania. His first instrument was the piano and by the time he was thirteen he was so far advanced that he was leading his own band. He eventually switched to drums and cherished the work of bandleader-drummer Chick Webb as well as hard swinging Big Sid Catlett. He would someday surpass both in ability and popularity in the hierarchy of jazz drummers.

In his late teens he moved to New York to seek his fame and fortune as a musician. His first gig in the Big Apple was with Mary Lou Williams in 1942. A year later he joined Fletcher Henderson's orchestra and toured with it all across the country. His first attempt at leading a band in New York was a brief one and after a short few months he joined Billy Eckstine's new group that included Dizzy Gillespie, Charlie Parker and Sarah

Vaughan. Upon the break up of Eckstine's band, Blakey once again formed his own outfit called the Seventeen Messengers. In the late 1940s he recorded with his own group, then called the Jazz Messengers, the first incarnation of that ensemble.

In 1953, he joined forces with pianist Horace Silver and the two decided to form a group that also included Hank Mobley and Kenny Dorham. They called themselves Horace Silver and the Jazz Messengers and they played fast, hard bop that exploded with intimidating power. Blakey was the driving force behind the rhythm-powered band with his lightning-quick attacks that sounded like bombs and missiles flying from his drum kit.

For three years they were on the cutting edge of the new music and every release helped to further define the hard bop sound. Two of their most important recordings were *Horace Silver & the Jazz Messengers* and *At the Café Bohemia*. These works underlined the interaction between drums, piano and horns, the very essence of their musical message. They were the shining jewels of the hard bop set, and after Silver's departure in 1956, the members regrouped behind Blakey. From this point on the Jazz Messengers would be completely under his leadership.

As the main voice of the group, Blakey experimented with musical styles and even developed a taste for Latin rhythms. Both volumes of his subsequent album *Orgy in Rhythm* incorporated Latin and Afro-Cuban musical languages. Although he worked most often with his band, he also jammed with various artists, including McCoy Tyner, Sonny Stitt, Art Davis, Thelonious Monk, and Al McGibbon. Even more interesting were his battles with Max Roach, Elvin Jones, and Buddy Rich at the Newport Jazz Festival in 1964. Blakey was an invaluable figure of modern jazz as both leader of the Jazz Messengers and a session man on a number of important recordings.

Blakey was the flagship of the hard bop movement and endured rises and falls in popularity of the style throughout the course of his career. In the 1960s, while John Coltrane and Ornette Coleman were heralded as the new thing, Blakey continued to play hard blues bop. In the mid–1960s, with the lineup of Bobby Timmons on piano, Blakey, Lee Morgan on trumpet and Wayne Shorter on tenor saxophone, they delivered a funkier style than the current trend. Although the names and faces would change throughout the years, Blakey's band continued to play in the hard bop idiom.

Throughout the 1970s when jazz fusion had replaced avant-garde and free jazz as the most popular style, Blakey was not moved by the new wave. His emphasis on the elements of music of the 1940s bop evolution remained firm. He recorded dozens of excellent albums with the various lineups of his Jazz Messengers right through the 1980s. He continued to experiment with various rhythmic structures, drawing from his experiences of traveling throughout the world and listening with an open mind. In many ways, he was a world musician rather than just an American artist.

As jazz split in many different directions in the 1980s, Blakey's tenacious message of hard bop blues began to shine through. It had taken thirty years for critics and many fans to realize that while some jazz styles were doomed to make a big splash only to quickly fade away, hard bop was destined to leave an enduring legacy. However, Blakey himself was not immortal. On Oct. 16, 1990, in New York, the great rhythm maker died. He was 71 years old.

Art Blakey was the granddaddy of hard bop. He stubbornly continued to play in that style his whole career, ignoring new trends that gained popularity and often overshadowed his achievements. Yet, he made enormous contributions to jazz as a drummer, bandleader, session man, composer and arranger. He explored entire new dimensions in the world of rhythm and created his own universe, often forgoing the established sounds of European music for the more exciting and exotic African music and the polyrhythms of Latin music.

The power and energy in Blakey's drumming was the cornerstone of his sound. He was the king of the press rolls and made them sound like invading tides of dynamic force that often left the listener and those in his band stunned. His understanding of rhythm textures was second to none. In 1949, he traveled to Africa and brought back with him an encyclopedia of sounds that he unleashed upon the Western Hemisphere through his recordings and live performances.

Blakey was a superb bandleader, but also a harsh one. He was relentless in his attack on the drums and insisted that everyone exert the same tremendous energy on their individual instruments. He often exhausted younger players who were never able to coast as a member of the Jazz Messengers. But Blakey was teaching the young jazz hopefuls the essence of improvisation, power, and commitment the best way he knew how—by leading through example.

One of his major talents was the ability to discover young talent. A list of musicians who graduated from the Art Blakey school of jazz includes Lee Morgan, Wayne Shorter, Freddie Hubbard, Johnny Griffin, Jackie McLean, Donald Byrd, Bobby Timmons, Cedar Walton, Benny Golson, Joanne Brackeen, Billy Harper, Valery Ponomarev, Bill Pierce, Branford Marsalis, James Williams, Keith Jarrett and Chuck Mangione. Many of these musicians left the Jazz Messengers and went on to form highly influential groups of their own.

Blakey also had a hand in shaping the styles of Bill Buford, Frank Butler, Chuck Flores, Milford Graves, Chico Hamilton, Billy Hart, Louis Hayes, Elvin Jones, Philly Joe Jones, Sunny Murray, Tony Oxley, Dave

Bailey, Barry Miles, Norman Connors, Larance Marable, Lenny McBrowne, Charlie Persip, and Bobby Sanabria. Taking their cue from the granddaddy of hard bop, these jazz musicians became prominent in their own right and although they went on to explore different styles, a direct line of essential techniques could always be drawn to Blakey. He also had a large influence on the rock and roll set, including John Bonham, Ginger Baker, Keith Moon, John Densmore, and Cozy Powell. There is scarcely a student of rhythm that has not been touched by his exploits.

He gave the world a number of great songs, including "Moanin'," "The Preacher," "Dat Dere," "It's Only Papa Moon," Freedom Rider," "Buhaina's Delight, "Mosaic," "Free For All," and "Drum Suite." Every song that Blakey played was injected with his hard-swinging pile-driving style and sparked feelings in the listener that spanned the entire spectrum of human emotions. Although he was more than a credible composer, he never received the credit he was due as an arranger and songwriter. His fame rested on his musical abilities rather than his creative side.

More than a decade after his death he remains one of the giants of jazz of the past half century. There is no denying that Blakey changed the face of modern drumming across the musical landscape that encompassed jazz, blues, rock, soul, and funk. His ferocious approach always ensured that no one was more capable of driving a band from the drum stand than the freedom rider himself.

Discography

Art Blakey Messengers, Blue Note BLP1050.
Art Blakey and the Jazz Messengers, Session 110.
Art Blakey/Sabu, Blue Note BLP1520–20.
Art Blakey & His Jazz Messengers: A Night at Birdland Vol. 1 & 2, Blue Note 521–1522.
Art Blakey, EmArcy MG36071.
Art Blakey, EmArcy MG26032.
Art Blakey & His Jazz Messengers: At the Café Bohemia, Vol. 1 & 2, Blue Note 1507–1508.
Art Blakey & the Jazz Messengers, Columbia 897.
Art Blakey & His Jazz Messengers, Columbia FC38036.
Art Blakey & His Jazz Messengers, Hard Bop, Columbia 1040.
Art Blakey & His Jazz Messengers, Blue Note P7468582.
The Drum Suite, Columbia 1002.
The Hard Bop Academy, Affinity 773.
Orgy in Rhythm Vol. 1, Blue Note 1553.
Orgy in Rhythm Vol. 2, Blue Note 1554.
Art Blakey & His Jazz Messengers, Mirage-Savoy ZDS4409.
Selections from Lerner & Lowe, Bluebird 666612.
Art Blakey & His Jazz Messengers, Cadet 4049.
A Night at Tony's Take 4, Bluebird 666612.

A Night at Tony's Take 3, Bluebird 666612.
Social Call Take 4, Bluebird 666612.
A Night in Tunisia, Bluebird 6286–2RB-20.
Art Blakey & His Jazz Messengers, Cu Bop Jubilee 1049.
Art Blakey's Jazz Messengers with T. Monk, Jazz Connection, Atlantic 127.
Art Blakey & His Jazz Messengers (live), Calliope 2008.
Art Blakey & His Jazz Messengers, Hard Drive Bethlehem 6023.
Art Blakey Big Band, Bethlehem 6027.
Moanin, Blues Note 84003–20.
Art Blakey & His Jazz Messengers: Live in Holland, Bandstand 1532.
Holiday for Skins, Vol. 1, Blue Note 4004.
Holiday for Skins, Vol. 2, Blue Note 4005.
Art Blakey's Jazz Messengers: Paris Olympia, Fontana 8326592–20.
Live At the Club St. Germain, RCA 430043.
At the Jazz Corner of the World, Vol. 1, Blue Note 4015
At the Jazz Corner of the World, Vol. 2, Blue Note 4016
Les Liaisons Dangereuses, Fontana 680203.
Live In Copenhagen—1959, Royal Jazz RJD516.
Africaine, Blue Note lt1088.
Live in Stockholm Dragon182.
Paris Jam Session—Live at the Champ Elysees, Fontana 832692–20.
Are You Real—Art Blakey and the Jazz Messengers, Moon 071–2.
The Big Beat, Blue Note 4029.
Art Blakey, Alto 721.
Art Blakey, Alto 720.
Horray for Blake, Blue Note 84245.
A Night in Tunisia, Blue Note 4049–20.
More Birdland Sessions, Fresh Sounds 1029–20.
Meet You at the Jazz Corner of the World, Vol. 1, Blue Note 4054.
Meet You at the Jazz Corner of the World, Vol. 2, Blue Note 4055.
Live at Theatre de Beaulier Lausane, Vol. 1, TCB 02022.
Live at Theatre de Beaulier Lausane, Vol. 2, TCB 020023.
Live in Stockholm, Dragon 137.
A Day with Art Blakey, Vol. 1 & 2, Eastwind 707–708.
Tokyo 1961, Somewhere Else CJ 32–5503–20.
Pisces—Blue Note, King 3060.
Roots and Herbs, Blue Note 4347.
The Witch Doctor, Blue Note 84258.
The Freedom Rider, Blue Note 4156.
Art Blakey & the Jazz Messengers, Impulse 7.
A Jazz Hour with Art Blakey's Jazz Messengers, Blue Note 4090.
Buhaina's Delight, Blue Note 4104.
The African Beat, Blue Note 4097.
Three Blind Mice, Blue Note, Vol. 1 & 2, 784451–784452.
Birdland Broadcast, Session Disc 117.
Caravan Riverside, Blue Note 438.
A Jazz Message, Impulse 45.
Theme from the Golden Boy, Colpix 9003.
Free For All, Blue Note 4170.
Kyoto, Riverside 493.
Indestructible, Blue Note 4193.
Art Blakey & His Jazz Messengers, Limelight 82001.

Soul Singer, Limelight 82018.
Buttercorn Lady, Limelight 82034.
Hold On I'm Coming, Limelight 4023.
Moanin', Irc 9052.
Art Blakey Live, Trip 5034.
Mellow Blues, Moon 032–2.
Art Blakey & Jazz Messengers, Catalyst 7902.
Child's Dance, Prestige 10047.
Child's Dance, Vol. 2, Prestige 24130–20.
Buhaina, Prestige 10067.
Buhaina, Vol. 2, Prestige 24159.
Anthenagin, Prestige 10076.
Art's Break, Joker 2060.
Backgammon, Roulette 5003.
Gypsy Folk Tales, Roulette 5007.
In My Prime, Vol. 1, Timeless 114.
In My Prime, Vol. 2, Timeless 118.
In This Korner, Concord Jazz 68.
Reflections in Blue, Timeless 128.
One By One, Palcoscenico 15005.
Jazzbuhne Berlin '80, Repertoire 409.
Live at North Sea and Montreux Big Band, Timeless 150.
Live at Bubba's, Who's Who in Jazz 21019.
Art Blakey in Sweden, Amigo 839.
Straight Ahead, Concord Jazz 168.
Killer Joe, Storyville 4100.
Keystone 3, Concord Jazz 196.
Art Blakey and the All-Star Jazz Messengers, RCA 45365.
Oh By the Way, Timeless 165.
Caravan Art—Blakey and the All-Star Jazz Messengers, Baystate 8071.
Aurex Jazz Festival, Estworld 80270.
A Groovy Night with the Magnificent Six—Art Blakey All-Stars, Japan 2025.
New York Scene, Concord 4256.
Blue Night, Timeless 217.
Live at Sweet Basil, Paddlewheel 6357.
Live at Kimball's [recorded April 13, 1985], Concord Jazz CJ 307.
Live at Ronnie Scotts, Wadham 001.
Hard Champion, Paddlewheel 6472.
New Year's Eve at Sweet Basil, Vol. 1, Projazz 651.
New Year's Eve at Sweet Basil, Vol. 2, Projazz 624.
Farewell, Paddlewheel 41412.
Blue Moon, Sounds 2720010.
Not Yet, Soul Note 1105.
Standards, Paddlewheel 6026.
I Get a Kick Out of Bu, Soul Note 12155.
Feeling Good, Delos 4007.
Feel the Wind, Timeless 307.
The Jazz Messengers: Legacy of Art Blakey, Telarc 83407.
Art Blakey Alumni: A Groovy Night with the Magnificent Six, Baystate 1053.
Art Blakey Alumni: Caravan, Baystate 8071.
Art Blakey Alumni: Aurex Jazz Festival '83, East World 80270.
Art Blakey Alumni: Art Blakey and the All-Star Jazz Messengers, RCA 45365.

DAVE BRUBECK (1920–)

Take Five

Throughout the history of jazz certain artists have been able to successfully tap a commercial nerve in the public consciousness. Like someone hitting a gusher, these musicians rode their finds to great success yet never tampered with their rich formula. Dave Brubeck, who told the world to take five, was one of these individuals.

Dave Warren Brubeck was born on December 6, 1920, in Concord, California. He started playing the piano at an early age. He received lessons from his mother, but he had no interest in music as a young boy, preferring to play ball with the neighborhood kids. However, by his late teens he had developed into a sound pianist and was destined to make his living as a musician. He studied at the College of the Pacific for four years.

His musical career was sidetracked in 1942 when Uncle Sam came calling. Brubeck served under General George S. Patton; while in Patton's army Brubeck led a service band, making sure to play all of the general's favorite songs. The experience proved invaluable.

Once the war was over, Brubeck studied at Mills College under the tutelage of classic composer Darius Milhaud, a noted jazz buff. Like other keen students, it was here that Brubeck finished his musical education. It was also during this period that he made his first recordings with the Dave Brubeck Octet, which consisted mostly of fellow classmates. Although they might have been mere music students, the songs they recorded were sophisticated pieces with complex time signatures and polyrhythms. It was a foreshadowing of his future musical direction.

Brubeck pared down his octet into a trio in hopes of securing more gigs. The trio consisted of drummer-vibraphonist Cal Tjader, bassist Ron Crotty, and Brubeck. They were one of the best local groups around but before they could explode on the national scene they broke up. A short time later, Brubeck injured himself in a swimming accident and remained inactive for months. It was one of his more desperate moments, but he would not be deterred and found the courage to carry on.

In 1951, having recuperated from his injuries, he joined forces with altoist Paul Desmond to form a quartet. Paul Desmond would play an important part in Brubeck's career; he was born in New York City in 1924 and from an early age had a keen interest in music. His instrument of choice was the alto saxophone and despite the influence of the great Charlie Parker, Desmond took a different path. He desired to play more laidback, California cool jazz than the frenetic sounds that made Bird famous. Like every other musician, Desmond paid his dues playing in many different groups, gaining valuable experience while waiting for his big break. He sought a kindred spirit in the jazz world and found one in Brubeck.

Together the two sounded like a dream. Desmond's style had a lighter feel to it and offset Brubeck's heavy-handed piano playing. There was also a commercial appeal in their collaboration that would eventually make both of them household names. While they were a formidable one-two punch, the rest of the quartet was a revolving musical lineup. Joe Dodge replaced Cal Tjader after his departure. Later, in the late 1950s, Joe Morello replaced Dodge on drums. After the quartet went through a number of bass players, the position was stabilized with the arrival of Eugene Wright in 1958.

By the late 1950s Brubeck and Desmond had settled on a winning formula. They had switched from Fantasy Records to Columbia and scored some big sales. After a long struggle they struck it rich in 1960 with the Desmond-penned classic "Take Five." The song was an international hit that catapulted the quartet into the spotlight as the deans of the cool jazz scene. Although many of the critics dismissed the group for their lack of genuine swing, there was no denying the fact that they knew how to write a catchy tune.

For the next several years the Dave Brubeck Quartet were globetrotters delivering a solid set to enthusiastic audiences throughout the world. They were especially popular with college students. The showpiece of the entire concert was the song "Take Five," which by now had been covered by numerous other bands. Although they possessed enough momentum to carry them for another decade, they broke up in 1967.

Brubeck seemed to lose his vision for some time, recording religious works, but by the late 1960s he was back playing his brand of popular jazz and re-formed his quartet with Gerry Mulligan, another cool jazz practitioner. They enjoyed moderate success. Brubeck also occasionally played with his old bandmate Paul Desmond. Sadly, the infrequent reunions ended permanently in 1977 with the passing of the talented alto saxophonist.

In the latter part of the 1970s, Brubeck formed a group with sons Darius on keyboards, Chris on electric bass and bass trombone, and Danny on drums. They were billed as Two Generations of Brubeck. The group toured and made some interesting records. The proud father had taught his sons well and his offspring enjoyed moderate success as solo acts.

In the 1980s, Brubeck re-formed his quartet with tenor saxophonist Jerry Bergorzi and Bill Smith, who had been with the original octet back in the 1950s. As well, long time group member and altoist Bobby Militello played with the band on certain occasions. With many of his earlier recordings now on CD, Brubeck's popularity spanned time and generations. Despite various health problems, he continues to record and perform.

Dave Brubeck is a household name in jazz. Because of his international hit "Take Five" and his success throughout the years with his laid-back cool sound that is very accessible to the average jazz fan, he has maintained a cult following. While many artists attempted to complicate their individual sound by exploring different paths, Brubeck stayed the course and never changed his basic style in order to gain a wider fan base.

Although he is not regarded as the greatest piano player in the world, he is one of the most creative. From the beginning Brubeck was an experimenter with time signatures and rhythms. A spunky individual who never shied away from trying something new, he was always able to play into the hearts and minds of jazz listeners with a style bridging the gap between the classical influence and African roots.

To fully understand his approach one must understand his roots. All the great pianists in jazz history, including Teddy Wilson, Fats Waller, Erroll Garner, Art Tatum, and Duke Ellington heavily influenced Brubeck. However, the classical works of Beethoven and Bach also had a strong impact on his mature sound. When the two worlds collided, the delirious result was the style of Dave Brubeck.

He had the uncanny ability to combine many elements of classical, pop, jazz, and blues into one cohesive, accessible package that explained the reason for his immense popularity. An inventive player, he was able to utilize the strengths of the individuals in his band to create a sound that emphasized no one special player but everyone in the group. His ability to spotlight strengths into a fine blend of talent made his sound practically impossible to duplicate.

Brubeck had many followers, including Charlie Rich, Tomasz Stanko, Jiri Stivin, Neal Creque, Carsten Dahl and Lemon James. Although they were disciples of his style, none captured the widespread following that their idol managed. There was a unique element in his creative process that no one could repeat. The fact that he was able to successfully collaborate with Desmond was another secret to his global appeal.

He gave the world a number of memorable songs, including "Take Five," "In Your Own Sweet Way," "The Duke," "Blue Rondo a la Turk," and countless others. Although he was criticized for his deep classical roots and lack of swing, Brubeck had the intelligence to create music for the average suburban person. He understood the constitution of his large audience and provided exactly what they wanted.

Dave Brubeck is one of the most interesting figures in jazz history. From the beginning he was unwilling to compromise and because of this he achieved huge success as one of the most innovative individuals in the last half of the 20th century. No matter how hectic life or how stressed out an individual becomes, listening to his wisdom—to take five—always seems to make perfect sense.

Discography

So What's New?, Telarc 83434.
Time Out, Legacy Records 65122.
25th Anniversary Reunion, A&M Records 210 806.
Back Home, Concord Jazz 4103.
Blue Rondo, Concord Jazz 4317.
Brandenburg Gate: Revisited, Legacy Records 65725.
Brubeck Time, Legacy Records 65724.
Buried Treasures, Legacy Records 65777.
Concord on a Summer Night, Concord Jazz 4198.
Dave Digs Disney, Legacy Records 48820.
Double Live from the USA & UK, Telarc Jazz Zone 83400.
Featuring Paul Desmond in Concert, Fantasy Records 60013.
For Lola, Concord Jazz 4259.
Gone with the Wind, Legacy Records 40627.
Jazz at Oberlin, Original Jazz Classics 046.
Jazz at the College of the Pacific, Original Jazz Classics 047.
Jazz Goes to College, Columbia 45149.
Jazz Impressions of Eurasia, Legacy Records 48531.
Near-Myth with Bill Smith, Original Jazz Classics 236.
Paper Moon, Concord Jazz 4178.
Plays Music from West Side Story, Columbia 40455.
Reflections, Concord Jazz 4299.
Stardust, Fantasy Records 24728.
The Last Set at Newport, Rhino Records 1607.
Time Further Out: Miro Reflections, Legacy Records 64668.
Time Out, Legacy Records 65122.
Tritonis, Concord Jazz 4129.
Greatest Hits, Legacy Records 65417.
In a Dancing Mood, Magnum (import) 26.
In Montreux, West Wind Jazz 2131.
One Alone, Telarc 83510.
A Dave Brubeck Christmas, Telarc Jazz Zone 83410.
All the Things We Are, Rhino Records 1684.
Bravo! Brubeck, Legacy Records 65723.
Brubeck a la Mode, Original Jazz Classics 200.
Brubeck Plays Brubeck, Legacy Records 65722.
Immortal Concerts: Take Five, Giants of Jazz Recordings 53309.
In Montreux, West Wind Jazz 2131.
In Moscow, Boheme Music 909094.
In Their Own Sweet Way, Telarc 83355.
Interchanges '54: Featuring Paul Desmond, Legacy Records 47032.
Jazz Collection, Legacy Records 64160.
Jazz Impressions of New York, Legacy Records 46189.
Just You, Just Me, Telarc 83363.
Late Night Brubeck: Live from the Blue Note, Telarc 83345.
Love Songs, Legacy Records 66029.

Moscow Night, Concord Jazz 4353.
Nightshift, Telarc 83351.
Plays and Plays and Plays, Original Jazz Classics 716.
Someday My Prince Will Come, Jazz Hour (import) 73572.
Take 5 Quartet, Jazz Hour 73598.
Take Five, Prism Entertainment 625.
The 40th Anniversary Tour of the U.K, Telarc Jazz Zone 83440.
The Art of Dave Brubeck: The Fantasy Years, Collectables 6615.
The Essence of Dave Brubeck, Legacy Records 47931.
The Great Concerts ... Amsterdam, Copenhagen, Legacy Records 44215.
These Foolish Things, Drive 3510.
This Is Jazz #3, Legacy Records 64615.
This Is Jazz #39—Plays Standards, Legacy Records 65450.
Time Signatures: A Career Retrospective, Legacy Records 66047.
Triple Play, Telarc 83449.
Truth Is Fallen/Two Generations, Collectables 6403.
We're All Together Again for the First Time, Rhino Records 1641.
Young Lions and Old Tigers, Telarc 83349.
Angel Eyes, SONY SRCS-9368.
At Newport, SONY SRCS-9522.
Brubeck & Rushing, SONY SRCS-9524.
Jazz Impressions of Eurasia, SONY SRCS-9360.
My Favorite Things, SONY SRCS-9369.
Newport 1958, SONY SRCS-9361.
Truth Is Fallen, ATLAN 7567807612.

———————————

CHARLES MINGUS (1922–1979)
The Boss of the Bass

In the first half-century of jazz the celebrated soloists played cornet, trumpet, saxophone, clarinet, piano, or trombone. The rhythm instruments—the guitar, bass and drums—were relegated to a defined background role. However during the swing era things began to change—especially for the bass. The emergence of Jimmy Blanton enabled bassists to break out of the confinement that had been imposed upon them. Those that followed the young trendsetter expanded the limitations of the instrument. More than anyone, one individual managed through perseverance, sheer determination, and unmatched talent to make the bass a lead instrument in jazz. Because of his fortitude and forcefulness he became known as the boss of the bass. His name was Charlie Mingus.

Charles Mingus Jr. was born on April 22, 1922, in Nogales, Arizona. Although he was born in the Grand Canyon State, Mingus grew up in Watts, the ghetto section of Los Angeles where, like hundreds of other

African American children of the same period, he was introduced to music through the gospel he heard attending regular church services. Brought up in a strict religious household where popular music was forbidden, Mingus, a rebel from the start, would sneak around and turn the radio to the jazz station. His hero was Duke Ellington.

In order to imitate the musical sounds that captivated his imagination, Mingus tried to teach himself the trombone, but grew frustrated and turned to the cello in order to unlock the mysteries that held him spellbound. He advanced no farther with the cello than he had with the trombone and quit in disgust. But when he opted to play the double bass, the musical universe opened up to him. With his thick, strong fingers, he could make it perform magic; he had finally found his instrument of choice.

Although he had learned how to play the bass with the help of teachers (including Red Callender, a much-traveled jazz figure who worked with Louis Armstrong, and Nat "King" Cole), Mingus also developed quickly because of his own inner drive. More compelling were his compositional skills; even when Miegus was a teenager, it was evident that his abilities were something special. In 1941, he wrote "Half-Mast" and although it wouldn't be recorded for another twenty years, it demonstrated a marked maturity, as well as the direction he would pursue as a musician and composer.

Although the study of the theoretical side of jazz was a necessary step in his development, he was much more interested in the practical experience. He was given the chance to explore the latter in 1942 when he joined Barney Bigard's group, performing with the great trombonist Kid Ory. A year later he was playing with the immortal Louis Armstrong. While the big bands provided an interesting entrance exam for Mingus, he preferred the challenge of a different kind of music. Eventually he was able to produce a grittier side of the blues, as part of Lionel Hampton's Orchestra in 1948.

Mingus, as strong-minded an individual as there's ever been in jazz, was not one to follow orders with graciousness. By the end of the decade he was running his own groups, playing jazz with tinges of rhythm and blues under the grandiose name of Baron Von Mingus. However, it was during his brief stint with the Red Norvo Trio that he began to get noticed outside the Los Angeles area for the first time.

Although Los Angeles offered handsome opportunities for someone with Mingus's talent and imagination, he felt that it was time to explore different venues. He moved to New York and immediately found work with Billy Taylor, Stan Getz, and the legendary Art Tatum. Although he had gained his start in big bands, by this point in his career, he was firmly in the bop camp. He championed the cause and jammed with Diz, Bird, et al.

At the Massey Hall concert in Toronto in 1953, he proved he was a musician of exceptional quality and someone who could not only keep up with the likes of Dizzy Gillespie, Charlie Parker, Bud Powell and Max Roach, but could push them even further. That performance earned Mingus so much attention that he was asked to join the Duke Ellington orchestra. While the Massey Hall gig was a great triumph for him, the embarrassment of being the only musician to ever be fired by Ellington was a definite low point. Duke, who had been Charles's hero since boyhood, would not stand for the fiery bassist's attitude.

In 1952, Mingus, along with his wife, and Max Roach formed their own record company. With expansive visions, the three collaborators decided that Debut Records would be accessible to all musicians of all styles to record their material without suffering the usual hassles of the entertainment establishment. Once again Mingus was taking a lead in jazz circles.

The bold dream lasted but five years, but in that time span some classical material was released by the record company, as well as *Jazz at Massey Hall* by the quintet of Charlie Parker, Dizzy Gillespie and Bud Powell, along with Mingus and Roach. Several of Mingus's compositions were also released by the label. He had grown as a writer and arranger. A compositional genius from the Charlie Parker school of songwriting, he heard whole songs in his head and was able to dictate the various pieces to each band member rather than write them down.

It was about this time that Mingus met different musicians who were keen on working with the brooding genius: horn men Jackie McLean and J. R. Monterose, trombonist Jimmy Knepper, trumpeter Clarence Shaw, and Mingus's ever-faithful companion on drums, Dannie Richmond. The friendship with Richmond would endure twenty years, a rarity in the Mingus groups that always saw a high turnover in personnel because of clashes between the intimidating leader and his bandmates. Although he was considered something of a musical genius, in jazz circles he was known as someone extremely difficult to get along with.

While the size of his outfit varied from album to album, the various members constitute an interesting list of alumni: Eric Dolphy, Jackie McLean, J. R. Monterose, Jimmy Knepper, Rashaan Roland Kirk, Booker Ervin, and John Handy, among others. There would be altercations between Mingus and his various bandmates. For example, one night in 1962, he decked Knepper during the middle of a memorial service. The incident caused a sensation in the jazz world.

By 1956, Mingus was in full control of his own destiny for the first time in his musical career. He was creating interesting new material, was in firm leadership of his band, and was recognized in the musical community as a major force. He was creating free jazz and broadening his controversial reputation. For the next decade, he would enjoy unprecedented success.

Always a man on his own mission, he released during this period a series of albums that were of seminal importance. *The Clown, New Tijuana Moods, Mingus Ah Um, Blues and Roots,* and *Oh Yeah* were all tours de force pointing the way to a brave new jazz world. Mingus always exuded an aura of confidence that bordered on arrogance that few other artists possessed. Although it helped him blaze his own trail through the jazz world, it offended many musicians.

By 1966, Mingus began to experience personal and career problems. Always the rebel, he challenged the music establishment and didn't always win. His effort to upstage the powers that staged the prestigious Newport Jazz Festivals ended in disastrous results. Another attempt to establish his own record company ended in failure, and the rejection by the publishing world to have his autobiography, *Beneath the Underdog,* out to the public convinced him to quit the music business.

Three years later, the boss of the bass returned to take on the world with a renewed spirit and in need of money. Despite his reputation as someone who was very difficult to deal with, the Guggenheim Fellowship awarded him financial support for composition that gave him hope. The sale of the Debut masters to a major record company, his ability to finally find a publisher for his book, and the release of his first album of new material in years clearly signaled the return of the fiercest bassman in the business.

In 1974, he was further excited by the formation of a new quintet that included Jack Walrath, Don Pullen, George Adams and the ever-loyal Dannie Richmond. He also began to write film scores and regained much of the respect that he had lost. He was enjoying one of the best periods of his long, interesting career when he was stricken with Lou Gehrig's Disease.

Within a year, he was unable to play the bass, but continued to dictate orders from his wheelchair. He led some recording sessions and even traveled to the White House to receive honors shortly before his death. His last project was with Joni Mitchell, who provided lyrics to the music he had written.

On January 5, 1979, in Cuernavaca, Mexico, Charles Mingus, the moody bass player with the undeniable talent, died. He was 56 years old.

Charles Mingus was one of the most controversial jazz figures in history. Although there was never any criticism of his genius as arranger, songwriter and bassist, he was a difficult man who never won any prizes for congeniality. He was intimidating, powerful, cutthroat, and demanding. But he also made enormous contributions to the genre.

Undoubtedly, he made his greatest impact on jazz with his thunderous style. His music was one of brute force, an overlapping of thick textures that emerged from his rumbling instrument like an angry rhinoceros. His playing was one of extremes with volcanic climaxes erupting from his mighty, dexterous fingers.

Despite the savage nature of his music, he was a sophisticated player who was able to combine his unquestioned abilities with an emotional potency that was absolutely breathtaking. He freed the bass from years of narrow perceptions and brought it to the forefront of contemporary music. He proved that the bass could be a lead instrument on par with all others, including the mighty saxophone. If his authoritative command of the bass wasn't enough to make him a legend, his skills as a composer, combined with his musicianship, were more than enough to secure him a place in the pantheon of jazz greats.

A prolific writer, he recorded over fifty albums as a leader, an astonishing number considering his reputation as a taskmaster and a difficult personality that terrorized other musicians. He was the supreme creator of moody compositions, and one of his strengths was to include the entire team. He was always able to draw the most from his bandmates through bullying, sheer genius, and manipulative skills.

There was the impulse of spontaneity to his music because he often created as he went along. It was nothing for him to shout instructions to his alert bandmates throughout the course of a song. He didn't use scores and during rehearsals quarterbacked his group from the piano. He would give the soloists in the band a couple of starter notes and allow them to negotiate the rest of the piece themselves.

The music of Mingus flowed like the sea. There was always a push forward, but with a swirl to it, a counterattack on the previous notes played which built layers of interesting and diverse tides. He could sound like the sea on a stormy night with savage stabs, rapid riffs, and eruptions of unexpected sounds. He could also mirror the beauty of the sea by capturing its tranquility, while suggesting that a strong undercurrent lay beneath the surface. He was able to write and improvise instantaneously if the composition he was playing refused to be molded into the shape he desired.

Some of the songs that he created that suited his scrutinized, high levels of perfectionism include "Love Chant," "Foggy Day," "Percussion Discussion," "Pithecanthropus Erectus," "Duke's Choice," "Haitian Fight Song," "Ysabel's Table Dance," "Tijuana Gift Shop," "Wednesday Night Prayer Meeting" (gospel), "Moanin'," "Good Bye Pork Pie Hat," and "Hog Calling Blues." However, there are countless Mingus classics and an exhaustive list would take up half a book.

Despite a nasty reputation that followed him throughout his career and even after his death, he had a strong influence on a variety of bands and musicians. The list includes Pentangle, George Lewis, George Adams, Ted Curson, Anthony Davis, Mark Dresser, Ricky Ford, Dave Holland, Mingus Dynasty, James Newton, Orange Then Blue, Steve Swallow, Keith and Julie Tippett, Michael White, Michel Portal, Tommy Potter, Jon Jang, Mario Pavone, Stanley Clarke, Jaki Byard, and Kyle Eastwood. Also, Mingus had a special effect on the Marsalis Brothers, Wynton and Branford, two of the brightest lights in contemporary jazz.

He also influenced many of the rock bassists to emerge in the past forty years. John Paul Jones, Jack Bruce, Roger Glover and many other rock bassists owed a debt to Mingus. He proved that the bass was not an instrument of anonymity but one as powerful as the loudest electric guitar and horns. Blues great Willie Dixon and Charles Mingus were the two artists who many from the new generation of bassists cited as major influences.

Along with Art Blakey, Mingus was one of the prime forces behind the hard bop sound. The ferocity he drew from the bass strings echoed the harshness of city noises like emergency wailing sirens, flashes of gunshot, the frustration of gridlock, the repetitious drone of pounding jackhammers, and the subway's rumble emerging through the sidewalk, sounding like some angry metallic monster beneath the city streets. There was a definite urban element in his bass style that was absent from cool jazz.

After his death the Mingus Dynasty was formed and eventually evolved into the Mingus Big Band, a group that tackled the most challenging of the master's compositions. The reissue of his music in lavishly packaged box sets has also helped to maintain interest in his work. Unlike some jazz artists who have passed away and been forgotten by the general public as well as the jazz world, Mingus—the music and the legend—remain current.

Undoubtedly, Mingus was always his own boss, a man who didn't like to take orders from others. He was always ahead of the pack and was never afraid of ruffling anyone's feathers. Mingus was a complicated, sometimes difficult character who inspired both love and hate in the music world; because of this the boss of the bass left behind a legacy that will be debated for a long, long time.

Discography

Charles Mingus Sextet, Excelsior CM132.
Charles Mingus Sextet, Excelsior CM133.
Charles Mingus Sextet, Excelsior CM134.
Charles Mingus Sextet, Excelsior CM135.
Charles Mingus Sextette, Vol. 1 & 2, Excelsior 162.

Charles Mingus Sextette, Vol. 3 & 4, Excelsior 163.
Baron Mingus and His Octet, Vol. 1 & 2, Star 1105.
Baron Mingus and His Octet, Vol. 3 & 4, Star 1106.
Baron Mingus and His Octet, Vol. 5 & 6, Star 1107.
Baron Mingus and His Octet, Vol. 7 & 8, Star 1108.
Baron Mingus Presents His Symphonic Airs, Fentone 2001.
Baron Mingus Presents His Symphonic Airs, Fentone 2002.
Baron Mingus and His Rhythm, Vol. 1 & 2, Fentone 2003.
Baron Mingus and His Rhythm, Vol. 3 & 4, Hollywood Info, 200.
Baron Mingus and His Rhythm, Vol. 5 & 6, Hollywood Info, 300.
Charles Mingus and His Orchestra, Vol. 1, Rex Hollywood 28002.
Charles Mingus and His Orchestra, Vol. 2 & 3, Rex Hollywood 28014.
Village Gate, Ozone 19.
Newport in New York Jam Session, Cobblestone CST9025-2.
Charles Mingus, Blues & Roots, Rhino 1305.
Pithecanthropus Erectus, Rhino 8809.
Mingus Ah Um, Sony 65512.
New Tijuana Moods, Victor 68591.
Jazz Experiments of Charles Mingus, Rhino 75782.
The Clown, Rhino 90142.
Backtracks, Renaissance Records 611.
Thirteen Pictures: The Charles Mingus Collection, Rhino Records 71402.
Tonight at Noon, Label M 5723.
A Modern Jazz Symposium ... Music & Poetry, Bethlehem Music Company, Inc.
    76678.
Alternate Takes, Legacy Records 65514.
Better Git It in Your Soul, Charly 1013.
Blues & Roots, Atlantic 1305.
Blues & Roots, Rhino Records 75205.
Changes One, Rhino Records 71403.
Changes Two, Rhino Records 71404.
Charles Mingus and Friends in Concert, Columbia 64975.
Charles Mingus Presents, Candid Records 79005.
Charles Mingus with Orchestra, Denon Records 8565.
Cumbia & Jazz Fusion, Rhino Records 71785.
Debut Rarities Vol. 2, Original Jazz Classics 1808.
East Coasting, Avenue Jazz 79807.
Epitaph, Columbia 45428.
Fables Of Faubus, Giants Of Jazz Recordings 53161.
Final Work, Chrisly Records 15007.
Goodbye Pork Pie Hat, Jazz Hour 73516.
His Final Work, Master Tone Records 8471.
In a Soulful Mood, Music Club Records 50004.
Jazz Composers Workshop, Savoy 92981.
Jazz Portraits: Mingus in Wonderland, Blue Note Records 27325.
Let My Children Hear Music, Legacy Records 48910.
Lionel Hampton Presents Charles Mingus, Giants of Jazz Recordings 53331.
Live in Chateauvallon, 1972, Esoldun 134.
Live in Stuttgart 1964, RKO/Unique Records 1038.
Meditations on Integration, Band Stand 1524.
Mingus, Candid Records 79021.
Mingus at Antibes, Rhino Records 90532.

Mingus at Carnegie Hall, Rhino Records 72285.
Mingus at the Bohemia, Original Jazz Classics 045.
Mingus Dynasty, Legacy Records 65513.
Mingus in Europe, Enja 3077.
Mingus Mingus Mingus Mingus Mingus, Impulse! 170.
Mingus Moves, 32 Records 32131.
Mingus Plays Piano, Impulse! 217.
Mingus Revisited, EmArcy 826 496.
Mingus Three, Blue Note Records 57155.
New Tijuana Moods, RCA Victor 68591.
Oh Yeah, Rhino Records 90667.
Oh Yeah, Rhino Records 75589.
Orange, Moon Records 78.
Paris 1964, Le Jazz 019.
Paris 1967, Vol. 2, Le Jazz 38.
Parkeriana, Band Stand 1530.
Passions of A Man: The Charles Mingus Story, Rhino Records 72871.
Plays It Cool, Metro 29.
Pre-Bird, Verve 538 636.
Priceless Jazz Collection, GRP Records 9877.
Revenge! The Legendary Paris Concerts, 32 Jazz 32002.
Sound of Jazz Volume 5, Galaxy Sound Of Jazz 388605.
The Black Saint and the Sinner Lady, Impulse! 174.
The Complete 1959 Columbia Sessions, Columbia 65145.
The Complete Debut Recordings, Original Jazz Classics 4402.
The Complete Town Hall Concert, Blue Note Records 28353.
The Jazz Experiments of Charles Mingus, Avenue Jazz 75782.
The Very Best of Charles Mingus, Rhino Records 79988.
Three or Four Shades of Blues, Rhino Records 1700.
Town Hall Concert, Original Jazz Classics 042.
West Coast 1945–49, Uptown Records 2748.
Charlie Mingus Jazz Workshop, MASTE 502942.
Mingus in Europe Vol. 1, TOKUM TKCB-71970.

DEXTER GORDON (1923–1990)

West Coast Tenorman

While the alto saxophone of Charlie Parker dominated the bop scene, his was not the only important horn voice. Although the bebop sound was conceived on the East Coast the fire spread to the left coast, especially after Parker and Dizzy Gillespie journeyed to Los Angeles to truly ignite the bop revolution. Some of the aspiring musicians had long been converts to the new music and had already taken up the mantle, including the West Coast tenor man with a sound all of his own. His name was Dexter Gordon.

Dexter Keith Gordon was born on February 27, 1923, in Los Angeles, California. The son of a doctor whose father might have wanted him to pursue a career in the medical field, young Dexter was bitten by the music bug instead and his future path was set. Dexter's father was the personal physician to many jazz figures, including Duke Ellington and Lionel Hampton. The thriving West Coast music scene was the perfect training ground for an aspiring musician.

At the age of 13, Gordon took up the clarinet, but switched to the alto saxophone a couple of years later. He jammed with other young musicians in the neighborhood to give him practical experience and studied harmony and theory with local teachers. He absorbed all of the music that was around him and yearned to be a famous jazz cat. At seventeen he became a tenor man and quit school. He continued to pay his dues by playing at various clubs around the Los Angeles area. A rather large youth, his size belied his age and that allowed him to play in restricted clubs when he was just a teenager.

He joined a local group called the Harlem Collegians, but soon jumped to Lionel Hampton's big band. He remained with the master vibraphonist from 1940 to 1943, taking a second seat to Illinois Jacquet in the band. Although he had few chances to solo, the education he received in the orchestra was invaluable. Aside from studying Jacquet, Gordon received important guidance from alto saxophonist Marshall Royal, one of the most well seasoned members in the band.

Slowly, Gordon's style was emerging. There was a definite Jacquet influence, but Dexter, like so many other musicians of his generation, was under the spell of Lester Young. He incorporated the laid-back approach of the Prez into his own developing style. While still in high school he had been able to see his hero live when the great saxophonist swept through the West Coast as part of the Count Basie big band. But Gordon could also blow a mean tenor sax with the speed and musical imagination that would give Yardbird Parker a run for his money.

After leaving Hampton's band, Gordon spent a year scampering around Los Angeles, sitting in on sessions in clubs on Central Avenue and honing his skills. Also during this time, he began to establish the reputation as a very exciting soloist during recording sessions with the great Nat King Cole. He later joined a succession of big bands, including Lee Young's, Jesse Price's, Fletcher Henderson's, and Louis Armstrong's all-star outfit, of which he was a member for six months.

He moved on and found a spot in Billy Eckstine's band, which included Dizzy Gillespie, Sonny Stitt and Fats Navarro. As a member of Eckstine's group, Gordon was part of the unholy four that included Stitt, John Jackson, and Leo Parker. They rehearsed together and became close personal friends. They were all young jazz cats who dreamed of making it big in the music business. It was a period of good times, good friends and good music.

Tenor sax man Gene Ammons, the son of blues boogie-woogie pianist Albert Ammons, joined the group some time later. He and Gordon played cat and mouse, chasing and cutting each other with their instruments. The pairing was pure magic, the evidence clear on some of the sides that they recorded together, especially the song "Blowin' the Blues Away." Unfortunately, the tandem never reached its full maturity because Gordon left Eckstine's band in 1945 and headed for New York to be with Bird and Diz.

Once he was in New York it didn't take long for Gordon to sit in on the jam sessions that occurred nightly at Minton's on 52nd Street. He eventually joined a group that included Miles Davis, Charlie Parker, Max Roach, Bud Powell (replaced by Sir Charles Thompson), and Curly Russell. During his time in the Big Apple, he recorded often with a cast of characters that included Charlie Parker and Dizzy Gillespie. He also played on many sessions for Savoy as leader and as a sideman.

After eighteen months of life in the Big Apple, Gordon returned to Los Angeles and the thriving Central Avenue jazz scene. The hot sound of the time was bebop and he was one of the leaders after receiving invaluable experience with the East Coast revolutionists. He was revered among the West Coast jazz musicians because he had played with legends and his stories of life in New York enthralled all those around him. He also brought back a heroin habit.

He teamed up with Wardell Gray and the two sounded good together. They began to appear on stage as a duo around the clubs in Los Angeles and also cut a few sides for Dial. On one of these sessions the pair recorded "The Chase," one of the tenor saxophone masterpieces of the 1940s. He also recorded with different musicians, including Teddy Edwards and Melba Liston. Although Los Angeles was home, the jazz scene of 52nd Street beckoned him and Gordon found the call irresistible. So he returned to New York.

Dexter remained in the Big Apple for the next two years and found plenty of work. He recorded for Savoy with Leo Parker and Fats Navarro. He was part of Tadd Dameron's band that played a residency at different venues around the city. He also was part of an all-star group that included Bud Powell. Although he never recorded with the great pianist, they played the circuit of clubs around town. Gordon even spent time with Machito's Afro-Cubans, since Latin music was all the rage at the time. The combination of his powerful tenor saxophone with the intricate Latin-Cuban rhythms proved an interesting mix. Later, he returned to Dameron's big band before heading back to the West Coast.

In 1950, he reformed his partnership with Gray and the two cut many sides for Prestige and other labels. Although they hadn't played together for over two years, the reunion was a natural one. They created magic from the very first note that emerged from their respective horns. But by late 1952, the winds of change spelled trouble for Gordon. Cool jazz was the new thing and his hard swinging style fell out of favor.

Also, his involvement in drugs did not go unnoticed by the authorities. He spent some time in Chino, a West Coast prison without bars, for narcotics possession. Upon his release he tried to piece his life back together again but received a severe blow when Gray was found dead of a heroin overdose. The two saxophonists who sounded like they were born to play alongside each other would never share another stage or recording session.

The 1950s were a slow period in his career, as he recorded very little. In 1955, he cut two sessions for the Bethlehem label—one as a sideman for Stan Levey, and the other under his own name. He also waxed a record for Doontone Records, *Dexter Blows Hot and Cold,* which proved to all detractors that he had not lost any of his power and impressive skills. But the deaths of Charlie Parker (1955) and Lester Young (1959), his two main idols, was a crushing personal blow and he sank further into despondency.

Although his musical career was waning, other venues opened up for him. While in Chino Dexter had appeared in a movie about the famous prison. Although he didn't star in the production, he was seen playing the saxophone and that at least enabled him to keep his name in the minds of jazz fans. More importantly, other acting work came his way as a result of his first big-screen flick.

In 1960, he had a vital role in the play *The Connection.* He performed and wrote music for the work, which had a successful run, and suddenly he was a drawing card once again. He fully intended to build upon his renewed appeal and decided to reenter the music business. Soon new offers came his way, including a recording session with Cannonball Adderley, who oversaw the making of the album *The Emergence of Dexter Gordon.* This record opened doors that previously had been shut and led to other opportunities.

In 1961, Blue Note stepped in with a handsome contract offer and Gordon delivered a series of pacesetting albums for the label, including *Doin' Alright, Dexter Calling, Go, A Swingin' Affair, Our Man in Paris,* and *One Flight Up.* His robust playing was once again in fashion and the jazz world that had forgotten him now embraced him like a long-lost son.

Once his parole period ended he was free to travel again. He headed to Chicago, where he was reunited with Gene Ammons. The two jammed together and the overwhelming reception that they received from crowds only intensified his appetite to make his comeback real. He had renewed his jazz spirit and looked at life with a different, positive attitude.

Later that year he traveled to New York and appeared in clubs around the area, as he was able to obtain a cabaret card that allowed him to play in establishments that served liquor. But the following year when he was denied the card, Gordon, born with a traveling bone, moved to Europe and based his operations in Copenhagen. Throughout this period he had continued to record for Blue Note.

Across the Atlantic, where American jazz musicians were revered, Gordon enjoyed two successful years. He cut a number of albums that proved he had not lost any of his beefy sound and he thrived in his new home, but returned to his native country in 1964. Gordon cut more sessions for Blue Note and played in Chicago as well as both coasts. But the allure of life overseas called him back and he returned in 1965.

Gordon remained for the next eleven years in Denmark, where he played in the finest clubs and continued to cut records for foreign labels. He jammed with many of the American jazz artists passing through, including Don Byas and others. Like Kenny Clarke before him, Gordon loved the different cultural experiences and seemed to have no intention of ever returning to the United States.

However, in 1976, he made his way back to America and despite his long absence was surprised at his reception. He was hailed as one of jazz's golden warriors. Although he had recorded most of his challenging material years before, critics and fans welcomed his untimely return. He took full advantage of the unexpected attention to further enhance his legend. His new studio work and live appearances increased his fan base; a new generation of jazz enthusiasts who had never heard him except through records because of his long furlough in Europe rushed to see him perform.

By the mid–1980s, his health was declining. He began to fade into obscurity but his star was rekindled when he starred in the movie 'Round Midnight. While Dexter Gordon the tenorman with the muscular tone and killer attack had left his best playing days behind him, his career as an actor took on special significance. He was nominated for an Academy Award.

On April 25, 1990, in Philadelphia, Pennsylvania, the behemoth tenor saxophonist with a unique sound that could cut through a cement wall was silenced forever. He was 77 years old.

Dexter Gordon is a genuine jazz legend. His career was one of triumphs and tragedies, and while he may not draw the same continued focus of attention like Charlie Parker has, there is no denying his place in the genre's history. Undoubtedly, he was the best tenor saxophonist of the bop era and possessed a unique sound that was the culmination of the influence of three of jazz's major sax men.

He combined the relaxed approach of Lester Young, the big tone of Hawkins, and the reworked complex harmonies of Charlie Parker to create his own style. Gordon always exerted a sound that was driven and imaginative. He swung with an uncanny sense of rhythm and quoted lessons of power with his intimidating stance. Although he was eclectic, he was no mere imitator; he boasted a unique jazz voice.

Gordon was able to move audiences with his ability to bring a ballad to life. He possessed the power, imagination, and knowledge to take a song down paths that were unexpected yet sounded so naturally right. He also had the touch of making notes march together like well-trained soldiers in a perfectly executed drill exercise without making it sound rote and mechanical.

He was an architect of the bop revolution that occurred on the West Coast. While Bird was doing his thing in the Big Apple, Long Tall Dexter, as he was known because of his intimidating and imposing stature, was blowing fiercely and exploring new ideas in the California sunshine. Gordon made a serious impact wherever he played, whether it was in Los Angeles, New York, Chicago or Europe.

He had a lasting effect on many of the most important tenors that came after bop. They include Gene Ammons, Hadley Caliman, Allen Eager, Booker Ervin, Karin Krog, James Moody, Sonny Rollins, Hilton Ruiz, David Schnitter, Alice Coltrane, John Coltrane, Eric Gale, Benny Golson, Jackie McLean, Grover Washington, Jr., Marcus Printup, and Rebecca Martin. Not only was he a leading voice in the bop revolution, but he neatly set down the formula for the cool jazz school and later exploits into free jazz. The fact that the cool school, hard bop and free jazz all claimed him as one of their own sheds proper light on the wide range of his multiple abilities.

Gordon recorded an impressive body of work that continues to be relevant more than a decade after his death. Some of his best known songs include "Blue 'n' Boogie," "Dexter's Minor Mad," "Blow Mr. Dexter," "Dexter Rides Again," "The Chase," "The Steeplechase," "Rocks 'n' Shoals," "The Duel," "Move," "Guess I'll Hang My Tears Out to Dry," and "You've Changed." Many of these were recorded with the elite of the bop crowd— Dizzy Gillespie, Bud Powell, Tadd Dameron, Art Blakey, Max Roach, Leo Parker, Wardell Gray, Teddy Edwards and Kenny Clarke, among others.

Dexter Gordon cut a lasting image in jazz lore with his towering physical presence and the sheer muscle of his playing. He was outspoken, an ambassador for the music, and a firm believer in the art that he was creating. He always exuded an air of supreme confidence because of his immense skills. His popularity wavered through periods of low appeal and then soared as he became fashionable again. A genuine rebel, he was determined from the start to chart his own path of success and he managed to accomplish his goals; he also became a legend at the same time. But no matter the level of his fame, there is no forgetting the West Coast tenorman.

Discography

Live at Carnegie Hall, Legacy Records 65312.
Our Man in Paris, Blue Note Records 46394.
1943–1947, Classics Jazz 999.
1943/1946, EPM 158792.
A Gordon Cantata, West Wind Jazz 2079.
A Swingin' Affair, Blue Note Records 84133.
Ballads, Blue Note Records 96579.
Blue Dex: Dexter Gordon Plays the Blues, Prestige Records 11003.
Body and Soul, 1201 Music 9004.
Bouncin' with Dex, SteepleChase 31060.
Ca' Purange, Original Jazz Classics 1005.
Cabu Collection, Masters of Jazz 8021.
Come Rain or Come Shine, Jazz Hour 73508.
Daddy Plays the Horn, Charly 121.
Daddy Plays the Horn [remaster], Bethlehem Music Company, Inc. 75991.
Dexter Blows Hot and Cool, Boplicity 6.
Dexter Calling, Blue Note Records 46544.
Dexter Rides Again, Savoy 0120.
Doin' Alright, Blue Note Records 84077.
Generation, Original Jazz Classics 836.
Gettin' Around, Blue Note Records 46681.
Go! [Remaster] Blue Note Records 98794.
Homecoming: Live at the Village Vanguard, Legacy Records 46824.
It's You or No One, SteepleChase 36022.
Jazz Classics, Aurophon Records 36002.
Live at the Amsterdam Paradiso, Le Jazz 28.
Love for Sale, SteepleChase 36018.
More Power, Original Jazz Classics 815.
One Flight Up, Blue Note Records 84176.
Our Man in Paris, Blue Note Records 46394.
Settin' the Pace, Savoy 17027.
Sophisticated Giant, Legacy Records 65295.
Take the "A" Train [Remaster], 1201 Music 9025.
The Art of the Ballad, Prestige Records 11009.
The Best of Dexter Gordon: The Blue Note Years, Blue Note Records 91139.
The Jumpin' Blues, Original Jazz Classics 899.
The Other Side of Round Midnight, Blue Note Records 46397.
The Panther!, Original Jazz Classics 770.
The Resurgence of Dexter Gordon, Original Jazz Classics 929.
The Tower of Power!, Original Jazz Classics 299.
Volume 2: Young Dex 1944–1946, Masters of Jazz 128.
Volume 3: 1946–47, Masters of Jazz 156.
Best of Dexter Gordon, BLUEN TOCJ-66047.
In a Soulful Mood, MCI MCCD394.
Jazz Masters, EMI G 4991592.
Saxophone Moods, Dial TOCJ-6205.
Swinging Affair, BNOTE TOCJ-9216.
There Will Never Be Another You, BCD JTM8105

WES MONTGOMERY (1923–1968)

Little Brother

While the guitar has never been one of the dominant instruments in jazz, there have been some fine contributors on the instrument. Eddie Lang, Lonnie Johnson, Charlie Christian, and Django Reinhardt were some of the prime players. In later years, another guitarist appeared on the scene and quickly claimed the jazz guitar crown. His career was brief, like Charlie Christian's, but Little Brother still made a very strong impact. His name was Wes Montgomery.

Wes Montgomery was born John Leslie Montgomery on March 6, 1925, in Indianapolis, Indiana. Like other great jazz artists he was self-taught, but he didn't begin the study of the guitar until he was eighteen. Although he was a late bloomer, he advanced quickly and five years later had secured the coveted six-string chair in Lionel Hampton's band. From the beginning, Wes didn't use a pick because he preferred the tone achieved with his fingers and thumb.

From 1948 to 1950, Montgomery toured with Hampton, learning much from the veteran jazz performer. He made a few records and the basics of his style—the double octave runs—were present. Upon his departure from the group, Montgomery moved back to his hometown and performed with his two brothers, Buddy, a vibe player, and Monk, a bassist. For most of the 1950s, Wes lived a civilian life working a regular job and playing on the weekends with his siblings. He seemed content to allow the world of jazz to slip by him.

But when his two brothers (calling themselves the Mastersounds) began to attract attention, it spurred Wes to return to the music scene at the age of thirty-four. Some of the legends of jazz, including Charlie Parker, Bix Biederbecke, Bunny Berigan, Clifford Brown, Chick Webb, Eddie Costa, Jimmy Blanton, and Charlie Christian, died younger or at the same age that Little Brother was when he began making his true musical mark.

After cutting a few records with Buddy and Monk, he set out on his own. Through his friendship with bop alto saxophonist Cannonball Adderley, Wes was able to secure a contract with Riverside Records in the late 1950s. During the Riverside period (1959–1963), Montgomery established his legend. His unique picking style combined with his double octave runs, the lyrical smoothness, and magic touch brought him the fame that had eluded him for so long.

The small combo setting in which Montgomery excelled was captured on his second release, *The Incredible Jazz Guitar of Wes Montgomery.*

The trio included the driving organ of Melvin Rhyne, who pumped out an even stream of bluesy riffs while Montgomery rode over and under the rhythm with his slick guitar licks. Despite a brief time in a group with John Coltrane and Eric Dolphy, Wes continued to perform and record within a small combo format. Some of his bandmates included Tommy Flanagan, James Clay, Victor Feldman, Hank Jones, and Johnny Griffin.

His release *While We're Young* demonstrated a maturity with his brilliant single note runs juxtaposed to his chunky chordings. He built up speed and enthusiasm, creating a tension that was pure excitement. His silky tone was appealing to all jazz listeners and by the end of the 1950s and early 1960s he had inherited the crown from Charlie Christian as the greatest guitarist in jazz.

When Riverside went bankrupt, Montgomery moved to Verve and remained there for two years (1964–1966) in what is acknowledged as his Verve period. During this time he recorded more complicated material that was a balance between jazz and an orchestral setting. Despite the unfamiliar environment, he was able to add to his reputation, although many jazz purists cringed at the inclusion of lush strings on some of his recordings, rather than the small combo setting that he was better suited to. On some of the records he worked with the Wynton Kelly Trio and organist Jimmy Smith.

The third recording period of his career (1967–1968) featured Montgomery on the A&M label, where he continued to put out best-selling albums, although his once crisp jazz sound had been watered down as he experimented with more of a pop-oriented style. It left some followers truly upset, but with these records he was able to interest fans outside of the genre, which only added to his popularity.

On one of these recordings, *Wes and Friends*, he teamed up with Milt Jackson and George Shearing. It was another success and only added to his burgeoning reputation. Montgomery was an absolute ace in a small combo setting because it allowed him to play rhythm and lead simultaneously. He was capable of stepping out and driving the music along with his classic style.

He recorded the album *Movin'* with Johnny Griffin. It was a hard blues affair with pile-driving songs that really swung hard and demonstrated Wes at his best. He tore through the repertoire with the skill and agility of a Charlie Christian, Muddy Waters, or Jimi Hendrix. Undoubtedly at the top of his game, he proved once and for all that he was the best jazz guitarist in the business.

For an eleven-year span—1957 to 1968—Wes Montgomery was the most recognized jazz guitarist on the planet, with few rivals. His soulful blues recordings had made him a very popular entertainer. It was a shock to the entire music world when on June 15, 1968, in Indianapolis, Indiana, he died of a heart attack. He was only 43 years old.

Wes Montgomery was a link in the jazz guitar chain. He arrived on the scene almost twenty years after Charlie Christian had passed through and assumed possession of the torch for the next decade. His immense fame that took so long to achieve erupted instantly and after that he never really looked back. He possessed a truly unique voice.

Like all good jazz musicians, Montgomery based his sound on the blues. But he blended his roots with a soulful touch that created a laid-back cool style. The key to his special touch was his intricate and deliberate use of octaves. By playing melodies and solos an octave apart, he skillfully added a depth that made it seem as if there were two guitarists playing instead of a solo performer. This technique made an impression on numerous musicians and although he wasn't the first guitarist to use the octave method, he perfected it.

Montgomery, with his bluesy, mellow style, had a huge impact on the future course of jazz guitar. He influenced a number of players, including Walter Washington, George Benson, Ted Dunbar, Robben Ford, Hubert Laws, Pat Martino, Pat Metheny, Terje Rypdal, Kazumi Watanabe, Jack Wilkins, Ryo Kawasaki, Buster Benton, Ron Affif, Airto Moreira, Egberto Gismonti, Kevin Eubanks, Bill Frisell, Dave King, Emily Remler, and Tim Sparks. He also shaped blues, soul, and rock. Jimi Hendrix was a keen student and great admirer of the Wes Montgomery school of guitar. In turn, Hendrix influenced every later guitarist who ever picked up the instrument.

But one of the most interesting links existed between Wes and Eric Clapton. They shared a love of the blues. They were both late bloomers, picking up the guitar in their late teens. They also excelled in a small combo setting rather than larger musical formats. Each enjoyed reign of extreme popularity, although Clapton's run has lasted much longer than Montgomery's. As individuals they also influenced a great number of guitarists outside their respective musical realms.

But the greatest similarity was in their respective styles. Undoubtedly, Wes was the epitome of the laid back, cool jazz predominant in the 1950s. Two decades later, Clapton, after earning his badge with Cream and his band Derek and the Dominos, was dubbed "Slowhand" for his ability to play calculated blues lines with an easy groove that astonished listeners. Clapton did in rock and blues what Montgomery had done in jazz.

Montgomery left behind a number of classics for the world to enjoy. They include "Tune Up," "Airgun," "Four on Six," "Finger Pickin'," "Old Folk," "Twisted Blues," "West Coast Blues," "Double Deal," "Delilah," "Born to be Blue," "Blues 'n' Boogie," "In Your Sweet Way," "Movin' Along," "Ghost of a Chance," "Work Song," and "Theodora." He also reworked many familiar songs, including "Eleanor Rigby," the Beatles' chestnut, into something new and exciting.

Although Montgomery's Riverside years—1959 to 1963—were arguably his most fruitful, his two other periods cannot be overlooked. That he managed to remain on top of the guitar jazz throne for a more than a decade clearly illustrates that he had that special touch in any setting, including small combo, orchestra, and pop. His talent was undeniable.

Wes Montgomery's name remains current in musical circles more than thirty years after his untimely death. The music he created is considered necessary study for all serious guitar students. All aspiring six-string slingers can learn much from his impressive catalog. There is no doubt that Little Brother was a genuine jazz guitar genius.

Discography

The Montgomery Bros. Quintet, Columbia 38509.
Montgomery Bros. and 5 Others, LBS 83178E.
The Mastersounds, CEMA CD S21-56913.
The Montgomery Brothers, Pacific Jazz CDP7 94475-2.
The Wes Montgomery Trio, Riverside 12RCD 4408-1.
The Incredible Jazz Guitar of Wes Montgomery, Riverside 12RCD 4408-1.
Work Song, Riverside 12RCD 4408-2.
West Coast Blues, Riverside 4408-3.
Movin' Along, Riverside 12RCD 4408-5.
The Montgomery Brothers, Milestone MCD 47076-2.
The Montgomery Brothers: Grooveyard, Riverside 4408-6.
The Montgomery Brothers in Canada, Milestone MCD 47076-2.
Wes Montgomery: So Much Guitar, Riverside 12RCD 4408-7.
Montgomery Brothers: Live at Jorgies, Magnetic MRCD 124.
George Shearing and the Montgomery Brothers: Love Walked in, Riverside 12RCD 4408-8.
Milt Jackson: Bags Meets Wes, Riverside 12RCD 4408-9.
Wes Montgomery Quintet Live: Full House, Riverside 12RCD 4408-10.
Wes Montgomery and Strings, Riverside 12RCD 4408-11.
Boss Guitar, Riverside 12RCD 4408-12.
The Last Riverside Sessions, Riverside 12RCD 4408-13.
Movin' Wes, Verve 810 045-2.
Stretchin' Out Live, Suisa JZCD 378.
Impressions, JICL 89228 9.
Solitude, JICL 89228 9.
Live in Paris, France Concert FCD 108.
Live in Europe, Philology W 97-2.
Straight No Chaser, Bandstand BDCD 1504.
Body and Soul, Jazz House CD JHAS 604.
Wes Montgomery: Bumpin', Verve 539 062-2.
Wes Montgomery: Smokin' at the Half Note, Verve J33J 25011.
Wes Montgomery: Willow Weep for Me, Verve POCJ 1902.

Wes Montgomery: Goin' Out of My Head, Verve 825 676–2.
Tequila, Verve 831 671–2.
Wes Montgomery—Radio Interview, VGM 0008.
California Dreamin', Verve CD 827 842–2.
The Dynamic Duo, Verve 821 577–2.
Further Adventures, Verve 519 802–2.
A Day in the Life, A&M 0816.
Down Here on the Ground, A&M 0802.
Road Song, A&M 0822–2.
A&M Gold Series, A&M 397076–2.

MAX ROACH (1925–)

Driva Man

While Kenny Clarke had opened up a whole new world for timekeepers with his innovative approach, he took it only so far. In order to complete the full evolution, another stickman was needed who could expand on Clarke's basic innovations and further the sound of bop. The individual arrived on the scene with the typical cockiness of a drummer and created a storm with his "Driva Man" style. His name was Max Roach.

Maxwell Roach was born on January 10, 1925, in Newland, North Carolina, but moved to Brooklyn with his family when he was four years old. He boasted a musical background; his mother was a gospel singer, and his aunt was a pianist who taught him the rudiments of the instrument. A few years later, at age nine, he was playing piano at the local Baptist church. Although the influence of gospel made a lasting impression, Roach had broader visions.

He discovered the drums at the age of ten and was enrolled in the Manhattan School of Music to further his education. But Roach was a musical sponge. He absorbed all kinds of styles, including March music, jazz, ragtime, and swing. Although Jo Jones, who had brought a new technique to the art of drumming, was his main idol, he also admired Chick Webb, O'Neil Spencer, Big Sid Catlett, Cozy Cole, and Kaiser Marshall. Max was enthralled with the art of broken rhythms that Jones was pioneering with the use of the lighter touch of the high-hat. But before he found fame, like every other musician he had to pay his dues.

Part of this process included listening to as much jazz as possible. Roach and his teenage friends Leonard Hawkins, Ray and Lee Abrams, and Cecil Payne would spend their free time at the Apollo Theatre. They also frequented the Savoy Ballroom, where they soaked up the good jazz bands that came through. He also played in rehearsal groups that jammed on the popular stuff of the day, like the songs of Glenn Miller, Jimmie Lunceford, and Count Basie.

Before he graduated from high school Roach was able to enter and even played gigs in Monroe's Uptown Club, where he met Bird Parker, Bud Powell and Thelonious Monk. Upon graduation, he dived into the thriving music scene of 52nd Street. He played at Kelley's Stables alongside Coleman Hawkins for much of 1943 and 1944. At the start of 1944, he received his first real break when Gillespie and Pettiford hired him for a date at the Onyx. In the early part of the year he was able to record with Dizzy, but not much of his mature drumming style was evident on those recordings.

Although the excitement that existed all around the Village and 52nd Street was something that drew Roach in like a magnet, the chance to play for Benny Carter's orchestra was too good an opportunity to turn down. It was during his stint with Carter that Roach began to receive recognition on recording sessions and live performances. He also met J. J. Johnson, the talented trombonist who would make the instrument go bop. Roach recorded with Carter, Coleman Hawkins, and Nat King Cole on a special session titled *The International Jazzmen*.

Upon his return to New York, he jammed with Gillespie and Parker. Later he would record with Dizzy and Miles Davis. His work on "Ko Ko," "Billie's Bounce," and "Now's the Time" indicated a drummer who had not achieved complete command of the bebop style. After participating on the ill-fated Gillespie big band tour of the South, Max returned to New York and freelanced instead of accepting the offer to go to the West Coast with Dizzy and Bird.

Roach jammed up and down 52nd Street with Allan Eager, Dexter Gordon, Coleman Hawkins and J. J. Johnson. He recorded with each one of these artists at different sessions as well as the great, unpredictable pianist Bud Powell. On these dates Roach displayed a more mature bop style than ever before. In order to be as close to the action as possible, he moved into an apartment on 52nd Street with fellow drummers Stan Levey and Art Mardigan. In a contradictory move, Max, firmly in the bebop mold, briefly recorded with big band stalwart Duke Ellington. The result was *Money Jungle* and on the record the young drummer challenged and pushed the elder Ellington into new heights of creativity. It was a satisfying endeavor for everyone involved.

When Parker finally returned from the West Coast in 1947, Roach became his regular drummer. He had developed into one of the top stickmen on the jazz scene, as he was young and very hungry. He was also the perfect bandmate because of his great chops and his keen enthusiasm to be playing in any situation; he loved to jam. It was not always easy putting up with the unpredictable Bird, but Roach recorded with Parker on the important Savoy and Dial sessions. It was at this point that he had reached his mature style that fit nicely with the genius' magic on the alto saxophone.

Roach spent three different periods with Parker: 1945, 1947–49, and one last time in 1951–1953. He was the perfect accompanist for the freewheeling Parker, because he was able to not only run with the great alto saxophonist, but challenge him at every turn. It drove the virtuoso Parker to revel higher in the fire. Roach also played on the seminal *Birth of the Cool* recording with Miles Davis.

Roach possessed a seemingly endless abundance of energy, for when he was not jamming with Parker and Miles, he was moonlighting with Louis Jordan and Henry "Red" Allen. As well, he entered a business partnership with the surly bassist Charlie Mingus as the two formed their own record company. Although it was an unsuccessful business venture, they were able to record some interesting albums on the label.

Roach also played on sessions with Bud Powell and Sonny Stitt in 1949–59 for the Prestige label. When he left Parker in 1949, he started to lead his own group at Soldier Myers. He also performed with J. J. Johnson and John Lewis. Roach rejoined Parker later in the year in order to go to France and play in the Paris Jazz Festival.

In 1952, he toured Europe as a member of Jazz at the Philharmonic, getting more exposure to European audiences and establishing a fan base across the Atlantic. Upon his return to America, he led his own quartet that recorded on the label he and Mingus had created. The drummer with the sharp hard bop licks was very much in demand and had eclipsed Clarke at this point by extending the boundaries that his predecessor had laid down. Roach's most serious rival was the great Art Blakey.

It was Roach who was behind the drum kit at the famed Massey Hall concert in 1953 that featured the powerhouse lineup of Parker, Gillespie, Powell, and Mingus. It was one of the most glorious moments in bebop history and once and for all proved that the style was not a passing fad but the real direction of jazz. While bebop had been in existence on record for nearly a decade, it had received an incredulous amount of bad press from critics who didn't understand the music. But that night at the Massey Hall all detractors finally realized what all the bebop artists were trying to achieve.

Although he was an asset in any session he took part in, Roach truly enjoyed leading his own group. He formed a quintet in Los Angeles that included the trumpeter Clifford Brown and Sonny Stitt. It is essential to provide some detailed biographical information on Brown because of his importance in the emergence of bebop and his professional relationship to Roach.

Clifford Brown was born on October 30, 1930, in Wilmington, Delaware. He started playing the trumpet when he was fifteen, and by his late teens he was jamming with the giants of bebop: Parker, Gillespie, Clarke, Powell, Monk, Davis, Roach, and Fats Navarro. Brown made his recording debut with Chris Powell's Blues Flames, but it was his stint with Lionel Hampton in Europe that established his reputation. He worked briefly with Art Blakey, then joined forces with Max Roach.

The partnership between Roach and Brown was very successful. There was a strong musical and personal chemistry between the two that quickly catapulted the quintet to the forefront of the jazz world. Aside from Roach and Brown, the group also included Richard Powell on piano, and Sonny Rollins or Harold Land on tenor sax. They would record several important albums together. However, on June 26, 1956, in Pennsylvania, Clifford Brown, one of the great bop trumpet players, died in a car accident. The jazz community had lost one of its most enterprising performers. Richie Powell and his wife also died in the tragedy.

The Roach-Brown partnership held so much promise but tragically, that full potential was never realized. One can only wonder at the many classics that they would have recorded together if Brown's life had not ended prematurely. However, in the short time that they did spend together they made the most of it. Later the group recorded "Clifford's Axe," one of the most memorable hard bop songs in Max's entire catalog.

Although he resumed performing and recording, Roach was never the same. He was devastated by the loss of Brown, who was replaced in the band by Kenny Dorham and Sonny Rollins as the lead horns. Roach remained one of the main hard bop attractions during the 1950s and the personnel in his quintet would change frequently with Booker Little, George Coleman, and Hank Mobley being some of the players that came through and left.

Roach was moving on with his life, but sadly, tragedy struck again when Booker Little died of uremia in 1961. From the time of Brown's death Roach had taken on a different personality. He drank heavily, making him sour to the point that he would berate friends, acquaintances and total strangers. It seemed as if the demons that haunted him from the Brown accident would never leave him alone. He eventually sought professional help and in time learned how to live with himself.

Like other African American artists of the 1960s, he developed a social conscience and began to write compositions that reflected his new point of view. Despite the ambitious "We Insist / Freedom Now Suite" collaboration with Oscar Brown Jr., Roach spent much of the 1960s away from the jazz scene. He recorded irregularly for a couple of labels and performed at various venues emphasizing his political views, which hampered his popularity.

Much of the work he recorded in the 1960s was found on the albums of others, including Thelonious Monk's *Brilliant Corners,* Sonny Rollins's *Saxophone Colossus,* and Thelonious Monk and Denzil Best's *Bemsha Swing.* During the decade he married singer Abbey Lincoln and backed her on her *Straight Ahead* album. Lincoln, a singer who grew disenchanted with the music scene, joined Roach in his projects that included *Tryptich: Prayer, Protest and Peace,* as well as *Tears for Johannesburg.* They were outspoken members of the Civil Rights movement and became one of the most highly visible African American couples working for improving the plight of their people.

In 1970, Roach returned to the jazz forefront with a ten-piece percussion ensemble called M'Boom. An interesting project, the group incorporated elements of classic contemporary music in their style to create something fresh and exciting. By this time he had shifted from hard bop to avant-garde, joining the likes of Anthony Braxton, Archie Shepp, and Cecil Taylor among others. Although he was much more active during this decade than the previous one, Roach never did recapture his lost popularity that he had enjoyed throughout the 1950s.

Always one to experiment, he began recording and performing with a double quartet in the 1980s. Aside from his regular foursome that included Odean Pope, Cecil Bridgewater, and Tyrone Brown, he combined the talents of the Uptown String Quartet. One of the featured members of the latter group was his daughter, Maxine, who played the viola. The enlarged group made some interesting recordings, but never found their particular musical niche.

He continued to participate in unique projects throughout much of the 1980s and 1990s. One of these was the concert duet with bop giant Dizzy Gillespie. Although the reunion of the two longtime friends was less than satisfying, it proved that their musical ideas had survived the test of time. Roach also conducted and composed the ambitious *Festival Journey,* a concerto that included jazz and classical elements.

The older Roach becomes, the more he refuses to live on past laurels; he always looks towards the future and experiments with different rhythmic, melodic, and harmonic structures. He continues to record and perform.

Max Roach is genuine jazz jewel. He has been a force for the past half-century and remains a name of the past that has challenged the present with great courage. He is one of the best stickmen of any era and along with Kenny Clarke changed the face of jazz drumming forever. Many young drummers hold him in awe.

Like Clarke, Roach shifted the emphasis of his playing from the bass drum to the hi-hat to create a rhythm of breakneck speed that allowed Parker, Davis, Gillespie, Navarro, Brown, Monk, Powell, J. J. Johnson, and others to play their quick, intoxicating brand of jazz. But Roach also added his own unique dimensions.

He played with an endless drive, he added a tremendous solo ability that intimidated other drummers, and he mixed pitches and timbres to produce a thicker layer of sound than other contemporaries. He was a master with the brushes creating a rhythmic universe of his own. He was always able to keep a steady beat while adding his special vocabulary to every song.

Roach was a tireless innovator who was never satisfied with the status quo; he demanded more from himself and the members in his various outfits. He always felt the need for the music to grow and evolve naturally, flowing down paths that his vivid imagination directed. He was always experimenting with whatever musical ideas piqued his curiosity and was never afraid to express his liquid thoughts, no matter how different they seemed.

He was a leader of African Americans as an outspoken voice who supported civil rights. He was a rebel and followed the course of his decision no matter where it might lead him. Although he made some unpopular comments that earned him severe criticism, he never backed down from his point of view.

Because of this fortitude he was also a major influence on the younger generation. A partial list includes Toshiko Akiyoshi, Ran Blake, Michael Carvin, Jack DeJohnette, Chico Hamilton, Slide Hampton, Beaver Harris, Louis Hayes, Philly Joe Jones, Bob Moses, Dannie Richmond, Art Taylor, Dave Bailey, Ron Jefferson, Barry Miles, Norman Connors, J. C. Heard, Albert "Tootie" Heath, Jon Hendricks, and Paul Motian.

His peers and others also recognized Roach for his numerous contributions to jazz. He received a MacArthur Foundation "genius" grant—one of the few jazz musicians to be given that honor. But he was also able to give back to the community as much as he received.

He was an articulate lecturer, and a distinguished spokesman for the music he loved so much. He helped spread the gospel of jazz throughout the world as much as anyone else. He always spoke with enthusiasm and sheer heartfelt emotion about the wonderful music that he spent more than half of his life creating and perfecting. He taught at the Lenox School of Jazz and was also a professor of music at the University of Massachusetts, Amherst.

Max Roach remains an ambassador of jazz. He has played thousands of concerts all over the world, delighting audiences with his musical abilities as one of the finest drummers in the entire run of the genre. Whether he was leading his own groups that consisted of trios, quartets, quintets and large ensembles, or was part of a working group, Roach rarely failed to incite the crowd or his bandmates.

Roach is also a jazz historian. He was present during the creation of bop. He was a leading force in hard bop, participated in the avant-garde movement, and has even experimented with the union of jazz, rap, and hip hop long before it was stylish to do so. With the deaths of Davis, Gillespie, Clarke, Monk, Parker, Mingus, Gordon, Johnson, Powell, Brown, and Navarro, Roach remains one of the last major voices of the bop evolution.

Throughout his career, Roach was able to deliver an exciting brand of jazz that highlighted all that was good with the genre. Like Blakey, he possessed a surging drive that never seemed to relent. A true individual in a world where individualism was always cherished, he set standards that are still vital in the present. While the history of jazz is full of exciting drummers with abundant talent, there was and always will be only one Driva Man.

Discography

Award Winning Drummer, Bainbridge Records 1042.
Deeds, Not Words, Original Jazz Classics 304.
Featuring the Legendary Hasaan/Drums Unlimited, Collectables 6256.
It's Christmas Again, Soul Note 121153.
It's Time, Impulse! 185.
Lift Every Voice and Sing, Koch Jazz 8516.
M'Boom, Legacy Records 57886.
Max, Chess 825.
Max Roach 4 Plays Charlie Parker, Verve 512 448.
Members, Don't Git Weary, Koch Jazz 8514.
Mop Mop, Le Jazz 44.
Percussion Bitter Sweet, Impulse! 122.
Plus Four, EmArcy 822 673.
Survivors, Soul Note 121093.
Variations on the Scene, Jazz Hour 73589.
Les Incontournables, WEA 9548358792.
Max Roach Quintet, VOGUE BVCJ-37022.

JIMMY SMITH (1925–2005)

Funky Cool Blues

One of the main branches of the jazz explosion in the 1960s was soul jazz. The combination of the classical elements of the genre with a rootsy rhythm and blues personality created interesting music. The main instrument of the style was the organ, one that had never made a large impact in the entire history of the genre. The greatest single exponent of soul-jazz was the organist who did it with his funky cool blues. His name was Jimmy Smith.

James Oscar Smith was born on December 8, 1925, in Norristown, Pennsylvania. Initially a pianist, he taught himself the rudiments of the instrument until he was proficient enough to play in front of an audience. However, a stint in the Navy interrupted his progress for a couple of years.

Upon his release, Smith furthered his musical education at the Hamilton and Ornstein schools of music. Although he was a good piano player, Smith began to explore the possibilities of the Hammond organ in 1951 and eventually adopted it as his main musical voice. A tap dancer of considerable skill, Smith used this ability to work the foot pedals of the organ to magically create early versions of his funky cool blues.

The trend of the day in the mid–1950s was hard bop/cool jazz, so he adapted to the latter style and soon found success. He formed a trio in 1955 and recorded some outstanding albums with Blue Note. Although many musicians had once reviled the organ, Smith had the knack of making the instrument sound like it belonged in jazz.

He never lacked partners. In 1956, he recorded *The Incredible Jimmy Smith* with Art Blakey and it caused a sensation. No one had ever heard such tasty, robust rhythms emerge from the organ or compositions of the ilk that he delivered with cool overtones. He was hailed as a star and teamed up with Hank Mobley, Jackie McLean, Ike Quebec and Lou Donaldson on subsequent recordings, such as *Open House, The Sermon,* and *A Date with Jimmy Smith.*

In the 1960s, the foundations that Smith had laid down in the previous decade exploded, much to his delight. Soul-jazz became a very lucrative market and Smith was its king. His music took on more of a funky sound, but still contained powerful strains of jazz. A great improviser, he combined his love of different styles to create his own cool universe.

With albums like *Back at the Chicken Shack, Rockin' the Boat, Prayer Meetin', Softly as a Summer Breeze* and *Crazy Baby,* he left little doubt as to who was the emperor of soul-jazz. He was at forefront of the African American musical outburst in the 1960s. He also toured extensively throughout the United States and the world, delighting audiences with his special blend of musical styles.

Although the 1970s were not as kind to him as the late 1950s and the entire decade of the 1960s had been, Smith carried on and collaborated with many important jazz figures, including Kenny Burrell, Lee Morgan, Tina Brooks, and Stanley Turrentine, usually in small combo settings. He also organized big band sessions where his playing never sounded funkier. However, by the 1970s, Smith was no longer a novelty in jazz circles; many other organists had jumped on the soul-jazz bandwagon, like Jimmy McGriff and Brother Jack McDuff. Also, the introduction of the electric piano had eclipsed the popularity of the organ.

Nevertheless, Smith carried on. Although his original sound was diluted by the recording company trying to cash in on his crossover appeal, he still was a force to be reckoned with. He toured Israel and Europe frequently in the 1970s and continued to deliver albums that combined soul, gospel, blues and jazz, including *Bashin'* and *The Monster*. Although the musical tastes of the general public had changed, he still retained an audience with his style of cool soul jazz.

By the 1980s, his career had slowed down considerably and his popularity was but a mere shadow of what it had been during his heyday in the 1960s. However, he continued to tour and record fully aware that his blend of funky blues never went totally out of style. By this time the music world was full of organ players who all owed a considerable debt to Smith. Many of them sounded too much like him, which did nothing for their careers, but added special tones to his.

In the 1990s, Smith marked his fortieth anniversary in the music business. He released some interesting albums that by this time were deeply rooted in gospel, more so than in blues, jazz and soul. Although he took some time off, he returned for the new millennium with a bluesier project called *Dot Com Blues*. He remained one of the most interesting voices on the organ until his death on February 8, 2005.

Jimmy Smith was a jazz pioneer. Before he demonstrated that the organ could be used as a dominant instrument in jazz, it had remained in obscurity with only Count Basie and Fats Waller making a handful of important recordings with it. No one had ever dedicated their efforts to stretching out the possibilities of the instrument. Smith was also the forefather of a number of musical directions that continue to this day.

He was a masterful organist. His expert use of the pedals brought the instrument to life. He provided crispness in his approach. His speedy attack was incredible and stunned listeners who had associated the organ solely with skating rinks and gospel music. He pumped out his own bass line, then spun fast single-note runs and sustained chords that fueled his remarkable improvised solos.

He was the founding father of soul-jazz, but he also signaled the jazz fusion mania that would occur in the late 1960s and early 1970s. He was also one of the main proponents of the cool jazz style practiced by Dave Brubeck, Wes Montgomery, Chet Baker, Paul Desmond, Miles Davis, Gil Evans, Jimmy Giuffre, Gerry Mulligan, Shorty Rogers, and Lennie Tristano. As well, along with Ray Charles, Sam Cooke, Jackie Wilson and others, Smith introduced soul into the musical mix. Many of the groups in the 1960s and 1970s like Chicago, Blood Sweat and Tears, Sly and the Family Stone, and dozens more can trace some of their roots to Smith.

He had a large influence on a number of players including Bill Doggett, Johnny "Hammond" Smith, Charles Earland, Richard "Grooves" Holmes, Brother Jack McDuff, Jimmy McGriff, Don Patterson, Big John Patton, Shirley Scoot, Lonnie Smith and Larry Young. All of the keepers of the jazz organ flame today owe a great debt to Smith, including Joey DeFrancesco, Barbara Dannerlin, Larry Goldings, Greg Hatza and John Medeski. He also had a major impact on electric piano players Keith Jarrett, Herbie Hancock, Chick Corea, Joe Zawinul, and Jan Hammer.

Because of his ability to blend many types of musical elements into a funky, cohesive style, he had a strong influence on organ players outside of jazz. Blues player Lucky Peterson was inspired by Smith. Rock legends such as Ray Manzerek, Keith Emerson, John Paul Jones, Jon Lord, Greg Rollie and so many others were also touched by Smith's magic.

With his supercharged performances Smith gave the world a treasure trove of songs. They include "The Duel," "All Day Long," "Plum Nellie," "The Preacher," Midnight Special," "A Walk On the Wild Side," "Goldfinger," "Slaughter on Tenth Avenue," and "Bluesette," as well as remakes of such standards as "Bye Bye Blackbird," "I Didn't Know What Time It Was," and "Mood Indigo." He could take any song, whether it be one of his original compositions or a cover version, and breathe life into it like no one else had done before him or since.

Jimmy Smith enjoyed a long, exciting career. He brought many innovations to the genre and his popularity spilled over into other styles. He was a crossover artist long before the term was coined and blazed that path that so many musicians followed. The man responsible for his funky cool blues certainly shook up the jazz world and added his own distinct chapter.

Discography

Bashin'—The Unpredictable Jimmy Smith, Verve 539 061.
Dot Com Blues, Blue Thumb Records 543 978.
Jimmy Smith's Finest Hour, Verve 543 598.
Six Views of the Blues, Blue Note Records 21435.

The Sermon, Blue Note Records 24541.
A New Sound ... A New Star ... Vol. 1–3, Blue Note Records 57191.
Angel Eyes: Ballads & Slow Jams, Verve 527 632.
Any Number Can Win, Verve 557 447.
Back at the Chicken Shack, Blue Note Records 46402.
Best of the Blue Note Years, Blue Note Records 91140.
Bucket, Blue Note Records 24550.
Christmas Cookin', Verve 513 711.
Compact Jazz, Verve 831 374.
Crazy Baby, Blue Note Records 84030.
Damn!, Verve 527 631.
Fourmost, Milestone Records 9184.
Got My Mojo Workin' / Hoochie Cootchie Man, Verve 533 828.
Groovin' at Small's Paradise, Blue Note Records 99777.
Home Cookin', Blue Note Records 53360.
House Party, Blue Note Records 24542.
I'm Movin' On, Blue Note Records 32750.
Immortal Concerts, Giants of Jazz Recordings 53114.
Jazz 'Round Midnight, Verve 521 655.
Midnight Special, Blue Note Records 84078.
Off the Top, Elektra Musician 60175.
Open House/Plain Talk, Blue Note Records 84269.
Organ Grinder Swing, Verve 543 831.
Peter and the Wolf, Verve 547 264.
Prayer Meetin', Blue Note Records 84164.
Prime Time, Milestone Records 9176.
Root Down, Verve 559 805.
Softly as a Summer Breeze, Blue Note Records 97505.
Standards, Blue Note Records 21282.
Sum Serious Blues, Milestone Records 9207.
Talkin' Verve: Roots Of Acid Jazz, Verve 531 563.
The Cat, Verve 539 756.
The Sermon, Blue Note Records 24541.
Ultimate Jimmy Smith, Verve 547 161.
Walk on the Wild Side: Best of the Verve Years, Verve 527 950.
At Club Baby Grand Vol. 1, BLUEN TOCJ-1528.
At Club Baby Grand Vol. 2, TOSHI TOCJ-1529.
At The Organ Vol. 1, BLUEN TOCJ-1551.
At The Organ Vol. 2, BLUEN TOCJ-1552.
Best Of Jimmy Smith, BLUEN TOCJ-66037.
Champ, BNOTE TOCJ-9204.
Jimmy Smith Plays Fats Waller, BLUEN TOCJ-4100.
Livin' It Up, POLY POCJ-2589.
Midnight Blues, MASTE 502932.
Plays Pretty Just for You, BLUEN TOCJ-1563.
Rockin' the Boat, EMI TOCJ-4141.

MILES DAVIS (1926–1991)
The Cool One

Throughout the history of jazz there have been many innovators. Louis Armstrong switched the emphasis of the ensemble to the individuals and solos became all the rage. Coleman Hawkins took the saxophone from obscurity to the main voice of jazz in a span of ten years. Dizzy Gillespie and Charlie Parker spearheaded a new movement known as bop that all of modern jazz is built on. One of these bop players would take his cue from his two mentors and go on to reinvent jazz many times over. He was able to transcend all barriers in order to achieve a superior level of popularity as the Cool One. His name was Miles Davis.

Miles Davis was born Miles Dewey Davis III on May 25, 1926, in Alton, Illinois. The son of a prominent dentist from East St. Louis, Miles was bitten by the musical bug at an early age. There was no cure and he started taking private lessons when he was ten. By the time he entered his teenage years music consumed all of his attention.

He started playing gigs around the East St. Louis area and earned the reputation as a decent trumpet player. His musical background was a mixture of rural blues, gospel, and a love for the black big bands, including those of Duke Ellington, Count Basie, Lionel Hampton, Jimmie Lunceford, and Louis Armstrong. On his thirteenth birthday, Davis received a new trumpet from his father.

In high school, he played second trumpet in the band. It was also around this time that he met Terry Clark, one of his early idols. After playing gigs and jamming with friends around his hometown and neighboring districts, Davis joined Eddie Randall's Blue Devils. For the first time in his life he was a working, breathing musician. During his stint with Randall, he learned how to run a band and write and arrange music, all the while expanding his skills on the trumpet.

In 1944, Davis left Randall's outfit and joined Adam Lambert's Six Brown Cats, but his time with this group only lasted a few weeks. Although East St. Louis provided ample opportunities for him to grow as a musician, the lure of the bop evolution in New York was hypnotizing. Besides, it was in the Big Apple that Dizzy and Bird were playing, and that was where young Miles wanted to be.

He moved to New York City in the fall of 1944 and entered the prestigious Juliard School of Music. But he was more interested in hanging out at Minton's with Bird, Dizzy, Fats Navarro, Kenny Clarke, Max Roach, Thelonious Monk, Bud Powell, and all the other bop cats than going to school. Eventually he left Juliard to embrace the hot jam sessions that were going down all over 52nd Street. He soaked up all the musical education he could in those dark, smoke-filled nightclubs listening to Bird and Dizzy. It was a romantic time to be an aspiring jazz musician and he lived the life to the fullest. Eventually, he and Charlie Parker joined forces.

Charlie Parker was an original, brilliant jazz player but possessed an insatiable destructive streak in him that would lead to his premature death. Davis joined Benny Carter's band for a brief stint, but most of the recording he did during this period was with Bird. He traveled to the West Coast for a few months and helped spread the bop gospel along with Parker and Gillespie to the hip jazz brethren in Los Angeles.

Davis returned to New York and joined Billy Eckstine's band for a short time, then rejoined Bird when the latter returned from the West Coast. However, Bird who was sinking in the morass of his heroin habit, and eventually was unable to operate a working jazz band. After a feud over money, Davis left Bird's band. He played with Tadd Dameron for a while, then joined Oscar Pettiford's group.

In 1949, Davis made two incredible strides toward achieving the immense popularity that he would later enjoy. One, he traveled to Europe where he played at the Paris Jazz Festival with Dameron, Kenny Clarke, James Moody, and Pierre Michelot. It was also around this time that he released the *Birth of the Cool* album that ushered in the cool jazz era. It would not be the only time that Davis would reinvent the music and start a new movement.

The lineup on *Birth of the Cool* featured Davis, Lee Konitz, Gerry Mulligan, Bill Barber, Kenny Clarke, Max Roach, J. J. Johnson, Kai Winding, Al Haig, and Joe Shulman. Recorded over three sessions, the seminal release included such classics as "Jeru," "Move," "Godchild," "Budo," "Moon Dreams," and "Boplicity." It was different than other bop recordings because some of the songs a person could hum to and make a connection with the music. The challenging, furious playing of Bird and Dizzy was spellbinding, but it was also intimidating. While 1949 was a good year for Davis, the early 1950s would not be so kind.

From 1950 to 1954, the "Lost Years," Davis had a heroin habit that nearly cost him his life. Although he was still playing and recording, much of the material at this point was sub-par to what he had done on *Birth of the Cool*. However, unlike his hero Parker, Davis managed to overcome his habit. Once he emerged from his drug haze in 1954, he was ready to resume his career and assume his position as one of the greatest voices in jazz.

He returned to New York and recorded *Miles Davis, Volume 2* and *Miles Davis Quartet*. He had Art Blakey on drums, Percy Heath on bass, and Horace Silver on piano. They were important comeback albums for Davis, who immediately resumed where he had left off. He was creating exciting jazz that was as good as, and in many cases better than, anything anyone else was making. Later on in the year he would record *Miles Davis and the Modern Jazz Giants* with a group that included Milt Jackson, Thelonious Monk, Percy Heath, and Kenny Clarke. The death of friend, mentor, and collaborator Charlie Parker in 1955 was a huge blow to him, but he carried on.

From 1954 to 1960, Davis delivered some of the greatest records in jazz history, including *Blue Moods, Basic Miles, Miles Ahead, Milestones,* and *Kind of Blue,* all with the Miles Davis Quartet. During this period, he influenced hundreds of aspiring jazz musicians with his cool tone. Miles was into the modal style and he dominated the charts, polls and award ceremonies. He began to tour around the world, taking the various lineups of his band to Europe, Brazil, and Africa. He was also a major draw throughout the major cities and small towns in North America.

Although there were other famous jazz musicians around this time, none were Miles Davis. He opened the door for many other musicians in terms of better money, playing conditions, and the ability to record. A prolific artist, he recorded over sixty albums in this six-year span. One of his famous quartets contained Red Garland on piano, Philly Joe Jones on drums, Davis, and a young sax player named John Coltrane. At one point his group would include Coltrane as well as the unknown Cannonball Adderley.

Although he continued to record from 1960 to 1964, the free jazz-/avant-garde wave overshadowed his efforts. While he was gifted enough to play in any style, Davis was not interested in the new thing. He made a number of records during this time including *Sketches of Spain, Directions, Live Miles, Sorcerer, Quiet Nights,* and *Blue Christmas.* But Davis regrouped and by 1964, he was ready to resume his position as one of the leading forces in jazz.

He formed a band with Wayne Shorter, Herbie Hancock, Ron Carter and Tony Williams that was probably the best combination that he ever assembled. This marked the beginning of his electric period. This era saw him invent a new movement that took away the limelight from the free jazz/avant-garde style, of which Davis had been an outspoken critic.

The electric era produced *Filles de Kilmanjaro, In a Silent Way, Nerfertiti, Circle in the Round,* and *Bitches Brew.* The 1970s would be known as the jazz fusion decade and many of the musicians who had played with Davis during the better part of the 1960s were leading their own band and melding jazz with other styles, including rock, pop, and soul. Wayne Shorter, Airto Moreira, John McLaughlin, Chick Corea, Herbie Hancock, Keith Jarrett, Joe Zawinul, Dave Holland, Ron Carter, Billy Cobham, Jack DeJohnette, Harvey Brooks and Larry Young were all Davis alumni.

He was hailed as a superstar in the 1970s, but had achieved this status many years before. His name was synonymous with jazz and he continued to build on his legend with albums like *Get Up with It, On the Corner, Agharta,* and *Pangaea.* However, at the end of the decade he suffered health problems that drastically curtailed his live appearances and recording efforts. There was also the fact that his popularity was cemented and there was no longer the urge to create music to make money since he was quite wealthy. He lost his drive to make jazz.

But Miles was first and foremost a musician; music was in his blood. In 1980, after a five-year absence, he decided to return to the world of jazz that hadn't been the same without his effervescent presence. Although he released albums throughout the rest of the decade, his most creative years were behind him. However, *The Man with the Horn, Star People, Decoy, Tutu, Amandla,* and *Aura* proved to be interesting additions to his lengthy catalog. He continued to perform but his touring schedule was not as hectic as it had been in previous eras. His health was not the best and he no longer had a burning desire to appear in public.

On September 28, 1991, in Santa Monica, California, Miles Davis, one of the greatest innovators and trumpet players in the history of jazz, died. He had suffered from cancer for a long time and finally succumbed to the disease. He was 65 years old.

Miles Davis was a genuine master of jazz. Arguably, he is the most important jazz musician of the latter part of the twentieth century, and one of the most celebrated names in twentieth century music. He was a brilliant songwriter, arranger, player and bandleader. He was also an open critic and spokesman. His contributions to the genre are enormous and his legacy continues to have an impact on the music more than a decade after his death.

Miles Davis was one of the greatest trumpet players of all time. There was accessibility to his music because of his lyrical facility. He had a way of writing songs that slipped into people's subconscious and found them humming the tune without even realizing it. His playing, throughout his career and many periods of changes, was always sweet, smooth, and spacious. His golden touch affected people; it hit a particular nerve.

He was an incredible bandleader. It was Davis who gave John Coltrane his start. A complete list of those who were part of his band would fill a book, but the most notable include Herbie Hancock, Chick Corea, Joe Zawinul, Ron Carter, Tony Williams, John McLaughlin, Wayne Shorter, Cannonball Adderley, Keith Jarrett, and Philly Joe Jones.

He played with some of the greatest names in jazz, including Bird, Diz, Max Roach, Charles Mingus, Thelonious Monk, Bud Powell, Kenny Clarke, Art Blakey, John Coltrane, Benny Carter, Coleman Hawkins, J. J.

Johnson, Paul Chambers, Tommy Potter, Red Garland, Al Haig, and Roy Haynes.

It was Miles who spearheaded two of the biggest schools in jazz history. He ushered in the cool school of jazz that was particularly strong on the West Coast and that influenced Gerry Mulligan, Chet Baker, Sonny Rollins, Horace Silver, Wes Montgomery, Herbie Mann, Sonny Stitt, Dave Brubeck, Paul Desmond, Shelly Manne, Modern Jazz Quartet, Lennie Tristano, Lee Konitz, and Wayne Marsh.

Davis was also the founding father of the jazz fusion style that dominated the late 1960s and 1970s. Corea, Hancock, Freddie Hubbard, McLaughlin, Zawinul, Shorter, Jaco Pastorius, Stanley Clarke, Ron Carter, Larry Coryell, Billy Cobham, and Keith Jarrett were just a few of those that carried on the ideas of electric jazz. Zawinul and Shorter later formed Weather Report, one of the best jazz-rock outfits ever created.

Davis also helped shaped the sound of countless other jazz musicians outside of his medium. They include Mtume, Anthony Braxton, Johnny Coles, Urszula Dudziak, Sonny Greenwich, John Klemmer, Steve Kuhn, Steve Lacy, Albert Mangelsdorff, Pat Metheny, Lee Morgan, James Newton, Cecil Taylor, Larry Willis, Luis Gasca, Michal Urbaniak, Deodato, Brian Jackson, Carlos Santana, and David Toop. He was a special inspiration to Prince, Michael Jackson, and many other African Americans who followed the path he created in the music business. An outspoken individual for the belief and welfare of his race, he touched all people, black, white, Muslim, Asian—anyone who heard his music.

He delivered a number of gifts to the world. A partial list includes "Back Seat Betty," "Blue Demon," "Boplicity," "Cherokee," "Circle in the Round," "In a Silent Way," "Lazy Susan," "Kilimanjaro," "Milestones," "Neferetiti," "My Funny Valentine," "'Round Midnight," "Star on Cicely," "Walkin'," "Warmin' Up a Riff," "Yesterdays," "The Leap," "Take-Off," "Bags Groove," "The Man I Love," and countless others. His songs have found their way into the catalog of every major and minor jazz musician of the past fifty years.

Miles Davis was a high profile star. He drove a fancy car (a Ferrari or Camero), was married to well-known actress Cicely Tyson, and lived hard and fast. Often the subject of gossip magazines, he lived his life the way he saw fit and never had any regrets. Perhaps his entire vision could be traced back to the album *Birth of the Cool*, because he displayed an enormous amount of confidence that truly made him the Cool One. There has never been nor will there ever be another one like him.

Discography

Chasin' the Bird—Live at the Royal Roost, Arpo 1.
Young Miles, Vol. 2, Masters of Jazz 151.
All Stars Live 1958–1959, JZBA 2101.
Ballads & Blues, 1953–1958, Bluebird 36633.
Agartha, Columbia 33967.
Basic Miles, Columbia 32025.
Big Fun, Columbia 32866.
Bitches Brew, Columbia 33042.
Black Giants, Columbia 33402.
Blue Moods, Fantasy 86001.
Capitol Jazz Classics Vol. 2, Capitol 11026.
Conception, Prestige 7744.
Miles Davis, Blue Note 815501/81502.
Miles Davis at Carnegie Hall, Columbia 8612.
Miles Davis at Fillmore, Columbia 30038.
Miles Davis' Greatest Hits, Columbia 9808.
Miles Davis' Greatest Hits, Prestige 7457.
Miles Davis in Concert, Columbia 32092.
Miles Davis in Europe, Columbia 8903.
Miles Davis in Person, Columbia 25820.
Miles Davis Plays for Lovers, Prestige 7352.
Miles Davis Plays Jazz Classics, Prestige 7372.
Decade of Jazz, Vol. 2, Blue Note 159–32.
Dig, Prestige 24054.
Early Miles, Prestige 7674.
Ezz-Ethic, Prestige 7827.
Filles de Kilimanjaro, Columbia 9750.
Four & More, Columbia 9253.
Get Up with It, Columbia 33236.
Green Haze, Prestige 24064.
In a Silent Way, Columbia 9857.
Miles Davis: a Tribute to Jack Johnson, Columbia CK 47036.
Jazz at the Plaza, Vol. 1, Columbia 32470.
Kind of Blue, Columbia 8163.
Lenny, United Artists 359–11.
Live-Evil, Columbia 30954.
Miles Ahead, Columbia 8633.
Miles, Prestige 7822.
Miles & Monk at Newport, Columbia 8978.
Miles in the Sky, Columbia 9628.
Miles Smiles, Columbia 9401.
Milestones, Columbia 9428.
My Funny Valentine, Columbia 9106.
My Old Flame, Up Front 171.
Nefertiti, Columbia 9594.
Odyssey, Prestige 7540.
Olea, Prestige 7847.
On the Corner, Columbia 31906.
Porgy & Bess, Columbia 8085.
Twofer Giants, Vols. 1 & 2, Prestige 1–2.

Quiet Nights, Columbia 8906.
Roots of Modern Jazz, Olympic 7135.
'Round Midnight, Columbia 8649.
Seven Steps to Heaven, Columbia 9951.
Sketches of Spain, Columbia 8271.
Someday My Prince Will Come, Columbia 8456.
Something Else, Blue Note 169.
Sorcerer, Columbia 9532.
Steamin', Prestige 7580.
Tallest Trees, Prestige 24012.
25 Years of Prestige, Prestige 24046.
Walkin', Prestige 7608.
Water Babies, Columbia 34396.
Workin' & Steamin', Prestige 24034
Tune Up, Prestige 24077.
Aura, Columbia Sony B00004WK3E.
Amandla, Warner Bros. 25873.
Tutu, Warner Bros. 25490.
You're Under Arrest, Sony 40023.
Decoy, Sony 38991.
Star People, Sony B00002644H.
We Want Miles, Sony Int'l B000026KPV.
The Man with the Horn, Sony 36790.
Pangaea Live, Sony 46115 CBS.
Birth of the Cool, Bluebird 92862.
From Bebop to Cool, EPM 159662.
L'ascenseur Pour L'echafaud, PLG 836305-C.

HORACE SILVER (1928–)

Finger Poppin' Jazz

Despite the eclectic nature of the modern jazz styles, improvisation remained one of the essential ingredients. Perhaps more than any branch of bop, hard bop required a definite flexibility and understanding of rhythmic structures. The practitioners of the gritty, hard edged, bluesy sound balanced their cutting edge approach with a harmonic and melodic tone, especially the man known for his finger poppin' jazz. His name is Horace Silver.

Horace Ward Martin Tavares Silver was born on September 2, 1928, in Norwalk, Connecticut. Although he would make his mark in jazz, Silver's initiation into music was the Portuguese folk music that his father played. In his teens, Horace honed his skills on the saxophone and the piano in local bands. He was also listening to the great boogie-woogie pianists as well as the bop revolutionists Thelonious Monk and Bud Powell. It was the latter in particular who really shaped Silver's early musical style. He eventually settled on the piano as his instrument of choice.

Silver hung around Connecticut waiting for his big break and it came in 1950 when he was hired to back Stan Getz. Getz was so impressed with Silver's trio—sidemen Walter Bolden and Joe Calloway—that all three were asked to join his band. Silver jumped at the opportunity and remained with Getz for a year, learning invaluable performing lessons.

In order to be in the Getz big band, Silver had to relocate to New York. An enterprising young man, he had always desired to play in the Big Apple, the heartbeat of jazz at the time. After his departure from the Getz band, he found plenty of work jamming with Coleman Hawkins, Lester Young, and Oscar Pettiford.

In 1952, he recorded with Lou Donaldson, but it was his teaming with Art Blakey a year later to form the Jazz Messengers that truly catapulted Silver to the top of the heap. He had made some recordings as leader but the albums he made with the great drummer were his best work so far. A hard bop pianist, Silver had extended the essential elements of Powell and to a lesser degree Thelonious Monk to create that definitive sound.

In three years with the Jazz Messengers, Silver sealed his popularity. They were arguably the best hard bop group around. Horace pounded out dangerous, hard-edged piano licks and drummer Blakey added his dynamic press rolls and bombs. Their debut album, *Horace Silver and the Jazz Messengers,* was of seminal importance and featured some of Horace's best writing, including "The Preacher," "Doodlin'," and "Room 608." However, despite the success and future promise in the band, he left the Jazz Messengers in 1956.

As a solo performer he proved that he was ready and very capable of creating exciting hard bop jazz. He delivered such classic albums as *Blowin' the Blues Away* and *Song for My Father.* He also formed his own outfit and although he was the natural focus of the group, he armed himself with talented sidemen, including Blue Mitchell and Junior Cook. Undoubtedly, Horace was one of the top composers and pianists of the era, if not the very best, since Powell suffered from mental breakdowns and Monk's odd brand of jazz had not yet gained widespread acceptance.

Despite the advent of free jazz and the avant-garde movement in the 1960s, Silver continued to deliver hard bop to interested audiences. His group featured a variety of musicians and included at times tenor men Hank Mobley and Joe Henderson, trumpeters Joe Gordon, Carmell Jones, Woody Shaw and Art Farmer, and drummers Louis Hayes, Roy Brooks and Roger Humphries. The group recorded some milestone albums: *The*

Stylings of Silver, Silver's Serenade, Six Pieces of Silver, and *The Cape Verdean Blues.*

Horace Silver and his Messengers and Blakey's Jazz Messengers best practiced the hard bop style that was overshadowed by free jazz and avant-garde. The two groups were in top form and although they didn't play complicated selections, their music was effective, finger poppin' jazz that catered to the tastes of a large segment of the listening audience. By this time Silver was recognized as one of the grand masters of the modern piano sound.

For twenty years, from the 1950s to the end of the 1970s, Silver recorded for Blue Note. But when the label went out of business, he started his own record company called Silveto. Although he kept somewhat of a low profile throughout much of the 1980s, he continued to record and perform around the country and internationally. While he didn't stray from his hard bop flavor, his work took on different dimensions, as he wrote lyrics to his compositions and ventured down various avenues with his music. Like other jazz artists during the decade, Silver expanded his creative muscle.

Because of his vast talents and proven track record, Silver was signed to Columbia Records in the 1990s. The prestige of a powerful label was the exact tonic that he needed to reestablish himself as one of the leading voices in jazz. His *Hardbop Grandpop* album clearly stated that he was one of the founders of the hard bop movement and was very proud of his vast accomplishments within that style. He continues to record and perform.

Horace Silver is a genuine jazz messenger. He has delivered the gospel of jazz for the past forty years with a power and fire that has rarely been matched. He is a commanding talent on the piano who has taken the blue note and ventured down avenues that had remained dark until he explored them. He has been a superb bandleader, a notable asset in the studio for his own projects and on the sessions of others.

Silver is a hard driving pianist whose roots are clearly embedded in the old boogie-woogie, barrelhouse style of the 1920s and 1930s. In the beginning, he was a firm disciple of Powell but eventually developed his own unique style. His furious attack on the piano coupled with his imaginative licks are just part of his style. He has been able to take the essential elements of the blues, the repetitive phrases, the single note runs the major and minor chord combinations, and shape them into his musical voice.

A breakdown of his style incorporates the magic collaboration of both hands. He played boogie figures with his left hand, hitting the top of the beat with single note bombs and alternating with chordal hammerings with his right hand. This created a bluesy, funky style of jazz with percussion overtones that has never been truly duplicated.

Throughout much of his career Silver wallowed in the confines of hard bop. Like his one time bandmate Art Blakey, he never had the desire to play the new thing. They both proved that hard bop was a rich vein that could launch and sustain a career for decades. As a prime architect of the style, he established the foundation that all modern piano is built upon.

Like Powell, who influenced him, Silver in turn has had a large impact on a number of artists over the years. They include piano players as well as organ players in a variety of styles. A short list includes George Cables, Sonny Clark, Ted Dunbar, Bill Evans, Russ Freeman, George Gruntz, Herbie Hancock, Geoff Keezer, Chris McGregor, Horace Parlan, George Shearing, Cecil Taylor, James Williams, Allan Gumbs, Kenny Kirkland, Claude Williamson, Brian Jackson, Chick Corea, Big John Patton and Jimmy Smith. It is hard to think of where modern jazz piano would be without Silver's contributions.

He wrote an incredible number of songs, including "Quicksilver," "Doodlin'," "The Preacher," "Home Cookin'," "Sweet Sweetie Dee," "Let's Get to the Nitty Gritty," "Filthy McNasty," "Señor Blues," "The Cape Verdean Blues," "Song For My Father," "Calcutta Cute," and dozens more. His material ranges from funky blues to exotic blues, from hard-driving bop to haunting ballads, from pure jazz to finger poppin' tunes. But despite the wide spectrum that his compositions cover, there is no mistaking that they are Silver's creations.

Silver is a superb leader. The influx of talent that graced his bands include Junior Cook, Hank Mobley, Joe Henderson, Joe Gordon, Carmeil Jones, Woody Shaw, Blue Mitchell, Art Farmer, Louis Hayes, Roy Brooks, Roger Humphries, Donald Byrd, Joe Henderson, Benny Golson, and the Brecker brothers. He also worked with Art Blakey, Sonny Rollins, Milt Jackson, Donald Byrd, Kenny Dorham, Philly Joe Jones, Oscar Pettiford, Curly Russell, Michael Cuscuna, Thelonious Monk, Max Roach, and John Lewis.

Horace Silver has made many contributions during his long stay on the scene, five decades of playing his boogie-woogie figures within a hard bop context. He is the dominant piano voice of the style and has given the world a bluesy, funky brand of jazz with percussion overtones that has never been quite duplicated. A dedicated hard bop artist, he never substituted his vision for the new thing. When all is said and done, it is obvious that he has created a hall of fame career with his finger poppin' jazz.

Discography

Jazz ... Has ... A Sense of Humor, Impulse! 293.
A Prescription for the Blues, GRP Records 238.

Best of Horace Silver—The Blue Note Years, Blue Note Records 91143.
Best of Horace Silver, Vol. 2, Blue Note Records 93206.
Greatest Hits, EMI-Capitol Special Markets 57589.
Horace Silver & The Jazz Messengers, Blue Note Records 46140.
Horace Silver Trio, Blue Note Records 81520.
Re-Entry, 32 Records 32005.
Retrospective, Blue Note Records 95576.
Safari, Giants of Jazz Recordings (import) 53131.
Serenade to a Soul Sister, Blue Note Records 84277.
Six Pieces of Silver, Blue Note Records 25648.
Song for My Father, Blue Note Records 99002.
The Baghdad Blues, Giants of Jazz Recordings 53138.
The Cape Verdean Blues, Blue Note Records 84220.
The Hardbop Grandpop, Impulse! 192.
The Jody Grind, Blue Note Records 84250.
The Tokyo Blues, Blue Note Records 53355.
Best of Horace Silver, BLUEN TOCJ-66034.
Finger Poppin', BLUEN TOCJ-4008.
Further Explorations, BLUEN TOCJ-1589.
Horace Scope, BLUEN TOCJ-4042.
Horace Silver & The Jazz Messengers, BLUEN TOCJ-1518.
Silver's Blue, EPIC ESCA-7762.
Silver's Blue, SONY COL4765212.
Stylings of Silver, BLUEN TOCJ-1562.
Tokyo Blues, BLUEN TOCJ-9068.

HERBIE MANN (1930–2003)

Flute Soufflé

The main instruments in the creation of jazz include the saxophone, trumpet, clarinet, trombone, piano, drums, guitar and bass. All others have taken a secondary role. For instance, the flute was considered a minor instrument capable of adding very little to a jazz ensemble. Although a handful of jazz artists doubled on other wind instruments and made some recordings with them, it wasn't until the arrival of the man playing his flute soufflé that the status of that instrument was elevated to a higher appreciation. His name was Herbie Mann.

Herbie Mann was born Herbert Jay Solomon on April 16, 1930, in Brooklyn, New York. He started playing the clarinet when he was nine and later added the flute and the tenor saxophone to his abilities. Although the clarinet and tenor saxophone were well respected in jazz circles, the flute wasn't, so Mann was determined to change this. By his late teens he was a proficient musician and gigged around the New York area.

He served in the Army for a couple of years and upon his discharge returned to his music career. He joined Mat Mathew's quintet for a couple of years and then assumed leadership of his own outfit. During his first few years as leader, Mann was known as a bop musician and joined forces with a number of jazz figures, including Phil Woods, Buddy Collette, Sam Most, Bobby Jaspar and Charlie Rouse. During the late 1950s, Mann demonstrated his versatility as a musician by recording on tenor sax, bass clarinet and his most stunning work to date—an unaccompanied flute album.

Mann was one of the few jazz artists who took advantage of opportunities to write for television, a brand new medium in the 1950s. After some success he decided to form another band. It was a strange group, an Afro-Jazz combination that included several percussionists, Johnny Rae, Hagood Hardy and Dave Pike at various times. They became known for the different flavor they delivered as well as their constant globetrotting, even into Africa and Brazil. Although they presented an alternative sound compared to other bands on the circuit, Mann's group was entertaining and provided a different side of the music. He was creating his own universe and converting many followers to his cause.

What set apart Mann from prior flutists was his penchant for experimentation. He explored a variety of sounds, including bossa nova, and proved that with dedication, practice and confidence, one could play anything with the instrument. He recorded in Brazil something few jazz artists had ever done before. He also displayed his commercial side with his early 1960s hit "Comin' Home Baby." Around this time he recorded with another experimenter, Bill Evans.

Mann's courage to incorporate the rhythms, harmonies, and melodies of various cultures only endeared him to a larger audience. He also added an element of pop to his jazz repertoire, which only enhanced his growing popularity. As a leader, Mann also had a keen eye for talent. He showcased young musicians like the pianist Chick Corea, as well as Attila Zoller and Roy Ayers, who would all be leaders of the 1970s jazz-rock fusion. In 1972, Mann played at the Newport Jazz Festival with an ensemble that boasted young musicians David Newman and Sonny Sharrock.

Always a step ahead of the competition, Mann had developed an interest in the technical side of making records and had taught himself how to produce. He worked for Embroyo, one of the subsidiaries of the giant Atlantic label, and became a respected producer with a keen ear for a unique sound. He possessed the ability to mix different styles to create something fresh and new. For much of the 1970s, Mann fused jazz with elements of rock, pop, and reggae, and even experimented with disco.

Once this enterprising figure had learned everything he could while on the staff of Atlantic records, he formed his own label, though it was not very successful. Later he recorded with Chesky Records, collaborating with Dave Valentin. The great flutist always found some worthwhile project to work on and never seemed to rest on past accomplishments.

For much of the 1980s, he continued to lead his own group, make some interesting records, and build on his unique legend. Although the decade proved to be such an unstructured musical adventure with a myriad of styles dominating the scene, the schizophrenic nature of it all only helped Mann. He greatly benefited from the eclectic tastes of the record buying public, because a bearded flutist playing cool and experimental jazz fit right in with the other diverse forms.

In the 1990s he formed the Kokopelli label that gave him the creative freedom he needed to record his visionary music. Since the genre fractured into a variety of styles, it was a true open-minded individual like Mann who was able to introduce the new sound to a broad audience. After all, he delivered his own brand of jazz to interested crowds for fifty years.

On July 1, 2003, Herbie Mann, the dynamic flutist who brought the instrument unprecedented respect in jazz circles, died in Pecos, New Mexico, of prostate cancer.

Herbie Mann was an original. He was always interested in creating his own music and never worried about classifications or trends. Although he is certainly included in the cool jazz movement of the 1950s, because of his vast experimentation it is impossible to categorize him. His adventures into the realms of rock, pop and soul enabled him to extend the parameters of jazz. In the process of following his own musical muse, he became the greatest flutist the genre has ever produced.

Mann became famous playing the flute and carved out a career with his ability to deliver simple, catchy melodies. Although his music was always different, it was never overly complicated and this is one of the most important aspects of his playing. An intelligent musician, he always understood the limitations of the instrument, but was never afraid to stretch its limitations in various settings. He demonstrated an incredible versatility with the flute by playing all kinds of styles with it.

Herbie was not the first important flute player in the history of jazz. Albert Socarras claims that honor and was first to record on an album with the instrument. He also played saxophone and clarinet, paving the way for future artists. Wayman Carver was another early flutist who arrived on the scene after Socarras. While both were competent musicians, neither made the impact Mann did.

Although he is acknowledged as the greatest flute player in jazz, Mann's one serious rival was Frank Wess. The latter was born Frank Wellington Wess on January 4, 1922, in Kansas City, Missouri. He was a multi-instrumentalist, arranger, composer and first class flutist. Although he would play in many different settings throughout his long career, it was with the Basie Band (1953–1964) that Wess made his name. He would later go on to play with Clark Terry's outfit, as well as lead his own sessions. Slightly older than Mann, Wess certainly blazed the path, but never achieved the same popularity as Mann.

Another important flute player was Buddy Collette, who managed to bring the instrument a larger share of the spotlight. He made some important recordings as a leader, including *Man of Many Parts* on the Contemporary label in the 1950s. Later, in the 1960s, Rahsaan Roland Kirk and Yusef Lateef would utilize the flute in strange and different ways, expanding its range. Yet, despite all of the talented individuals mentioned above, Herbie Mann remains the main practitioner of the flute.

In the 1950s, Mann was the epitome of cool jazz with his dark shades, bebop hat and goatee. He ushered in a new era along with other practitioners, including Dave Brubeck, Miles Davis, Gerry Mulligan, Chet Baker, Paul Desmond, Gil Evans, Jimmy Giuffre, Shelly Manne, John Lewis, Milt Jackson, Shorty Rogers, Frank Rosolino, Sonny Clark, Hampton Hawes, Stan Levy and Claude Williamson. He made the flute a cool instrument to play as well as a valuable addition to any jazz ensemble.

His structured solos inspired a generation. He had a large influence on Ian Anderson, leader of the rock group Jethro Tull, and Bobbi Humphrey. The unsinkable Tull combined rock, pop, blues, soul, folk, and jazz to carve out their own niche in the competitive music business. In all, Mann influenced anyone who ever picked up the flute in the past half-century.

He also has worked with an interesting selection of jazz figures: Zoot Sims, Wendell Marshall, Joe Newman, Ron Carter, Roy Ayers, Carlos "Patato" Valdes, Jimmy Jones, Jerome Richardson, Quincy Jones, Chris Connor and Phil Woods, to name a few. He toured with trumpeter Doc Cheatham throughout the African continent in the 1960s. He helped Chick Corea develop into one of the prime exponents of the jazz fusion style, as well as guitarist Larry Coryell and others. The cool flutist also served as a sideman for a diverse number of jazz artists, including singer Sarah Vaughan. Mann left an imprint in numerous jazz corners.

Herbie Mann was an innovator, a creative individual who was able to translate the sounds in his head into his playing, and he achieved great success. Although he might not have stuck with one particular genre his entire career, he is still the king of the cool jazz flutists. He was always keen on spreading the power, beauty and uniqueness of his flute soufflé, and because of his commitment, dedication and incredible talent, he was able to do so.

Discography

65th Birthday Celebration: Live At, Lightyear 54185.
America/Brasil, Lightyear 54233.
At the Village Gate, Rhino Records 1380.
Caminho de Casa, Chesky 40.
Concerto Grosso in D, Wounded Bird Records 1540.
Do the Bossa Nova/My Kinda Groove, Collectables 6245.
Flautista! Herbie Mann Plays Afro-Cuban Jazz, Verve 557448.
Herbie Mann Plays, Bethlehem Music Company, Inc. 76681.
Just Wailin', Original Jazz Classics 900.
London Underground, Wounded Bird Records 1648.
Memphis Underground, Rhino Records 1522.
Monday Night at the Village Gate, Wounded Bird Records 1462.
Opalescence, Kokopelli 1298.
Peace Pieces, Lightyear 54193.
Push Push, Rhino Records 532.
Returns to the Village Gate, Wounded Bird Records 1407.
Standing Ovation at Newport, Wounded Bird Records 1445.
Stone Flute, Wounded Bird Records 520.
Sultry Serenade, Original Jazz Classics 927.
The Best of Herbie Mann, Rhino Records 1544.
The Evolution of Mann, Rhino Records 71634.
The Man, Drive Archive 41086.
Yardbird Suite, Savoy 0193.
Flautista, POLYG POCJ-2778.
Mann & a Woman, ATLAN AMCY-1242.

JACKIE MCLEAN (1932–)

Jackie's Bag

Every jazz artist has borrowed ideas from those who came before them. It is one of the traditions that link the generations together through variations of styles and techniques. Every alto saxophonist to come along in the aftermath of Charlie "Yardbird" Parker's legacy was instantly compared to him; they were unable to escape his shadow. However, some players were able to emerge with their own distinct sound including, the man responsible for "Jackie's Bag." His name was Jackie McLean.

John Lenwood McLean Jr. was born on May 17, 1932, in New York City. He developed an early interest in music since his father, John McLean, Sr., was a guitar player in Tiny Bradshaw's band. Jackie started on the alto sax at fifteen and progressed quickly. He practiced with some of his neighborhood friends, including Bud Powell, Sonny Rollins, and

Thelonious Monk. All would later make enormous contributions to the bop revolution.

McLean's initial influence was Charlie Parker; they met and jammed at various locations on the bop scene, mostly along 52nd Street in New York. Although McLean had his own style, it was impossible not to incorporate some of Bird's stylings into his own. While at the beginning of his career there is no doubt he sounded like any one of the dozens of Charlie Parker imitators, he would eventually emerge from the shadow and develop his own voice.

McLean continued to keep heavy company in the recording studio. He made his debut with the cool one, Miles Davis, on the album *Dig.* While his time with Davis certainly enhanced his reputation, his playing really came into its own as a member of the Charles Mingus outfit. He took part in the classic *Pithecanthropus Erectus* as well as the *Blues & Roots* effort. On these two albums he developed his tonal strength and learned how to express himself in a freer, clearer style.

Like Parker, Mingus had a way of dictating the future a jazz musician would take. The boss of the bass was a controversial figure, but also a brilliant composer and arranger and superior musician. As a member of the Mingus ensemble, it was difficult for McLean not to pick up at least some of the traits of his bandleader.

He left Mingus and joined Art Blakey's Messengers of Jazz for a three-year stint in the mid–1950s. He was featured in the front line and his cutting edge was one of the essential dimensions of the group's overall sound. McLean and Blakey's individual styles meshed together rather nicely. All who were ever part of the Messengers of Jazz played furiously in order to ride along with the leader's powerful drumming. Because of his close association with the granddaddy of hard bop, Jackie was classified as a practitioner of that style.

In the late 1950s, he was finally given the chance to lead his own sessions and demonstrated that he had reached his full musical maturity. There was intensity, a relentless drive that displayed his ability to play economically. He had stopped trying to imitate the note-infested solos of Parker and settled into a sparser style. In many ways, McLean played the saxophone the way Mingus played the bass. There was a brute force, a total self-expressionism, but also impeccable timing and a harmonic logic.

Once he began to record under his own name for the Blue Note label, he started to receive the credit that had always eluded him. Although he had been a featured member in the outfits of both Mingus and Blakey, McLean was never the sole focus of the band. His new sound of starkness and economy was heard explicitly in a series of recordings he made, including *Swing Swang Swingin', Bluesnik, Capuchin Swing, New Soil, A Fickle Sonance, Let Freedom Ring,* and *Destination Out.*

On these albums his best is delivered by the accompaniment of great drummers, including Pete La Rocca, Art Taylor and Billy Higgins. The communication between McLean and his percussionists had a tribal characteristic. They were musically and spiritually in tune with each other and above the harsh, haunting rhythms, Jackie recorded some of his greatest solos that dripped with a killer drive and perfected tonal distortion.

Once he had established himself as a first rate sax player, other offers came his way. For example, he was asked to participate in the play *The Connection* written by Jack Geiber. He made an acceptable stage debut and also performed with the band that was part of the story. The play opened in New York and although he didn't win a Tony award for his efforts, it was a satisfying experience.

In 1963, McLean fell under the influence of Ornette Coleman and John Coltrane, who were changing the way the saxophone was to be played. This forced him to evaluate his musical direction and he began to pursue a freer route clearly evident on *Let Freedom Ring.* While the relentless drive and brilliant inventions were still present in his playing, there was also a broader range of sound from the lowest notes to the highest peaks. He had smartly expanded his musical vocabulary without losing the essential elements that had earned him respect.

His musical adventure had begun with bop, moved through to hard bop, and finally into the realm of free jazz. As a firm disciple of Coleman and Coltrane,   he jammed with a group of young musicians who explored the same territory: Grachan Moncur II, Anthony Williams, and Bobby Hutcherson. They collaborated on *Destination Out, One Step Beyond* and *Evolution,* all fine free jazz albums. Later McLean would join forces with trumpeter Charles Tolliver and the pair would record *Action, It's Time* and *Jacknife* together.

In 1967, McLean finally had the opportunity to work with one of his earlier idols, Ornette Coleman. The two combined their creative genius and produced *New and Old Gospel.* Although the union was a fruitful one, it demonstrated that McLean was less a free player than Coleman. Despite serious intentions of trying to become a total practitioner of that style, he was too deeply rooted in bebop and extensions into hard bop. But the opportunity to jam with Coleman was a positive experience for both participants.

McLean would work with the West Coast tenor sax champ Dexter Gordon and with Gary Bartz. Although in the 1970s jazz fusion was all the rage, Jackie continued to blow hard bop jazz. His association with Blue Note ended in 1967, and five years later he recorded for Steeplechase, sounding as good as ever. The albums *The Meeting, Ode to Super,* and *New York*

Calling, all on his new label, demonstrated an alto saxophonist that had returned full circle.

While he continued to perform and record on a fairly regular basis throughout the 1970s, he also devoted much of his time to teaching jazz. It wasn't until a decade later that he returned to a more full time schedule of musical activity. One of his projects was the band The Cosmic Brotherhood, in which he shared the spotlight with his young son Rene. He also recorded numerous albums for the Triloka, Antilles and Blue Note labels. Into his sixties the intensity and emotional power continued to be trademarks of his distinguished sound. He continues to record and perform.

Jackie McLean is a jazz explorer. A player who has never been satisfied with staying strictly within the confines of bop, he has moved through the various styles with considerable ease and success. With his unmistakable talent and open mind, he has carved his own special place in the modern history of the genre.

No matter the style he has delved in, there are trademarks to his individual sound, even though it has evolved and matured over the years. There has always been an unusual intensity to his playing that is definitely one of his badges of honor. There is also the probing element of his sound. McLean always played a cutting edge brand of alto saxophone that pushed and expanded the mind of the listener to debate the possible avenues his playing could venture down. There was sharpness to his sound that was not overbearing, but still strongly persistent enough to create tension and dynamics.

To truly understand McLean's vast contributions to jazz, one must compare him to contemporaries. Unlike Art Blakey, who remained a proponent of the hard bop school, Jackie experimented with free jazz. In many ways he had the ability to transcend styles and labels while other artists were unable to escape a particular branding. With the possible exception of Miles Davis, there are few practitioners from the bop talent pool that have excelled in three different forms of jazz.

The universe of Jackie McLean contains many of the most important names of the modern jazz era. His main musical heroes were Dexter Gordon, Sonny Rollins, Ornette Coleman, John Coltrane, and Charlie Parker. He has collaborated with a variety of jazz figures, including Billy Higgins, Hank Mobley, Philly Joe Jones, Michael Cuscuna, Horace Silver, Gene Ammons, Kenny Burrell, Percy Heath, J. J. Johnson, Kenny Clarke, Charles Mingus, Miles Davis, Donald Byrd, and Grachan Moncur II. In turn, he had a special influence on Anthony Braxton, Michael Carvin, Oliver Lake, David Sanborn and Bobby Watson.

Jackie's bag includes a number of jazz classics: "Pithecanthropus Erectus," "Moanin'," "Little Melonae," "Stanley's Stiff Chickens," "Bluesnik," and "Francisco," to name a few. In any situation, he has always added an excellent musical presence.

Today, he teaches and serves as the Founding Artistic Director at the Hartt School of the University of Hartford African American Music Department. It was renamed the Jackie McLean Institute of Jazz in 2000. Also together with his wife they founded the Artists Collective, Inc. some thirty-five years ago. The organization is an arts program that helps Hartford youth develop an appreciation for African culture.

Jackie McLean possesses one of the most recognizable alto saxophone sounds in jazz history. While many Parker imitators faded away, McLean was able to take the best elements of Bird's sound and make them the very cornerstones of his own style. Jackie's Bag continues to hold one spellbound with its magical qualities.

Discography

Nature Boy, Blue Note Records 23273.
4, 5 and 6, Prestige Records 7048.
A Fickle Sonance, Blue Note Records 24544.
A Long Drink of the Blues, Original Jazz Classics 253.
Bluesnik, Blue Note Records 84067.
Destination Out, Blue Note Records 32087.
Jackie McLean & Co., Original Jazz Classics 074.
Jackie's Bag, Blue Note Records 46142.
Let Freedom Ring, Blue Note Records 46527.
Makin' the Changes, Original Jazz Classics 197.
McLean's Scene, Original Jazz Classics 098.
One Step Beyond, Blue Note Records 46821.
Jacknife, Blue Note B00006J3KW.
Swing, Swang, Swingin', Blue Note Records 56582.
Tippin' the Scales, Blue Note Records 84427.
Vertigo, Blue Note Records 22669.
Best of Jackie McLean, BLUEN TOCJ-66046.
Capuchin Swing, BLUEN TOCJ-9156.
Demon's Dance, BLUEN TOCJ-9112.
Let Freedom Ring, Blue Note B0000BV20X.
New & Old Gospel, EMI TOCJ-4262.
New Soil, BLUEN TOCJ-4013.
Quintet 1962, Blue Note TOCJ-4116.

PART THREE

Free Jazz and the Avant-Garde

The fractured forms of jazz best known as avant-garde and free jazz dominated the scene during the late 1950s, and throughout the 1960s, and they continue to boast practitioners to this day. Although each style attracted its fair share of critics, each direction produced some incredible musicians and composers that altered the course of musical history. The two genres shared some similarities and substantial differences.

Avant-garde originated from the attempt to break out of the confines of hard bop and cool jazz. One of the forefathers of the movement was Lennie Tristano, whose music possessed more of the elements of avant-garde than cool jazz, although he was often mistakenly lumped into the latter category. George Russell, John Lewis, and Cecil Taylor, like Tristano, also desired to play outside the traditional parameters of the established styles of the day.

Free jazz was essentially the mission to throw off the shackles that had locked up players for decades. There was very little structure to the form and the key to the style was imagination. While improvisation had always been one of the main ingredients, in free jazz, the ability took on an entirely different dimension.

Although both styles consisted of elements that were interchangeable, there was one vast difference that set them apart. Avant-garde was experimental in nature, but also featured some structure, whereas free jazz had little or no structure. However, both styles were considered more radical than predecessors cool jazz, hard bop and bop. Fans of the big band era that seemed a distant memory were shocked when the first recordings of free jazz and avant-garde hit the market.

The two main centers for the new music were Chicago and New York. In Chicago, the Association for the Advancement of Creative Musicians was established. In New York, the Knitting Factory was its equivalent. Each group was formed to promote various types of experimental music, record their respective artists, perform concerts, and present jazz to schools.

The avant-garde artists who gave the style definition and substance included saxophonists Anthony Braxton, Eric Dolphy, Albert Ayler, Archie Shepp, Julius Hemphill, Oliver Lake, Hamlet Bluiett, David Murray, Muhal Richard Abrams, Joseph Jarman, Gerry Hemingway, pianist Paul Bley, and trumpeter Don Cherry. It also featured multi-instrumentalist Rahsaan Roland Kirk, bassists Charlie Haden, Niels-Henning Orsted Pedersen, Gary Peacock, and drummer Ronald Shannon Jackson.

The free jazz camp boasted saxophonists Ornette Coleman, John Coltrane, Pharoah Sanders, Sun Ra, Arthur Blythe, Roscoe Mitchell, Henry Threadgill, John Zorn, pianists Andrew Hill, Cecil Taylor, Don Pullen, Marylin Crispell, trumpeter Lester Bowie, violinist Leroy Jenkins, drummer Sunny Murray, guitarists Sonny Sharrock and James "Blood" Ulmer. Elvin Jones was the definitive free jazz drummer.

However, it is impossible to permanently place one artist in one specific category. For instance, Ornette Coleman and John Coltrane were the leaders of the free jazz movement, but are easily classified as avant-garde players. Cecil Taylor always had one foot in each style. The most important theme that underlies every artist in this section is that they attempted to break away from the current trends to establish something new and fresh.

Sun Ra was from another world and his experimental sound blazed the path that many would follow. Although he was on the fringe of the free jazz movement, his brave adventures encouraged others.

Yusef Lateef deserves a category all of his own. The multi-instrumentalist brought shades to jazz never heard before or since. An experimenter with wood instruments, he was a main cog in the Detroit jazz scene of the 1950s and 1960s.

John Coltrane is the greatest saxophone player in jazz since Charlie Parker. He was a free jazz player but in the latter part of his career experimented with avant-garde.

Elvin Jones was the prime drummer of the free jazz style. His partnership with Coltrane in the early 1960s established him as a giant of the school. Although Jo Jones, Art Blakey and Max Roach had a special influence on him, he carved out his own musical universe.

Eric Dolphy is one of the giants of post-bebop alto saxophone. From his earliest days his driving style proved that he was something special. His premature death was a severe blow to the avant-garde movement.

Cecil Taylor was the premier avant-garde/free jazz piano player. He thumped the keys with a ferocity and emotion that created a serious debate over whether his music was a new, exciting direction or mere cacophony. The debate still rages on to this day.

Ornette Coleman is credited with being the originator of the free jazz movement, though it was only years later, when the style had gained its proper respect, that he finally received the credit that he was due.

Rahsaan Roland Kirk is the stuff of legends. His abilities as a multi-instrumentalist, his inventiveness, and his showmanship enabled him to write a unique page in jazz history.

Archie Shepp, another talented saxophonist, is a noted sideman and leader of avant-garde jazz groups. His early association with Cecil Taylor and Don Cherry was crucial to the movement.

Charlie Haden was the definitive avant-garde bass player and his association with Ornette Coleman and Don Cherry enabled him to build a grand reputation.

Anthony Braxton is an avant-garde giant and arguably its main spokesman. A richly talented individual and an intellectual, his genius is overwhelming. The author of a complex musical output, his contributions as a player, arranger, and composer can never be denied.

SUN RA (1914–1993)

Cosmic Tones

The avant-garde/free jazz movement was one of great experimental and the exploration of specifically chosen paths. Its cast includes some of the most brilliant jazz minds as well as some of the strangest. The creators of the new style were keenly interested in pushing the music beyond conventional borders, taking it in dark and disturbing directions. One of the leaders of the free jazz explorations was the man who gave the world his cosmic tones. His name was Sun Ra.

Sun Ra was born Herman Sonny Blount on May 22, 1914, in Birmingham, Alabama. While Alabama was his official birthplace, Ra often claimed that he was from another planet. However, his early days seemed normal enough. He grew up listening to Duke Ellington, Albert Nichols, and Fletcher Henderson, an experience he shared with countless other jazz figures of his generation. Later he would count on Tadd Dameron and Gerry Mulligan as special inspirations. But somewhere the catacombs of his imagination were opened and the energy that flowed forth was never turned off during his interesting career.

Ra was a piano player who began the study of the instrument at an early age. By the time he was in his twenties he was leading his own band and already some of his uniqueness was showing through. But in the depth of the economic depression there was no room for his flair of experimental music. The jazz world was firmly rooted in the classical style and the big band era loomed like a giant balloon just over the horizon.

Ra, who at this time was still using his birth name, Sonny Blount, earned a living as a freelancer in the Midwest in 1934. He worked with one of his early heroes, Fletcher Henderson, as a pianist and arranger and gained valuable lessons in leading and composing during his tour of duty with the great jazz pioneer. Ra, who had a much different musical outlook, was only biding his time.

He continued to work with various big bands, accumulating the raw material of these experiences that he would later mold into his own vision. It wasn't until 1948 that he began to experiment with his obscure brand of jazz. He made some interesting records that year, but returned to the laboratory to create what would be some of the most bizarre and intimidating music ever produced.

By 1953, all the pieces were in place. He was no longer using his birth name but Sun Ra, an appropriate title for the kind of spaced out music he was set to unleash on the world. He named his band Arkestra and gigged around the Chicago area. Although he started off playing an advanced version of bop, Ra never limited himself to any confining musical idea. His creations were the stuff of improvisation and a vast imagination that borrowed from the ancient civilization of Egypt, as well as the future of Buck Rogers. Considering that this was the early 1950s, when space exploration was still a few years off and science fiction was in its infancy, Ra's music was considered radical.

He played electric keyboards long before the jazz fusion era and led his unique band from his astro space organ. Often dressed in a cape and a sorcerer costume, Ra directed like a concert maestro. His earliest albums, *Sun Song* and *Sound of Joy*, were harbingers of future directions. Despite his unique take on jazz, he had no problems recruiting members. Pat Patrick, a baritonist, and John Gilmore, a tenor saxophonist, remained with Ra for two decades. He allowed his players an incredible amount of freedom in the creative process—an alluring proposal for any jazz artist.

Ra moved his entire production to New York in 1961 and continued to record some of the strangest yet most advanced sounds in jazz. He had preceded the new thing by years and at this point his creations didn't seem like such fringe music anymore. He greatly profited from the avant-garde/free jazz movement of the 1960s simply because he had been playing that music for the past decade.

In 1970, he moved to Philadelphia. One of the underlying themes to Ra's music, vision, and creation was that he always sought a fresh environment. Because of this his music never grew stale, but remained buoyant.

Throughout the decade he continued to experiment, adding elements of mystical group chants to his swinging, freestyle base. Undoubtedly, by this time he was considered the strangest character on the jazz scene; in a style that preached individuality, this was quite the claim.

During the fragmented 1980s when myriad musical ideas invaded the radio and concert halls, Ra was still a leader in experimental music. In a strange yet brilliant way he was still ahead of his time. The new wave rock thing was the philosophy that Ra had been preaching all along, proving that the style was not so original as it claimed to be, but based on prior elements including Sun's own recordings. With a renewed interest in neo-traditional music in the 1980s, Ra's science fiction space-outs seemed out of flavor. However, there were always elements of swing in his music that aligned him with the new players who pursued the tradition of classical unplugged jazz.

On May 30, 1993, Sun Ra, the great experimenter who had pointed many towards the new directions that jazz would pursue for three decades, died. He was 79 years old.

Sun Ra was one of the most colorful fringe figures in jazz history. Once he arrived on the scene with his planetary music and band, the traditionalists as well as the modernists did not know what to make of him. He was completely different from anything anyone had ever seen, heard, or experienced. Despite his totally unique vision, Ra made many contributions to the genre.

He was always a step ahead of the rest of the jazz world and ushered in new movements years before they took hold. Once the avant-garde and free jazz movement had been assessed in the 1960s, it was clearly evident that Ra had been a major influence on all the practitioners. Throughout his career he demonstrated an ability to anticipate the next musical trend.

He was one of the first keyboard players to go electric and in the process he influenced a number of fusion figures, including Herbie Hancock, Chick Corea, Keith Jarrett, Joe Zawinul, and others. His astro space organ and use of the moog synthesizer were years ahead of their time. Although not an exceptional keyboard player, he could hold his own in any contest because of his ability to improvise as well as his unique musical vision.

Although he might have seemed otherworldly, Ra's music was clearly accessible. There was a sense of rhythm and harmony that was removed from the mainstream but still appealing. He was constantly evolving in technique and approach. He was never afraid to alter the lineup of his outfit. Throughout his long career, the name of his musical ensembles underwent numerous changes. It went from the original Arkestra to Solar Arkestra, to Sun Ra Arkestra, to Sun Ra Omniverse Arkestra, to Sun Ra

& His Cosmo Discipline Arkestra, to Sun Ra & the Astro Infinity Arkestra, and finally to Sun Ra & the Year 2000 Myth Science Arkestra. No matter the name, his group rarely failed to deliver something bizarre, fresh and exciting.

Although somewhat an object of ridicule, he had a large influence on a number of jazz figures, including Joseph Celli, Brian Ritchie, Courtney Pine, Lonnie Liston Smith, Clifford Thornton, Matthew Shipp, Annie Gosfield, Marvin "Hannibal" Peterson, DJ Spooky, and Olivia Tremor. But his spacey music with its science fiction elements also made a large impact on Pink Floyd and the entire progressive rock movement. Also of note, John Gilmore, a long time member of Ra's various aggregations, had a strong influence on John Coltrane.

Another musician that Ra's music and vision affected was David Bowie, the avant-garde chameleon rock star. The Thin White Duke began as a folkie with strange lyrics and constantly experimented, using rock as a starting point. He moved from blues to soul to new wave without losing his fan base. Like Ra, Bowie was very much into the spacey side of music. His lyrics, his costumes, his vision always seemed otherworldly. Bowie had a strong influence on much of the rock music that emerged in the past twenty-five years.

Ra was more than just a musician; he was an innovator who understood the importance of both the sound of music and the visual aspect of a live performance. Members of his groups were often outfitted in their space robes and light-up hats. There was back-projected film, dancers and, in later years, fire-eaters. The circus-like atmosphere of his later shows prompted detractors to claim all fanfare denigrated the music. But years later when many rock acts incorporated a strong visual presence into their live shows, they seemed to take a page from Ra's handbook.

Ra was a shrewd businessman and set up his own label, Saturn, well aware that no one would record his bizarre take on jazz. But on his own label he could follow his particular vision and that is exactly what he did. He understood the need for a complete package and that he was in the entertainment business. He delighted audiences with his multi-layered compositional themes, as well as the brilliant improvisational abilities of himself, Gilmore, Patrick, and alto saxophonist Marshall Allen. He catered to all senses.

Sun Ra was never taken seriously by jazz purists despite his many contributions to jazz. He was too different, too original for the taste of many traditional fans and critics. But looking back on a career that spanned almost forty years, there is no denying that the man who gave us his cosmic tones wrote a very unique chapter in jazz history—one that will certainly never be duplicated.

Discography

Concert for the Comet Kohoutek, Get Back Records 1011.
Cosmic Tones for Mental Therapy/Art Forms of Sun Ra, Evidence 22036.
Heliocentric Worlds Vol. 1, Calibre 1014.
Heliocentric Worlds Vol. 2, Get Back Records 1005.
Janus, 1201 Music 9012.
Mayan Temples, Black Saint 120121.
Monorails & Satellites, Evidence 22013.
My Brother the Wind Vol. 2, Evidence 22040.
Nothing Is, Get Back Records 1007.
Other Planes of There, Evidence 22037.
Solo Piano Vol. 1, I.A.I. (Improvising Artists) 123850.
Somewhere Else, Rounder Records 613 036.
Sound of Joy, Delmark 414.
Space is the Place, Impulse! 249.
St. Louis Blues Solo Piano, I.A.I. (Improvising Artists) 123858.
Standards, 1201 Music 9019.
Strange Celestial Road, Rounder Records 613 035.
Sun Song, Delmark 411.
The Futuristic Sounds of Sun Ra, Savoy 0213.
The Great Lost Sun Ra Albums, Evidence 22217.
The Singles, Evidence 22164.
Visits Planet Earth/Interstellar Low Ways, Evidence 22039.
We Travel the Spaceways/Bad & Beautiful, Evidence 22038.
Hours After, Black Saint 120 111.
Jazz in Silhouette, Evidence 22012.
Live at Pit-Inn, Tokyo, Japan, DIW 824.
Live at Praxis '84, Golden Years of New Jazz 5.
Live from Soundscape, DIW 388.
Love in Outer Space, Leo Records 54.
Reflections in Blue, Black Saint 0101.
Sound Sun Pleasure!, Evidence 22014.
Super-Sonic Jazz, Evidence 22015.
A Quiet Place in the Universe, Leo Records 198.
Cosmo Sun Connection, ReR Recommended #SR1.
Friendly Galaxy, Leo Records 188.
Greatest Hits: Easy Listening, Evidence 22219.
Lanquidity, Evidence 22220.
Live in London 1990, Blast First 60.
Meets Salah Ragab in Egypt, Golden Years Of New Jazz 1.
Out There a Minute, Blast First 42.
Second Star to the Right (Salute to Walt Disney), Leo Records 230.
Stardust from Tomorrow, Leo Records 235.
Atlantis, Evidence 22067.
Holiday for Soul Dance, Evidence 22011.
Pathways to Unknown Worlds/Friendly Love, Evidence 22218.
Angels and Demons at Play/The Nubians of Plutonia, Evidence 22066.
Fate in a Pleasant Mood/When Sun Comes Out, Evidence 22068.
When Angels Speak of Love, Evidence 22216.
Outer Space Employment Agency, Total Energy 3021.
Space is the Place, Evidence 22070.

YUSEF LATEEF (1926–)

An Eastern Taste

Perhaps one of the most striking features of free jazz and the avant-garde schools was their broad musical philosophies. In an effort to push beyond the normal boundaries established by bop, hard bop and cool jazz, all practitioners searched for something different to attach to their new vision of jazz. One individual who was never afraid to experiment with his approach was Yusef Lateef, the man with the Eastern taste.

Yusef Lateef was born William Evans on October 9, 1920, in Chattanooga, Tennessee. A late bloomer, he didn't pick up the tenor saxophone until he was seventeen, but made up for his delayed start quickly. Evans had moved to Detroit when a young boy and upon his introduction to music began to investigate the thriving city nightclub scene. Although the Motor City could not boast the same kind of activity as New York City or even Chicago, it was a solid breeding ground for jazz musicians in the post-war era.

His first break came when he played with Lucky Millinder's band just after the war. Lateef, a keen student of all types of music, was well aware of the bop revolution and became a quick convert to the cause. It was Lateef that spearheaded the bop explosion on the Detroit jazz scene. He had many disciples, including pianists Tommy Flanagan, Barry Harris, and Hank Jones, drummers Louis Hayes and Elvin Jones, trumpeters Thad Jones and Donald Byrd, guitarist Kenny Burrell and baritone saxman Pepper Adams.

After leaving Millinder's band, he worked with Hot Lips Page, Roy Eldridge and Dizzy Gillespie. In the 1950s, he returned to Detroit and once again immersed himself in the local scene while studying music at the local university. He was also expanding his musical capabilities by learning how to play alto, soprano, and baritone saxophone, as well as the oboe and other woodwinds. His multi-instrumentalist abilities would place him in a selective group among jazz artists.

Although he had done some recording, he assumed leadership of his own sessions for the first time in 1955 for the Savoy label. The entire Detroit group of hard bop practitioners—Byrd, Harris, the Jones Brothers, Burrell, and Eddie Farrow—all played on these sessions. It was also during this period that Lateef established his reputation for experimentation of fusing jazz with Eastern and African rhythms. Although he wasn't the first to do this, he did it with a unique touch.

Undoubtedly he was the kingpin of the Detroit jazz scene and one of the most respected musicians on the circuit. He could have enjoyed a fine career in the Motor City, but decided he needed a change of environment, so he relocated to New York in 1959. In the Big Apple he found work with Charles Mingus and fellow Detroiter Donald Byrd. Perhaps his most important association at the time was with the Cannonball Adderley Sextet. Lateef remained with the alto saxophonist's outfit from 1962 to 1964.

Because of his immense talent, Lateef was once again able to lead his own sessions for the Impulse label, which greatly enhanced his already burgeoning reputation. He was years ahead of his time because he could successfully weld different parts of world music into one solid, cohesive sound. He was predating universalism by at least a decade.

With each successive album release he was increasing his power in jazz circles. But it was his Atlantic sessions that in many ways sealed the deal on Lateef's total appeal. He fused the most intricate Middle Eastern and African rhythms with good old-fashioned American swing and bop strains to crystallize the definitive framework of universalism that many jazz practitioners were beginning to explore.

Perhaps he was able to create such a truly appealing breed of music because he himself was a worldly individual. He saw the would not in terms of divided countries and borders, but as one endless linked chain of spiritualism and harmony. Lateef had always been intent on proving that the planet was really one giant neighborhood and that everybody was a neighbor. He continued to roam the earth in the 1980s and added a teaching stint in Nigeria to his list of lengthy cultural experiences.

Of course, while in Nigeria, Lateef, always a musician, didn't miss the opportunity to teach enthusiastic Nigerians the beautiful art of jazz. He was able to encourage the use of African rhythms, since he possessed an incredibly deep vocabulary of them, with Western melodic influences. No matter where he went in the world he was determined to teach all that music was an international language that transcended any limitations humans tried to impose on it.

Lateef, never satisfied with repeating himself, branched out into what would later be dubbed new age music in his recordings during the 1980s. Mood or new age music was an extension of what he had accomplished with universalism. Although the jazz content in these releases was questionable, it is interesting to note that he was once again ahead of the times and trying to spearhead a new movement.

He returned in the 1990s with more jazz flavored albums and regained the audience he had lost while experimenting with the new age ideas of the previous decade. Many of the CDs were on the YAL label, Lateef's own company. His music now contained the spontaneity that it boasted back in the 1960s and 1970s. His noted sidemen included Ricky Ford, Archie Shepp and Von Freeman.

Yusef Lateef is one of jazz's greatest experimenters. He was never afraid to expand and break through the boundaries of contemporary jazz. No matter how radical the new trend proved to be, Lateef was always three steps ahead, pushing the music into different avenues that shook up the jazz world. In some circles, he isn't even rated as a true jazz artist since his music incorporated so many different musical ideas outside the genre.

Lateef is one of the most incredible multi-instrumentalists in the history of the genre. He mastered instruments such as the tenor saxophone (common in jazz), the flute (a rarity in the genre) the oboe (an even more rarely used instrument) and the uncommon bassoon. He also expanded the parameters with a variety of strange noisemakers. He coaxed a new sound out of the argol (a double clarinet that resembles a bassoon), a shanai (akin to the oboe) and numerous varieties of Middle Eastern flutes. It was his ability to play each of them with a superior touch and to integrate the various sounds they could produce into one cohesive package that truly established his place in jazz history.

His understanding of foreign rhythmic, melodic and harmonic textures is second to none. Although other jazz artists had experimented with Latin flavors and African rhythms, Lateef also borrowed heavily from the Middle East sound bag and tied all of the various ends together to create something new and bold. In interviews, he often stated that he wasn't a jazz player but a world music practitioner. Upon listening to his work and examining the procedure he undertook to record his extensive catalog, it is difficult to disagree with the man.

Lateef was the prime architect of universalism. The style borrows elements from numerous musical strains to create something fresh. He understood the possibilities of this union better than anyone before or since. There was something in his inquisitive nature, multi-abilities, and vision that allowed him to pursue this path of world music. The underlying task was never a simple one but he made it look relatively easy.

Since he has such a reputation as a trailblazer, his influence is both deep and long. The immediate jazz list includes Bennie Maupin, Azar Lawrence, John Almond, Albert "Tootie" Heath, John Coltrane Quartet and Greg Burk, Don Cherry, Rahsaan Roland Kirk, Sun Ra, Sam Rivers, Dewey Redman, Roscoe Mitchell, Charlie Mariano, Joseph Jarman, George Coleman, and Anthony Braxton.

However, as the father of universalism and world fusion, his sphere of influence extended well beyond the world of jazz. Those who owe a debt to Lateef include Rabih Abou-Khalil, Vishwa Mohan Bhatt, David Amram, Manu Dibango, Sandy Bull, Hamza el Din, Trilok Gurtu, Kip Hanrahan, Lou Harrison, Fred Ho, Paul Horn, Antonio Carlos Jobim, Zusaan, Kali Fasteau, Zakir Hussain, Harry Partch, Lakshminarayana

Shankar, Hossam Ramzy, Shakti, Collin Walcott and Paul Winter. Actually, anyone who has attempted to fuse different elements of world music together is a follower of Lateef. His reach spills into every style of music.

The fact that he excelled on so many different instruments also makes him unique in the annals of jazz. Perhaps the only modern exponent of the genre that can make the same claims of a strange multi-instrumentalist command as Lateef is Rahsaan Roland Kirk. Both were excellent flute players as well as masters at introducing into jazz contexts instruments never heard there before. They were never afraid to experiment with different styles to create their personal vision of world music.

Yusef Lateef remains one of the most important modern figures in jazz. He broke down many barriers while delivering music that was not always popular with the masses. He was intent on creating his own sounds to satisfy his own tastes and this path of individualism made the man with the Eastern tastes a legend.

Discography

Detroit, Collectables B00006GFBA.
Golden Flute, Impulse Records B00014AURS.
The Diverse Yusef Lateef Suite 16, Rhino Records B000003363.
Live at Pep's, Grp Records 134.
Live at Pep's 2, Polygram Records B0000296VK.
Souls Song/Diverse Yusef Lateef, Collectables Records 6620.
Blue Yusef Lateef, Label M. B000058TH2.
Hush n Thunder, Collectables B00006GFB7.
Complete, Collectables B00006GFB9.
Meditations, Collectables B00005NG45.
Last Savoy Sessions, Savoy Jazz B00004R8S3.
Gentle Giant, Atlantic 1602.
Prayer for the East, Savoy Jazz 210.
Sounds of Yusef, Orig. Jazz Classics 917.
Jazz Moods, Savoy Jazz 237.
Part of the Search, Collectables B00006GF9E.
In the Garden, Meta (City Hall) B0000WN0Q4.
Autophisiopsychic, Sony B000160YZE.
Nocturnes, Atlantic B000002IO9.
Before Dawn, Polygram Records 557097.
Plays Piano Sonata No. 2 By Yusef Lateef, YAL YAL984.
Other Sounds, Orig. Jazz Classics 399.
Cry/Tender, Orig. Jazz Classics 482.
Yusef Lateef's Little Symphony, Atlantic B000002IL6.
Concerto for Yusef Lateef, Collectables B00005NG43.
Concert for Yusef Lateef, Atlantic B00004VOYP.
The Three Faces of Yusef Lateef, Orig. Jazz Classics 759.
The Centaur and the Phoenix, Original Jazz Classics 721.
Eastern Sounds, Original Jazz Classics 612.

Into Something, Orig. Jazz Classics 700.
Beyond the Sky, Meta (City Hall) B000053F09.
Encounters, Collectables B00005NG40.
World At Peace—Music for Twelve Musicians, Meta (City Hall), 753.
Contemplation, Collectables B000066JEP.
African American Epic Suite, Act Music 9214.
Doctor is In and Out, Collectables B00006GF9F.
Every Village Has a Song, The Yusef Lateef Anthology, Rhino Records 71551.
Lost in Sound, Collectables 5792.
First Flight: Yusef Lateef with Donald Byrd, Delmark 407.
The Man with the Big Front Yard, Jazz Records 32059.
Live in London, Harkit B00007GXUS.
1984, Impulse B00000JA5S.

JOHN COLTRANE (1926–1967)

Giant Steps

After the death of Charlie Parker, the modern school of jazz needed a new leader to continue propelling the changes in the music that had been taking place over the past decade. It required a saxophone player with the imagination, excitement, technique and sheer fuel of Yardbird. While there were many pretenders and contenders for the throne, one individual emerged and was able to take the giant steps necessary to move the music ahead: his name was John Coltrane.

John William Coltrane was born on September 23, 1926, in Hamlet, North Carolina. He began to study music at an early age and by his teens had made the alto saxophone his instrument of choice. Like so many other sax players of his generation, his hero was the Prez, Lester Young. Coltrane learned Young's solos note for note and aspired to one day be as famous as his idol. He gigged with bands around his hometown, but before he could launch his career proper he found himself serving in the Navy, courtesy of the draft.

Coltrane further honed his skills as part of a Navy band and was anxious to become a professional musician. Upon his release, he took a step toward attaining that goal in 1946 when he recorded four privately released songs; however, none of them made the impact he had hoped. He resettled in Philadelphia and began the first true phase of his stellar career.

He toured with King Kolax for a year, playing alto saxophone. Like every other musician Coltrane was paying his dues, an arduous task but a very necessary process. When he joined Eddie "Cleanhead" Vinson's band in 1947, Coltrane switched to tenor. A year later he left to join Dizzy Gillespie's big band. On the radio broadcasts with the outfit, a slight hint at the magic he would create later on in his career was evident.

He left Gillespie and moved on to Gay Crosse's group for a brief spell, then joined Earl Bostic's Orchestra. He also played with Johnny Hodges, the Duke's main saxman, for a year, before returning to Philadelphia to work with the organ king of the laid back cool sound, Jimmy Smith. Although he didn't achieve wide acclaim during his early days, they were a very important part of his maturation as a musician.

In 1955, Coltrane began the second phase of his career when he joined the Miles Davis Quintet. At this point, he was a twenty-eight year old tenor saxophonist who had not made a truly strong impression with any of the numerous bands he had played in. But Davis had a way of unearthing hidden talents of the musicians in his group and he began to polish Coltrane's rough edges. The year and a half that he spent with the trumpeter greatly enhanced his development, but his personal problems were mounting. He had acquired a heroin addiction and was fired by the bandleader because of his sickness.

He kicked his habit and joined Thelonious Monk's group in order to revive his fledgling musical spirit. This was an important turning point in Coltrane's life because he realized that his addiction would ruin his ambitions and eventually kill him. Davis, who had also suffered and survived a heroin addiction, knew full well the far-reaching, disastrous effects it had on a musician's abilities.

This third phase of his career is commonly called "sheets of sound," because he produced an incredible and adventurous wall of music, boldly exploring previously uncharted territory. The mutual respect between Monk and Coltrane helped both musicians achieve a greater degree of fame. It was also a musical friendship that armed Coltrane with a new confidence and it was during this period that he led his first recording session. The result was *Blue Train*, a great record that catapulted him into the position as the number one tenor saxophonist in the world.

In 1958, Coltrane rejoined Davis. It was a different Coltrane who played in Davis' band this time because he had made giant steps as a musician and was playing the best tenor saxophone of his life. He ripped the music apart with speedy solos of imaginative chordal improvisations and single note runs that left everyone stunned. He played on the *Milestones* and *Kind of Blue* albums, which only added to his star status, and he was quickly turning into a superstar.

Upon signing a contract with Atlantic, Coltrane began to put together the kind of works that Davis and a few others had known he was capable of while he was still a struggling musician. The excellent "Giant Steps" and "Naima" proved that he was ready to lead his own band. In 1960, he took the initiative and began the fourth phase of his career, the classic quartet period.

By this time he had begun to change his style, going from playing many chords to stretching out emotionally over one- and two-chord riffs. He was moving into free jazz territory. He recruited pianist McCoy Tyner and drummer Elvin Jones to his new quartet. After a long search for a bass player that saw several auditions for the coveted seat, he settled on Jimmy Garrison. One of the keys to the success of the new group was the carte blanche Coltrane was given by the executives of Impulse to record anything he wanted. An enterprising musician, he had recently added the soprano saxophone to his musical arsenal and made full use of it on his first album for his new label. The fresh approach he brought to the soprano inspired others to pick it up and explore its possibilities.

During his quartet period Coltrane's sound continued to evolve. He added avant-garde artist Eric Dolphy to his quartet and the two dueling saxophone players cut some very interesting music. He moonlighted from the group to record with Duke Ellington and singer Johnny Hartman. His role as session man demonstrated a different side to his vast talents. It was hard to imagine that the talented young saxophonist genius was the same player who not long ago couldn't buy his way into someone's session, much less successfully lead his own.

While his studio work was gaining attention, it was his live performances that were rocking the jazz world. Coltrane would solo for ten minutes or an hour until he felt that he was finished. Each solo was a spiritual search for something greater than he had ever experienced before and he took the audiences on these special adventures. Also, his solos often rode above, below, and all around the same two-chord pattern that provided the foundation of most of the songs he was turning into classics, including "Impressions" and "Afro Blue," among others.

In 1965, Coltrane changed directions again. His constantly evolving interest was caught up in the sound of new thing players Ornette Coleman, Albert Ayler, Archie Shepp, and Pharoah Sanders. He eliminated the melodies from his playing in pursuit of emotional explorations in sounds. In order to play this new music he expanded his quartet to include Archie Shepp, Pharoah Sanders, John Tchicai, Marion Brown, Freddie Hubbard, Dewey Johnson and Art Davis. It was this group that recorded the album *Ascension*. There were personnel changes, including the departure of Elvin Jones, who was replaced by Rashied Ali, a musician better suited to play the type of music Coltrane desired to create.

The fifth and final phase of Coltrane's career, his avant-garde period, began in 1965. Although many critics and fans would question Coltrane's new direction, he did enjoy some success. The album *Meditations* was a classic, but some of his releases during this time were grounded in confusion. By 1966, he was down to a quintet that featured his wife Alice, Sanders, Ali, himself, and Jimmy Garrison. Coltrane played some of his best jazz of his career until his experimentation with the avant-garde was abruptly terminated.

On July 17, 1967, in New York City, John Coltrane, one of the greatest tenor saxophone players in the history of jazz, died of liver cancer. He was only forty years old.

John Coltrane was on a spiritual quest his entire career. Throughout his five major phases he was always searching for the answers to the many questions he pondered so seriously. In the process, he created a body of music that includes some of the most exciting and vital work of the last forty years. He had much to contribute to the world of jazz and in many ways the genre needed him more than he needed it.

The Coltrane sound is unmistakable. His free, soaring solos were pieces of beauty as he managed to go outside a song without losing control. He added an odd array of noises like squawks, honks, bleats and the sweeping sound of his breath to his basic foundation. His use of modal compositions a preoccupation with exploring all the possibilities in a single key instead of several keys, was also an integral part of his style. Coltrane, along with Davis (on the trumpet), pioneered this concept.

Although he was part of different big bands, Coltrane made his best music in his famous quartet. The scaling down of groups from large ensembles to only a few players changed the very face of jazz. This allowed Coltrane the creative freedom he needed to realize his loftiest ambitions, and in the process made him famous. A pure soloist like Coltrane needed the creative space to achieve his spiritual quest.

Like every other jazz figure in history, Coltrane drew inspiration from diverse sources. His use of African rhythms foreshadowed the 1960s movement of black pride and the emotional struggles of a people. He always seemed to be ahead of his time and certainly his portrayal of the plight of the African American certified his authoritative role in jazz.

Another of his influences was Sidney Bechet, whose use of the soprano saxophone thirty years before had remained dormant. Coltrane, an intelligent individual, closely studied Bechet's technique and ability before he took up the instrument. His revival of the soprano sax as a vital voice in jazz influenced Wayne Shorter, among others.

Although he was known for his impossibly long solos, his understanding of rhythms and their various combinations was also impressive. He teamed up with strong drummers like Elvin Jones to unlock the mysteries of rhythm and in the process created new patterns and subtexts. While

Coltrane was soloing for countless minutes, he was also creating an exciting tension within his group by juxtaposing his uncanny sense of rhythm against those of his bandmates.

Coltrane was one of the greatest improvisers in the history of jazz. His ability to create new songs on the spur of a moment was truly remarkable. He freed jazz from prior constraints with his ability to follow different harmonic, rhythmic and melodic paths. Many of his songs were entirely improvised, a fact that only enhances his credited genius.

He gave the world a number of treasures that have been performed by the entire spectrum of jazz players. A few of his gems include "Round Midnight," "God Bait," "Lush Life," "Training In," "Naima," "Mr. P.C.," "Harmonique," "My Favorite Things," "Chasin' the Trane," "A Love Supreme," "Blues Minor," "Transition," "Out of This World," "Offering," "I Want to Talk About You," "Spiritual," "Amen," "A Theme for Ernie," "Monk's Mood," and "Nutty."

Because of the many innovations he brought to the world of jazz, it is notwithstanding that he would be a major influence on many that came after he had passed through. A partial list includes George Coleman, Booker Ervin, Terumasa Hino, John Klemmer, Hubert Laws, Charlie Mariano, Edward Vesala, Kazumi Watanabe, Norma Winstone, Vincent York, Eddie Henderson, Lenny White, Roland Alphonso, James Carter, Alice Coltrane, Joe Farrell, Don "Sugarcane" Harris, Howard Shore, and T. K. Blue.

His legacy lives. In the Church of John Coltrane in San Francisco, they use the spiritual power of his songs as the basis for their sermons. His music also lives on in New York in Greenwich Village, where he performed hundreds of concerts. His spirit is alive in that quarter and he is talked about as if he were still jamming at the various clubs. Any jazz enthusiast who picks up a saxophone is immediately intimated and in awe of his musical contributions.

John Coltrane was an innovator who revolutionized the genre. He is, along with Charlie Parker, considered a messiah of the modern jazz movement. Whether he ever achieved the end of his spiritual quest remains one of the great unanswered questions in jazz. No matter the end result, he certainly made giant steps towards taking the music into the twenty-first century.

Discography

Ballads, Mobile Fidelity Sound Lab 731.
Ballads, Impulse! 156.
Coast to Coast, Moon Records 035.

Coltrane, Impulse! 215.
Crescent, Impulse! 200.
The Classic Quartet: Complete Impulse! Studio, Impulse! 8280.
The Complete Africa/Brass Sessions, Impulse! 2168.
The John Coltrane Quartet Plays, Impulse! 214.
Giant Steps, Atlantic 1311.
Coltrane Jazz, ATL 1354.
The Ultimate Blue Train, Blue Note 53428.
A Love Supreme, Impulse! 155.
Interstellar Space, Impulse! 543 415.
My Favorite Things, Atlantic 1361.
The Very Best of John Coltrane, Atlantic 79778.
A John Coltrane Retrospective, Impulse! 119.
Afro Blue Impressions, Pablo Records 101.
Ascension, Impulse! 543 413.
Best of John Coltrane, Pablo Records 2405 417.
Black Pearls, Original Jazz Classics 352.
Blue Train, Blue Note Records 46095.
Blue Trane: John Coltrane Plays the Blues, Prestige Records 11005.
Bye Bye Blackbird, Original Jazz Classics 681.
Coltrane, Original Jazz Classics 020.
Coltrane for Lovers, Impulse! 549 361.
Coltrane Jazz, Rhino Records 1354.
Coltrane Jazz: Deluxe Edition, Rhino Records 79891.
Coltrane Plays the Blues, Atlantic 1382.
Coltrane Time, Blue Note Records 84461.
Coltrane's Sound, Atlantic 1419.
Dakar, Original Jazz Classics 393.
Dear Old Stockholm, Impulse! 120.
Expression, Impulse! 131.
First Meditations, GRP Records 118.
Immortal Concerts, Giants of Jazz Recordings 53068.
Impressions, Charly 1009.
In a Soulful Mood, Impulse 1699.
Jazz Showcase, Original Jazz Classics 6015.
John Coltrane and the Jazz Giants, Fantasy Records 60014.
Kulu Se Mama, Impulse! 543 412.
Like Sonny, Blue Note Records 93901.
Live at Birdland, Impulse! 198.
Live at Birdland—1962, Le Jazz 58.
Live at the Half Note, Laserlight 17193.
Live at the Village Vanguard Again, Impulse! 213.
Live at the Village Vanguard: The Master Tapes, Impulse! 251.
Live in Antibes, 1965, Esoldun 2119.
Live in Japan, Impulse! 4102.
Live in Paris, Le Jazz 31.
Live in Seattle, Impulse! 2146.
Live in Stockholm, 1961, Le Jazz 57.
Live in Stockholm, 1963, Charly 33.
Live!, RKO/Unique Records 1031
Living Space, Impulse! 246
Lush Life, Original Jazz Classics 131.

Meditations, Impulse! 199.
More John Coltrane, GRP Records 9915.
Newport '63, Impulse! 128.
Ole Coltrane, Atlantic 1373.
Plays It Cool, Metro 15.
Settin' the Pace, Original Jazz Classics 078.
Soultrane, Prestige Records 7142.
Spiritual, Drive 3513.
Standard Coltrane, Original Jazz Classics 246.
Stardust, Original Jazz Classics 920.
Stellar Regions, Impulse! 169.
Sun Ship, Impulse! 167.
The Art of John Coltrane, Blue Note Records 99175.
The Believer, Original Jazz Classics 876.
The Best of John Coltrane, Rhino Records 1541.
The Bethlehem Years, Avenue Jazz 75987.
The Complete 1961 Village Vanguard, Impulse! 4232.
The Complete Graz Concert, Charly 8262.
The European Tour, Pablo Records 2308 222.
The Gentle Side of John Coltrane, Impulse! 107.
The Heavyweight Champion, Rhino Records 71984.
The Last Giant: The John Coltrane. Rhino Records 71255.
The Last Trane, Original Jazz Classics 394.
The Major Works of John Coltrane, Impulse! 2113.
The Paris Concert, Original Jazz Classics 781.
The Prestige Recordings, Prestige Records 4405.
Trane's Blues, Blue Note Records 98240.
Bahia, Original Jazz Classics 415.
Ballad Trane, IMPUL MVCJ-19171.
Impressions in Blue, MASTE 502992.
Spiritual Trane, IMPUL MVCJ-19173.
Standard Trane, IMPUL MVCJ-19172.
Training In, PREST VICJ-60423.

ELVIN JONES (1927–2004)
Heavy Sounds

The constant evolution of jazz has required experimenters, innovators, and leaders who were not afraid of breaking away from traditional sounds in order to forge a new direction. Some of these creators earned major acclaim while others never received the credit they were due. During the free jazz movement, one drummer was at the forefront of the birth of that style with his heavy sounds. His name was Elvin Jones.

Elvin Ray Jones was born on September 9, 1927, in Pontiac, Michigan, into a musical family. His brother Hank, the eldest of the Jones trio, became a noted jazz pianist. Thad Jones was a well-received trumpeter. Elvin himself became interested in music at an early age and his desires were fueled by the ambitions of his two big brothers. He jammed with them in clubs around his hometown until he joined the army in 1946.

Upon his release in 1949, he became involved in the booming Detroit jazz scene of the early 1950s that included his brothers, Louis Hayes, Donald Byrd, Barry Harris, Tommy Flanagan, Kenny Burrell, Yusef Lateef, and Pepper Adams. These young lions would be instrumental in shaping the future of hard bop, free jazz, and jazz fusion. It was during this period that Jones honed his developing skills as a drummer.

When he moved to New York in 1955, he began the second phase of his apprenticeship and worked with a number of acts, including Teddy Charles and the Bud Powell Trio. He was fortunate enough to record with Miles Davis and Sonny Rollins, who enabled him to spread his wings as a musician. He also began to attract serious attention. He padded his resume even further when he played with J. J. Johnson, the great bop trombonist, for a year, as well as Donald Byrd, one of his old friends from Detroit, Tyree Glenn and Harry "Sweets" Edison. This long road eventually led him to the John Coltrane quartet.

During his five-year tenure with the band the volcanic drumming of Jones fueled Coltrane's best solos. They rode and explored different themes of music with Coltrane, blowing for hours and taking the song every which direction that was humanly possible. Jones, like a loyal companion, was with the tenor man all the way. The chemistry between the two, how they complemented each other's individual style, sparked the imagination of a generation of listeners.

Perhaps the high point of their partnership was best represented on the song "Chasin' the Trane," a duet that featured one of Coltrane's most headlong solos fueled by Jones' relentless attack. There was a boundless energy exuded by both of them and the sheer fuel was never matched. They opened up doors and avenues that no one had ever thought possible. It sounded as if the two were born to play together.

Although his years in Coltrane's quartet were very productive, when the great sax man added drummer Rashied Ali to the band, it initiated the dissolution of the great partnership. Eventually, Jones left the group.

After a tour of Europe with the Duke Ellington Orchestra, Jones fronted his own outfit for the first time. His trio with saxophonist Joe Farrel and bassist Jimmy Garrison was successful. Subsequent sidemen included Frank Foster, George Coleman, Pepper Adams, Dave Liebman, Pat LaBarbera, Steve Grossman, Andrew White, Ravi Coltrane, Sonny Fortune, Nicholas Payton, Dollar Brand, Willie Pickens, Jan Hammer, Richard Davis, Wilbur Little, and Gene Perla, among others. All benefited from Jones' ability to complement his accompanist's individual style with his flexible, fluid drumming.

He was the leader of many sessions, including a reunion with brothers Thad and Hank. The three leading lights of the free and avant-garde scene followed their own individual careers but often crossed paths. The result was a satisfying meeting every time that they decided to work with one another. One of the highlights for any jazz fan was to witness all three performing together on the same stage.

Some of the other sessions Elvin led included the avant-garde pianist McCoy Tyner. Tyner wasn't an ordinary pianist but attacked the instrument like a man possessed; he required a different type of drummer to provide the perfect accompaniment. Jones was that drummer.

When he wasn't in the studio, he was on the road performing in many venues—including prisons—with the Elvin Jones Jazz Machine. An interesting crop of musicians passed through his outfit, including saxophonists David Liebman, Steve Grossman, Sonny Fortune, and Azar Lawrence, guitarist Roland Prince, and bassists Gene Perla and David Williams. In recent years younger players Delfeayo Marsalis, Nicholas Payton, James Moody, Joshua Redman, David Sanchez, Javon Jackson, and Ravi Coltrane (John's son) were part of Jones' impressive outfit. As an elder statesman of jazz, he had the dubious honor of passing the torch to the younger generation.

Sadly, on May 18, 2004, the passing of the torch came to an end when Elvin Jones, the great free jazz drummer, passed away. He was 76 years old.

Elvin Jones was a master drummer. He was at the jazz forefront for the past forty years and was an integral part of the development and popularity of Coltrane's music. He was a major influence to young percussionists for the past five decades and continues to be a hero to many. Any aspiring stickman's musical 'education' consists of closely studying the enormous recorded catalog of Jones' long, illustrious career.

It was Jones who bridged the gap between hard bop and free jazz and avant-garde. Although he started out as a hard bop drummer, he found a medium between the two styles. His idea of freer accompaniment was a logical extension of post-bop drumming. He broke away from the regular cymbal beat, launching a barrage of accents and rhythmic patterns that offered endless possibilities to the soloists.

Although there were other drummers in jazz that had parallel careers, including Billy Higgins, Dannie Richmond, Tony Williams, Sunny Murray, Ed Blackwell, Clifford Jarvis, Ronald Shannon Jackson, and Kevin Mahogany, none had the same power and imagination as Jones. While his contemporaries were very good musicians, they lacked that extra punch that he was able to provide in a group setting. He was—with the exception of hard bop granddaddy Art Blakey—the greatest stickman of the post-bop era.

The great trinity of jazz drummers—Max Roach, Kenny Clarke and Art Blakey—had a large influence on Jones. As well, Roy Haynes and Philly Joe Jones (no relation) shaped his style. But of all those, it is Blakey that necessitates a closer comparison. Although both graduated from the bop school, they went different directions. Blakey remained a hard bop enthusiast throughout his career, while Jones explored free jazz as well as the avant-garde. Simultaneously, they were considered the best two drummers on the circuit despite their different approach and techniques.

Jones was an inspiration to a generation of young drummers and other musicians, including Roy Brooks, Michael Carvin, Peter Erskine, Trilok Gurtu, Jan Hammer, Pete LaRoca, Tony Oxley, John Stevens, Collin Walcott, Dave Bailey, Lenny White, Phil Wilson, Norman Connors, Joe Farrell, Dave Liebman, and Lenny McBrowne. Many of the aforementioned combined the best that Jones and Blakey had to offer to create something new and fresh.

Throughout his career Jones worked with a number of major jazz figures. The list includes John Coltrane, Tommy Flanagan, Paul Chambers, Art Davis, Sonny Rollins, Freddie Hubbard, Wynton Kelly, Herbie Hancock, Richard Davis, Stan Getz, Reggie Workman, McCoy Tyner, James Moody, Joshua Redman, Delfeayo Marsalis, Wayne Shorter, Kenny Burrell, Eric Dolphy, and Thad and Hank Jones. The wealth of jazz mates represents a cross section of artists in the hard bop, avant-garde, free jazz, jazz fusion and contemporary styles.

Elvin Jones was the most important jazz musician to emerge from the fertile Detroit area. Beginning in the late 1940s and 1950s, the Motor City produced a solid crop of young artists that were keen revolutionists. Donald Byrd, Milt Jackson, Ron Carter, the three Jones boys, Tommy Flanagan, Barry Harris, Louis Hayes, Kenny Burrell, and Pepper Adams all played a vital role in putting the state of Michigan on the jazz map. While only a handful of players in the first half century of jazz boasted an authentic Great Lake State birth certificate, the second generation made up for it. Although each of the new school enjoyed good careers, none equaled that of Elvin.

Jones was also a leader of the free jazz school and along with Coltrane blazed the trail for all to follow. But he could never be confined to one particular style. Although free jazz and avant-garde have often been pitted against each other, Elvin was a student and leader of both trends. His vast abilities allowed him to excel in any style.

Elvin Jones was a respected man who enjoyed a distinguished career.

He was one of the most creative drummers in the history and his association with John Coltrane is the stuff of legends. A favorite among all jazz fans, his recordings are an essential part of every music collection and study guide for every aspiring drummer. Undoubtedly, the man who gave the world his heavy sounds will forever occupy an important seat in modern jazz history.

Discography

And Then Again/Midnight Walk, Collectables 6242.
Dear John C, GRP Records 126.
ELVIN! Riverside 409.
Elvin!, Original Jazz Classics 259.
It Don't Mean A Thing, Enja 8066.
Very Rare, Evidence 22053.
Familiar Ground, West Wind WW 2104.
Fumio Karashima/Moon Flower, AMJ ABCJ-49.
Jazz Machine, TRIO ABCJ-9.
Jazz Machine Vol. 2, TRIO ABCJ-32.
Live at Lighthouse, EMI TOCJ-9240/1.
Live at the Village Vanguard, ENJA TKCB-71690.
Very Rare, TRIO ABCJ-10.
Youngblood, ENJA ENJ0006.
Youngblood, TOKUM TKCB-71981.
On the Mountain, One Way Records 30328.
The Main Force, Universal Records 24.
Philly Joe Jones and Elvin Jones Together!, Atlantic 1428.
Illumination! Elvin Jones and Jimmy Garrison, Impulse IMPD250.
The Ultimate Elvin Jones, Blue Note BST84305.
Heavy Sounds, MCA—Elvin Jones and Richard Davis, Impulse A9160.
Puttin' it Together, Blue Note BST84282.
The Prime Element, Blue Note BNLA506H2.
Mr. Jones, Blue Note BNLA110F.
Poly-Currents, Blue Note Records 84331.
Coalition, Blue Note BST84361.
Merry-Go-Round, Blue Note BST84414.
Genesis, Blue Note BST84369(.
Live at the Lighthouse, Vol. 1, Blue Note B2-84447.
Live at the Lighthouse, Vol. 2, Blue Note B2-84448.
At This Point in Time, Blue Note 724349338524.
New Agenda, Vanguard Universe 15.
Summit Meeting, Vanguard VSD 79390.
Time Capsule, Vanguard Universe 38.
Remembrance, MPS15523.
Mr. Thunder, EastWest EWR7501.
Very R.A.R.E., Evidence E524119.
Love & Peace, Storyville STCD 5006.
Live in Japan 1978, Storyville STCD4153.
Elvin Jones Live—The Town Hall, PA-7111.
Skyscrapers, Vol. 1–4, Honeydew HD6602–5.

Soul Train, Denon 7004.
Heart to Heart, Denon 7146.
Earth Jones, Palo Alto PA8016.
Live at Pit Inn, 1985, CBS/Sony 4878992.
In Europe, Enja PAP9111.
Youngblood, Enja 7051.
It Don't Mean a Thing, Enja 8066.
When I was at Aso Mountain, Enja 70812.
Going Home, Enja 70952.

ERIC DOLPHY (1928–1964)

Outward Bound

The sphere of influence that Yardbird Parker exerted on succeeding generations of saxophonists is incalculable. The one lesson he taught all his disciples who hailed him as the messiah was to play their own thing, no matter how strange it might sound. One of Parker's fervent students took this lesson to heart and his music was always outward bound. His name was Eric Dolphy.

Eric Allan Dolphy was born on June 20, 1928, in Los Angeles, California. He was interested in music from an early age and learned how to play the alto sax. His main influence was Charlie Parker; however, unlike his hero, who was first and foremost a sax man, Dolphy would add the bass clarinet and the flute to make himself a multi-instrumentalist.

He gigged around the Los Angeles area, playing in many bands, honing his skills, and moving up the ladder of success. He joined Roy Porter's Orchestra and it was during this period that Dolphy made his first recordings. The union was a good one but before he could build up any momentum, he was drafted into the army. After two years of service he returned to his native city to pick up the threads of his once flourishing musical career. However, it seemed that the club scene had left him behind as he played in a number of forgettable bands waiting for his big break. He craved a change in direction.

In 1958, after having paid his dues for a long period, Dolphy joined Chick Hamilton's Quintet. The exposure enabled him to step to the forefront for the first time and also gave him much needed confidence. A year later, he moved to the right coast and found work in the Charles Mingus Quartet. In the Big Apple, things really began to happen for him. He recorded on his own for the first time and received much attention from fans and also critics because of his sterling work in the Mingus quartet.

By this time Dolphy had developed a highly advanced style that was often misunderstood, but it did not stop him from securing work with a variety of other musicians. He teamed with Booker Little and the two cut some impressive live albums at the Five Spot nightclub. He also recorded with Ornette Coleman, who would become a soul mate; they would eventually lead the way for free jazz and avant-garde practitioners. He also sat in on sessions that included the great drummer Max Roach. That Dolphy was accorded this kind of respect from the jazz community indicated that he had come a long way.

However, his major break came when he joined the John Coltrane quartet in 1961. He had built a solid reputation but his popularity exploded as he traded impossibly long solos with Coltrane, enraging some critics and bedazzling the other jazz artists. The chemistry between the two towers of power was exceptional as they explored the uncharted territories of free jazz and the avant-garde.

The uniqueness of their individual sounds and the combination of their imagination, abilities, and fluid thoughts resulted in a mixture of pure excitement and confusion. They were simply too far ahead of their time to be appreciated by many, except a short list of people who shared their unique vision. It is a tribute to Coltrane and Dolphy that they never allowed the criticism to deter them from playing the sounds they heard in their heads.

Undoubtedly, with the pair as the leading "frontman," the great innovator Elvin Jones on drums, the radical McCoy Tyner on distorted piano, and the steady Jimmy Garrison trying to hold it all together, the John Coltrane Quintet was the wildest group on the scene. The twin pairing of Dolphy and Coltrane was likened to having two great lead guitarists in a band such as the Yardbirds with Jeff Beck and Jimmy Page. Every night the two talented saxophonists were creating their own universe fueled by the energetic pulse of Jones and the advanced thinking of Tyner.

Despite the fact that there was no other act like it on the jazz circuit at the time, and the twin towers of sax power turned the jazz world on its ear, like all good things it came to an end. During their time together they dared to reinvent the genre in a way no one thought possible. Although their partnership was brief, it made a lasting impact on jazz and both benefited from the experience.

After leaving Coltrane, Dolphy joined Gunther Schuller and Orchestra U.S.A. He toured and recorded with the group but his tenure there was short-lived. He moved on and rejoined Charles Mingus' sextet. He remained with the meanest bass player in jazz long enough to participate in the Great Concert of Charles Mingus. In the interim, Dolphy was leading his own group and recorded the classic *Out to Lunch* in 1964.

That same year, he decided to remain in Europe rather than return to the United States. Sadly, on June 29, 1964, Eric Dolphy died of diabetes in Berlin, Germany. The young genius left us much too early. He was 36.

Eric Dolphy was a genuine jazz giant. In just a few short years he established himself as a well-respected musician whether in the role of sideman or leader. He established the foundations of avant-garde jazz, along with Ornette Coleman and John Coltrane. Dolphy did very much in so little time and his early death was an irrevocable loss to the jazz world, as well as to the international music community.

He was a multi-instrumentalist with certain dimensions. Although the alto saxophone was his prime instrument, he also excelled on bass clarinet and flute. It was his solo efforts on the bass clarinet that brought the instrument greater respect. While he wasn't the first to pick up the flute in jazz, along with Yusef Lateef and Rahsaan Roland Kirk, he brought it into the avant-garde realm.

But it was the alto saxophone with which he built his fame. In the modern era, there are four giants of the instrument: Charlie Parker, John Coltrane, Ornette Coleman and Dolphy. Each possessed his own unique voice, each was misunderstood, each was heavily criticized for playing the sounds in his head that were labeled revolutionary. All were prime innovators that changed the sound of jazz forever. Interestingly, all but Coleman died young.

Dolphy, along with soul mates Coltrane and Coleman, was a pioneer of the free jazz/avant-garde movement. Eric played long, intricate solos that often mesmerized his audience for the sheer brilliance of their creation. He was a mood painter able to create dark undertones that hinted at fantastic adventures and whole universes not yet explored. However, in some ways he went further than both Coltrane and Ornette because of his ability to play three instruments (very well) and to make significant recordings with each one. He created entirely new dimensions of solo voicing in the avant-garde/free jazz styles.

He had a strong influence on a variety of players, including Hamlet Bluiett, Tony Campise, John Handy, Dave Holland, Eric Kloss, Ken McIntyre, Tony Oxley, Don Pullen, Sonny Simmons, Barbara Thompson, Bennie Wallace, Jack Walrath, Michael White, Vincent York, Michel Portal, and Freddie Hubbard. Dolphy's music was not for the timid and required an essence of understanding that was often out of the reach of most listeners. Yet, those that heralded him as an important voice in jazz knew a good thing when they heard it. Like Coltrane, Coleman and Parker, he was shunned by traditionalists and critics for trying to create something new that was outside normal taste boundaries.

He was a noted composer and wrote the "African Brass" movement that Coltrane recorded. Dolphy also gave the world "245," "The Prophet," "Love Me," "What Love," "Alone Together," "Music Matador," and "Gazzelloni." The musical gifts he gave the world were limited because of his short life, but the work he managed to deliver was mostly excellent. All of his albums became collector's items.

Eric Dolphy remains an important name in jazz despite his death over thirty-five years ago. Like all other artists who die young, the biggest question that surrounds him is what he would have produced had he lived longer? The promise he held was never fully tapped. However, the music he did give us will always maintain that he was outward bound.

Discography

Berlin Concerts, ENJA TKCB-71694.
The Caribe with the Latin Jazz Quintet, Orig. Jazz Classics 819.
Conversations, Jazz World 226.
The Complete Prestige Recordings, Prestige Records 4418.
The Complete Uppsala Concert Vol. 1, Pony Canyon B00005QYI5.
Dolphy Sound, Jazz World 314.
The Essential Eric Dolphy, Prestige Records 60–022.
Eric Dolphy Memorial Album [live], Prestige 353.
Eric Dolphy, 1928–1964, Collectables B00005YDKU.
Far Cry, Original Jazz Classics, 400.
Fire Waltz, Eric Dolphy & Booker Little Remembered ... Vol. 2 [Live] Evidence 22074.
Green Dolphin Street, Art Union B00008CH1C.
Here and There, Original Jazz Classics 673.
The Illinois Concert, Blue Note Records 99826.
Immortal Concerts [live], Giants of Jazz 53013.
In Candid Dolphy, Candid Records 79033.
In Europe, Vol. 1, Original Jazz Classics 413–20.
In Europe, Vol. 2, Original Jazz Classics 414.
In Europe, Vol. 3, Original Jazz Classics 416.
Iron Man, Vol. 1, Jazz World 225.
Jitterbug Waltz, Casablanca Giants of Jazz B00009KUA.
Last Date, Verve 822 226.
Late Date, Universal B000065E97.
Left Alone, Art Union B00008CH1G.
Les Incontournables, Wea International 35821.
Live! At the Five Spot, Vol. 1, Original Jazz B0002IQFUO.
Live! At the Five Spot, Vol. 2, Original Jazz 247.
Live in Germany, Magnetic Records 130.
Looking Ahead, Original Jazz Classics 252.
Music Matador, Jazz Hour 73593.
Naima, West Wind B000008ARI.
Original Ellington Suite, Blue Note Records B00004UB9B.
Other Aspects, Blue Note Records 48041.
Out There, Original Jazz Classics 023.
Out to Lunch, Blue Note Records 98793.

Outward Bound, Prestige Records 8236.
The Quest, Prestige 82.
Quiet Please, Past Perfect B00007BKE8.
Softly, as in a Morning Sunrise, Natasha Imports 4001.
Stockholm Sessions, Enja B00000E7D1.
Straight Ahead, Orig. Jazz Classics 99.
This Is Eric Dolphy, Varese Records B0000BWVO4.
Vintage Dolphy, GM Recordings 3005.
Where?, Orig. Jazz Classics 432.
Wherever I Go, (No Label) B00005AT7U.

CECIL TAYLOR (1929–)

The Note Painter

Jazz has often been called the great American art form with musicians compared to painters in their ability to create a united visual and audio portrait of pure individual expressionism. In art, one of the more controversial styles was abstract. The equivalent in jazz was the avant-garde and one of its most controversial practitioners was the man known as the note painter. His name was Cecil Taylor.

Cecil Percival Taylor was born on March 15, 1929, in New York City. He began his musical career at the age of six when he discovered the magic he could make on the piano. He continued to develop and his maturation process as a musician was exceptional. During his early years he was particularly fond of Duke Ellington, Art Tatum, the boogie-woogie threesome of Meade 'Lux' Lewis, Pete Johnson and Albert Ammons, and later, Dave Brubeck. From myriad influences Taylor created his own unique style.

After attending the New York College of Music and the New England Conservatory, he found work with Johnny Hodges during the latter's split from Duke Ellington for a brief time in the 1950s. Taylor also worked with Hot Lips Page. But from the very beginning it seemed that he was destined to lead his own groups because of his unconventional approach to the piano. His problem was finding someone who could blend properly with his manic attacks.

He formed his first quartet in the 1950s with Steve Lacy on soprano, bassist Buell Neidlinger and drummer Dennis Charles. Taylor and his new group landed a regular gig at the Five Spot Cafe and later played at the Newport Jazz Festival. But due to his very unique approach to playing the piano, he was shunned from many promoters and work was hard to find.

Personnel changes didn't help matters, but the addition of saxophonist Archie Shepp was a step in the right direction.

Throughout much of the 1960s Taylor struggled to establish himself. Despite numerous recordings for the Candid label, live dates remained scarce. By 1962, he had acquired new sidemen in Jimmy Lyons on alto and Sunny Murray on drums. They were better suited to blend with Taylor's kamikaze-like attack on the piano, which by this time had gained some widespread attention and more mixed reviews. During his stint in Europe he hooked up with saxophonist Albert Ayler and although they played a few dates together (no doubt raising the eyebrows of the European audiences), they never recorded together. Upon his return to the United States, Taylor found himself in the same rut as before. His music was so advanced that it was out of public favor.

But he persisted and did record some strong albums for Blue Note, including *Unit Structures* and *Conquistador;* both masterpieces. He also was one of the founders of the Jazz Composer's Guild and played on a record by the Jazz Composer's Orchestra. The latter project did not do much for his career; the slow progress was very frustrating for someone as brilliant and diverse as Taylor.

By the dawn of the 1970s Taylor's fortunes improved, as his music became more readily acceptable to jazz fans. He was also involved in a variety of projects that enhanced his career. He recorded frequently with his own group, the Cecil Taylor Unit and his touring schedule became hectic with several excursions in Europe, where he received more favorable reviews. His collaboration with Max Roach, the great bop drummer, proved to be an interesting adventure that nicely fueled his blossoming reputation.

Taylor was also involved in projects outside of the jazz idiom, including terms as a teacher at the University of Wisconsin, Antioch College, and Glassboro State College. He received much needed financial support from the Guggenheim Fellowship and performed at the White House during President Jimmy Carter's administration. In all, he enjoyed a much better decade than the previous one, but he still hadn't broken through as much as he desired.

As the 1980s unfolded, Taylor continued to record and perform on a regular basis. By now his music was tolerated and appreciated in different circles. He was still far advanced as an avant-garde artist, but there was a certain quality about his style that lured listeners in. Although personnel changes in his band occurred—including the death of Jimmy Lyons in 1986—the pianist carried on.

Today, Taylor has garnered sufficient recognition, including a run of nine consecutive years as the number one pianist in *Down Beat* magazine's international critic's poll. In 1986 the Berlin Free Jazz Society sponsored a "Cecil Taylor Week." In 1999, he played a concert at the Library of Congress in Washington, D.C. Interestingly, he has always been more readily accepted in Europe than in the United States. While he was never popular on a large scale, he has carved a definite niche for himself in the fragmented musical world.

Taylor continues to explore his brand of jazz through studio and live performances. He is one of the most diverse voices of jazz piano. He has developed a reputation as someone who is way out there, a pianist whose technique and skill are regarded as too advanced for the casual listener to decipher. But there is a genius to his playing that many have discovered over the years. He remains one of the prime painters in jazz.

He is an avant-garde artist, and probably one of the movement's most outspoken individuals. Although he suffered through lean times before his music was accepted, he never relinquished his goals. He had a strong inner drive and perseverance that enabled him to finally enjoy the success he deserved. He is one of the more interesting jazz experimenters of the last fifty years.

The Taylor piano technique has often left listeners breathless. He has always combined atonality with a deep respect for those who influenced him, including Fats Waller, Duke Ellington, Thelonious Monk and Bud Powell. He was also keen on composers Stravinsky and Bartok. Although there are definite traces of past jazz pianists, he was able to turn all of the elements he acquired into something that sounded like it was from another world. His music lacked the harmonic and melodic familiarity that had characterized jazz piano for over sixty years.

If what he played wasn't enough to deter the average listener, then his method of delivery certainly did. His wild piano attacks were akin to a voodoo ceremony. He pounced on the piano with the wild abandon of an angry, lion producing a cacophony of angry, disjointed sounds, but was able to coordinate everything into one irregular package of raw emotion and sound images. Every song in every concert was a different mood painting. Like an artist trying to fill an empty canvas, Taylor attempted to fill his audience's minds with his sound notes.

The physical routine of his live act often left the audience bewildered. The energy that ran through his body during a performance forced him to never settle on a satisfactory position. It was physically exhausting to watch him alternate quickly between sitting and standing throughout an entire set. But there was a rhythm to his movement, including the visual delight of his tightly wound dreadlocks flowing to the wild music created by his unrelenting passion. He gave everything he had in every performance and delivered it as if it were his last. He looked as if he was in a trance and the scene could be visually shocking.

Taylor influenced a number of jazz artists. A partial list includes Geri Allen, Stanley Cowell, Anthony Davis, Steve Lacy, Chris McGregor, Enrico Rava, Archie Shepp, Lonnie Liston Smith, Keith Tippett, Julie Tippett, Yosuke Yamashita, Khan Jamal, Frank Lowe, Marilyn Crispell, Glenn Horiuchi, Matthew Shipp, Brian Jackson, Frank Kimbrough, and Marvin "Hannibal" Peterson. His techniques have spread throughout the world and many have been able to find some essential kernel in Taylor's playing to help shape their own individual sound.

He gave the world a number of classics, including "Excursions on a Wobbly Trail," a direct homage to Duke Ellington's "Take the A Train" and Thelonious Monk's "Little Rootie Tootie." Other notable songs include "This Nearly Was Mine," "Ari," "D Trad," "That's What," "Into the Hot," "Enter Evening," "Communications II," "Spring of the Blue J's," "Silent Tongues," and "Indent." Each composition provided a distinct look at Taylor's artistry and was another strike for the avant-garde movement.

Taylor was one of the main architects of the avant-garde jazz period. Yet, despite being a spokesman for the style, he never forgot his roots and attempted to turn the old into something new and acceptable. He encouraged everyone in his band to explore the strange side of their musical personality and discouraged the idea of limiting one's creative genius.

After fifty years in the music business Taylor can look back on a successful career that has taken him to many places and down many different roads. Although his music is not for every jazz fan, those that are able to break through the initial barriers are pleased that they have done so, because they admire the breadth and depth of the note painter's musical gift.

Discography

Jazz Advance, Blue Note Records 84462.
3 Phasis, New World Records 303.
Chinampas, Leo Records (Jazz) (import) 153.
Conquistador, Blue Note Records 84260.
For Olim, Soul Note (import) 121150.
Iwontunwonsi—Live at Sweet Basi, Sound Hills (import) 8065.
Jumpin' Punkins, Candid Records 79013.
Looking (Berlin Version), FMP Records 28.
Nefertiti, the Beautiful One Has Come, Revenant 202.
Olu Iwa, Soul Note (import) 121139.
Silent Tongues, 1201 Music 9017.
The Cecil Taylor Unit, New World Records 201.
Tzotzil/Mummers/Tzotzil, Leo Records 162.
Unit Structures, Blue Note Records 84237.
1955–1961, GOJ CD53172.
Akisakila, TRIO ABCJ-30/1.
Always a Pleasure, FMP FMPCD69.

Crossing, NA JHR73505.
Dark Unto Themselves, ENJA ENJ20842.
Double Holy House, FMP FMPCD55.
Erzulie Maketh Scent, FMP FMPCD18
Indent, BLACL CD41038.
Live in Bologna, LEORE LRCD100.
Looking, FMP FMPCD28.
Tree of Life, FMP FMPCD98.
Unit Structures, EMI TOCJ-9235.

ORNETTE COLEMAN (1930–)

Tone Dialing

Once the musical restraints had been lifted off jazz artists, an entirely new vocabulary of innovations found its way into everyone's sound. The 1950s and beyond were a time of great experimentation and by the middle of the 1960s many critics and fans were questioning the future of the music. Where was jazz heading? One contemporary artist was never confused as to the direction of the music, since he helped shape its sure path with distinct tone dialing. His name was Ornette Coleman.

Ornette Coleman was born on March 9, 1930, in Fort Worth, Texas. Like so many saxophone players, he was inspired by Bird Parker and started playing the alto when he was fourteen in order to emulate his idol. A couple of years later he added the tenor sax to his musical arsenal. Also like his mentor, Ornette was very keen on reproducing the sounds he heard in his head. His evolution as a musician was slow and frustrating at times, but it was also rewarding when he broke down another barrier towards achieving his ultimate goal.

He gigged around his home state mostly with rhythm and blues bands, including apprenticeships in Pee Wee Crayton's and Red Connors' outfits. From the beginning he was an original voice, but his individual style that was years ahead of its time met with utter disdain from audiences and fellow musicians. Coleman required patience and time before he would be able to unleash his musical vision onto the jazz world.

He moved to Los Angeles in 1952 for a change of scenery and to try and get his musical career off the ground. He met with disappointment during his first attempts and was forced to find a day job as an elevator operator. In his spare time he was studying music books, but his true education took place in jam sessions with other young cats that sympathetically understood his vision. Don Cherry, Charlie Haden, Ed Blackwell, Bobby Bradford, Charles Moffett, and Billy Higgins were the first jazz figures that Coleman could bond with on a musical and spiritual level.

Despite this sign of encouragement, Coleman still suffered lean times until 1958, when he was given his first major break by the brass at Contemporary Records. He was able to record his musical ideas and the results were two albums, *Something Else* and *Tomorrow Is the Question*, with a group of kindred spirits who were able to understand his complicated theory of harmolodics. His stint with Paul Bley's Quintet around this time also gave his career a much-needed boost while also serving notice that there was a new force on the jazz scene.

Due to the underground respect that Coleman received from the release of his two albums, he was able to find more work, including a long residency at the Five Spot in New York. Trumpeter Don Cherry, bassists Charlie Haden, Scott LaFaro or Jimmy Garrison, and drummers Billy Higgins or Ed Blackwell backed him on concert dates. Coleman also secured a contract with Atlantic, which was willing to take a chance on the daring innovator. While everyone was trying to find their way out of the maze of chord progressions, Coleman bypassed the problem by playing improvisations on rhythmic and melodic planes and developing his solos along a freer logical extension. This was the basic tenet of his musical philosophy, harmolodics.

The albums *The Shape of Jazz to Come, This Is Our Music, Change of the Century, Ornette!, Art of the Improvisers, Ornette on Tenor, Free Jazz* and *Twins* ushered in the free jazz movement and attracted many converts to the cause, including John Coltrane, Eric Dolphy, Pharoah Sanders, Lester Bowie, Henry Threadgill, and John Zorn. His regular studio group included the faithful Cherry, Haden, Higgins or Blackwell. On these sessions Coleman used the tenor saxophone, including on the album *Ornette on Tenor*. By this time an entire new school of players had grouped behind him.

Coleman, an ambitious musician, experimented with a double quartet that included Eric Dolphy, Freddie Hubbard, Scott La Faro, Higgins, Blackwell, Haden, and Cherry, and that delivered some of the most radical music in jazz history. On the album *Free Jazz* they expanded the boundaries of what Ornette had already attempted. The session clearly distanced itself further from earlier forms. The music that he and his mates created challenged the establishment to a greater degree than the radical tones of bop that had slated Gillespie and Parker against the big band/swing enthusiasts.

But Coleman was a different breed of jazzman and continued to explore a new path. He stripped down his double quartet to a trio that included bassist David Izenson and drummer Charles Moffett. On the album *Town Hall* the various directions that Coleman followed were highlighted. He experimented with a string ensemble on the record that further pushed the envelope.

Oddly, at the height of his newfound popularity he quit. He remained outside of jazz for three years and during his self-imposed retirement he taught himself the violin and the trumpet. As well, he composed a fresh batch of songs that clearly indicated the future path that he intended to pursue.

Upon his return to the jazz world in 1965, he appeared at the Village Vanguard with his trio, still comprised of himself, bassist Izenson and drummer Moffett. He traveled to England and appeared at different venues there, including the legendary concert at Fairfield Hall. Although the British had been exposed to traveling American jazzmen for four decades they were somewhat unprepared for Coleman's brand of jazz. Nevertheless, there were those who liked his music and he added them to his ever increasing fan base.

He would release two albums that year on the Blue Note label, including *At the Golden Circle,* a live set. He was asked to provide the score for the film *Chappaqua Suite,* and although it contained some of his finest work, it was not used in the movie. The masterwork that Coleman had written included an eleven-piece band of woodwinds, strings, and brass, as well as the addition of tenor player Pharoah Sanders. It showed another side of Coleman's musical genius.

Coleman would augment his group to a quartet with the addition of Dewey Redman, as well as Haden or Blackwell on bass in place of Izenson, and his son Denardo Coleman on drums. Denardo was only ten years old and his position in the band raised a few eyebrows. The elder Coleman also jammed with Don Cherry, his best friend from the early part of his career when he was a struggling musician.

In the early 1970s, Coleman, ever the experimenter, formed Prime Time, a group that had two guitars, two electric bassists, two drummers, and two horns. It proved to be an interesting exercise that featured some of the most intense, thick jazz ever created. By this point, he had fully developed his theory of harmolodics, which placed an equal emphasis on harmony, melody, and rhythm. Some critics labeled the music he made during this period free funk because of the vast chunks of soul that he incorporated with his jazz ideas. Some of the main contributors of Prime Time were drummer Ronald Shannon Jackson, bassist Jamaaladeen Tacuma, and Denardo Coleman.

Although they played a different brand of jazz, Prime Time did have its strong points and attracted the attention of other jazz musicians, including converts Steve Coleman and Greg Osby. Ornette also jammed with Jerry Garcia of the Grateful Dead, as well as Pat Metheny, one of the best-known jazz fusion guitarists. While his music remained on the cutting edge, by this time he had so many imitators that Coleman did not stand out as much as he had in the past.

In the 1980s, he reunited with some of his old friends, including Don Cherry, Pharoah Sanders, and Billy Higgins. Despite his advancing age, Ornette's music still contained some of his old grit. His *Opening the Caravan of Dreams* mid-decade effort was a spicy contribution to the later avant-garde movement by the man many consider the granddaddy of the style. He had proven to all of the many detractors that his musical idea of harmolodics had withstood the test of time.

In the 1990s, Coleman showed no signs of slowing down. His *Tone Dialing* and *Sound Museum* CDs clearly demonstrated that he was still quite capable of producing hot jazz. His occasional live performances were genuine experiences in power and color as he utilized the trumpet, the violin, and the tenor and alto saxophones to entertain the audience. He has never veered from his initial vision and remains one of the greatest spokesmen of modern jazz.

Ornette Coleman is a jazz revolutionist. He changed the face of jazz improvisation with his theory of harmolodics and his incredible ability on the alto saxophone. Not only was he an original thinker, he had enough talent to push these theories across despite meeting with many obstacles, confusion and outrage. However, he was not deterred by some of the hostility that was directed towards him and what he was trying to accomplish. He was a visionary who refused to compromise his musical ideas.

Coleman was an abstract painter on the alto and tenor saxophones. Rather than base his music on subjects, he built his style around feelings, emotions, and impressions. Although his music was criticized as non-jazz, his sheer ability to improvise, his distinct voice, and his inclusion of swing and blues assured that it was the real thing. His style was different, which didn't make it inferior, just different.

The key to Coleman's sound was his incredible gift of improvisation. He dethroned the use of harmony, an act that caught the old guard flatfooted. His unshakable belief that the music be centered on his theory of harmolodics eventually proved that he was right. A long list of followers indicates that he did indeed have an insight and solution to the problem of the seemingly inescapable maze of chord progressions.

He influenced Karl Berger, Carla Bley, Anthony Braxton, Don Cherry, Hal Galper, Joe Henderson, Albert Mangelsdorff, Dewey Redman, Archie Shepp, John Stevens, Klaus Doldinger, Gerd Dudek, Tomasz Stanko, Silver Apples, James Blood Ulmer, Ronald Shannon, Jackson Tortoise,

Jamaaladeen Tacuma, Jackie McLean, and Henry Threadgill. But his ideas had an effect on a larger group of individuals, including those in the jazz fusion school. Along with John Coltrane, Coleman stands out among saxophonists during the late 1950s until the present.

He gave the world a number of outrageous classics, including "Gave the World Lonely Woman," "Peace," "Ramblin'" "Kaleidoscope," "Beauty Is a Rare Thing," "C & D Congeniality," "Monk and the Nun," "The Fifth of Beethoven," "Cross Breeding," "Mapa," "Falling Stars," "Antiques," "Dee Dee," "Faces and Places," and "Song for Che." Whether covering someone else's work or debuting one of his self-penned tunes, he possessed the ability, confidence, and drive to deliver the song in its fullest context. His compositions have been studied, broken down, and re-evaluated by each jazz generation.

Coleman traveled around the globe to deliver his theory of harmolodics to lukewarm audiences who did not understand what he was trying to say, as well to enthusiastic and knowledgeable fans who were in his corner pulling for him to conquer the jazz world. Despite a divided opinion of his work, he acquired a considerable reputation as someone with an incredible amount of talent. Many of his live concerts were recorded for posterity and serve as a testimony to the man and his vision.

Coleman worked with a number of jazz figures. His young son played on the albums *The Empty Foxhole, Ornette at 12,* and *Crisis.* He also collaborated with Elvin Jones on the albums *New York Is Now* and *Love Call.* But he had the most success with Charlie Haden, Don Cherry, Billy Higgins, Dewey Redman, Ed Blackwell, David Izenon, Jamaaladeen Tacuma, Jimmy Garrison, Scott LaFaro, and Charles Moffett. He also worked with Francis Wolff, Bern Nix, Nesuhi Ertegun, Charles Ellerbee, Al Macdowell, Paul Bley, Yoko Ono, Geri Allen, Nathan Goldstein, and Dave Sanders.

Ornette Coleman was a pioneer of the avant-garde/free jazz style with an open imagination and improvisational ability to create the rich pasturage of musical self-expressionism. Although his music did not always win over every jazz critic and fan, he still managed to become a legend. His refusal to compromise assured that his tone dialing survived the test of time.

Discography

Tone Dialing, Harmolodic Records 527 483.
Virgin Beauty, Portrait 44301.
At the Golden Circle, Stockholm, Vol. 1, Blue Note Records 84224.
At the Golden Circle, Stockholm, Vol. 2, Blue Note Records 84225.
Free Jazz, Atlantic 1364.
In All Languages, Harmolodic Records 531 915.
Skies of America, Columbia 63568.

The Complete Science Fiction Sessions, Columbia 63569.
The Shape of Jazz to Come, Rhino Records 1317.
Beauty Is a Rare Thing, Rhino Records 71410.
Body Meta, Harmolodic Records 531 916.
Broken Shadows, TriStar Music 35096.
Change of the Century, Atlantic & Atco Remasters 81341.
Chappaqua Suite, Legacy Records 65469.
Dancing In Your Head, Verve 543 519.
Free, Giants of Jazz Recordings 53212.
Free Jazz, Giants of Jazz Recordings (import) 53214.
Harlem's Manhattan, Giants of Jazz Recordings (import) 53225.
Live at Jazzbuhne Berlin '88, Repertoire 6/88.
Love Call, Blue Note Records 84356.
New York Is Now, Blue Note Records 84287.
Sound Museum: Hidden Man, Harmolodic Records 531 914.
Sound Museum: Three Women, Harmolodic Records 531 657.
The Art of the Improvisers, Rhino Records 90978.
The Best of Ornette Coleman—The Blue Note Sessions, Blue Note Records 23372.
The Complete Science Fiction Sessions, Columbia 63569.
The Music of Ornette Coleman: Something Else!!!, Original Jazz Classics 163.
Tomorrow Is the Question!, Original Jazz Classics 342.
Town Hall Concert 1962, Calibre 1006.
Beauty Is a Rare Thing, Rhino Records 71410.
At the Golden Circle Vol. 1, BNOTE TOCJ-9161.
At the Golden Circle Vol. 2, BNOTE TOCJ-9162.
Empty Foxfall, EMI TOCJ-9236.
Friends & Neighbors—Live At Prince Street, BMG 74321477952.
Of Human Feelings, POLY PHCR-4036.
This Is Our Music, ATLAN 7567807672.

RAHSAAN ROLAND KIRK (1936–1977)

Saxophone Concerto

The history of jazz is rich with colorful individuals who made enormous contributions to the genre by following their own paths. Charlie Parker, Billie Holiday, Dizzy Gillespie, Ornette Coleman, John Coltrane, and Louis Armstrong all became legends because of their determination to do things on their own terms. One of the most eccentric characters in the genre followed the sounds in his head in order to give the world his saxophone concerto. His name was Roland Kirk.

Rahsaan Roland Kirk was born Ronald T. Kirk on August 7, 1936, in Columbus, Ohio. It seemed from the very beginning that no matter what obstacles he faced trying to achieve his goals, he had the drive to overcome them all. He became blind by the age of two; however, in the next nine years would discover music and develop his skills rapidly. By the age of eleven he could play the bugle, trumpet, clarinet, C-melody sax and a variety of homemade instruments. He possessed a facility in music, a genuine and natural gift.

He started playing in rhythm and blues bands before his teens and four years later was leading his own outfits. By this time he had added the manzello and stritch to his arsenal of musical abilities. Kirk, an experimenter, managed to invent a circular breathing system that allowed him to play any of the saxophones, in addition to the flute, nose flute, clarinet, police whistle and siren. He was truly a one-man band.

He also understood the subtle texture of showmanship and was able to entertain the audience drawing on vaudeville performance tricks. The ability to play three horns simultaneously was a novelty never seen before in jazz annals. Despite his multi-instrumental abilities, his showmanship, and knowledge of musical textures, fame was slow to arrive. In many circles he was considered more of a buffoon than a true jazz artist.

He recorded his first album, *Triple Threat,* in 1956, but the record didn't make an immediate impact. Kirk took his show on the road and toured throughout the United States, earning a divided opinion among jazz fans about the true value of his talents. On the one hand, there was no doubting his ability, while on the other hand, his buskerish approach in concert made him so different from anyone else on the circuit he was ignored in many mainstream circles.

Kirk spent time in Louisville, Kentucky, then headed to Chicago in 1960. His second album, *Introducing Roland Kirk,* brought him a wider appeal. It included saxophonist-trumpeter Ira Sullivan and if nothing else proved that Kirk had the respect of some of his peers. However, it was his fortune to spend three months with Charles Mingus, one of the giants of jazz in the early 1960s, that sealed his acceptance despite his eccentric nature. It was agreed that his music and performing ability now possessed a charming quality.

From this point on, he led his own band, called the Vibration Society, and began to build his legend with outlandish concerts where he stunned audiences by playing three instruments at one time. It gave him more freedom to create a greater layer of sound with his varied musical arsenal. As well, in an era where free jazz and avant-garde baffled many jazz fans, Kirk arrived on the scene with a much simpler sound to entertain the crowds. There was something familiar in his live music that people could connect to.

Throughout the 1960s, Kirk released a number of very good albums, including *The Art of Rahsaan Roland Kirk, We Three Kings, The Inflated*

Tour, and *Bright Moments.* Although personnel in the Vibration Society turned over quickly, the group toured regularly all over North America and the world. His show-stopping techniques were by now the stuff of legends. He knew how to play an audience and feed their desires to see something grand, but he never lost control, demonstrating his professional skills as a first-class entertainer.

In the 1970s, Kirk, who was an established star, began to use his muscle to spread his message of social equality throughout the world. He headed the Jazz and People's Movement, a group dedicated to elevating the number of opportunities for African Americans in all of the arts. His activities took nothing away from his music, but instead added a dimension to his character that proved he was more than just a performing clown, as he had once been labeled, and was indeed a serious artist.

He reunited with Mingus in the mid–1970s to play on the *Mingus at Carnegie Hall* album. All doubts about his ability as a serious musician were wiped out on this work. He was challenged by formidable tenorman George Adams and Kirk displayed a fervent energy that took the music to a place only he could occupy. In any cutting contest, his multi-instrumental ability as well as his facility in playing more than one instrument at one time usually earned him a decisive victory.

In 1976, Kirk had a stroke that severely limited his mobility. However, despite being paralyzed on one side, he continued to play one-handed concerts and recaptured some of his past versatility. He received numerous messages from fans that he had touched from around the globe, but they were not enough to help him overcome the final obstacle.

On December 5, 1977, in Bloomington, Indiana, Rahsaan Roland Kirk, the extravagant performer who had played his way into the hearts of millions of music fans around the world, died. He was 41 years old.

Rahsaan Roland Kirk was a jazz phenomenon. His firm musicianship—which included expertise on a range of instruments and his encyclopedic knowledge of different styles—and his classification as a world class performer made him a legend. Behind the somewhat clownish performances was a serious student of blues, jazz rock, pop, and soul who understood musical textures and subtleties that were beyond the grasp of most other artists.

It is hard to establish how many instruments Kirk could actually play. He was proficient on manzello, stritch, tenor saxophone, police whistle, flute, clarinet, the nose whistle, the piccolo, the siren, and the harmonica. He also designed his own instruments, including the trumpophone, a trumpet with a soprano sax mouthpiece, and a slidesophone, a small trombone that also sported a sax mouthpiece. He was constantly developing new instruments to play in concerts and add dimension to albums. It was because of his homemade gizmos that he was almost impossible to imitate.

He was a spectacular showman of superhuman strength who could dazzle a crowd with his street performing techniques and his sheer talent. He possessed incredible breathing ability that allowed him to push the music across like a tsunami. He wore a complex network of straps and adhesive tapes that allowed him to have all kinds of outlandish instruments at his fingertips. For example, he would play the tenor with his left hand, finger the manzello with his right hand, and sound a note on the stritch. All of his skills were self-taught.

It is difficult to categorize Kirk's music because of its depth and breadth. He played everything from the very roots of the New Orleans tradition to swing and bop and free jazz. Perhaps he was most comfortable in free jazz because it allowed him to play his multitude of instruments and create new sounds with few confinements. Without a doubt, Kirk was one of the most creative artists in the history of music.

Some of his most memorable songs include "Saxophone Concerto," "Eat That Chicken," "Creole Love Call," "The Seeker," "You Did It; You Did It," "A Sack Full of Soul," "The Inflated Year," and "Bright Moments." Any self-penned material or covers possessed the Kirk magical touch. Although he was a brilliant writer, he played numbers from the classic jazz books of Duke Ellington, Billy Strayhorn, Hal David, Burt Bacharach, Tommy Peltier, Ira Gershwin, Richard Rodgers, Mort Dixon, Charlie Parker, Ray Henderson, Henry Mancini, George Gershwin, Oscar Hammerstein II, Louis Ferrari, Dubose Heyward, Johnny Mercer, Bud Green, and John Coltrane. Because of his self-confidence, he was never afraid to attempt any song.

Due to his uniqueness, his outlandish musical abilities, and charisma, Kirk had a special influence on a small but important group of artists. The list includes Jethro Tull, Iain Ballamy, Bob Moses, Barbara Thompson, John Almond, James Carter, Jeff Coffin, Charlie Hunter, and Steve Turre. But his impact could be felt in many subtle ways throughout the world of jazz, blues, rock, and pop. His showmanship had a special effect on Jimi Hendrix, who could play guitar behind his back or with his teeth, and who even lit the instrument on fire.

Rahsaan Roland Kirk was one of the most exciting performers in the history of jazz. He was a total package of musical ability, invention, historian, and showmanship skill. His level of intensity displayed was rarely matched by anyone that appeared before him or after. His legend rests on his ability to excite audiences with his saxophone concerto.

Discography

Dog Years in the Fourth Ring, 32 Jazz 32032.
I, Eye, Aye, Rhino Records 72453.
A Standing Eight, 32 Jazz 32100.
Aces Back to Back, 32 Jazz 32060.
Bright Moments, Rhino Records 71409.
Does Your House Have Lions, Rhino Records 71406.
Domino, Verve 534 445.
Gifts & Messages, Ronnie Scott's Jazz House 55.
Here Comes the Whistleman, Label M 5720.
I Talk with the Spirits, Verve 558 076.
Introducing Roland Kirk, GRP Records 821.
Left Hook, Right Cross, 32 Jazz 32142.
Live in Paris 1970, Vol. 1, Esoldun 2109.
Rahsaan: The Complete Mercury Recordings, Mercury 846 630.
Rip, Rig & Panic/Please Don't You Cry Beautiful, Verve 832164.
Simmer, Reduce, Garnish & Serve: The Warner Bros. Recordings, Warner Archives
    45811.
Talkin' Verve: Roots Of Acid Jazz, Verve 533 101.
The Inflated Tear, Rhino Records 75207.
Three for the Festival, Le Jazz 006.
We Free Kings, Verve 826 455.

ARCHIE SHEPP (1937–)

The Articulate Spokesman

Every era and school of jazz has featured leaders, brave individuals who were seriously intent on broadcasting their art. It is these warriors who have kept the long and proud tradition of the genre alive. One of these figures who has always been keen on celebrating the avant-garde/free jazz movement was the articulate spokesman. His name is Archie Shepp.

Archie Vernon Shepp was born on May 24, 1937, in Fort Lauderdale, Florida. Although he can claim an authentic birth certificate from the Sunshine State, Shepp was raised in Philadelphia, the City of Brotherly Love, from an early age. Despite being surrounded by music, his passion did not truly surface until he was in college studying dramatic literature. He picked up the alto saxophone and discovered that he possessed a special talent on the instrument.

After an intense period of practicing and honing his skills, Shepp made his debut on clarinet rather than the alto sax with R&B bands around the Philadelphia area. Later he moved to New York in hopes of discovering a wider set of musical opportunities. To pay the bills he was also writing and acting in various plays, something he had done back in Philadelphia. As well, he was jamming with Latin bands in an effort to broaden his musical horizons. Because of his diverse and multiple activities, his evolution as a musician was considerably accelerated.

Shepp caught his first break in 1960 when he met and teamed up with pianist Cecil Taylor. He toured and recorded with the abstract piano player, altering on alto as well as tenor saxophone. His recording debut on the album *Air* (with Taylor) demonstrated Shepp at an interesting point in his development, sounding like an amalgam of Sonny Rollins and John Coltrane. Although his contributions to the record were solid, it was obvious that he hadn't yet reached his full maturity.

Shepp also played on Taylor's *Into the Hot,* and spent time in Don Cherry's group before they joined forces and formed the New York Contemporary Five. The NYC5 also included altoman John Tchicai and free drummer J. C. Heard. They released one album, *Archie Shepp & The New York Contemporary Five,* which gained the alto saxophonist some important attention. However, the project was short-lived and each went their separate ways before the promise that the group held could be fulfilled.

Some time later he formed his own outfit with trumpeter Bill Dixon, trombonists Roswell Rudd and Graham Moncur III, and vibraphonist Bobby Hutcherson. They released the *Bill Dixon–Archie Shepp Quartet* collection, which was a step in the right direction. It was at this point that he attracted much attention as one of the most impressive new players, making him a serious rival of John Coltrane.

Like other young jazz revolutionaries in the early 1960s, Shepp was in awe of Coltrane, who was designated the leader of the first wave of the new thing. It was difficult not to be influenced by Trane, the most innovative saxophonist to arrive on the scene since the demise of Charlie Parker. Shepp and Coltrane became good friends due to the admiration they had for one another. Through the connection, Archie was able to land a recording contract with the Impulse label.

Shepp emerged with his own individual sound and recorded in the mid–1960s during the height of the avant-garde movement. Although he and Coltrane collaborated on the album *Ascension* with a number of the new thing players, the duo was not to last. They were heading in different musical directions—each was following the sounds he heard in his head. On the album *Ascension,* Shepp stands out with his ferocious, coarse efforts that initiated comparisons to the great Ben Webster.

Shepp played at the Beat Festival in Chicago with Coltrane and widened his circle of admirers. He also appeared at the Newport Festival and proved that the avant-garde style was more than just a passing fad.

He was on the cutting edge of the new jazz with his double-threat alto and soprano saxophone sound. Although he was making positive noise in the music world, he also found time to stage one of his plays in New York. He was an all-around artist.

After his Coltrane phase, Shepp stretched out as a writer with the inventive record *Fire Music* on the Impulse label. It marked a giant step in his acceptance as a first rate composer. He also extended his sphere of influence by recording a series of politically oriented albums, including *Malcolm, Malcolm, Live in San Francisco, New Thing at Newport, Things Have Got to Change,* and *Attica Blues.* This series also had him return to working with some of his old collaborators, including Hutchinson, Rudd, and Moncur III.

Shepp was something of a complex figure; some critics considered him to be a free jazz player while others saw him as a definite soldier of the avant-garde army. He was one of those artists talented enough to play and excel in both styles. It was also about this time that he began to experiment with Sousa marches, complex R&B pieces, and a general direction opposite of where he had been heading earlier in his career.

Whatever category he was placed in, by the mid–1960s he had made a name for himself in the jazz world as a brilliant player with the fire and passion of a dozen saxophonists. His tours and records sold well, and he matured as a composer. When not establishing his essential musical credentials, he was writing and staging his own plays that reflected the new identity that African Americans were trying to promote during the turbulent times.

Like many of the new thing players, he traveled to Europe in the late 1960s. During his foreign period he recorded an interesting number of albums, including *Yasmina, A Black Woman, Black Gypsy, Archie Shepp & Philly Joe Jones* and *Coral Rock.* Lester Bowie, Roscoe Mitchell, Hank Mobley, Leroy Jenkins, Anthony Braxton, Noah Howard, Clifford Thornton and Sunny Murray backed him on various projects. Many of them were avant-garde artists but fit in perfectly with Shepp's versatility.

He was also performing all over the world. In 1969, he played at the Pan African Festival in Algiers and remained in Europe until 1970. During his time in France, the country was experiencing major student revolts. The outspoken Shepp identified with the rebelliousness of the students and played a few concerts in sympathy for their cause. Whether it was the plight of his own people or that of others, he was always ready to come to the defense of the oppressed.

In 1971, Shepp returned to the United States after securing a dedicated fan base throughout various parts of Europe. Back in America he divided his time between creating music and teaching it, as well as teaching literature at the University of Massachusetts. Eventually, he became an associate professor at the school, but it didn't cut into his continued musical journey.

He recorded with the singer Joe Lee Wilson on *Things Have Got to Change* and *Attica Blues*. Although he was still a prime figure in jazz, Shepp turned to a less aggressive style that saw him expand the base of his sound to include rock, blues, bop, and rhythm and blues. He projected a wider image that was aligned with the new black consciousness. In the jazz fusion era, he was a fighter of the new style with his ability to mix different musical strains into one cohesive and coherent sound.

He eventually formed another group that included Charles Greenlea on trombone, Dave Burrell on piano, Cameron Brown on bass, and Beaver Harris on drums. He also recorded duo albums with Max Roach, the great bebop/hard bop drummer. Shepp, who had never forgotten his roots, also partnered with Horace Parlan to pay tribute to the greats of the past, including Charlie Parker and Sidney Bechet.

In the 1980s, Shepp was far distanced from the free jazz/avant-garde player of his youth. He had matured into a more complete player who appealed to a broader audience. He had added the soprano saxophone to an arsenal that already included the clarinet, the piano, and tenor and alto saxophones. Although he had mellowed and the urgency and anger of his playing had subsided, he continued to pad his extensive resume with touring and recording in the United States and Europe. Some of his European collaborators included Horace Parlan, Niels-Henning Orsted Pedersen and Jasper Van't Hof.

He rolled on in the 1990s but with less success. He produced exciting blues-filled works that demonstrated his abundant musical ability. However, like other artists that mature and lose their angry edge, he experienced a decline in popularity. Although he continues to make good records, he is remembered mostly for his past achievements.

Archie Shepp is a cornerstone of the free jazz/avant-garde movement. Since its inception he has contributed much to the music through his playing and his outspoken point of view. In a career that has spanned over forty years, he has ensured that his work was not to be ignored. An important stylist, he has written his own chapter on the history of the tenor saxophone.

His original sound consisted of a fierce blend of hoarse cries, rasps, loose vibrato and pure clarity. He demonstrated a clear and dramatic control of dynamics with a genuine feeling for the blues as well as an overwhelming emotional intensity that set him apart from many of his contemporaries. His tenor work boasted a commanding sound and even today, he remains one of the kings of the instrument.

He has given the world an array of great music: "Trio," "Speed'a Song Flute," "Niema," "Acension," "In a Sentimental Mood," "Prelude to a Kiss," "Hambone," "Los Olivadados," "Malcolm, Malcolm," "Attica Blues," "Portrait of Robert Johnson," "Damn It," "Rain Forest," "Yasmina, A Black Woman," and "Black Gypsy." The songs are scattered throughout his catalog and range from robust ballads, deeply moving blues poems, magnificent spirituals, and pure modern jazz. Few artists of the modern era can match the breath, depth and total of Shepp's compositions.

When he first broke in during the 1960s, he was very much into black power and the African American social conscience. He was a fiery radical and channeled the anger he felt about social injustice into his playing. In the 1970s he changed direction, taking on more of a swinging rhythm and blues approach. In the 1980s, he played a mixture of straight bebop, ballads and blues—the sound of a contemplative veteran. Despite this change in attitude and vision, he continued to gain respect in jazz circles.

Although noted for his fervent musical ability, he was always more than just a one-dimensional artist. He made important contributions outside the music world as a noted playwright. Two of his more famous plays include *The Communist* and *Lady Day: A Musical Tragedy*. The latter was a tribute to Billie Holiday. Both works display the anger and fire of a young artist.

Archie Shepp is now one of the senior statesmen of jazz. He has mellowed with age but his playing remains exceptional. The unique tone of his sound has not lost its edge over the years. No matter the decade or the circumstance, he remains forever the articulate spokesman.

Discography

A Sea of Faces, Black Saint 0002.
Attica Blues, MCA MVCI-23038.
Attica Blues Big Band, EPM 151982.
Ballads for Trane, Denon Records 8570.
Bird Fire: Tribute to Charlie Parker, EPM 151 962.
Black Ballads, Timeless 386.
Blase, Blase/Live at Pan-African Fest, Le Jazz 26.
Blue Ballad, Venus Jazz B00003WGAS.
Blues, Absor B00005MIBI.
Blues Quartet, Phantom B00005661H.
Body and Soul, Enja 7007.
California Meeting Live, Soul Note Records 121122.
Conversations, Delmark 514.
Cry of My People, Impulse Records B00014AUTG.
Day Dream, Denon Records 8547.
Déjà vu, Japanese Import B00007K4QE.
Down Home New York, Soul Note 121102.

Duet: Archie Shepp/Dollar Brand, Denon Records 8561.
Fire Music, GRP Records 158.
Four for Trane, GRP 218.
Freedom, Jmy 1007.
French Ballad, Venus Jazz B00005MIKD.
Goin Home, Steeplechase B000027UJJ.
The Good Life, Varrick 005.
House I Live In, Steeplechase B000027T4S.
Hungarian Bebop, Budapest Music B00006B1Q0.
I Didn't Know About You, Timeless Records 370.
I Know About the Life, Sackville 3026.
Kwanza, Uni B000006ZWR.
Lady Bird, Denon Records 8546.
Little Red Moon, Soul Note Records 121112.
Live in Antibes 1 & 2, Varese Records B000078JK1.
Live at the Donaueschingen Music, Polygram B00005HPVP.
Live at the Totem Vol. 1, EPM 152172.
Live at the Totem Vol. 2, EPM 152202.
Live in San Francisco, GRP Records 254.
Live in New York, Universal B0000560N7.
Looking at Bird, Steeplechase B000027UDE.
Long March 2, (No Label) B00008F7E4.
Loverman, Timeless Holland B000026GXV.
Magic of Ju-Ju, Impulse! Universal B00024Z98M.
Mama Rose, Steeplechase B000027UBQ.
Mama Too Tight, GRP Records 248.
Montreux Vol. 1 Live, Freedom-Navarre 741027.
New Thing at Newport, Polygram Records B00004SST5.
New York Contemporary Five, Storyville 8209.
On Green Dolphin Street, Denon Records 77262.
On This Night, GRP Records 125.
One for the Train, Phantom B0000566IJ.
Painted Lady, tm [Tko Magnum] B00008F8HT.
Parisian Concert Vol. 1, EPM 152062.
Poem for Malcolm, Sunspots B000091EDW.
Rising Sun Collection [LIVE], Just a Memory 5.
St Louis Blues, Jazz Magnet 2006.
Shepp Live Quartet, Phantom B0000566IK.
Something to Live, Timeless Holland 439.
Sophisticated Lady, Westwind Records B00008G26R.
Soul Song, Enja 4050.
Steam, Enja 2076.
Swing Low, Elephant B00005LJF0.
The Way Ahead, GRP Records 272.
There's a Trumpet in My Soul, Freedom, Navarre 741016.
Things Have Got to Change, MCA MVCI-23081.
True Ballads, Venus Jazz Japan B00003WGAT.
True Blue, VENUS TKCV-35080.
Tray of Silver, Denon Records 8548.
Tribute to Duke Ellington, Phantom B0000566IL.
Trouble in Mind, Steeplechase B00004S6H6.
Yasmina, a Black Woman, Le Jazz 51.

CHARLIE HADEN (1937–)

Haunted Hearts

The evolution of bass playing has undergone many innovations in the hands of those with the skill and imagination to make the changes happen. Since the inventiveness of Jimmy Blanton every subsequent bassist has added their own distinct touch, including the man who rose to the challenge of bringing the instrument into the realms of the free jazz/avant-garde movements with his haunted hearts. His name is Charlie Haden.

Charles Edward Haden was born on August 6, 1937, in Shenandoah, Iowa, into a musical family. He began his study of the bass at an early age and played country music with his family on their radio show. Although he was quite young when Blanton came through, Haden was able to study what the great virtuoso had accomplished. More importantly, during Haden's adolescence, Charles Mingus was making some huge rumblings that would have a profound effect on Haden's overall development.

Although musical opportunities existed for Haden in his native Iowa, he decided to seek his fame and fortune on the West Coast and arrived in Los Angeles in 1955. He was armed with an abundance of talent and radical sounds swirling in his head. He found work with Art Pepper, Hampton Hawes, and Paul Bley during the 1950s and though he was making a living as a musician, he still yearned for more creative freedom. His experimental bass sound would have to wait.

He was finally given the opportunity to expand his musical vocabulary when he met Ornette Coleman, who was in the process of formulating his radical musical theory called harmolodics. Haden, Coleman, and trumpeter Don Cherry all met while playing with Bley at the Hillcrest Club and left to form their groundbreaking quartet in 1959. The three had much to prove because their ideas were considered too far out there.

Up to this point Ornette Coleman and Charlie Haden were two very frustrated jazz musicians. Like Charlie Parker before them and John Coltrane, one of their contemporaries, all the two young musicians wanted was to play the sounds they heard in their heads. However, no one was interested in the music that existed in their fertile imaginations. Nonetheless, once they joined forces they gave each other the necessary confidence to pursue their individual musical paths.

Haden played on many of Coleman's most classic recordings, including *The Shape of Jazz to Come,* the work that boldly pointed to the direction that the music would take for the next few years. Coleman, who had tried unsuccessfully to find sidemen who could play within the structure of his harmolodics, thought Haden was heaven sent. The brilliant bassist was a perfect foil to Coleman's saxophone exercises; he had the imagination, technical skill, and fluidity to pull it off.

During the three years they were together the duo firmly established the free jazz school as a force to be reckoned with. The style was the logical extension of the hard bop and cool jazz styles that had dominated the genre for the past few years. The sweeping changes that Haden and Coleman brought to jazz ushered in a new period.

But like all good things the partnership came to an end. The two brilliant musicians had outgrown each other and they split up. Haden left Coleman in 1961 to pursue other musical interests and worked with Denny Zeitlin for two years from 1964 to 1966. He then left in search of new adventures. There was always a never ending quest to go beyond established boundaries and it was this drive to constantly evolve that kept him on the move physically and musically.

Although they no longer played together, Coleman and Haden had many reunions over the years and the magic always remained vibrant. They also recorded together on occasion, sounding as strong as they had during their golden days in the late 1950s and early 1960s. In between stints with Coleman, Haden was kept busy playing with a variety of musicians, including the avant-garde tenor saxophonist Dewey Redman. While there was plenty of work as a sideman, Charlie desired to lead his own outfit.

By the mid–1960s, Haden was cultivating a strong social opinion and at the end of the decade formed the *Liberation Music Orchestra.* The subsequent album Liberation Music Orchestra was a classic example of contemporary free jazz. The work's subject matter swung from homespun Spanish American War songs to the hard-edged politics of the 1968 Chicago Democratic Convention. Although he had played within the free jazz idiom with Coleman, Haden became an avant-garde artist in the 1970s and his Liberation Music Orchestra reflected this outlook.

He participated in the outfit Old and New Dreams in the 1970s, adding his distinct bass tone to the group's overall sound. He continued to make contributions to various ensembles, including a trio with Jan Garbarek and Egberto Gismonti. He even found time to teach music at California Arts College.

As well as aforementioned recordings with Coleman, he shared studio time with Keith Jarrett, the jazz fusion pianist who had played with Miles Davis, and Alice Coltrane. Haden dabbled with jazz fusion before returning to his free jazz roots. By this time he had stretched the limitations of the bass and redefined the role of the instrument in a group setting. But despite two decades of innovative work, he still had plenty to say as an artist.

During much of the 1980s he led a new band called Quartet West that included Ernie Watts, Alan Broadbent, and Larance Marable. The group instilled their music with the creeping effect of the noir novels and movies that gave their sound mystery, darkness, and a genuine dangerous edge. No matter what individual or group he hooked up with, Haden was able to create something that was unique in jazz.

He also continued to record outside of the group on a regular basis throughout the years, including a series of duets with Hank Jones on the *Haunted Hearts* CD in 1995. They concentrated on old favorites like "Swing Low, Sweet Chariot," and "Nobody Knows the Trouble I've Seen." There was a delicate beauty that permeated each cut, as well as a definite power that begged for release. He had pulled off another emotionally triumphant collection of jazz songs. He continues to be a force in the jazz world.

Charlie Haden has been an important voice on the bass for over four decades. Although he began as an obscure sideman, he rose to the top of the bass heap and has been one of the finest practitioners of the instrument ever since. He is a vital link in the long line of bassists and is responsible for establishing its boundaries in free jazz and the avant-garde styles.

There is an undercurrent in his playing. His subtle ability to state a theme without killing it is pure genius. Some of his more chilling, haunting creations conjure reflections of the eerie noises of the ocean. There is much freedom in his playing, an ability to complement the soloists in the band, as well as to move in an independent direction. His oscillating notes flow dependently of each other, but stand alone as true symbols of power like each wave of the great sea.

His respect in the music world is incredible. He earned the admiration of many fellow bass players, including Ron Carter, Charles Mingus, Gary Peacock, Niels-Henning Orsted Pedersen, Cecil McBee, Ray Brown, Stanley Clarke, Charles Duvivier, Percy Heath, Rufus Reid, and Miroslav Vitous. He has been a special inspiration to the new generation of bassists, most specifically Christian McBride, Mark Dresser, Steve Swallow, and Peter Epstein. He is more than just a link in the chain that includes Pops Foster, Jimmy Blanton, Slam Steward, and Oscar Pettiford; he occupies a special place in the succession of bass players. Even the great Charles Mingus was a fan.

Haden has worked with Jack DeJohnette, Denny Zeitlin, Roswell Rudd, Tony May, Jan Erik Kongshaug, Gonzalo Rubalcaba, Joe Lovano, Ron Carter, Jean-Philippe Allard, Hank Jones, Keith Jarrett, Alice Coltrane, John Scofield, Joe Henderson, and Gato Barbieri, among others. His ability to fit into any new situation without compromising his own individual sound is a cornerstone of his musical identity. But, of course, he will forever be best remembered for his association with Ornette Coleman.

Charlie Haden is also famous for the musico-political element in his work. The bold statements found on his Liberation Music Orchestra album during one of the most turbulent times in American history clearly demonstrated his stance. He recorded "Song for Che" in praise of Che Guevara the famous South American revolutionary who took Castro from the foothills of Cuba into absolute power.

Haden is a deserving annual poll winner. He is an excellent bass player with a wide range of ideas that flow freely with grace and beauty as well as a subtle anger. He has taken the bass into unexplored territory with successful results. There is no limit to the catalog of greatness that lies in the music of his haunted hearts.

Discography

Liberation Music Orchestra, Impulse! 188.
None but the Lonely Heart, Naim Audio 022.
Quartet West, Verve 831 673.
Silence, Soul Note 121172.
The Ballad of the Fallen, ECM Records 811 546.
The Montreal Tapes/Liberation Music Orchestra, Verve 527 469.
Closeness Duets, POLY 3970002.
Dream Keeper, DIW DIW-844.
The Art of Song, Verve 547 403.
Always Say Goodbye, Verve 521 501.
Haunted Heart, Verve 513 078.
In Angel City, Verve 837 031.
Now Is the Hour, Verve 529 827.
Steal Away, Verve 547 403.
Works 1986–1999, POLYG UCCV-4002.
Liberation Music Orchestra, Impulse! 39125.
Night and the City, Verve 314539 961-2.
As Long as There's Music, Verve 513534-2.
Year of the Dragon, JMT 834 428.
Segments, DIW 833.
Live at the Village Vanguard, DIW 847E.
Etudes, Soul Note 121162-2.
Charlie Haden and Al Foster, Red CD123215-2.
Memoirs, Soul Note 121240.
Dialogues, Antilles 422–849 309.

ANTHONY BRAXTON (1945–)

The Professor's Approach

There have been countless attempts to specifically define the term "jazz." However, because of the creative depth and breadth of its practitioners, it is impossible to pigeonhole the music into one simple and narrow concept. The blues-based notes that emerge from the fertile imaginations of jazz artists are one of the most striking features of the music. Every performer possesses his or her individual vision, including the man known for his professor's approach. His name is Anthony Braxton.

Anthony Braxton was born on June 4, 1945, in Chicago, Illinois. He was the middle of five children on the South Side of Chicago where Muddy Waters, Howlin' Wolf, Little Walter, Willie Dixon, Elmore James, and other blues greats were creating their own legends. However, Braxton was not seduced by the lovely, enchanted music until his teenage years. He learned how to play the clarinet in high school and studied music for a brief semester at Wilson Junior College.

Disenchanted with his studies at school, Braxton joined the army for a couple of years during peacetime. During his stint in Uncle Sam's private club he extended his musicianship by adding the alto saxophone. Once he returned to Chicago he began to put his musical act together.

One of the most important steps he took to advance his career was joining the Association for the Advancement of Creative Musicians based in Chicago. This group included forward thinking individuals Muhal Richard Abrams and Roscoe Mitchell. The AACM was on the cutting edge of the avant-garde style of jazz that was in its infancy but would quickly mushroom into a dominant style. Braxton provided the organization with an added dimension of intellectual depth.

Braxton formed his first group, eventually dubbed the Creative Construction Company, with Leroy Jenkins and Leo Smith. Their first release, *Three Compositions of New Jazz* in 1968, brought a fresh voice to the genre, a voice that relied on sound, space, and texture—directly opposed to the stylistic ideas established by John Coltrane, Ornette Coleman and their disciples. Undoubtedly, Braxton was a student of the avant-garde and would soon move into the role of supreme professor.

One of the philosophies of the AACM was every player's ability to be a multi-instrumentalist, which Braxton keenly adopted as one of his badges of honor. He expanded his musical vocabulary by learning how to play all the saxophones—soprano, alto, tenor, and bass—plus the flute, the contrabass clarinet, the piano, and percussion instruments. His debut album also displayed his philosophical advanced ideas of formula music.

One of the brashest jazz artists to emerge in the last half-century, he never backed down from a challenge. A pure intellectual with a taste for the experimental, he recorded a double album of solo saxophone—the first time anyone had attempted such a bold act. Critics, fans, and fellow musicians were torn between the merit and confusion over the project. Braxton was weaving his magical spell.

In 1969, he took his group to Paris; unfortunately while in Europe they disbanded. Upon his return to America, he spent a brief time with Ornette Coleman, one of the leading voices of free jazz. But Braxton had much different ideas and found himself out of the music business. Instead of earning his living as a musician, he became a professional chess player, a source of income that he has turned to in lean times. The fact that he could earn a living playing chess demonstrates that he was quite different from the average jazz artist.

But music was in his blood and in 1970, Braxton and jazz fusion pianist Chick Corea, bassist Dave Holland, and Barry Altschul formed the group Circle. Although the band held much promise due to its talented lineup, Circle broke up due to philosophical differences. Braxton, dispirited over the failure of the band, returned to Paris.

In the City of Lights, he found eager colleagues who shared the same musical vision. He played with some of the great European avant-garde musicians, including the Alex Von Schlippenbach's Globe Unity Orchestra, as well as Derek Bailey's Company festivals. While his musical career prospered across the Atlantic, Braxton was lured back to the United States with a contract offer from Arista Records. Although he had managed to push across his very distinct ideas in jazz, he had never been given carte blanche in recording the sounds in his head.

He formed a new group, calling on his old bandmates Holland and Altschul, as well as Kenny Wheeler. Wheeler would eventually leave the group and be replaced by George Lewis. For the first time in his career, Braxton was given the chance to deliver his sophisticated musical ideas to the jazz world. He made the most of the opportunity.

Braxton, who always lived in his own universe, gave the world a complex series of jazz albums that expanded the boundaries beyond capability, then rearranged everything in a logical, calculus-like fashion. His albums—*For Trio, For Four Orchestras,* and *For Two Pianos*—catapulted him at the head of the avant-garde school. The listener required a Ph.D. in advanced musical theory in order to understand what Braxton was trying to say. Also, the fact that his compositions came with enigmatic diagrams only served to further confuse people and enhance his reputation as one of the most eccentric figures in jazz. His music contained all the complexity of a chess player mapping out his strategy.

But there was an undeniable depth to his music, as he extended the parameters of jazz to include the classical ideas of Schoenberg and Stockhausen and the dark truths of the avant-garde experiments of John Cage's work. Jazz—which has often been called American's classical music—was given a boost with Braxton's contemporary freshness. He gave the genre a sophistication that it had never seen.

Despite his foray into musical styles that were far removed from jazz, one could hear the influence of Coltrane in his style. Like all other individuals who ever decided to follow their own paths and go against the established norm, Braxton teetered on the edge between visionary and lost individual. His *Two-Tradition* album was a combination of both the new thing and traditional jazz that sparked the return of the classics a decade later.

It was obvious that he was not an ordinary jazz artist and this was greatly reflected in the material he recorded in the late 1970s. Two tribute albums, one in honor of Thelonious Monk and the other paying homage to Lennie Tristano, were both cherished efforts. He also united forces with bebop drummer Max Roach and their improvised duets were interesting adventures. Braxton demonstrated that even though avant-garde was a thinking man's music, it also could include ideas of the past. His collection of big band pieces were astonishing.

In the 1980s, his interest in mysticism and theatre formed the central ideas of his work. He composed a series of ceremonial recordings that explored themes of astrology and numerology. The result of this experimentation was *Trillium*, a fantastic creation of a series of twelve operas that further explained his calculus- like musical approach.

For much of the decade he was preoccupied with chromesthetic music, a type of music based on sounds with a particular color and shape. Chromesthesia is a form of synesthesia, a condition in which normally separated senses become intermingled. It's rare in general but more common among musicians; a chromesthete hears a particular note and at the same time "sees" it as a corresponding color and shape. But he was also continuously expanding his musical theories and introduced such complex concepts as pulse track structures, multiple logics music, and other diversions that only added to his reputation as the deepest thinker among all jazz artists.

Although his musical ideas were far advanced and the normal jazz musician was confused as to what he was attempting to accomplish, he did find some kindred souls in Marilyn Crispell, Mark Dresser and Gerry Hemingway. These three musicians were part of the quartet that recorded with him through much of the 1980s and into the early 1990s. It was difficult for Braxton to find musicians able to complement and challenge him at the same time.

He also became an important jazz writer with the publication of his *Tri-Axium Writings*. The three-volume set explained in precise detail his musical philosophy. He further added to his credentials as an author when the five volumes of his composition notes were made available to the public. For the first time, fervent disciples had the opportunity to decipher his incredibly complex musical theories. The professor was attempting to teach his students.

While he established his reputation as a musically creative giant over the past twenty years, he also found time to teach at Wesleyan College. Despite his duties as an instructor he has not forsaken his musical endeavors. He found time to record as a solo performer, as well as in duets, trios, quartets and more ambitious ensembles. He has also collaborated with the ROVA Saxophone Quartet and the London Jazz Composers Orchestra. Although his music is intimidating because of its abstract and complex format, Braxton continues to be on the cutting edge of jazz. His brilliance, fortitude, and undeniable skill on a variety of instruments should not be overlooked. He also continues to confound all that have tried to unravel his musical thoughts.

Anthony Braxton is an intellectual jazz figure of incredible proportions. This deepest of thinkers he has made innumerable contributions that have remained obscured because of their complexity. Although he has been derided by critics and jazz players alike, his sense of blues and his grand ability to improvise makes his style one of the most unique in the realm of modern music.

He is a multi-instrumentalist, but most of his work has been recorded on alto sax. He has taken the instrument down paths that few understand or could ever duplicate. His complicated lines, staccato attack, and versatility make for interesting listening. He has recorded some of the toughest, most savagely violent jazz in history. Yet, he also possesses a soft touch and can communicate more through silent passages than most players can with note-infested solos.

His work on other instruments, including the soprano saxophone, the contrabass clarinet, the clarinet, and piano, have allowed him to interpret a wide range of traditions from bebop to cool and avant-garde to straight jazz. But no matter the instrument he has used or the style he has toyed with, one can be assured that the music was always imaginative, challenging, creative and strange.

To truly understand its roots one must examine the influences on Braxton. The large variety of names includes artists of the first wave including Cecil Taylor, Eric Dolphy and Muhal Richard Abrams. There are the free jazz thinkers Ornette Coleman and John Coltrane. There is the classical stamp of Karlheinz Stockhausen and Arnold Schoenberg. There is also the hard bop/cool school influence of Miles Davis, Jackie McLean, Lee Konnitz, Paul Desmond and others. Another special influence was Warne Marsh.

Despite the complexity of his music Braxton has made an impact on a number of jazz artists. They include Ray Anderson, Leroy Jenkins, Kenny Wheeler, Affinity, The Earons, Fred Hess, John Zorn, Francois Houle, Kevin Norton, Kit Clayton, and Rajesh Mehta. While he has shaped the sound of many individuals because of his style and the coded nature of his music, he has also alienated those who felt that his material was just too confusing.

In any assessment of Braxton one must look at both sides of the equation. Perhaps his music is for only the high intellectual and not the masses. However, he challenged fans and critics to seriously attempt to decipher his music. On the other hand, like many jazz artists before him, including Duke Ellington, Charlie Parker, Dizzy Gillespie, Miles Davis, Ornette Coleman, and John Coltrane, Braxton was just simply playing the sounds he heard in his head. A true measure of his talents and contributions to jazz will take years to grade because of his professor's approach.

Discography

B-X x NO/147.
Alto Saxophone Improvisations 1979, Arista A2L 8602.
Anthony Braxton Solo (Milano) 1979 Vol. 1, Leo/Golden Years of New Jazz GY20.
Anthony Braxton/Derek Bailey, Royal Volume 1 Incus 43.
Anthony Braxton Trio and Duet, Sackville 3007.
Anthony Braxton Quartet: Live at Moers Festival, Ring Records 01010–11.
Anthony Braxton: Five Pieces 1975, Arista AL4064.
Anthony Braxton: The Montreux/Berlin Concerts, Arista AL 5002.
Anthony Braxton: Creative Orchestra Music 1976, RCA Bluebird 6576-2-RB.
Anthony Braxton/George Lewis Duo: Elements of Surprise, Moers Music 01036.
Anthony Braxton/Richard Teitelbaum: Time Zones, Black Lion BLCD760221.
Anthony Braxton with Muhal Richard Abrams: Duets, Aristra AL 4101.
Anthony Braxton/Evan Parker/Derek Bailey: Company 2, Incus 23.
Anthony Braxton & George Lewis: Donaueschingen (Duo) 1976, hatART 6150.
Anthony Braxton: Dortmund (Quartet) 1976, hatART 6075.
Anthony Braxton Quintet (Basel) 1977, hatOLOGY 545.
Anthony Braxton for Trio, Arista AB 4181.
Anthony Braxton Solo (Koln) 1978, Leo/Golden Years of New Jazz GY17.
Anthony Braxton Creative Orchestra (Köln) 1978, hatART 6171.
Anthony Braxton for Four Orchestras, Arista A3L 8900.
Anthony Braxton Performance (Quartet) 1979, hatART 6044.
Anthony Braxton featuring John Lindberg: Six Duets (1982) Cecma 0042.
Anthony Braxton Quartet (London) 1985, Leo CDLR 200/20.
Anthony Braxton Quartet (Birmingham) 1985, Leo CDLR 202/203.
Anthony Braxton Quartet (Coventry), Leo CDLR 204/205.
Anthony Braxton: Five Compositions (Quartet) 1986, Black Saint BSR 0106.

Anthony Braxton/Derek Bailey: Moment Precieux, Victo 02 Sound Aspects SAS 023.
Anthony Braxton/Gino Robair Duets, Music & Arts 1026.
Anthony Braxton: 19 (Solo) Compositions, 1988, New Albion NA 023.
Anthony Braxton Solo (London), Impetus 18818.
Anthony Braxton Ensemble (Victoriaville) 1988, Victo 07.
Anthony Braxton/Ensemble Braxtonia 2 Compositions (Järvenpää), Leo CDLR 233.
Anthony Braxton: Four Compositions (Solo, Duo and Trio), # 1–3 on hatART 6019.
Anthony Braxton Four Compositions (Solo, Duo and Trio), # 4 on hatART 16003.
Anthony Braxton & Ran Blake: A Memory of Vienna, hatOLOGY 505.
Andrew Voigt/Anthony Braxton: Kol Nidre, Sound Aspects SAS 031.
Anthony Braxton & Robert Schumann String Quartet, Sound Aspects SAS 00.
Anthony Braxton for Two Pianos, Arista AL 9559.
Anthony Braxton & Giorgio Gaslini: Four Pieces, Dischi Della Quercia Q28015.
Braxton/Bailey Live at Wigmor, Inner City IC 1041.
Composition No. 94 for Three Instrumentalists, Golden Years of New Jazz GY3.
Composition 98, hatART 1984.
Composition 96, Leo CDLR169.
Composition 113, SoundAspects SAS 003.
Creative Music Orchestra, Ring Records 01024/5/6.
Donna Lee, America 30AM6122.
Eight (+3) Tristano Compositions 1989 for Warne Marsh, # 1–12 as hatART 6052.
Eight (+3) Tristano Compositions 1989 for Warne Marsh, # 13–15 on hatART 16004.
Eugene, Black Saint 120137.
For Alto, Delmark DS-420/421.
Four Compositions, Denon YX-7506-ND.
Four Compositions (Solo, Duo and Trio) 1982/1988, hatART 6019.
Four Compositions (Quartet) 1983, Black Saint BSR0066.
If My Memory Serves Me Right, WestWind 004.
Max Roach/Anthony Braxton Birth and Rebirth, Black Saint BSR0024.
Neighbors with Anthony Braxton, GNM Vol. 3 120754.
News from the 70s, New Tone 7005.
New York Fall 1974, Arista AL 4032.
Open Aspects (Duo) 1982, hatART 6106.
Prag 1984 (Quartet Performance), Sound Aspects SAS 038.
Recital Paris '71, Futura 23.
Roscoe Mitchell Duets with Anthony Braxton, Sackville 3016.
Saxophone Improvisations Series F, America 30AM011/012.
Seven Compositions, Moers Music, 01066.
Seven Compositions (Trio), # 1–5 as hatART 6025.
Seven Compositions (Trio), # 6 on hatART 16003.
Seven Standards 1985, Volume I, Magenta 02003.
Seven Standards 1985, Volume II, Magenta 0205.
Six Compositions: Quartet, Antilles 422–848 585–2.
Six Compositions (Quartet) 1984, Black Saint BSR120086.
Six Monk's Compositions, Black Saint 120116–2.
Solo—Live at Moers Festival, Ring Records 01002.
This Time, BYG 529.347.
Three Compositions of New Jazz, Delmark DD 415.
The Complete Braxton, Arista/Freedom 1902. Freedom 40112/3.
Town Hall (Trio & Quintet) 1972, hatART 6119.
What's New in the Tradition, SteepleChase SCCD-37003.
Woody Shaw with Anthony Braxton: The Iron Men (+), Muse MR 5160.

Anthony Braxton/Marilyn Crispell, Duets Music & Arts 611.
2 Compositions (Ensemble) 1989/1991, hatART 6086.
Anthony Braxton with Peter Niklas Wilson: 8 Duets, Music & Arts 710.
2 Compositions (Ensemble), hatART 6086.
Willisau (Quartet), hatART 61001/2/3/4.
Anthony Braxton/Georg Gräwe Duo, Okkadisk OD12018.
Composition No. 165 (for 18 instruments), New Albion NA 050.
David Rosenboom/Anthony Braxton: Two Lines (+), Lovely Music 3071.
Anthony Braxton Quartet: Victoriaville, Victo 021.
Wesleyan (12 Altosolos), hatART 6128.
4 (Ensemble) Compositions, Black Saint.
Anthony Braxton with Mario Pavone: Nine Duets, Music & Arts 786.
Anthony Braxton & the Fred Simmons Trio: 9 Standards (Quartet), Leo CDLR 237/238.
Anthony Braxton/Evan Parker Duo (London), Leo CDLR 193.
12 Compositions: Live at Yoshi's, Music & Arts 835,
Anthony Braxton Quartet (Santa Cruz), hatART 6190.
Anthony Braxton: Charlie Parker Project, hatART 6160.
Anthony Braxton with Ted Reichman Duo, Music & Arts 848.
Anthony Braxton: Knitting Factory (Piano/Quartet) Vol. 1, Leo LRCD 222/223.
Anthony Braxton, Knitting Factory (Piano/Quartet) Vol. 2, Leo LRCD 297/298.
Anthony Braxton Composition 174, Leo CDLR 217.
Anthony Braxton & Richard Teitelbaum Duet: Live at Merkin Hall, Music & Arts 949.
Anthony Braxton Piano Quartet, Music & Arts 849.
Anthony Braxton Small Ensemble Music, Splasc(h) 801,
Abraham Adzinyah/Anthony Braxton Duo, Leo CDLR 228/229.
Anthony Braxton Composition 173, Black Saint 120166-2.
Anthony Braxton/Mario Pavone Quintet: Seven Standards, Knitting Factory Works KFW168.
Anthony Braxton/Brett Larner: 11 Compositions (Duo), Leo LRCD 244.
Anthony Braxton Piano Music (Notated) 1968–1988, hatART 6194.
Anthony Braxton with Joe Fonda: 10 Compositions (Duet), Konnex 5071.
Anthony Braxton: Four Compositions (Quartet), Braxton House BH-005.
Anthony Braxton Sextet (Istanbul), Braxton House BH-001.
Anthony Braxton Solo (Skopje), Braxton House BH-002.
Anthony Braxton Octet (New York), Braxton House BH-006.
Anthony Braxton Ensemble, Braxton House BH-007.
Anthony Braxton Solo Piano (Standards), No More 2.
Anthony Braxton Composition No. 102 for Orchestra &
Puppet Theatre, Braxton House BH-003.
Anthony Braxton 14 Compositions (Traditional), Leo CDLR 259.
Borah Bergman/Anthony Braxton/Peter Brötzmann: Eight By Three, Mixtery 1.
Anthony Braxton/Lauren Newton: Composition 192, Leo CDLR 251.
Anthony Braxton Tentet (New York) 1996, Composition 193. Braxton House BH-004.
Anthony Braxton Trillium R: Shala Fears for the Poor, Composition No. 162 for 9 Singers, 9 Instrumentalists and Orchestra, Braxton House BH-008.
Anthony Braxton Compositions 10 & 16 (+101), hat[now]ART 108.
Anthony Braxton Ninetet (Yoshi's) 1997 Vol. 1, Leo LR 343/344.
Anthony Braxton Ninetet (Yoshi's) 1997 Vol. 2, Leo LR 382/383.
Anthony Braxton: Two Compositions (Trio), Leo LR 367/368.
Anthony Braxton: Four Compositions (Washington, D.C.), Braxton House BH-009.

Kevin Norton Ensemble and Anthony Braxton for Guy Debord (in nine events), Barking Hoop BKH-001.
Anthony Braxton: Four Compositions (GTM), Delmark 544.
Anthony Braxton Composition N. 247, Leo CDLR 306.
Anthony Braxton/Brandon Evans Composition No. 249, Parallactic 27.
Brandon Evans/Anthony Braxton Elliptical Axis 15, Parallactic 28–30.
Anthony Braxton: Ten Compositions (Quartet) 2000, CIMP 225.
Anthony Braxton: Nine Compositions (Hill) 2000, CIMP 236.
Anthony Braxton & Scott Rosenberg: Compositions/Improvisations, Barely Auditable 222.
Anthony Braxton Composition No. 169 + (186 + 206 + 214), Leo 320/321.
Anthony Braxton with Alex Horwitz: Four Compositions (Duets), CIMP 235.
Anthony Braxton: Six Compositions (GTM), Rastascan BRD 050.
Anthony Braxton Eight Compositions (Quintet), CIMP 243.
Anthony Braxton Quartet: 8 Standards (Wesleyan), Barking Hoop BKH004.
Anthony Braxton/Taylor Ho Bynum: Duets, Innova 576.
Anthony Braxton Solo (NYC), Parallactic 53.
Wadada Leo Smith & Anthony Braxton: Organic Resonance, Pi Recordings PI06.

WITH CIRCLE

Early Circle, Blue Note CDP 784465-2.
Circle: Paris Concert, ECM 1018/19.

PART FOUR

Jazz Fusion

For more than six decades jazz remained mostly a pure form. Its progression developed not by incorporating other styles, but through internal evolution. However, in the 1960s that all changed. For the first time, the practitioners began to mix elements of soul, pop, rock, and country with a jazz base to create something different and exciting. As well, acoustic instruments were replaced with electric ones. Because of the melding of various musical styles and the amplification, this new direction was called fusion or electric jazz.

At the forefront of the jazz fusion school was Miles Davis, whose ability to unite swing, improvisation, and distinctive solos—all trademarks of unplugged jazz—with elements of rock and funk created a new stream. His two albums *In a Silent Way* and *Bitches Brew* were experiments in electric music. The departure from the traditional acoustic instruments caused an uproar in jazz circles.

In many ways, jazz fusion was a style developed by those who were not interested in pursuing the free jazz/avant-garde paths. One of the outstanding spokesmen against the aforementioned trend was Davis, who followed a different avenue than players such as Coltrane, Coleman, Braxton, Dolphy, Taylor and the rest of the cast.

Many would follow Davis's lead. Some of the major jazz fusion figures included bass players Ron Carter, Stanley Clarke, Alphonso Johnson, John Lee, Will Lee, Jaco Patorius, and Miroslav Vitous. The important brass men were Davis, Randy Brecker, Freddie Hubbard, and Chuck Mangione. On drums, Gerry Brown, Billy Cobham, Steve Gadd, Alphonse Mouzon, Narada Michael Walden, Lenny White and Tony Williams starred. On guitar, John Abercrombie, Joe Beck, George Benson, Philip Catherine, Larry Coryell, Al Di Meola, Steve Khan, Earl Klugh, John McLaughlin, Pat Martino, and Ralph Towner were the premier stylists. Brian Auger, Chick Corea, George Duke, Jan Hammer, Herbie Hancock, Bob James, Keith Jarrett, Patrice Rushen, Richard Tee, and Joe Zawinul rocked everyone with their groovy keyboard exploits. On percussion, Airto Moreira and

191

Ralph McDonald made their presence felt. The vibraphone players Roy Ayers, Gary Burton, and Mike Mainieri plugged in. Jean-Luc Ponty played electric violin to maximum effect. Gato Barbieri, Mike Brecker, Joe Farrell, John Klemmer, Ronnie Laws, David Liebman, Tom Scott, Wayne Shorter, and Grover Washington, Jr., added their woodwinds to the mix.

Those featured in this book are some of the brightest students of the jazz fusion school.

Wayne Shorter was a brilliant saxophone player but gained as much recognition for his abilities as composer, arranger, and producer. Along with Zawinul, he was a creative force behind Weather Report.

Herbie Hancock, another ex–Miles Davis sideman, created his own universe with his electronic gadgets. He was one of the founders of techno pop, techno funk, and other electric based musical styles.

Chick Corea was a prime keyboard player and one of the many ex–Miles Davis sidemen to go on and lead his own highly touted jazz fusion group, Return to Forever.

John McLaughlin, a British guitarist with deep roots in blues, rhythm and blues, and pop, formed his influential Mahavishnu Orchestra in the early 1970s. He also spent time in Davis's outfit.

Fusion guitarist Larry Coryell practically invented the style. His affiliation with rock figures proved his versatility.

Tony Williams was a powerhouse drummer and another discovery of Miles Davis. His untimely death in the late 1990s made everyone grateful that he had begun his professional career at a young age.

Billy Cobham was one of the definitive fusion drummers whose style was perfectly suited for the genre. He recorded with Miles Davis and was also a member of the Mahavishnu Orchestra.

Stanley Clarke was a good example of the modern jazz player. He was university educated and was equally adept at the electric and acoustic bass. He played in Return to Forever with Chick Corea.

Jaco Pastorius was an extraordinary bass player who took the instrument down the fertile avenues of his imagination. His best work can be heard on the records of others, including Joni Mitchell. He also played with Weather Report.

WAYNE SHORTER (1933–)

Ju Ju's Blues

The electric jazz era is one of the most interesting chapters in the history of the genre. As an art form the style changed the face of the music and explored dimensions that had been previously uncharted territory. Many artists emerged during the period to make significant contributions to the new style, including the man playing his Ju Ju's Blues. His name was Wayne Shorter.

Wayne Shorter was born on August 25, 1933, in Newark, New Jersey. One of his earliest musical influences was the street parties held in his Newark neighborhood as he grew up. The different cultures all championed their own folk sound and from a very young age he was exposed to the rhythms, harmonies, and melodies of world music. In many ways, his education was akin to someone growing up in New Orleans around the turn of the twentieth century. He also listened to the radio in order to expand his musical knowledge.

In an attempt to reproduce the music that was all around him, he picked up the clarinet in his teens. A year later, he acquired his first saxophone. Because of his excellent background, he was a walking encyclopedia of various styles that he carefully stored away for future reference. At first his attempts to emulate the sounds brought only frustration, but slowly he began to find his way.

He attended the High School of Music and Art in Newark. He performed with local bands, building up his proficiency on the tenor saxophone, and was enthralled with bop. He started to compose songs during his teens and refined his skills. This gradual self-improvement would enable him to write many classics for the various groups that he would play in. Music became the main focus of his life before he was twenty years old.

Shorter continued his musical education after high school in a variety of ways. He studied art and music theory at New York University, but it was the informal jam sessions that truly propelled his evolution. He majored in playing hooky to hear all the bop artists that were jamming nearby: Dizzy Gillespie, Charlie Parker, Kenny Clarke, Thelonious Monk, Max Roach, and Bud Powell among others. He frequented jazz venues to listen to the big bands of Stan Keaton, Woody Herman, who played bop, and Duke Ellington and other practitioners of the big band/swing style.

Once he had graduated from college with a degree in music education, it was time to utilize all of the theory and practical experiences he had accumulated to his advantage. But before he could do that he served two years in the army. Upon his return, he played in a few bands, and continued to compose as well as arrange songs.

His big break came in 1959 when he was asked to join Art Blakey's Jazz Messengers. During his stay in that celebrated group, Shorter contributed many classics, including "Lester Left Town," "Children of the Night," "This Is for Albert," and "Free for All." After five years with the great bebop drummer, Shorter joined the Miles Davis Quintet.

During his six years with Davis, Shorter matured as a musician and composer. He began to play the soprano saxophone and after long hours of solid practice boasted a strong command of the instrument. He also continued his songwriting, adding "E.S.P.," "Iris," "Orbits," "Footprints," "Dolores," "Limbo," "Vonetta," "Prince of Darkness," "Masqualero," "Nefertiti," "Fall," "Pinocchio," "Paraphernalia," and "Sanctuary" to his cannon. In a world where many jazz artists played one instrument properly, Shorter was a double threat, as well as a first-class arranger and composer. In 1970, Shorter left Davis to form Weather Report with Joe Zawinul.

Joe Zawinul was born on July 7, 1932, in Vienna, Austria, and grew up in Europe during the Second World War. He caught the fever listening to the Vienna folk music he heard in the streets and his parents singing at home. Later he enrolled at the local conservatory and furthered his education in college. He arrived in America in 1959 and played with Maynard Ferguson, Slide Hampton, Joe Williams, Dinah Washington and Cannonball Adderley for a stay of nine years. He also had a short stint in Miles Davis' outfit. Zawinul, the first musician to record jazz on a Fender Rhodes piano, also played the acoustic piano in Weather Report.

The experimental band that also included bassist Miroslav Vitous, percussionist Airto, and drummer Alphonse Mouzon created a jazz-rock sound that catapulted them to the heap of the fusion pile. Their music not only appealed to the jazz crowd; rock audiences also bought their albums and attended their concerts. The members of the group were implementing the lessons learned from their time spent with Miles Davis.

In 1976, Shorter left Weather Report to play in V.S.O.P., a reunion with fellow Davis alumni Tony Williams, Herbie Hancock, and Ron Carter. The group added trumpeter Freddie Hubbard (in place of Davis) to complete the quintet that toured and recorded. Shorter also contributed his talents on Steely Dan's *Aja* album, as well as Joni Mitchell's *Don Juan's Reckless Daughter*.

Shorter returned to Weather Report after his stint with V.S.O.P., but left the band again in the mid–1980s. After more than two decades as one of the leading lights in jazz, he fell on hard times and his career took a downward turn. Although he continued to record, none of his releases made a commercial or critical impact.

He disappeared from the scene in the late 1980s, but returned in the middle of the 1990s with his new band, High Life, featuring Rachel Z. on keyboards. Shorter, who had experimented with jazz structures from his earliest days, has not strayed from his vision in the last few years. Although not of all of his projects gained mainstream appeal, but they remained interesting because of his vast talents as musician, songwriter and arranger.

When not leading his own outfits, he has collaborated with a variety of artists, including Carlos Santana, and has held a reunion with his old cohorts from the V.S.O.P. project. The group performed a tribute for their deceased leader, Miles Davis. The sets were well received and proved that Shorter had not lost any of his fire or imagination. He continues to record and perform.

Wayne Shorter is a jazz traveler. He began his career playing hard bop as a member of Art Blakey's Jazz Messengers and moved on to play exciting electric jazz in the 1960s. He has made a large impact on the genre for his brilliant composition abilities. Although he has suffered some tough times, he has, for the most part, remained a prominent figure in the modern era.

He is one of the great tenor saxophonists of the past forty years. Although initially influenced by John Coltrane, he eventually developed his own individual style. His playing contained an unusual intensity and a rugged tone that was brash and exciting. However, on soprano, he employed a lighter touch with a more pleasing sound. This dual saxophone personality was yet another of the many weapons in his arsenal and is a tribute to his vast musical talents.

Although he has worked with a large number of artists, including Jimmie Merritt, Bobby Timmons, Curtis Fuller, Cedar Walton, Reggie Workman, Michael Cuscuna, Chick Corea, Joni Mitchell, Teo Macero, Jaco Pastorius and Airto Moreira, Shorter is best known for his work with Davis and as a member of Weather Report. It was with the latter that he displayed his delightful electric jazz fusion licks that made the band one of the best in that field. In any group situation, he was a definite asset because of the many dimensions he brought with him.

Also of major importance are his compositional skills. He contributed a great number of songs to every group he has ever been a part of, including the Jazz Messengers, the Miles Davis Quartet and Weather Report. Undoubtedly, his most productive period was with Davis. His creative genius was responsible for some of the Cool One's best songs, including "E.S.P.," "Pinocchio," "Nefertiti," "Sanctuary," "Footprints," "Fall" and "Prince of Darkness."

He was a prime influence on the young lions that emerged in the 1980s, particularly Branford Marsalis and his brother Wynton. Others who have been touched by the Shorter magic include Urszula Dudziak, Hal Galper, Carlos Garnett, Bennie Maupin, Roscoe Mitchell, Horace Arnold,

Steve Grossman, Onaje, Allan Gumbs, Azar Lawrence, Brian Jackson, Dave Liebman, and Kurt Elling. His group Weather Report had a far-reaching effect, spilling over jazz boundaries into the realms of rock, soul, and pop.

Shorter was a prime architect of the jazz fusion style. While many made significant contributions, including Davis, Hancock, Corea, McLaughlin, Tony Williams, Stanley Clarke, Ron Carter and a host of others, the talented double threat from New Jersey held a slight edge over everyone. His multi-faceted abilities enabled him reach a little deeper than his contemporaries.

Since he has accomplished much in his long, distinguished career, Shorter occupies a special place in jazz history. His prime years were the 1960s and 1970s, when he was at the forefront of activity. It was during this period that he established his legend and although he became less active in the past twenty years, there is no denying the important contributions from the man who gave us his Ju-Ju's blues.

Discography

Introducing Wayne Shorter, Vee-Jay VJ-3006.
Two Stars at Birdland, Roulette RB2.
Second Genesis, Vee-Jay VJS3057.
Wayning Moments, Vee-Jay VJ-3029.
Night Dreamer, Blue Note BLP-4173.
Ju-Ju, Blue Note BLP-4182.
Speak No Evil, Blue Note BLP-4194.
The Soothsayer, Blue Note CDP7-84443-2.
The Collector, Blue Note 3059.
The All Seeing Eye, Blue Note BLP-4219.
Adam's Apple, Blue Note BLP-4232.
Schizophrenia, Blue Note BLP-4297.
Super Nova, Blue Note 84332.
Moto Grosso Feio, Blue Note BN-LA014-G.
Odyssey of Iska, Blue Note, BST-84363.
Native Dancer, Columbia PC33418/CS 25DP-5305.
Atlantis, Columbia FC-40055/CS 32DP-277.
Phantom Navigator, Columbia FC-40373 CS 32DP-628.
Joy Ryder, Columbia FC44110/CS 32DP-5073.
High Life, Verve 314 529 224-2.
Free Form, Blue Note 84118.
Wayne Shorter, Crescendo 2-2075.
Shorter Moments, Blue Note 5009.
Search for the New Land, Blue Note 84169.
Some Other Stuff, Blue Note 84177.

WITH WEATHER REPORT
Weather Report, Columbia KC-30661.
Weather Report: Osslach Live, BASF49-21119-3/1-3.

I Sing the Body Electric, Columbia KC-31352.
Live in Tokyo, Columbia (Japan) SOPJ-12–13.
Sweetnighter, Columbia KC-32210.
Mysterious Traveler, (Columbia KC-32494.
Tale Spinnin', Columbia PC-33417.
Black Market, Columbia PC-34099.
Heavy Weather, Columbia PC-34418.
Mr. Gone, Columbia JC35358.
Weather Report: 8:30, Columbia PC2–36030.
Havana Jam / various artists, Columbia PC2 36053.
Havana Jam, II / various artists, Columbia PC2 36180.
Night Passage, Columbia JC-36793.
Procession, Columbia FC 38427.
Weather Report, Columbia FC-37616.
Sportin' Life, Columbia FC-38427.
Domino Theory, Columbia FC-39147.
This Is This, Columbia FC-40280.

HERBIE HANCOCK (1940–)

The Chameleon

The fusion of jazz with other musical styles requires a vast knowledge of harmonies, melodies, and rhythms. Also, a deep understanding of dynamics, textures, and space are essential, as well as excellent instrumental ability. One best jazz fusion musician who has been able to appeal to a cross-section of fans because he possesses all of the aforementioned qualities as well as an encyclopedic knowledge of musical styles is The Chameleon, Herbie Hancock.

Herbie Jeffrey Hancock was born on April 12, 1940, in Chicago, Illinois. He started taking piano lessons when he was seven and learned how to read music from the first instructor. His second teacher taught him the nuances of music. These two different methods served as the foundation for his approach to the piano. Hancock, who would make a large impact on jazz, was more interested in classical and gospel at this point in his development than other styles.

In high school, he met Don Goldberg, who had a large influence on him. Goldberg was much more advanced musically than Hancock and taught his new friend the dimensions of space and sound, among other things. At the time, the hot jazz sounds were the West Coast cool style and hard bop. Herbie was a student of both strains. He listened closely to what Chet Baker, Gerry Mulligan, Shorty Rogers, George Shearing, Art

Blakey, Max Roach, and Horace Silver were putting down. As well, he was paying close attention to the music that the cool one, Miles Davis, was creating.

His immersion in music was complete. He not only played, but also began to study theory and harmony while still in his teens. Hancock, a gifted student, learned quickly and already his understanding of jazz textures was far superior to many of the people he played with at the time that were his age and much older. To put it in perspective, if he would have displayed the same ability in sports, he would have been called a blue chip prospect.

Although there were many great jazz players in the mid–1950s that impressed him, it was Miles Davis that had the biggest impact on Hancock. As well, John Coltrane, who was in Davis's band, had a hand in shaping Herbie's final mature sound. Although he was playing gigs in various bands while in high school, he was not interested in a musical career at the time.

He enrolled at Iowa's Grinnell College and majored in engineering. Eventually he realized that his true calling was music and changed his major to music composition. It was also at this time that he formed a seventeen-piece band that he composed and arranged for. Despite attending college for four years, Hancock never graduated and left school to join Donald Byrd's outfit. He remained with Byrd for three years until 1963, when he joined his idol, Miles Davis.

During his tenure with the Cool One, Hancock grew tremendously as a musician in every aspect. After all, the informal classes that Professor Miles taught were the best school any young scholar could ever attend. The education received was equivalent to years of formal study in a credited institution of higher learning. It was during his stay in the great trumpeter's band that Hancock began to explore the dimensions possible with the electric piano.

In 1962, Hancock started his solo recording career on Blue Note and produced a series of highly influential albums, including *Takin' Off, My Point of View, Inventions and Dimensions, Empyrean Isles, Maiden Voyage, Speak Like a Child,* and *The Prisoner.* One of the songs from *Takin' Off,* "Watermelon Man," was a sizeable hit. He was one of the few artists able to enjoy a solo career while participating in one of the most influential groups of the period. In fact, the quintet consisting of Hancock, Davis, drummer Tony Williams, saxophonist Wayne Shorter, and bassist Ron Carter was considered the number one group on the circuit from 1963 to 1968. Some believe they were the greatest jazz outfit in the genre's history of more than 100 years.

After his departure from Davis's band, Hancock formed his own sextet. Their musical direction was sealed with the albums *Fat Albert Rotunda,*

Mwandishi, Crossings, and *Sextant.* He created electronic jazz-funk that would enjoy immense crossover success. Although primarily a jazz artist, he found himself performing in rock venues because of the immense appeal of his music.

In 1972, Hancock, searching for a change of scenery, moved to Los Angeles and disbanded his sextet. He re-formed a different version of his band and was determined to play funky, commercial music for the masses. At this point in his career he had paid enough dues to be able to play anything that he desired.

His subsequent album, *Headhunters,* featured the song "Chameleon," a huge hit that was played on rock, pop, R&B, jazz, and soul radio stations. A multi-talented songwriter, he also found time to write the scores to the films *Blow-Up* and *Death Wish,* as well as for the Bill Cosby's cartoon *Fat Albert.* By the mid–1970s, Hancock had found many different creative outlets in which to plug his vast abilities.

In 1976, a reunion with Miles Davis alumni resulted in a series of concerts and some recording dates. Ron Carter, Tony Williams, Wayne Shorter, Freddie Hubbard, and Hancock comprised one of the best modern jazz groups of the era. They called their outfit V.O.S.P. and played acoustic jazz fusion that was on the cutting edge. They broke up a couple of years later and reunited infrequently throughout the years.

At the beginning of the 1980s, Hancock had been a professional musician for twenty years and had created a spectacular body of music. However, he didn't rest on his laurels; he continued to set trends instead of following them. An intelligent artist, he took full advantage of the new MTV program to score a hit, "Rockit." The accompanying video was ahead of its time. At this point in his career, he began to experiment with electronic music on a regular basis and became one of the forefathers of the techno craze.

In the past twenty years he has toured and recorded regularly. He has also continued to write film scores, including *Ghostbusters.* The hypnotic ten-minute-plus theme song paved the way for the movie's blockbuster success. Later a cartoon would be adapted from the movie and the intro song played in millions of living rooms all over the world further spreading his genius. Almost twenty years later it remains one of the most instantly recognizable movie soundtracks ever created.

An exciting live artist, Hancock became a regular on the festival circuit, playing with a host of other jazz artists—the new young lions like Wynton Marsalis, Marcus Roberts, Kenny Kirkland, Mart Whitfield, Keith Eubanks, Jeff "Tain" Watts and Joey DeFrancesco, to name a few. His concerts were extravaganzas in electronic music and experiments in the vast field of sound. He performed this wild, electric magic as a solo artist as well as within a group context.

He also continued to release albums that combined elements of contemporary jazz, pop, rock, soul, and funk. He left Columbia after a fifteen-year association and signed with Verve without missing a beat. No matter the label, Hancock continued to produce and record exciting, pacesetting jazz fusion CDs as well as experiments in electronic sound.

He also formed a musical friendship with Foday Musa Suso and they recorded the album *Africa* together. One of the outstanding jazz albums of the 1980s, it demonstrated Hancock's taste for exploring new directions in electronic sound once again and kept his name current in jazz circles. He continues his interest in cutting edge gadgetry as host of the weekly BET Jazz program *Future Wave*. He remains one of the giants of contemporary jazz and continues to record and perform.

Herbie Hancock is a jazz chameleon. Throughout his career he has made important contributions to every jazz movement he has participated in. As a young man he was strictly an acoustic player, then later in the 1960s he began to experiment with electric keyboards. His flair for discovering new dimensions in electronic sound remained the vibrant element of his artistry. However, he returned to an acoustic format in the 1980s with the arrival of the young lions and became an important figure in yet another era.

Hancock is one of the true wizards of piano, keyboard and synthesizer. His innovations on electric keyboard propelled Miles Davis into the forefront of the electric rock–jazz fusion scene. When Hancock broke away from his mentor he continued to create astonishing electronic music that had enough commercial appeal to make him one of the leaders of the techno-funk era. He has remained a force on a number of musical fronts and has reached millions with his creative abilities.

It is a tribute to Hancock's multi-faceted dimensions that he was able to switch from acoustic piano to Fender Rhodes electric piano and Hohner clavinet with ease and without changing his style significantly. But he took the electric experiment further than anyone else with his electronic gadgets, computers, and other assorted inventions. He was to the jazz synthesizer what Jimi Hendrix was to the electric guitar in the rock-blues genre.

Because of his talent and abilities, forthright vision, and controversial attitude, it is not surprising that Hancock developed a large following. Some of his disciples include Joe Bonner, George Cables, George Duke, Adam Makowicz, Tom "Bones" Malone, Bob Mintzer, Hilton Ruiz, Collin Walcott, Larry Willis, Prince, Mickey Tucker, Mike LeDonne, Matthew Shipp, Brian Jackson, Jeff "Tain" Watts, Steve Gadd, Carl Craig, Kirk Degiorgio, and Wynton Marsalis. No matter the era or the style of music that dominated the scene, Hancock was usually in the midst of the action.

He gave the world an entire package of strange and wonderful classics, including "Watermelon Man," "Dolphin Dance," "Rock-It," "The Maze," "Blind Man," "The Omen," "Sorcerer," "Madness," "Riot," "Fat Mama," "Ostinato," "Mwandishi," "Hidden Shadows," "Chameleon," and "Black Byrd," among others. The songs represent nearly every major musical movement and trend of the past forty years. The recording studio was always like a laboratory for him, where like a brilliant scientist he created something new and strange from his vast knowledge of alchemist musical elements.

Herbie Hancock has always been a controversial figure. It is this tension that surrounds him that has appealed to fans for the past four decades. He is a bold adventurer and not afraid to try a new path. His versatility has allowed him to create a vast body of legendary electronic music during his illustrious career. The Chameleon remains a vital force in modern music.

Discography

Adam's Apple, Blue Note 84232.
Takin' Off, Blue Note 84109.
My Point of View, Blue Note 84126.
Inventions and Dimensions, Blue Note 84147.
Empyrean Isles, Blue Note 84175.
Maiden Voyage, Blue Note 84195.
Speak Like a Child, Blue Note 84729.
The Prisoner, Blue Note 84312.
Fat Albert Rotunda, Warner 1834.
Crossings, Warner 2617.
Sextant, Columbia 32212.
Head Hunters, Columbia 32731.
Thrust, Columbia 32965.
In Concert, Vol. 2 [live], CTI 6049.
Love Me by Name, A&M 4565
Man-Child, Columbia 33812.
Secrets, Columbia 34820.
V.S.O.P.: The Quintet, Columbia 34976.
Death Wish (movie soundtrack), Columbia 33169.
Best of Herbie Hancock, Vol. 1, Blue Note 89907.
Contours, Blue Note 84206.
Free Form, Blue Note 84118.
Happenings, Blue Note 84231.
Herbie Hancock, Blue Note LA399-H2.
Piano Giants, Prestige 24052.
Succotash, Blue Note La-152-G.
Traces, Up Front/Spingboard 194.
Treasure Chest, Warner Bros. 2W S 2807.
Una Mas, Blue Note 84127.
Future Shock, Legacy Records 65962.
Gershwin's World, Verve 557 797.

Headhunters, Legacy Records 65123.
Best Of Herbie Hancock (Blue Note Years), Blue Note Records 91142.
Blow-Up (Soundtrack), Rhino Movie Music 72527.
Cantaloupe Island, Blue Note Records 29331.
Dedication, Legacy Records 65461.
Dis Is Da Drum, Mercury 522 681.
Feets Don't Fail Me Now, Columbia 35764.
Future Shock, Legacy Records 65962.
Greatest Hits, Columbia 36309.
In Concert, Legacy Records 65463.
Inventions and Dimensions, Blue Note Records 84147.
Jammin' with Herbie, Prime Kutz 2112.
Jammin' with Herbie Hancock, Collectables 6134.
Mwandishi—The Complete Warner Bros., Warner Archives 45732.
Perfect Machine, Columbia 65960.
Sound-System, Columbia 65961.
Tempest In, Legacy Records 65465.
The Best of Herbie Hancock: The Hits, Legacy Records 65963.
The Complete Blue Note Sixties Sessions, Blue Note Records 95569.
The New Standard, Verve 529 584.
The Piano, Legacy Records 65458.
The Prisoner, Blue Note Records 46845.
Trio '77, Legacy Records 65464=20.
Dance Singles, SONY SRCS-7542.
Dancin Grooves, COLUM SRCS-8856.
Flood, SONY SRCS-9341.
Lite Me Up, SONY COL4865732.
Monster, SONY COL4865712.
Mr. Funk, SONY COL4927862.
Mr. Hands, SONY COL4712402.
Riot, BLUEN TOCJ-66021.

―――――――――

CHICK COREA (1941–)

Man on a Mission

Jazz musicians have always seemed to have something to prove, particularly those in the last half of the twentieth century. Perhaps it is because they were exploring new territory and trying to convince the old guard, critics, and fans that the path they were following was a vital one. Whatever the reason, it resulted in some very interesting and incredible music. In the jazz fusion era there seemed to be one person determined to unite jazz with other elements successfully; he was truly a man on a mission. His name was Chick Corea.

Chick Corea was born Armando Anthony Corea on June 12, 1941, in

Chelsea, Massachusetts. He came from a musical family; his father was a jazz trumpeter, bassist, composer, and arranger. Chick began his formal studies when he was four years old and developed nicely under the tutelage of his father, discovering one of the most important lessons any musician could ever learn: that music was fun.

Aside from his idolized father, his first important influence was the classical music that gave him a strong foundation. He studied piano for a few years with a classical pianist from the Boston area and developed a taste for all the old masters like Bach, Beethoven, Mozart, Bartok, Stravinsky, Scarlatti, and Chopin. At this point in his development there was a very good chance that he would become another Tchaikovsky.

His greatest lessons occurred while touring with his father around the Boston and New England areas. These early concerts enabled him to advance far ahead of his peers, as many were not exposed to this kind of musical "education." The experience of performing before a live crowd at such an early age would prove very beneficial later in his career.

Although he loved the great composers, in his teens he began to listen to the beboppers, particularly Dizzy and Bird. Even though they were horn players, Corea was a keen enough student of music to realize their genius. He was also amazed at the power display of Bud Powell, and the mood spaces in the music of Thelonious Monk. Later on he would cite Horace Silver, the hard bop artist, as one of his favorite piano players and main idols.

In high school, like most normal teenagers interested in music, Corea played in a variety of neighborhood bands. He expanded his listening tastes to include rock, blues, soul, country and Latin rhythms, an element that would eventually become an important part of his unique sound. His ability and desire to keep an open mind to all possibilities accelerated his development and enhanced his encyclopedic knowledge of music.

In 1959, upon graduation, he was poised to make his mark on the world. He moved to New York City to attend Columbia University, but left before the end of the first semester. He later enrolled in the prestigious Juilliard but grew disenchanted with the courses that were offered there. Instead, he decided to pursue the music that he wanted to play through practical rather than scholastic avenues.

He paid his dues in bands with Mongo Santamaria and Willie Bobo. He served later apprenticeships in the groups of Herbie Mann, Blue Mitchell, and Stan Getz. As a musician he was stretching out, honing his skills and learning much from others. A stint with the great vocalist Sarah Vaughan was another name to add to his increasingly impressive resume. The Stan Getz Band was arguably the best group that Corea had been up to that point; then he joined the Miles Davis outfit.

In 1968, Davis was entering his electric phase. Corea, who had been mostly an acoustic player, was forced to explore the world of the electric piano. It allowed him to expand his horizons and soon he was hammering away at an electric Fender Rhodes piano. He would play on the *Bitches Brew* sessions, and record eight albums altogether while a member of Davis' quartet. The veteran jazz trumpeter was instrumental in helping the young pianist acquire the right attitude and confidence to head his own outfit.

Corea left Davis and formed a group called Circle with bass player Dave Holland, drummer Barry Altschul, and saxophonist Anthony Braxton. They recorded a couple of albums but after only a year together broke up. As a solo artist he now had the freedom to explore different musical territories without having to comprise his vision.

His next project was Return to Forever, a jazz fusion group. This enabled him to create the type of music that he had wanted to for some time, combining his love of various styles. By this time he had mastered an entire array of different keyboards, including acoustic and electric piano as well as synthesizer. He had also grown as a composer and arranger.

Despite the many personnel changes Return to Forever endured throughout their lifespan, they still managed to become one of the leading jazz fusion groups of the 1970s. At various times, the lineup included bassist Stanley Clarke, reedman Joe Farrell, percussionist Airto, singer Flora Purim, drummer Lenny White, and guitarist Al Di Meola. They were able to combine the improvisation of jazz with the hard cast of rock. The driving impulse of the band was the leader's layered, multi-dimensional keyboards. In the era of electric jazz, Return to Forever was one of its main exponents.

After the breakup of his trendsetting group, Corea teamed up with another luminary of the period, Herbie Hancock, in a series of piano duets. They toured the United States and Europe entertaining crowds with their brand of electronic music. The dynamic chemistry between the two keyboard players gave their sound a raw edge seldom heard in jazz before. Both were highly respected composers who had made a large impact throughout their respective careers and the combination of their talent, their vast musical knowledge and showmanship made for a very interesting listening adventure.

Apart from his duets with Hancock, Corea remained busy with several different projects, including time spent in various groups with Michael Brecker, Miroslav Vitous, and Roy Haynes, among others. He also wrote a monthly column for *Contemporary Keyboard*. Since he was so well respected in the music world, he was considered one of the main keyboard players. However, he was beginning to grow stale and needed to rejuvenate his musical vision.

He began a new phase of his long career in the 1980s when he resurfaced with a project called the Electric Band. The group consisted of bassist John Patitucci, guitarist Frank Gambale, saxophonist Eric Marienthal, and drummer Dave Weckl. He would also create the Akoustic Trio with Patitucci and Weckl in order to explore another side of his multifaceted musical personality. Despite the departure of the highly regarded Patitucci and other lineup changes, Corea was able to keep the group intact, and remained one of the leaders of creative jazz. He also participated in many side projects, including all-star touring packages.

In the 1990s he continued to create great jazz. He formed a band called Origin that recorded on Stretch, a company that he established with his manager in the early part of the decade. Bob Berg, John Patitucci, Eddie Gomez and Robben Ford were some of the first artists to record for the label. Corea also collaborated with Gary Burton, the London Symphony Orchestra and the St. Paul Chamber Orchestra. He continues to record and perform.

Chick Corea is a jazz experimenter. Throughout his forty-year career, he has stretched his musical boundaries with each new project. His contribution to the jazz fusion style is immeasurable, but has also dabbled in avant-garde, classical and new age sound. He is a wizard of the keyboards—acoustic and electric. He possesses a wide range of weapons with the ability to play energetic, fierce chords or bouncy blues rhythms, and to rock with the hardest all the while displaying a definite artistic touch.

Corea stands out on his own, despite the fact that throughout much of his career he has shared the spotlight with other noted keyboard players like Herbie Hancock, Keith Jarrett, Joe Zawinul, Gary Burton, Joe Bonner, Michel Camilo, Bobby Enriquez, John Hicks, and Bennie Green. Along with Hancock, Jarrett, and Zawinul, he was at the forefront of the jazz fusion scene. He made as large an impact as anybody else, and in many cases an even stronger mark.

He has had a large influence on a number of keyboard players for his acoustic as well as his electric work. A partial list includes The Dixie Dregs, Richie Beirach, Hal Galper, Frank Gambale, Horace Arnold, David Sancious, Abraham Burton, Gerry Niewood, and Melon Baller. Corea's influence also spilled over into other areas and he left his stamp on the playing of Keith Emerson, Lucky Peterson, and others of the rock-blues fraternity.

Corea is a superb bandleader and has worked with a number of important jazz figures including Wayne Shorter, Steve Gadd, John Patitucci, Grady Tate, Ron Moss, Tony Williams and Dave Weckl to name a few. He is also credited as a founding member of Return to Forever, Circle, Electric Band, and Akoustic Trio. Always willing to experiment, he has ventured down various paths without ever losing his focus or identity.

The story of Chick Corea is one of talent, diversity, enthusiasm, leadership and perseverance. A devout Scientologist, his music has always seemed destined to serve a higher purpose than that of simple entertainment for the masses. His work is a sacred effort from the man who has always been on a mission to free the world from the shackles it has imposed on itself.

Discography

Tones for Joan, Vortex 2004.
Now He Sings, Now He Sobs, Solid State SS 18039.
Song of Singing, Blue Note LA 472-H2.
Piano Improvisations, Vol. 1, Polydor ECM 1014.
Piano Improvisations, Vol. 2, Polydor ECM 1020.
Circling In, Blue Note BST 84353.
A.R.C., ECM 1009.
Circle, Paris Concert, ECM 1018.
Circle, Paris Concert, ECM 1019.
Inner Space, Atlantic SD 2–305.
Crystal Silence, ECM 1024.
Chick Corea, Blue Note LA 395-H2–0798.
The Leprechaun, Polydor PD 6062.
My Spanish Heart, Polydor PD 2–9003.
Bliss, Muse 5011.
Mad Hatter, Polydor 1–16130.
Originals: Solo Piano Part One, Stretch Records 9029.
Standards: Solo Piano Part Two, Stretch Records 9028.
Children's Songs, ECM Records 815 680.
ECM Works, ECM Records 20–20.
Early Days, Laserlight 17082.
Expressions, GRP Records 9774.
Friends, Polydor 849 071.
Music Forever & Beyond, GRP Records 59819.
Sundance, Beast Records 1288.
Tap Step, Stretch Records 9006.
The Beginning, Laserlight 17083.
The Best of Chick Corea, Blue Note Records 89282.
Three Quartets, Stretch Records 9002.
Touchstone, Stretch Records 9003.
Trio Music Live In Europe, ECM Records 827 769.
Circle: Live In Germany, UNI MVCR-237.
Circle 2: Gathering, UNI MVCR-238.
Gold Collection, RETRO R2CD40–28.
Live From the Country Club, STR MVCR-243.
Solo Piano (From Nothing), UNI MVCR-244.
Solo Piano: Compositions, MCA MVCL-24023.
Solo Piano: Standards, MCA MVCL-24024.
Three Quartets, STRET MVCL-17003.
Tones For Joan's Bones, ATLAN 8122753522.

WITH RETURN TO FOREVER

Light As A Feather, Polydor PD 5525.
Hymn of the Seventh Galaxy, Polydor PD 5536.
Where Have I Known You Before, Polydor PD 6509.
No Mystery, Polydor PD 6512.
The Romantic Warrior, Columbia PC 34076.
Best of Return to Forever, Columbia 36359.
Musicmagic, Columbia 34682.
Return to Forever, ECM Records 811 978-20.

JOHN MCLAUGHLIN (1942–)

Mahavishnu Blues

Since the innovator Charlie Christian burst upon the scene in the 1930s with his wild-eyed, electric guitar licks, the instrument has developed a more prominent role in jazz. With the fusion of the genre to other styles—particularly rock—the amplified sound became an essential element. There have been many remarkable electric players, but one talented individual wrote his own interesting chapter with his unique Mahavishnu Blues. His name is John McLaughlin.

John McLaughlin was born on January 4, 1942, in Yorkshire, England. When he was seven he was struck by the beauty of classical music and like many curious children he wanted to recreate that sound. He began to play piano shortly thereafter and then at the age of twelve he picked up the guitar for the first time. Initially influenced by classical music, McLaughlin expanded his tastes to include blues, rhythm and blues, jazz, and pop. His first guitar hero was the exotic Django Reinhardt. Later he discovered Christian, trumpeter Miles Davis and saxophonist John Coltrane.

Primarily a self-taught musician, McLaughlin eventually took some guitar lessons when he was in his teens. It was also around this time that a musical revolution was taking England by storm. The records of the first generation of American rock and rollers Elvis Presley, Chuck Berry, Buddy Holly, and others had trickled across the Atlantic. A tour by Muddy Waters and his band in the late 1950s also made a lasting impact. McLaughlin soaked up all of these sounds with eagerness.

By the early 1960s, R&B was the new musical trend in England. Every aspiring musician who wanted to make it big in the music world based their craft in blues. McLaughlin hung around the Ealing Club and London Marquee Square, both blues venues that Jack Bruce, Brian Jones, Ginger

Baker, Mick Jagger, Jimmy Page and Eric Clapton, among others, frequented with regularity. All in attendance were keen blues scholars. Eventually, McLaughlin would play with the Graham Bond Organization, as well as Georgie Fame and Brian Auger.

In the mid–1960s, McLaughlin, baritonist John Surman, and bassist Dave Holland formed a group whose sound was based more on free jazz than R&B. The band recorded *Extrapolation* and although the album was not a great commercial success, it did gain the attention of many in the business, including Tony Williams, who called for McLaughlin to come to America.

McLaughlin arrived in the United States in 1969 and immediately joined Williams's band, Lifetime. He appeared on two of the group's albums, *Emergency* and *Turn it Over.* Williams, who had been part of the Miles Davis Quintet, introduced the great jazz trumpeter to McLaughlin. It was this meeting that would later result in the guitarist taking part in two seminal Davis albums, *Bitches Brew* and *In a Silent Way.* As well, he found time to record another solo effort called *Devotion* that included the fine earthy drum work of Buddy Miles.

During this period many musicians developed an interest in Indian teachings and music initially inspired by the Beatles. McLaughlin was a firm disciple of the ways of Sri Chinmoy and this seriously altered his musical vision. Later, Carlos Santana would also follow the teachings of the guru. It was during this period that McLaughlin adopted the name Mahavishnu.

In 1971, McLaughlin formed the Mahavishnu Orchestra with bassist Rick Laird, keyboard player Jan Hammer, vocalist Jerry Goodman, and drummer Billy Cobham. They wove elements of Indian music and rock with jazz to create a totally unique sound. McLaughlin played a double-barreled guitar that added further layers to their fusion sound. The group was one of the most admired innovators on the scene.

The band recorded *Inner Mounting Flame* for Columbia and set down the basic foundation of what people could expect from this experimental outfit. The collective ensemble of noted virtuosos, the Mahavishnu Orchestra, created a wall of sound that featured more personal adventures than a cohesive front. Although their output seemed confusing at times, it was interesting for the average listener. They delivered fine examples of their musical philosophy on the recordings *Birds of Fire* and *Between Nothingness and Eternity.* They spawned many imitators that attempted to duplicate the group's style but were unable to do so.

Unfortunately, after the third album, Jan Hammer and Billy Cobham left the group to pursue solo careers. Hammer would eventually hook up with Jeff Beck and record some interesting jazz-rock fusion albums in the latter part of the 1970s. Meanwhile, McLaughlin retooled the group, adding Jean-Luc Ponty, the French electric violinist, drummer Michael Walden, bassist Ralphe Armstrong, keyboardist-vocalist Gayle Moran, and a horn section comprised of Steve Frankovitch and Bob Knapp. It was this second version of the Mahavishnu group that recorded *Apocalypse* featuring the London Symphony Orchestra.

Although the group held much promise and did record *Visions of the Emerald Beyond* in 1975, after the album *Inner Worlds,* McLaughlin broke up the band. He then formed an alliance with an acoustic Indian group called Shakti. They collaborated on the albums *Shakti* and *A Handful of Beauty,* which did much to restore the guitarist's fading career. The unique fusion of jazz, Indian music, rock, blues, and a touch of soul were like nothing heard at the time.

Despite producing a totally individual sound, McLaughlin, a restless musician, ended the experiment after only two studio albums with Shakti. He then formed a new group called the One Truth Band, with Stu Goldberg on keyboards, Woodrow Theus on drums, Tom Stevens on bass, and L. Shankar on violin. However, like many of his previous projects, the One Truth Band was a short-lived adventure.

Throughout the 1980s and 1990s, McLaughlin participated in many different jazz outfits that featured his brilliant electric and acoustic guitar playing. He played in a trio with Al Di Meola and Paco De Lucia and together they recorded the masterful *Passion, Grace, and Fire.* He also guested on a couple of Miles Davis records. He even re-formed the Mahavishnu Orchestra for a brief spell with famed saxophonist Bill Evans.

In 1993, he toured with organist Joey DeFrancesco and drummer Dennis Chambers. A later album featured the hurricane drumming of free jazz stalwart Elvin Jones, as well as the cool tones of DeFrancesco. Later in the decade, McLaughlin also recorded many interesting solo albums for the Verve label, including a tribute to Bill Evans called *Time Remembered: John McLaughlin Plays Bill Evans.*

Because of his constant shift in musical tastes, there is no telling what McLaughlin will offer up to the public in the future. But it is a safe bet that he will remain active as a performer and recording, artist blazing his own path in the jazz fusion realm.

John McLaughlin is a genuine jazz guitar ace. From the very beginning in the 1960s' R&B craze that swept through London throughout his forty-year career, he has proven his mettle with his six-string abilities. His time signatures, his blisteringly fast ever-ascending runs, his tasty yet elusive harmonies and his razor-sharp rhythmic patterns that are part of their own universal dimensions have enabled him to write his own chapter in jazz history.

To understand how McLaughlin achieved his unique sound, it is best to investigate his influences. Interestingly enough, they are split evenly between blues guitarists like the rural acoustic player Big Bill Broonzy and the electric Mojo Man Muddy Waters. The magic Django Reinhardt created is an important source. Like so many of McLaughlin's generation, Miles Davis also had a large part in the shaping of his sound. Barney Kessel, the definitive bop guitarist, makes the list, as does Tad Farlow, who debuted as a bebop player but became known as a solid practitioner of the cool jazz school. As well, the great sitar player Ravi Shankar encouraged McLaughlin's interest in world music.

In turn, McLaughlin had an influence on a wide range of guitarists, including Steve Kindler, Eric Johnson, Steve Morse, Joe Satriani, Steve Vai, John Abercrombie, Philip Catherine, David Sancious, Egberto Gismonti, Kevin Eubanks, Vernon Reid, Niacin Richard, and Leo Johnson. The cross section of musicians that followed the path he blazed is an indication of his versatility. His contribution to the genre is a definite study book for all aspiring six-string gunslingers, no matter the style.

He remains prominent for many of his past accomplishments. In the late 1960s, at a time when Eric Clapton, Jimi Hendrix, Jimmy Page, Jeff Beck and Duane Allman were the top names in guitar rock-blues, McLaughlin's name was often added to this incredible list. Undoubtedly, he was the best jazz guitarist in England during the 1960s and into the 1970s.

McLaughlin will forever be remembered as the leader of the Mahavishnu Orchestra, one of the founding groups of jazz-rock in the 1970s, and certainly one of the best. Although the last twenty years have not been as commercially successful for him, it is not a deterrent of his music. He remains a giant of jazz guitar with his Mahavishnu blues.

Discography

Extrapolation, Polydor 5510.
My Goals Beyond, Douglas 6003.
Devotion, Columbia 32034.
The Heart of Things, Verve 539 153.
The Heart of Things: Live in Paris, Verve 543 536
After the Rain, Verve 527 467.
Electric Guitarist, Legacy Records 46110.
Plays Bill Evans: Time Remembered, Verve 519 861.
The Promise, Verve 529 828.
Belo Horizonte, WEA 2292570012.
Collection, CONNO VSOPCD279.
Music Spoken Here, WEA 0630171572.
Tokyo Live, POLYG POCJ-1220.

Love, Devotion and Surrender, Columbia 32034.
Johnny McLaughlin: Electric Guitarist, Columbia 35326.

WITH THE MAHAVISHNU ORCHESTRA
Inner Mounting Flame, Columbia 31067.
Bird of Fire, Columbia 31996.
Between Nothingness and Eternity, Columbia 32766.
Apocalypse, Columbia 32957.
Visions of the Emerald Beyond, Columbia 33411.
Inner Worlds, Columbia 33908.

WITH SHAKTI
Shakti with John McLaughlin, Columbia 34162.
Natural Elements, Columbia 34980.
A Handful of Beauty, Columbia 34372.

LARRY CORYELL (1943–)
The Electric Jazz Warrior

The Texas guitar legacy boasts many heroes. Blind Lemon Jefferson, Aaron "T-Bone" Walker, Lightnin' Hopkins, Freddie King, Charlie Christian, Johnny "Guitar" Watson, Billy Gibbons, Johnny Winter, and the Vaughan Brothers are just some of the great six-string gunslingers from the Lone Star State. From a jazz perspective, Charlie Christian is considered the most important guitarist in the history of the genre. Another axe man to emerge from Texas to add to the list is known as the Electric Jazz Warrior, Larry Coryell.

Larry Coryell was born April 2, 1943, in Galveston. Although he boasts an authentic Lone Star State birth certificate, Coryell cut his musical teeth in the state of Washington, after his family moved there when he was seven. After a few brief piano lessons, he switched to guitar. Although he did take some lessons in his teens, he was mostly self-taught.

Coryell soaked up different genres of music, including country, jazz, rock, and blues, incorporating it into his own developing style. One of his first musical heroes was Chet Atkins, the country fingerpicking legend who amazed everyone with his blinding speed and technique. Although considered primarily a country artist, Atkins would make an impact on numerous rock, blues and jazz guitarists. By the time he was sixteen, Coryell was in a high school band jamming on popular songs of the day.

Although he loved music, Coryell majored in journalism at the University of Washington. Eventually, he realized that music was his true calling and continued to explore all avenues. He was enamored with the sounds of non-string players like trumpeter Dizzy Gillespie, saxophonists Charlie Parker, and John Coltrane. He practiced constantly to hone his skills and also began to write music. In 1965, he moved to New York.

When he arrived in the Big Apple, he discovered the music scene was divided along generational lines between the traditional guard and the new breed. Many of the jazz musicians based there were from the old school and didn't have much respect for the young upstarts. But the music of Bob Dylan and the Beatles had to be taken seriously. Coryell, instead of getting in any kind of petty arguments over the old versus the new, simply soaked up all that he could while continuing to sharpen his axe.

He thrived in New York City, hanging around Greenwich Village and jamming with dozens of folk, blues, jazz, and rock acts. A few months after his arrival he joined Chico Hamilton's band, replacing legendary Gabor Szabo, who by this time had developed a serious heroin addiction. It was with Hamilton that Coryell made his recording debut, adding his distinct guitar touch to the session that resulted in the album *The Dealer*.

Coryell soon left Hamilton's band and joined forces with Chip Baker, Jim Pepper, Chris Hill and Bobby Moses in an outfit called the Free Spirits. The group, a few years ahead of their time, attempted to successfully fuse jazz with rock. The band's album *Out of Sight and Sound* was an interesting adventure that featured some of the slickest jazz-rock guitar licks heard at that time. Despite their innovations, the band broke up a year after its inception.

Coryell moved on to join Gary Burton's combo. He began to receive the attention that he deserved as one of the new players on the jazz scene with his blues-drenched, wild electric rock-jazz guitar sound. He had managed to bring all the styles together into one cohesive attack that placed him at the forefront of the jazz fusion scene. He added to his burgeoning reputation when he played on flutist Herbie Mann's seminal *Memphis Underground* offering.

Coryell also played and toured briefly with bassist Jack Bruce, drummer Mitch Mitchell, and Mike Mandel. Bruce, who had been with Cream, featuring Eric Clapton, and Mitch Mitchell, who had formed one half of the rhythm section of the Jimi Hendrix Experience, were rock musicians. It was a special thrill for Coryell to play with Mitchell since Hendrix had played such a vital part in the shaping of his overall development. Like every other guitarist, he was compared to the great Seattle guitarist. While he definitely added some of the Hendrix guitar vocabulary to his own dictionary of sounds, Coryell possessed his own distinct style.

In 1969, Coryell put together his first band, Foreplay, with Mandel and Steve Marcus. For the next six years he would be involved in his solo projects as well as that of the band. Foreplay would evolve into the Eleventh House. The lineup included the great drummer Alphonse Mouzon, among others. Despite achieving success on some of their earliest albums, including *Introducing the Eleventh House, At the Village Gate, Level One, Aspects,* and *Spaces,* the group suffered because of a true lack of direction.

In 1975, after building up a reputation as one of the premiere electric jazz guitarists, Coryell made an about face and pulled the plug. His first acoustic album, *The Lion and the Ram,* proved to be a satisfying project. The change stunned some listeners, but he was comfortable creating music that he heard, instead of what he was told to play. It was also around this time that he broke up the band Eleventh House.

In the latter part of the 1970s, he was very busy touring and recording albums as a solo artist, as well as in a small group context. Many of his bandmates were fellow guitar players, including Philip Catherine and Steve Khan. He also teamed up with John McLaughlin, John Scofield and Joe Beck. Around this time Coryell became a part-time guitar teacher when he wasn't on the road or in the studio. He even became a contributing writer to *Guitar Player* magazine.

In the 1980s, Coryell took part in many recordings, including one with McLaughlin and Paco Delucia. He participated in an all-star jam that included five guitar players—Larry Carlton, John Abercrombie, John Scofield and Tad Farlow. He also worked with a number of jazz legends, notably Charles Mingus, and Stephane Grappelli, the violinist who played with the great Django Reinhardt. Once again, Coryell was able to learn from someone who had played with one of his idols.

Coryell has remained an important name in music circles, even if some of the music he has recorded in the past ten years was considered non-jazz. A talented individual who can glide from one style to another with relative ease, he continues to explore musical ideas that suit his taste. A terrific guitarist who is beyond category, Coryell will forever be linked to the jazz-rock era despite his approach to different styles in the past two decades. He continues to record and perform.

Larry Coryell is one of the most famous names in modern jazz and has carved a special place for himself with his distinct guitar sound. He was a pioneer of the jazz-rock movement and was able to successfully merge the elements of jazz with other musical styles. His celebrity continues even today after a forty-year career that has seen its fair share of good times and bad times.

Coryell is a chameleon on the guitar. He possesses a distinctive touch that is unique. But more importantly, he has been comfortable in every style of music including jazz, blues, rock, and even country. His ability to play the most heavy-laden electric jazz with emotional note bends and a feeling of pure power are part of his legend. He is also able to cruise effortlessly through delicate passages, taking the listener away on a dreamy voyage.

Coryell burst upon the scene with his edgy guitar sound that was more akin to the blues cutting contests than to jazz. Along with Charlie Christian, Django Reinhardt, Barney Kessel, Wes Montgomery and George Benson, he brought the instrument more respect. He added another element to the possibilities of a guitar in a jazz context with heavy tones, and a down and dirty blues-rock element.

To understand Coryell's ability to elevate the guitar to noteworthy status in the jazz fusion mode, one must only look at his roots. The greatest influences on Coryell were Jimi Hendrix and Chet Atkins. From Hendrix, he created his fuzzy, blues-drenched electric guitar work. From Atkins, he learned how to pick and swing with a backing rhythm.

In turn, he has had a major influence on many jazz guitarists including Jan Akkerman, John Abercrombie, Philip Catherine, Kazumi Watanabe, and Al Di Meola, among others. But, he has also shaped the sound of all players to pick up the instrument in the past forty years. The Larry Coryell songbook is one of the essential courses that every aspiring guitarist must study in order to pass the musical exam.

Over the years, he has worked with a who's who of jazz figures: Steve Marcus, Buster Williams, Rudy Van Gelder, Miroslav Vitous, Chick Corea, Mervin Bronson, Charles Mingus, and Ron Carter, to name a few. He has sat in on hundreds of sessions with the Pat Metheny Group, Chet Baker, Sonny Rollins, and dozens more. But perhaps more than any other jazz guitarist of the modern era, he has also shared the stage and recording studio with a number of artists from different musical worlds.

Larry Coryell continues to build on a career that has seen him emerge as one of the best guitar stylists of the past forty years. Although his name is synonymous with jazz in the minds of many music fans, his popularity has spread to other corners of the music world. While he commands much respect, he will always be remembered for his major role in the fusion period as the Electric Jazz Warrior.

Discography

Free Spirit: Out of Sight and Sound, ABC 593.
Lady Coryell, Vanguard VSD-6509.
Coryell, Vanguard VSD-6547.
Spaces, Vanguard VSD-6558.
Larry Coryell at the Village Gate, Vanguard VSD-6573.
Fairyland, Philips 6369 411.
Barefoot Boy, Flying Dutchman FD-10139.
Offering, Vanguard VSD-79319.

The Real Great Escape, Vanguard VSD-79329.
Introducing the Eleventh House, Vanguard VSD-79342.
The Eleventh House—Level One, Arista AL 4052.
The Restful Mind, Vanguard, VSD-79353.
Another Side of Larry Coryell, Vanguard VSD-79360.
Planet End, Vanguard VSD-79367.
Basics, Vanguard VSD-79375.
The Eleventh House—Aspects, Arista AL 4077.
The Lion and the Ram, Arista AL 4108.
Twin House (with Philip Catherine), Elektra ACT 9202-2.
The Essential Larry Coryell, Vanguard Records 75.
Back Together Again, Wounded Bird Records B0000667PN.
Two for the Road (with Steve Kahn), Arista AB 4156.
Difference, EGG 90041.
Standing Ovation, Mood Records MOOD 22888.
European Impressions, Arista 3005.
Better Than Live, Direct 109.
Return, Vanguard VSD-79426.
Bolero, Philips, 6315 100.
Larry Coryell, Bolero 33850.
L'Oiseau de Feu, Petrouchka, Philips 812 864-1.
Quiet Day in Spring, Steeplechase B000027UAI.
Just Like Being Born, Flying Fish FF 337.
Comin' Home, Muse Records 1656 53034.
Equipoise, Muse Records 1656 53192.
Toku Du, Muse Records 1656 53504.
Air Dancing, Jazzpoint 1025.
Shining Hour, Muse Records 5360.
American Odyssey, DRG 2147 52134.
The Dragon Gate, Shanachie SHA 97005.
Twelve Frets to One Octave, Shanachie SHA 97015.
Fallen Angel, CTI 2464 672364.
I'll Be Over You, CTI 2464 672384.
Sketches of Coryell, Shanachie SHA 5024.
Spaces Revisited, Shanachie 5033.
Major Jazz, Minor Blues, Jazz Records 32058.
Cause and Effect, Tone Center 4002.
Monk, Trane, Miles & Me, High Note 7028.
Larry Coryell, Vanguard 6509.
The Eleventh House at Montreux, Vanguard, VSD-79410.
Out of Sight and Sound, ABC 593.

TONY WILLIAMS (1945–1997)

The Powerhouse

The ability to drive along the soloists while working with the members of the rhythm section is the strength of all great jazz drummers. This method did not lose any of its luster during the jazz fusion era; in fact it was highly emphasized. One of the main stickmen of the style was known as the Powerhouse for his creative spark and energy. He was Tony Williams.

Tony Williams was born Anthony Williams on December 12, 1945, in Chicago, Illinois, but grew up in Boston. He came from a musical family; his father was the saxophonist Tillmon Williams. The pair performed live together, playing mostly dance music and top forty songs that were popular on the radio. Despite this fine practical education, Tony was primarily self-taught and from the earliest age began to listen to a great range of musical styles, including jazz and blues.

A teenager during the first wave of rock and rollers, Williams listened intently to Bill Haley and the Comets, Chuck Berry, Elvis Presley, Fats Domino, Jerry Lee Lewis and others of that era. But he also liked the music of Count Basie, Miles Davis, and Max Roach, his first great idol on the drums. The synthesis of Williams's mature style was born from these myriad influences.

He received lessons from Alan Dawson for a period during his midteens, then joined saxophonist Sam River's band. Like every other musician, Williams loved to jam and did so with a number of groups in the Boston, area none of which ever gained any notoriety. Although Beantown offered ample opportunities for someone of Williams's highly developed ability, he decided to move to New York City in 1962.

Upon his arrival in the Big Apple, he joined Jackie McLean's band. The legendary hard bop saxophonist was thrilled at having in his group someone of Williams's caliber; even in his teens he could play as well as men twice his age. It was during his tenure with McLean that Tony began to draw comparison to the great Art Blakey, certainly an encouraging compliment for any young percussionist trying to make a name for himself in the jazz world. Although there was a promising future as part of McLean's outfit, Williams opted to join the cool one, Miles Davis.

A spot in the Miles Davis Quintet was one of the most coveted in all of jazz. The trumpeter was probably the number one figure in the genre in the early 1960s. Despite having jammed with Max Roach, Kenny Clarke and other top drummers, Davis could not believe the power Williams possessed. The young timekeeper would occupy the drum chair for seven years as part of Davis's outfit and appeared on seven albums. He also toured extensively throughout the United States, Europe, and Japan.

Williams was the spark that lit a fire under the solos of Davis, Herbie Hancock, Wayne Shorter, Chick Corea, and everyone else who passed through the quintet. He was only seventeen at the time he joined Davis, and before his twentieth birthday, Tony was being hailed as the new king of jazz drummers. He benefited greatly from the partnership and by the time that his stay with the cool one was over, Williams was a genuine star.

His maturation as a musician also included performing with a number of different important jazz artists while still a member of Davis's outfit. Noteworthy were Sonny Rollins, Eric Dolphy, Stan Getz, and Chet Baker, among others. This exposed him to a wide circle of distinct voices and allowed him to adjust to each individual while forcing them to learn how to mesh to his own abilities. Always willing to expand his horizons, he was listening to the classical works of Beethoven, Stravinsky, Wagner, and Tchaikovsky, as well as to the Beatles, Jimi Hendrix, and Cream. While the great free stickman Elvin Jones made a powerful impact on Williams, it was the young drummer who was the idol of every aspiring percussionist.

After playing on a number of groundbreaking sessions with Miles, including the electric *In a Silent Way* and *Filles de Kilimanjaro*, Williams left the band to form his own outfit called Lifetime. The group included British guitarist John McLaughlin, Larry Young and bass player Jack Bruce. Two years later upon the departure of McLaughlin, Lifetime disbanded. Williams continued to play in various jam sessions and recording dates, and also became a private teacher.

In 1975, Williams reformed Lifetime with Alan Holdsworth, Alan Pasqua, and Tony Newton; however despite the promise of the new lineup, it lasted just one year. However a much more viable project was V.S.O.P., the reunion with Davis alumni Herbie Hancock, Ron Carter, Wayne Shorter, and Freddie Hubbard. He toured and recorded with the group before forming his own outfit once again.

The Tony Williams Quintet, a hard bop group, was together for over a decade and made several recordings. Wallace Roney was perhaps the best known member of the various lineups aside from the group's leader. They toured extensively in the United States and abroad. Although the personnel shifted consistently, they remained together for a long period of time until Williams dissolved the band in 1995.

The famous drummer returned to work as a freelancer and recorded his own material for the remainder of his career. On February 23, 1997, the youthful Williams entered a hospital in Daly City, California, for a routine gall bladder operation. Unfortunately, due to medical complications, he suffered a heart attack and died at the age of 51. His loss was a severe blow to the jazz world.

Tony Williams was one of the most important jazz drummers of the past forty years. He defined the parameters of the rhythm keeper in the electric-jazz fusion era, and always provided a powerful punch on whatever gig he was in. He was an accomplished soloist, but more important was his ability to push everyone in the band to greater heights with his impeccable sense of rhythm and timing.

He was a fireplug drummer capable of unleashing a seismic attack at a moment's notice. But he was also a team player and often reverted to the role of timekeeper, allowing the soloists in the band to grab the spotlight. It was his facility and ability to excel in both situations that made him such a spectacular musician. In an era of great drummers that included Art Blakey, Elvin Jones, Alphonse Mouzon, Billy Cobham, John Bonham, Keith Moon, and so many others, Williams stood out.

Like nearly all other jazz fusion practitioners, Williams first came to prominence as part of the Miles Davis Quintet. The trumpeter had a keen eye for talent and accepted nothing but a full effort from each person in his group on every song cut in the studio, as well as every concert. Davis, with a legendary reputation as one of the toughest bandleaders because of his sheer brilliance and flair for experiment, was able to nurture Williams. It was during his time with the master trumpeter that the young drummer went from playing unplugged jazz to electric flavors. He made the conversion from one idiom to the other with very little change to his style, which displayed the range of his capabilities.

Williams had many admirers. Other jazz fusion artists like Ronald Shannon Jackson, Jack DeJohnette, Bill Buford, Roy Haynes, Billy Higgins, Marvin "Smitty" Smith, Steve Smith, Ed Blackwell, Clifford Jarvis, Alan Dawson, and Billy Cobham marveled at his ability to keep time from the simplest to the most complex rhythms. He never failed to astonish those who tried to keep up to him no matter what instrument they played. His ferocious attack always inspired others to play beyond their boundaries.

However, it was fellow band members that really appreciated Williams, because he provided them launching pads for their solos. He was revered by Eric Dolphy, Sam Rivers, Jackie McLean, Herbie Hancock, Ron Carter, Stanley Clarke, Bobby Hutcherson, George Benson, John McLaughlin, and Miles Davis, to name a few. He also worked with Teo Macero, Freddie Hubbard, Chick Corea, Alfred Lion, Rudy Van Gelder, Michael Cuscuna, Buster Williams, Stanley Clarke, Hank Jones, George Coleman, Paul Chambers, Great Jazz Trio, Dave Holland, Joe Henderson, Mulgrew Miller, and Wallace Roney.

In a career that spanned thirty-five years, Williams opened many doors for future rhythm keepers. A complete list of the drummers he influenced would fill a jazz encyclopedia. A partial list includes Jerome Cooper, Ted Dunbar, Lenny White, Simon Phillips, Jeff "Tain" Watts, Norman Connors, and Motohiko Hino. Like Williams, all of his followers were bold musicians who were never afraid to venture into uncharted rhythmic territory. He encouraged everyone with his youthful appeal to reach to the very depths of their creativity and imagination.

Despite his untimely death, there is no doubt that Williams made a strong impact on the jazz world. He was one of the foremost creators and keepers of the electric jazz–rock flame. No matter whether he was in front of thousands of fans or in a private jam session with a few close musician friends, Williams was always a Powerhouse.

Discography

Magic Touch of Tony, Philips.
Lifetime, Blue Note 84180.
Spring, Blue Note 84216.
Emergency, Polydor 25–3001.
Turn It Over, Polydor 24–4021.
Ego, Polydor 24–4065.
The Old Album's Rush, Polydor PD 5040.
Believe It, Columbia PC 33836.
Million Dollar Legs, Columbia PC 34263.
Joy of Flying, Scorpio 6500.
Foreign Intrigue, Blue Note Records 46289.
Civilization, Capitol B000008CL9.
Third Plane, Fantasy B00000DWM2.
Angel Street, Capitol B000008CL8.
Native Heart, Capitol B000008CLA.
The Story of Neptune, Capitol B000007O1G.
Carnaval, Orig. Jazz Classics B00006310L.
Tokyo Live, Blue Note Records B000008CLB.
Wilderness, Ark 21.
Young at Heart, Sony 69107.
Spectrum: The Anthology, Polygram Records 537075.
The Best of Tony Williams, Blue Note Records 53331.
Ultimate Tony Williams, Polygram Records B00000J2T1.
At the Village Vanguard, Vol. 1, East Wind EW 8053.
At the Village Vanguard, Vol. 2, East Wind EW 8046.
I'm Old Fashioned, East Wind EW 8037.
Kindness, Joy, Love & Happiness, East Wind EW 8056.
Tribute to Tony Williams, Phantom B0000568O1.

BILLY COBHAM (1946–)

The Panamanian Percussionist

Because of the globetrotting efforts of countless jazz musicians, the music spread to every corner of the world and the influence of American artists on other cultures was phenomenal. In Panama, where the spicy and thick Latin rhythms dominated the musical landscape, one individual was enchanted with the jazz beat and grew up to be the Panamanian Percussionist. His name is Billy Cobham.

Billy Cobham was born William C. Cobham on May 18, 1946, in Panama. He was surrounded by music from an early age; his father was a piano player. Cobham was amazed by the street music he heard during carnival time. He was also enthralled with the marching bands. The polyrhythms touched a particular nerve impulse that pointed him towards a career as a professional musician.

When he was almost eight years old, Cobham and his family moved to Brooklyn, New York, in search of greater financial opportunities. A self-taught drummer, he began to imitate the rhythms of the gritty, noisy streets of his new environment and incorporated the heady beats of his native homeland to stretch and enhance his overall sound. By his teens, he was proficient enough to play in various school groups, including the Jazz Samaritans, the Grover Washington Jr. band, Billy Taylor Trio and the New York Jazz Sextet. He was an asset to every band of which he was a member.

Cobham caught his first big break when he joined Horace Silver's outfit in 1968. He gained immediate attention and was chosen by Miles Davis to play on the latter's seminal *Bitches Brew* recording. The session was a great learning experience for Cobham and he incorporated his lessons to his next project, a jazz fusion band called Dreams. The group recorded two albums for Columbia, *Dreams* and *Imagine My Surprise,* but the project was short-lived.

A year later, after stints with Stanley Turrentine and Kenny Burrell, he joined the Mahavishnu Orchestra. His teaming with John McLaughlin made for a dynamic duo and the group's first album immediately propelled them to the forefront of the jazz fusion scene. Cobham played on the *Inner Mounting Flame, Birds of Fire,* and *Between Nothingness & Eternity* record sessions before moving on. Although he only remained in the band for a couple of years, he made major contributions and enhanced his reputation in jazz circles as well as in other styles of music.

After a decade of being the drummer in a number of outfits, recording as a sideman, and playing for films and jingles, Cobham formed his own group once again. Although it was a successful endeavor, he craved a new direction and after breaking up the outfit he teamed up with keyboard player George Duke. The duo was a formidable one-two jazz punch.

George Duke was born in San Rafael, California. When he was six his mother took him to a Duke Ellington concert that triggered the music switch inside him. He immediately started to play the piano, honing his skills quickly first with classical music and later with jazz, rock and blues. He learned to improvise and widen his style to include other genres and began to play regular gigs. Before he joined forces with Cobham, Duke had a lengthy stay in Frank Zappa's Mothers of Invention.

The partnership lasted for a short time but they did record one acclaimed album, *The George Duke/Billy Cobham Band Live on Tour in Europe*. Each remained prominent on the jazz fusion scene after the breakup and over the past twenty-five years they have crossed paths several times. Unfortunately, like many other short-lived collaborations, their true potential was never realized. One can only wonder what exciting musical jewels they would have delivered to the world had they remained together.

Cobham was one of the best drummers in jazz during the 1970s, and arguably the greatest jazz fusion percussionist of the era (with the possible exception of Tony Williams). His incredible and versatile talents were always highly in demand. One of his many projects at the time was the CBS All-Stars that also included Tom Scott, Alphonso Johnson, Mark Soskin, and Steve Khan. The tour was a success and added yet another satisfying adventure to his resume.

Since 1980, he has divided his time between leading his own group, touring with other artists and teaching. His outfit has featured a variety of names, including Gary Husband, Carl Orr, Stefan Rademacher, Joe Chindamo, Christian Diener, and Peter Wölpl. They have played around the world, touring in Japan, the Bahamas, Brazil, Argentina, Canada, Germany, Turkey, Macedonia, Latvia, Croatia, Israel, Egypt, France, and Scandinavia.

He has toured and recorded with Larry Coryell, Mose Allison, McCoy Tyner, Ron Carter, George Benson, Carly Simon, Gene Ammons, Gabor Szabo, Roberta Flack, Roy Ayers, Jack Bruce and Friends, Bobby and the Midnites, Gil Evans, Miles Davis, Peter Gabriel, Nordic, and many more. A masterful drummer, his skills have always been in great demand.

But perhaps his greatest achievement from a purely humanitarian point of view has been his relentless effort to pass on the magic of jazz through the countless drum clinics and workshops he has conducted. He is one artist who truly gives back to his community and has generously donated his time and led classes for various drum companies, including Yamaha. His deep knowledge of acoustic as well as electronic rhythm instruments gives him a wide dimension of teaching tools. A patient instructor, he has always insisted that his students follow their own path rather than a dictated one. He continues to record, perform and teach in a variety of capacities.

Billy Cobham is a rhythm ace. His ability to shift gears during a performance is astonishing. He can play many different polyrhythms during the course of one song, spurring on the soloists to blend styles and take the audience on a voyage of various periods of jazz. One of the most highly respected jazz fusion drummers, he has never taken an easy stride. From the very beginning he poured every ounce of energy he had into every drum lick.

There is an underestimated and unappreciated power to his drumming. He plays fast and furious but is never sloppy. He is a musical explorer venturing down avenues that only he seems able to envision. His inherent knack for rhythm is second to none and he is capable of doing more with one tiny drum kit than others can do on a big splashy set.

Among certain critics and in certain jazz circles, Cobham was considered the greatest jazz fusion drummer of the 1970s, a major accomplishment considering his contemporaries were Tony Williams, Lenny White, Bill Buford, Jack DeJohnette, Simon Phillips, and Narada Michael Walden. Cobham had the fire of a Tony Williams, the industriousness of Lenny White and the fortitude of Jack DeJohnette. The Panamanian percussionist added a dimension that the others did not seem to have because he was able to reach back into his native roots and deliver complicated rhythms and distinguished flares.

A valued asset, Cobham has worked with a number of jazz figures. Among them are Randy Brecker, Wayne Andre, Eric Gale, George Marge, Chick Corea, Ralph MacDonald, Marvin Stamm, Garnett Brown, Larry Coryell, Phil Bodner, Romeo Penque, Stanley Clarke, Michael Brecker, and James Buffington. He has also participated in a number of highly influential bands, including the Mahavishnu Orchestra, the New York Jazz Quartet, Bobby & The Midnites, and Dreams. He has played on sessions for Mose Allison, Gene Ammons, Roy Ayers, Gato Barbieri, Tommy Bolin, Bunny Burnel, Larry Coryell, and Woody Herman, to name a few.

Although his popularity has waned since the height of the jazz fusion period, he remains one of the best drummers in the business. He continues to stun audiences with his fiery brand of jazz that layers sound to weave a rich texture of possibilities. There is no denying the talent of the Panamanian percussionist.

Discography

Dreams, Columbia 30225.
Imagine My Surprise, Columbia 30960.
Crosswinds, Atlantic 7300.
A Funky Thide of Sings, Atlantic 18149.
Life & Times, Atlantic 18166.
Shabazz, Atlantic 18139.
Spectrum, Atlantic 7268.
Total Eclipse, Atlantic 18121.
Magic, Columbia 34939.
Inner Conflicts, Atlantic 19174.
Billy Cobham, Big Eye Music 4076.
Focused, Purple Pyramid/Cleopatra 482.
A Funky Thide of Sings, Koch Jazz 8527.
By Design, Purple Pyramid/Cleopatra 505.
Flight Time, Inakustik Records 8616.
Life & Times, Wounded Bird Records 8166.
Nordic, Purple Pyramid/Cleopatra 506.
Picture This, Purple Pyramid/Cleopatra 507.
Powerplay, Purple Pyramid/Cleopatra 508.
Shabazz, Wounded Bird Records 8139.
Spectrum, Rhino Records 7268.
The Best of Billy Cobham, Rhino Records 19238.
The Traveler, Purple Pyramid/Cleopatra 509.
Warning, Purple Pyramid/Cleopatra 519.

WITH GEORGE DUKE
Live on Tour in Europe, Atlantic 18194.

STANLEY CLARKE (1951–)
Individual Strings

The creation of jazz fusion demanded the amplification of the various instruments. Although the electric guitar had been a weapon in jazz for years, the bass had remained acoustic. Seemingly overnight a new crop of bassists appeared on the scene eager to plug in and explore the parameters of the electric bass sound. One of the outstanding warriors of the amplified style was the man who played his individual strings. His name is Stanley Clarke.

Stanley M. Clarke was born on June 30, 1951, in Philadelphia, Pennsylvania. One of a growing number of jazz artists to emerge from one of the larger metropolitan cities of the United States, his first instrument was the accordion. Since he didn't like the accordion, he turned to the violin and cello before picking up on bass. Although he would make a significant impact on the jazz world, his initial interests were rooted in classical music. He listened to the German composer Richard Wagner, as well as the great masters: Bach, Beethoven, Mozart, and Schubert.

Eventually Clarke discovered popular music and listened to rock and roll, jazz, soul, and the blues. His list of musical heroes shifted from the classical giants to jazz virtuosos like Paul Chambers, Charles Mingus, Scott LaFaro, and Billy Cox, the electric bassman who played with the late, great Jimi Hendrix. It was Cox who pointed Clarke towards the electric warrior direction; until that point Clarke had played solely acoustic.

Clarke worked in several rock outfits around the Philadelphia area as a teenager, but entered the professional jazz world when he joined Horace Silver's band at the tender age of eighteen. Despite his relative inexperience, he prospered under Silver's guidance and carved a reputation as one of the outstanding young bassmen in jazz. It was clearly evident that the youthful string player possessed a special talent.

Clarke then joined Joe Henderson's band, and later played with Pharoah Sanders, as well as bandleader Stan Getz. It was while a member of the latter's group that Clarke met Chick Corea. In 1972, Clarke took the plunge and joined Corea's group, Return to Forever. The jazz fusion outfit was tailor made for Clarke's individual talent and it was during this period that his reputation was established and cemented. He played on the albums *Hymn to the 7th Galaxy, Light as a Feather, Where Have I Known You Before, No Mystery, Romantic Warrior,* and *Musicmagic.* His layered, pulsating electric bass solos added a distinct muscular presence to the band's whole sound.

While he was creating magic with Corea in Return to Forever, Clarke was recording some very important solo material. The albums *Stanley Clarke, Journey to Love, School Days,* and *Children of Forever* were all well produced works that demonstrated another dimension to his musical personality; he was quite capable of leading his own outfit. In 1976, Clarke began to tour with his own band.

Although he was highly regarded in the jazz world as one of the leading voices on electric bass, over the past two decades Clarke has explored different styles. One of the many sidetracks from jazz he has taken is the formation of a group with George Duke, the keyboard player. The union of the two very unique musicians raised eyebrows throughout the jazz world. Many wondered what kind of strange and wonderful music the two would produce for everyone's listening pleasure.

Duke, who was a keen student of the jazz fusion style, worked in many bands, including those of Gerald Wilson, Dizzy Gillespie, Bobby Hutcherson, and Don Ellis. He performed and recorded with Jean-Luc Ponty, the brilliant electric violinist. Duke also had a lengthy stay in Frank Zappa's Mothers of Invention in the 1970s. Later he would team up with the Panamanian percussionist, Billy Cobham.

The combination of Clarke and Duke was a strange but interesting experiment. Each boasted a long list of credentials in various groups and as solo artists. The duo was in some ways a mini-super group. The two leading practitioners of the electric jazz movement were dynamic musicians and solid composers who united their interests and talents to create another dimension of the style that incorporated large chunks of funk.

After his breakup with Duke, he joined forces with guitarist Al Di Meola and violinist Ponty to record the acoustic *Rite of Strings*. Clarke also wrote film scores that demonstrated another side of his multi-talented ability. However, there was no denying his creative force, whether it was some solo or group project on the cutting edge of jazz or some commercial enterprise. He proved time and again that he was one of the most imaginative bass players of the modern era. His willingness to tackle and conquer any challenge underlined his superior versatility.

He remained active throughout his career in a variety of capacities. He cut several solo albums, each offering a different insight into his creative genius. He also toured throughout North America and abroad with his small group. Although he always surrounded himself with talented players, he was often the main focus of any outfit because of his strong musical presence. He continues to record and perform.

Stanley Clarke is a bass virtuoso. He has performed brilliantly on the acoustic as well as the electric bass throughout his distinguished career. His name is synonymous with the instrument. Although he has crossed the line and explored different styles of music, he remains one of the best jazz artists of the modern era.

There is a definite fluidity to his sound. He has the ability to improvise—a mark of all good jazz players—as well as straddling the bass line without venturing away from it. He is capable of covering a large amount of territory very rapidly with his lightning quick fingers as a solo artist, as team player in the rhythm section, or as the catalyst to spur on the horn soloists within a group context.

He was one of the great jazz fusion artists of the 1970s as he plugged in and played some very tasty, very funky bass. Along with Ron Carter, Alphonso Johnson, John Lee, Will Lee, Jaco Patorius and Miroslav Vitous, he blazed the trail and set down the parameters for the electric bass style. Although many of his contemporaries were very good musicians, Clarke possessed an extra dimension that enabled him to reach a larger audience than many of his peers because of his facility in switching from acoustic to electric without significantly changing his style. His uncanny sense of rhythm and tone allowed him to excel in any situation.

He worked with a number of artists, including Gary Burton, Flora Purim, John "J.R." Robinson, Tony Williams, Ron Carter, Steve Gadd, Al Di Meola, Erik Zobler, Jerry Hey, Gary Grant, Gerald Albright, Gayle Moran, Stan Getz, and Howard Hewett. However, he cultivated most of his fame during his association with keyboard wizard Chick Corea where, arguably, he delivered some of his best work. Later collaborations with George Duke, Jean-Luc Ponty and Al Di Meola also proved to be beneficial to his career.

Clarke influenced a number of jazz bassists. Among them are Charles Fambrough, Charnett Moffett, Robert Hurst, Christian McBride, Billy Sheehan, Gerald Veasley, and Les Claypool. However, since he has ventured into the realm of rock and funk, a number of other artists outside the jazz world emulated him. His style can be heard in the music of countless electric funk bands as well as hip-hop, rap, and techno funk.

Stanley Clarke was also part of the large contingent of modern jazz musicians who were from Philadelphia or elsewhere in Pennsylvania. A partial list includes bassists Paul Chambers, Alphonso Johnson, Jaco Pastorius, trumpeters Clifford Brown, Randy Brecker, and Lee Morgan, pianists McCoy Tyner, Keith Jarrett, and Bobby Timmons, saxmen Mike Brecker, Benny Golson and Jimmy Heath, guitarists Joe Beck, George Benson, and Pat Martino, and drummers Philly Joe Jones and Gerry Brown. Aside from perhaps Detroit, the City of Brotherly Love has provided more modern jazz artists than any other metropolitan area. Clarke was also one of the new wave players with a musical degree. In the first fifty years of the genre there were few artists that boasted a music degree. In fact, many had dropped out of school to pursue their careers.

Clarke carved a special place for himself in the music world through his perseverance, his skills, his hard work, and his brilliance. He remains one of the best jazz musicians in an industry that boasts thousands of practitioners. What separated him from all other bass players was his desire to play his individual strings down avenues that no one could ever follow.

Discography

Children of Forever, One Way 5531.
Stanley Clarke, Epic 431.
Journey to Love, Epic 433.
School Days, Epic 439.
I Wanna Play for You, Epic 64295.
Modern Man, Tristar B0000020H5.
Rocks, Pebbles and Sand, Epic 36506.

The Clarke/Duke Project, Vol. 2, Columbia B000026F2V.
Time Exposure, Epic 38688.
Find Out!, Epic 40040.
Hideaway, Epic 40275.
If This Bass Could Only Talk, Portrait 40923.
3, Stanley Clarke and George Duke, Epic 46012.
Passenger 57, Sony Music 53232.
East River Drive, Epic B0000251E6.
Live at the Greek, Epic 57506.
Live in Montreux, Jazz Door 1234.
Rite of Strings, Capitol 34167.
At the Movies, Epic 67286.
Live (1976–1977), Sony 48529.
Collection, Castle Music B0000241WP.
Portrait Stanley Clarke, Sony B00005YA5H.

WITH RETURN TO FOREVER

Return to Forever, ECM 1022.
Light as a Feather, Polydor PD 5525.
Hymn of the Seventh Galaxy, Polydor PD 5536.
Where Have I Known You Before, Polydor PD 6509.
No Mystery, Polydor PD 6512.
Romantic Warrior, CBS PC 34076.
Musicmagic, CBS PC 34682.

JACO PASTORIUS (1951–1987)

The Brazilian Bass Man

When Jimmy Blanton stepped up and proved that the bass was an instrument of power and beauty, he opened a whole new dimension of sound. After his untimely death, Oscar Pettiford and Ray Brown continued the cause. Charlie Mingus, Charlie Haden and Neils Pedersen took the bass into avant-garde/free jazz territory. With the advent of fusion, Stanley Clarke and Ron Carter plugged in to create an electric element. There was another disciple of fusion to make his mark: the Brazilian Bass Man, Jaco Pastorius.

Jaco Pastorius was born John Francis Pastorius on December 1, 1951, in Norristown, Pennsylvania. When he was seven his family moved to Fort Lauderdale, Florida. Jaco's father, a drummer and a singer, had a direct influence on his young son. Jaco played the drums, piano, saxophone, and guitar before settling on the bass as his instrument of choice. When he was thirteen he was already playing the drums in local groups, but an injury caused him to switch to the electric bass.

In his teens, Pastorius was able to hook up with many of the groups on tour passing through town. He gained invaluable experience as a temporary member of Wayne Cochran's group, the C. C. Riders, the Temptations, the Supremes and dozens more. He was also listened to a wide range of styles: soul, rock, blues, jazz, Cuban bands, and pop. Although he was known throughout the music business as an adventurous player who could really burn up the bass line, he had yet to record.

In the early 1970s fatherhood sidetracked his ambitions to be a successful musician, but he continued to hone his skills until he could challenge and defeat all other players within a group context. He was a solo force, yet also fit well in a band. He performed in many outfits, usually only one-night gigs since a tour across the country clashed with the commitment to his family.

In 1972, he began to work with Ira Sullivan, who taught him a great deal. At the time, Pastorius was an excellent bass player who had a totally different approach to playing the instrument. Although he had the knowledge and the ability, he was unsure how to incorporate his style into a jazz format. His time spent with Sullivan and later Peter Graves, a big-band leader, helped Jaco understand how he could turn the bass into a lead instrument within a jazz context.

An enterprising young man, he was obsessed with continuously improving his skill by jamming with a host of different musicians. He also taught music theory at the University of Miami. His arrangement and composition skills vastly improved during this time until they were polished to a fine, sharp edge. With all the pieces of the puzzle in place, he was ready to make his true mark on the jazz world.

Jaco, a well-liked individual in music circles, made friends easily. One of the most important connections he cultivated was with Bobby Colomby, who played the drums for the jazz-rock fusion group Blood, Sweat and Tears. With Colomby's help, Pastorius was able to finally record. Although his records were good they didn't provide the breakthrough he was seeking. His star really began to shine brighter when he joined Weather Report, the mid–1970s Rolls Royce of jazz-rock groups.

His first appearance with his new band was on the album Heavy Weather and his immediate contributions energized the group. Finally, after years of scuffling about dreaming of being a legitimate professional musician, he was receiving the attention he deserved. During Weather Report's live act, he drove the crowd frantic with his Hendrix-like virtuoso on the electric bass. He played with such power and originality that his talents did not go unnoticed by other artists in the music business.

He played on Joni Mitchell's *Hejira* and on the albums of the great Charles Mingus. He also recorded with the guitarist Pat Metheny, Blood,

Sweat and Tears, Paul Bley, Bireli Lagrene, and Ira Sullivan. No matter the studio or live gig, there was never any doubt as to identity of the bass player. He possessed such a distinct, thick sound on his Fender electric fretless instrument that his style was as recognizable as any other player in jazz, rock, blues, and pop at the time.

He also found time to record his own solo album, which received massive critical acclaim from a variety of sources. Pastorius left Weather Report in 1980 to lead his own band, Word of Mouth. They toured and recorded for the next four years as Jaco only enhanced his position as one of the great individual players in the music industry. An experimental project, Word of Mouth went through various personnel changes during its tenure, and the size of the band varied from a small combo to a larger ensemble, including for some time a big band setup.

Despite his success, Pastorius seemed to be playing on borrowed time. A noted drug user, his addiction began to affect his sanity and eventually destroyed his career. By the mid–1980s, he had already experienced his best days as a musician. His excessive alcohol intake did little to alleviate his problems and he slid down the slippery road to desperation.

It would be wonderful to write a happy ending to the Jaco Pastorius story, but sadly that cannot be done. The man who had once dazzled the music world with his incomparable technique, explosive imagination, and pure fire finished his life as a disoriented street person. On September 21, 1987, in Fort Lauderdale, Florida, Jaco Pastorius, one of the greatest virtuoso bassmen to ever play the instrument, died a violent death. He was only 35 years old.

Jaco Pastorius was a unique bass voice in jazz history. In the 1970s, he was at the top of his form and no one could match him for sheer imagination and fuel, perhaps with the sole exception of Stanley Clarke. He turned the bass from a simple rhythm instrument into a front line weapon with his spectacular displays of unchecked virtuoso.

He played an acoustic bass that was louder than those that plugged in. He possessed an amazing fluidity, a flowing motion that surged ahead like a tidal wave and assaulted all those who stood in its way. He took the instrument to the outer limits of his inventiveness and created a whole new circle of respect for it. As a performer, he often drew comparisons to the wizard of the electric guitar, Jimi Hendrix.

Jaco had a vivid imagination and lightning-quick fingers that produced swoops of sounds like the cries of the whales of the ocean. He could reproduce just about any sound on earth on his strapless, fretless bass. The strength of his hands was astonishing, as he was a physically powerful player and flexed his musical imagination and dexterity.

Although his time in the sun was cut short because of personal problems, Patorius left behind a solid body of work as a solo and session artist.

He backed Joni Mitchell, was a key member of Weather Report, and led his own recordings. He also worked with Airto Moreira, Robert Thomas Jr., Steve Gadd, Dave Bargeron, Kenwood Dennard, David Sanborn, Alphonse Mouzon, Brian Melvin, Michael Brecker, Othello Molineaux, and Manolo Badrena.

He also helped shape the sound and technique of Randy Coven, Randy Bernsen, Billy Sheehan, Jimmy Haslip, Gerald Veasley, Les Claypool, and Anatholi Bulkin. Like so many other artists of the jazz-rock fusion era, his exploits spilled into other styles. He was known as the wild man of the bass and challenged anyone who dared to outplay him. There were few takers.

It is a shame that Pastorius lost control of his life in the 1980s after contributing so brilliantly in the previous decade. However, one must remember his best years when he was at the zenith of his career. Thankfully, much of the material he recorded on his own and on the records of others remain with us, ensuring the Brazilian bass man's special place in jazz history.

Discography

Jaco [live], DIW, 312.
Jaco Pastorius, Epic PE 33949.
Jaco Pastorius, Epic 64977.
Honestly Solo Live, Jazz Point Records 1032.
Live in Italy, Jazz Point Records 1031.
Live in NYC, Vol. 1: Punk Jazz, Big World Music 1001.
Live in NYC, Vol. 2: Trio, Big World Music 1002.
Live in NYC, Vol. 3: Promised Land, Big World Music 1003.
Live in NYC, Vol. 4: Trio 2, Big World Music 1004.
Live in NYC, Vol. 5: Raca, Big World Music 1005.
Live in NYC, Vol. 6: Punk Jazz 2, Big World Music 1006.
Live in NYC, Vol. 7: History, Big World Music 1007.
The Birthday Concert, Warner Bros. Records 45290.
Word of Mouth, Warner Bros. Records 3535.
Best Improvisation, JAZZ TFCK-87560.
Good Stitch for Golden Roads, SOUND SSCD-8078.
Heavy 'N Jazz, JAZZP TFCK-87563.
Invitation, WEA WPCP-4932.
PDB, DIW DIW-827.
Rare Collection, A&M POCJ-1693.

PART FIVE

Contemporary Jazz

The long, illustrious history of jazz continues into the new millennium with a group of practitioners who have taken elements of the past and incorporated them into their own sound. In many ways, contemporary jazz is a catch phrase for the many different faces of the genre that are prevalent today.

Acid jazz, neo-traditional styles, smooth jazz, gentle instrumental, Latin Jazz, avant-garde, free jazz, fusion, and many others all have their fair share of supporters. This section of the book represents a mix of the many versions that make up the current scene. While those featured are considered the elite, they are not the only ones who must be acknowledged.

The new generation of saxophone players includes Michael Brecker, Kenny Garrett, Joe Lavano, Courtney Pine, Joshua Redman, Javon Jackson, Chris Potter, and Jesse Davis. Top trumpeters include Terrence Blanchard, Roy Hargrove, Leroy Jones, Nicholas Payton, and Wallace Roney, among others. A plethora of jazz vocalists is making fresh, exciting CDs, including Angela Higgenbottom, Karrin Allyson, Kurt Elling, Kevin Mohogany, Kitty Margolis, Dianne Reeves, and Cassandra Wilson, to name a few.

Today's prime pianists include Kenny Barron, Cyrus Chestnut, Mulgrew Miller, Renne Rosnes, Gonzalo Rubalcaba, and Jacky Terrasson, among others. Important organists are Joey DeFrancesco, Barbara Dennerlein, Larry Goldings, and Greg Hatza. Notable drummers include Roy Haynes, Shadow Wilson, Roy Brooks, Louis Hayes, Al Foster, Billy Higgins, Jake Hanna, Victor Lewis, Billy Hart, Grady Tate, Jimmy Bobb, and Danny Richmand.

The guitar tradition continues on with Joshua Breakstone, Lenny Breau, Bruce Forman, Peter Leitch, Emily Remler, Nels Cline, Ron Affif, and Jimmy Bruno. James Newton, Lew Tabackin, and Dave Valentin are prime flutists. Ray Anderson, George Lewis, Steve Turre, and Delfeayo Marsalis are wonderful modern trombonists.

There are hundreds of young musicians in jazz today pursuing their individual path and creating excellent music. The following are a sampling of the best of the contemporary scene, those who carry the torch that was lit so long ago in the late nineteenth century in New Orleans.

Kenny Kirkland was one of the prime piano players of the new generation. His association with the Marsalis brothers helped out his career tremendously. His premature death was a blow to the contemporary movement.

Jeff "Tain" Watts is the best drummer of his generation. A virtuoso capable of excelling in any style, he was the powerhouse that drove the early bands led by Wynton Marsalis.

Branford Marsalis, older brother of Wynton, has logged many miles as a jazz player. His recent experiment of melding traditional jazz with classical sounds proves that nothing is new.

Wynton Marsalis is the young lion who inspired a back-to-traditional jazz movement in the 1980s. He is the most vital jazz artist of the past twenty years.

John Medeski is a prime example of the groovy, acid jazz movement. He is one third of Medeski, Martin and Wood, one of the best trios in the business today.

Diana Krall is a wonderfully talented singer who has stolen a page from the past with an eye to the future. She can make a song melt into your mouth with her sultry, right as rain vocals.

Mark Whitefield is one of the modern guitar warriors. He has continued to bring the instrument respect, following the path Charlie Christian and Django Reinhardt established so long ago.

Christian McBride has assumed the bass throne as the main proponent of the instrument. His exploits are based on a hundred years of history, but he has a futuristic element in his style.

KENNY KIRKLAND (1955–1998)

The New Piano Thing

The piano has played an important role in every era in jazz and boasts some of the greatest musicians in the history of the genre. The foundation was laid by the early practitioners, Scott Joplin, Eubie Blake, James P. Johnson, Willie "The Lion" Smith, Jelly Roll Morton, and Fats Waller, and the swing/big band players Art Tatum, Earl Hines, Duke Ellington, Count Basie, and Teddy Wilson laid down the foundation. Oscar Peterson,

Bud Powell, and Thelonious Monk made the piano go bop while Horace Silver, Dave Brubeck, Cecil Taylor, Herbie Hancock, and Chick Corea took the instrument down hard bop, cool jazz, free jazz, avant-garde and jazz fusion avenues. The tradition continues in the contemporary period; an assortment of players have taken elements of previous styles to create something fresh. One of these innovators was the man keen on playing the new piano thing. His name was Kenny Kirkland.

Kenneth David Kirkland was born on September 28, 1955, in Newport, New York. He began playing the piano when he was six years old and discovered seven decades of good jazz. He continued to develop his skills at the Manhattan School of Music. He further expanded his education by delving into blues, rock and soul.

Unlike the early jazz performer, an aspiring pianist growing up in the 1960s had a back tradition of more than seventy years of piano. It stretched from the ragtime of Scott Joplin to stride pianists Fats Waller and James P. Johnson, and the big band swing of Count Basie, Teddy Wilson, and Duke Ellington. There were the unique bop piano stylings of Bud Powell and Thelonious Monk, who spoke in a language all their own. There was the hard bop message of Horace Silver, the free jazz/avant-garde distortion of Cecil Taylor and McCoy Tyner, and the jazz fusion of Herbie Hancock, Chick Corea and Joe Zawinul. Another dimension was the electric organ exploits of Jimmy Smith, Brother Jack McDuff, and others with their groovy, funky sound.

If all that wasn't enough to inspire a young pianist, then there was also the history of the blues that dated as far back as jazz piano. The important players to study included as Jimmy Yancey, Leroy Carr, Roosevelt Sykes, Sunnyland Slim, the boogie woogie trio Pete Johnson, Meade 'Lux' Lewis and Albert Ammons, as well as the Chicago blues of Pinetop Perkins and Otis Spann. There was also the first wave of rock and roll pianists, including Fats Domino, the wild Little Richard, and the Killer, Jerry Lee Lewis.

Kirkland absorbed all of these influences and incorporated them into his own style that he was honing by playing in a number of local groups and jamming with some of his friends from the neighborhood. His first professional gig was playing electric keyboards with Michal Urbaniak. Later he joined Miroslav Vitous's band and then Terumasa Hino's outfit. Later he played in a group led by the legendary free jazz drummer Elvin Jones. He added his Herbie Hancock–influenced electric and acoustic piano sound to every situation.

In 1981, after much travel, he joined Wynton Marsalis's outfit, the best jazz group on the circuit. Like so many other young enthusiasts, a spot in the great trumpeter's outfit was equivalent to a finishing school. Kirkland, a resident of Manhattan at the time, lived in a loft that became an informal jam center for all the young musicians in the area. There was some serious music being created at his place that would greatly affect the course of the contemporary sound.

Upon hearing his range on the piano, Marsalis, the talented young trumpeter, desperately wanted Kirkland in the group he was forming. The two hit it off famously and during his tenure with Marsalis, Kirkland established and expanded his reputation. The band also included Branford Marsalis on tenor saxophone, Jeff "Tain" Watts on drums, and Clarence Seay or Charles Fambrough on bass.

Kirkland played on a number of well-received Marsalis recordings, including *Notes from the Underground, Live at Blues Alley, Think of One, We Three Kings of Orient Are,* and *Wynton Marsalis,* among others. He also played on a number of Branford Marsalis's sessions. This period was a truly productive one for the pianist who blossomed under the leadership of the young lion.

The quintet traveled all over the United States and Kirkland played his Herbie Hancock–influenced keyboards better with each passing performance. The group was tight musically on stage as well as off stage because they were the brightest jazz artists on the scene. In the process of trying to earn a living as professional musicians, they were creating their own history. By the mid–1980s, Kirkland had established himself as one of the best young piano players around. Other musicians took note, including pop-rock star Sting.

In a move that angered Wynton, Kirkland and Branford joined Sting's world tour. The blind pianist Marcus Roberts, another prime member of the new traditionalists, took over Kenny's spot in Wynton's band. Once the Sting tour was done, Kirkland freelanced and played on a number of sessions that included the self-titled works of Michael Brecker and Buckshot LeFonque, as well as on the latter's *East River Drive,* and *This Is Jazz.* He could also be heard on Stanley Clarke's *Portrait* and bassist's Charles Fambrough's *Proper Angle.* By stretching out and flexing his creative muscle, Kirkland was adding significantly to his already solid reputation.

Finally, in 1991, after years of playing on the records of others, Kirkland led his first and only session. Although the album was a solid effort, he never received any other opportunities to record more of his material. The self-titled album is the only evidence that serves as a testimony of his abilities as the leader of a jazz ensemble.

Kirkland added another chapter to his interesting career when he joined the *Tonight Show* along with Branford Marsalis, who was at the time the popular television program's musical director. The two had worked well in the past and the pianist welcomed the opportunity. The television exposure helped him secure more sessions. But he eventually left the show and returned to freelancing.

On November 13, 1998, in Queens, New York, Kenny Kirkland, who just seemed to have begun tapping into his immense potential, died in his apartment of an apparent heart attack induced by a drug overdose. He was 43 years old.

Kenny Kirkland was a fine jazz pianist. Throughout his career he demonstrated a definite command of the instrument and reminded everyone of many of the greats that had passed through, including Teddy Wilson, Jimmy Smith and Chick Corea, but especially Herbie Hancock. Sadly, despite possessing an incredible amount of talent, Kirkland was never able to fully demonstrate everything he could do.

Many individuals had a large influence on Kirkland. Among them were Larry Willis and Kenny Barron, both fine contemporary players. Herbie Hancock, the electric warrior, also had a large impact on Kirkland. However, like most other jazz musicians of the 1980s and 1990s, one of his main inspirations wasn't even a pianist but the trumpeter Wynton Marsalis. The latter was able to coax the best out of Kirkland and help him blossom into a solid keyboard player.

The Kirkland style encompassed the entire history of jazz piano from the ragtime of Joplin, the swing of Basie, the bop of Powell and the electric adventures of Hancock. But Kirkland was able to amass the best of every strain to create something fresh that pointed to the path the instrument would follow for a very long time. He was equally adept at the acoustic and electric piano, and keyboards. He was able to switch from one to another quickly without altering his style.

Although he is forever known as one of the prime architects of the new piano thing, he also played blues, rock and soul. In his later years, he experimented with African American and Cuban rhythms. This was the new direction he was headed in when he was cut down. It would have been interesting to hear a full album of his polyrhythmic ideas.

Along with Marcus Roberts, Donald Brown, John Hicks, Joe Bonner, Cyrus Chestnut, Mulgrew Miller, Renee Rosnes, Gonzalo Rubalcaba, Jacky Terrasson, Jaki Byard, Roger Kellaway, Bill Cunliffe, Steve Kuhn, Billy Childs, Mike Garson, Geri Allen and Benny Green, Kirkland was one of the prime contemporary keyboard players. As one of the leaders of the new movement, he jammed with many of these artists. Each individual borrowed from one another and the sharing of ideas is the strength on which the entire jazz tradition is built.

But he was more than just an important cog in the new piano thing. He reached out and touched the careers of many other artists. A short list includes Donald Brown, James Williams, George Cables, Tommy Flanagan,

Hank Jones, Dave Kikoski, Dori Caymmi, Alejandro "Alex" Acuña, Daniel Ponce, Nestor Torres, Tania Maria, Claudio Roditi, Branford Marsalis, Wynton Marsalis, Giovanni Hidalgo, Joao Bosco, Charlie Sepulveda, and Leny Andrade.

Although he was forever tied to the Marsalis Brothers, Kirkland also worked with a number of other jazz artists. Among them were Dave Baker, Elvin Jones, Michael Brecker, Patrick Smith, Marcus Miller, Stanley Jordan, Janice Pendarvis, Tim Geelan, Kenny Garrett, Miroslav Vitous, Tom Scott, Kevin Eubanks, Mino Cinelu, Michal Urbaniak, and Lew Soloff. Although he only headed one recording session, he sat in on the efforts of many artists and his contributions live on through their material.

Kenny Kirkland was an important modern jazz pianist. He was an integral part in the contemporary scene and although his personal recording catalog is very slim, he still made significant contributions to the genre in a number of ways. The man who possessed a special touch will always be remembered for his new piano thing.

Discography

Kenny Kirkland, GRP Records B000008BHU.
Kenny Kirkland, Christian McBride, Polygram Records B00001QGP8.
Thunder and Rainbows, Sunnyside 1055.

JEFF "TAIN" WATTS (1960–)

Citizen Tain

Throughout the history of jazz, the city of Pittsburgh has produced more great drummers than any other urban center in the United States and the entire planet. Kenny "Klook" Clarke, the great bop drummer, hailed from Steel Town. As well, Art Blakey, the amazing hard bop drummer who dominated the scene for years with his Jazz Messengers, boasted a Pittsburgh birth certificate. In the 1980s, another timekeeper emerged from the city and carried on the tradition nicely as Citizen Tain. His name is Jeff "Tain" Watts.

Jeff Watts was born in January 20, 1960, in Pittsburgh, Pennsylvania. He learned how to play the drums at an early age and was open to a variety of influences, including stickmen Harvey Mason and Narada Michael Walden, the funk of Earth, Wind & Fire, and the John McLaughlin–led Mahavishnu Orchestra. The different rock, blues, and jazz acts helped shape his sound. He also listened closely to Gene Krupa, Dave Tough, Chick Webb, Jo Jones, Kenny Clarke, Max Roach, Elvin Jones, Tony Williams, Billy Cobham, Shelly Manne, and Roy Haynes. Although he was attempting to develop a modern style, he never passed on the grand tradition of earlier timekeepers Zutty Singleton and Baby Dodds. The fact that he had two of the prime stickmen—Clarke and Blakey—in his own back yard gave him a distinct advantage.

He gigged with groups around his hometown, dreaming of the day when he would become famous like his musical heroes. He later attended Duquesne University where he played tympani in the youth orchestra, as well as in ensembles that provided the background sound for operas and other productions. He was paying his dues and truly building up some important credentials.

Watts attempted to enroll in the New England Conservatory, but was not accepted and by a stroke of luck opted for the Berklee School of Music in Boston. It was here that he hooked up with Branford and Wynton Marsalis, a meeting that changed the path of his career forever. It was already apparent to Watts that Wynton was going to be a big star in jazz since he played with so much confidence and sheer ability. The young, budding musicians jammed together and shared ideas. They talked endlessly of being vital forces on the contemporary jazz scene.

When Wynton formed his quintet in the early 1980s, Jeff became the drummer. As the trumpeter was establishing himself as one of the premiere jazz artists of the 1980s, Watts was quickly gaining a reputation as one of the best young drummers in the business. In his three years with Marsalis's band, he played on the albums *Codes from the Underground* and *Wynton Marsalis,* among others.

His time with Wynton was important in shaping his style because it broadened his horizons. Although he had appreciated traditional jazz while playing in Marsalis's band, he heard the music with a new ear. He grew less interested in fusion, funk, and progressive rock, and put more effort in learning traditional jazz. That he was able to expand his range made him an in-demand drummer. Over the years he would appear on the recordings of pianist Geri Allen, saxophonists Michael Brecker, Kenny Garrett, Courtney Pine, and pianist Kenny Kirkland.

The time spent in Marsalis's quintet was vital for other reasons. It gave him a chance to travel all over the country and the world in a top-notch group. As well, the confidence that the leader exuded rubbed off on the rest of the band, including Watts. The young musicians grew together and became brothers on their way to assuming their top positions as the young lions. It was a period of good times, good music and good friends.

In 1992, Watts became the drummer for the *Tonight Show* band under the direction of Branford Marsalis. The decision to leave Wynton's band was a difficult one, but the experience and exposure of playing on television was a positive step in his career. Although a solid opportunity, he began to feel limited in the music that the *Tonight Show* band played. A drummer with an abundance of talent, he yearned for something more that allowed him a greater opportunity to display his other musical venues.

He left the *Tonight Show* in 1995 and began freelancing around New York City. At one point he had a trio consisting of Craig Handy on saxophone and James Genus on bass. The combo performed in cozy New York jazz clubs like the Zinc Bar, playing a mixture of styles including hard bop, traditional, rhythm and blues, funk, and progressive jazz. It was a good learning experience for Watts and also enlarged his fan base.

After years of being a sideman, in 1999, he was finally given the chance to lead his own recording session. The result was *Citizen Tain* and it surprised a lot of people for its rich texture and versatility. There were moments of pure emotion on such songs as "Bluetain, Jr." On the other side, "The Impaler" welded Afro-Cuban spice with straight-ahead jazz. "Muphkin Man" was a spitfire of a song with powerful pulse and snare riffs that allowed Watts to tip his hat to Philly Joe Jones. The song "Attainment" drew comparisons to the legendary Elvin Jones. Altogether, it was a strong debut that demonstrated the wide range of his expressionism. He continues to record and perform in all types of settings.

Jeff "Tain" Watts is an assimilator. He has taken the elements of every major jazz style in the history of the genre and incorporated it into his own playing. He can swing like Jo Jones, bop along like Kenny Clarke, kick out press rolls like Art Blakey, swim strongly in free jazz like Elvin Jones, and be a pure powerhouse like Tony Williams. As well, there are the usual influences of R&B, blues, soul, and even a smidgen of pop in his style.

There is energy to his art that rushes at the listener like a tidal wave. He is an explosive drummer who can attack with the speed and precision of an angry shark. He can also sit in the pocket and groove all day like a surfer riding the perfect, endless wave. A clever, well-seasoned drummer, he can create an entire spectrum of moods from his drum kit.

Although his personal recorded catalog is slim, Watts can be heard on the works of a number of individuals, including guitarist Paul Bollenbeck, organist Barbara Dennerlein, pianist Jason Robello, the Joey Calderazzo Trio (with John Patitucci), and pianist Dave Kikoski. His versatility allows him to play in any setting with maximum effect. He has been an asset to every session that he participated in and boasts solid credentials as a freelance artist.

Although he has worked with a number of individuals including

Michael Brecker, Steven Epstein, Reginald Veal, Ellis Marsalis, Stanley Jordan, James Genus, Terence Blanchard, James Williams, and Lonnie Plaxico, he will always be remembered as one of the young lions in Wynton Marsalis's breakthrough band of the early 1980s. It was this period that created a foundation for him and enabled Watts to progress further with his career. As well, his stint as part of the *Tonight Show* band also richly enhanced his career.

Watts is a perfect example of today's jazz drummer. He is full of vigor, ready to jump in on any gig, and has stretched his encyclopedic knowledge to include every major style of the past one hundred years. He has achieved on his own terms the fame that Kenny Clarke and Art Blakey enjoyed. In many ways, Citizen Tain has taken his place among the hall of fame of jazz drummers.

Discography

Citizen Tain, Columbia 69551.
Megawatts, Sunnyside B0001IXSXC.
Detained at the Blue Note, Half Note Records B0002VGQDM.
Bar Talk, Sony B00006DTZJ.
Wynton Marsalis Quartet, Live at Blues Alley, Columbia 40675.

═══════════════════

BRANFORD MARSALIS (1960–)
The First Family of Jazz

Jazz has included many family connections throughout its long history. Gene Ammons, the great tenor saxophonist of the hard bop set, was the son of Albert Ammons, known for his stomping boogie-woogie–jazz speckled piano style. Mercer Ellington was a longtime employee to Duke Ellington, and has remained the prime caretaker of his father's immense legacy. Ornette Denardo, Ornette Coleman's son, played drums on his father's albums. Then there is the Marsalis family. Ellis, the patriarch, has watched proudly as his sons Wynton, Delfeayo, James, and the oldest, Branford, have carried on the tradition of the first family of jazz.

Branford Marsalis was born August 26, 1960, in Breaux Bridge, Louisiana. Like his three brothers, he benefited greatly from having a father in jazz, as he was exposed to the music from an early age. The saxophone was his instrument of choice, and he eventually mastered the tenor, baritone, and soprano saxophones. With no shortage of musicians in the house to jam with, Branford honed his skills quickly and by the time he was in high school had developed a strong reputation as a player. While in their teens, he and Wynton led a funk band that played at dances and parties.

Like many modern jazz figures Marsalis, obtained a college degree, first at Southern University and then at the well-known Berklee School of Music in Boston. Once he had finished his formal studies, he began the most important part of his musical education when he joined Art Blakey's Jazz Messengers playing baritone saxophone. He was able to tour all over the country and Europe with the elder statesman of hard bop, picking up invaluable lessons not taught in a regular classroom. Later, he played with legendary swing trumpeter Clark Terry for a few months. A year later he returned to the Blakey fold.

In 1982, Branford joined Wynton's quintet and switched from alto to tenor sax at his brother's request. Together they ushered in the neo-traditional jazz renaissance of the 1980s. Their ability to create a new sound and pay respect to the great masters of the past demonstrated the deep talent that each possessed. While with his brother's band, Branford moonlighted with Herbie Hancock, joining the latter on his V.S.O.P. II tour. He was also fortunate enough to record with his idol, Miles Davis, a year later.

Branford, with his college education, talent, and practical experience, made enormous contributions to his brother's band. One of the most important sessions on a sentimental level was with Ellis called *Fathers and Sons*. Although an integral part of Wynton's rise to fame, Branford moved on after a falling out with his younger sibling when he joined Sting's world tour.

During the next few years Branford attempt to emerge from Wynton's enormous sphere of stardom. He went to work in an executive position for Sony Music. In 1986 he returned to the world of jazz, leading his own group with pianist Kenny Kirkland, bassist Bob Hurst and drummer Jeff "Tain" Watts. When Kirkland left the band they continued on as a trio.

In 1992, Branford became the musical director for the *Tonight Show*, hosted by funnyman Jay Leno. A year later he won his first Grammy for Best Jazz Instrumental Performance, Individual or Group, for his album *I Heard You Twice the First Time*, and another for Best Pop Instrumental Performance for "Barcelona Mona," a single he recorded with Bruce Hornsby for the Olympics in Spain. In 1994, he won his third Grammy for the *Contemporary Jazz* CD the same year that he left the *Tonight Show* to pursue his jazz ambitions.

Since then he has worked on a variety of projects, including the *Buckshot LeFonque* recording. He also joined his brother at the Jazz at the Lincoln Center concerts that signaled a period of reconciliation between the two. Eventually, they would perform together more often, including on the television special *The Marsalis Family: A Jazz Celebration* with family members Ellis, James and Delfeayo.

He also made his mark as a producer. Some of his credits include David Sanchez's *Obsesi* and *Melaza* efforts. Other productions include the albums of singer and keyboardist Frank McComb and pianist Joey Calderazzo. In the mid–1990s he formed his own label, Marsalis Music, and recorded Doug Wamble's debut *Country Libations* as well as Miguel Zen's first release.

Branford has also written the music for many soundtracks, including *Showtime, Mr. and Mrs. Loving, Single Dad, Once in the Life,* as well as three Spike Lee films: *Mo' Better Blues, Malcolm X* and *Clockers*. Other credits consist of *Sneakers, School Daze, Throw Momma from the Train* and *The Russia House*. There seems to be no limit to the breadth of his musical talents.

He has also made significant contributions as visiting scholar and part-time faculty member at Michigan State, San Francisco State and Stanford. But his teaching experiences go deeper. He initiated a program called Marsalis Jams that enabled young musicians to play with professionals before live audiences. The first sessions at Smith College and University of New Hampshire were enthralling experiences for everyone involved. About this time he recorded *Romare Bearden Revealed*, a tribute to the African American artist Romare Bearden that included the musical talents of his brother Wynton, as well as Harry Connick, Jr. and Doug Wamble. Branford continues to record and perform.

Branford Marsalis is a jazz fixture. During his career he has made a number of contributions in many areas. His soulful playing is one of the most distinctive voices on all the saxes. He had a hand in his brother's rise to stardom, as well as that of Kenny Kirkland and Jeff "Tain" Watts, among others.

In the beginning, Marsalis sounded like a cross between Wayne Shorter and John Coltrane before he developed his own individual voice. There is a strong emotional depth to his blues and soul saxophone style. He displays an incredible versatility in that he is adept at all three saxes. His multi-instrumentalist abilities became his musical badge in every situation that he participated in.

Although known primarily as a jazz artist, he has also recorded two classical albums. One was *Orpheus*, a collection of music drawing its inspiration from early 20th century French composers, including Milhaud, Ravel and Debussy, among others. He toured for the album strictly in the United States and Japan, backed by the Youngstown, Ohio, and Baltimore Symphony Orchestras.

He has worked with a number of important figures, including Mino Cinelu, Ellis Marsalis, Rob "Wacko" Hunter, Tim Geelan, Jerry Garcia, Michael Landau, Dave Grusin, Omar Hakim, James Taylor, Bruce Hornsby, Stevie Wonder, Bob Hurst, and Kevin Eubanks. The range of names indicates the respect he receives in the music business. Of course, he will forever be linked to his brother Wynton and the rest of the Marsalis family.

Branford was an architect of the return to the traditional jazz movement that began in the early 1980s. He ensured that the old masters were never forgotten for their enormous contributions to the genre, while simultaneously pointing the music towards a new frontier. The respect that he has paid to his predecessors is a credit to his musical vision and his outstanding character.

But he boasts another important credit. In modern times other cities in the United States—Chicago, New York, Detroit and Philadelphia—have produced great jazz musicians. However, Branford, along with his three brothers, has proudly carried on New Orleans's grand tradition as the cradle of jazz. He has upheld the honor of the Louisiana greats that have come before him: Buddy Bolden, King Oliver, Freddie Keppard, Kid Ory, Louis Armstrong, Jelly Roll Morton and Sidney Bechet, to name just a few.

The greatest single influence on Branford was his brother Wynton. The competition between the two from the very beginning fueled their desire to improve. There is a strong brotherly love that undercuts their rivalry. The first to praise one another in any interview, each remains a leading light in modern jazz.

Branford Marsalis is a classic example of the new breed of jazz artist. He has pointed music in a modern direction, while retaining respect for those that established the music. He continues to build on the foundation that he has already created as part of the second generation of the first family of jazz.

Discography

Bloomington, Columbia 52461.
Crazy People Music, Columbia 46072.
I Heard You Twice the First Time, Columbia 46083.
Random Abstract, Columbia 44055.
Renaissance, Columbia 40711.
Royal Garden Blues, Columbia 40363.
Scenes in the City, Columbia 38951.
The Beautyful Ones Are Not Yet Born, Columbia 46990.
Trio Jeepy, Columbia 44199.

Contemporary Jazz, Columbia 63850.
Requiem, Columbia 69655.
Footsteps of Our Father, Rounder 3301.
Eternal, Rounder 3309.

WYNTON MARSALIS (1961–)
The Young Lion

Ever since the bop evolution radically changed the music forever, purists had been crying for a return to traditional jazz. But the music moved through bebop, hard bop, cool jazz, avant-garde, free jazz, and jazz fusion, all experiments in a new direction. However, in 1980, one young lion returned the genre back to its roots. His name is Wynton Marsalis.

Wynton Marsalis was born on October 18, 1961, in New Orleans, Louisiana, into a musical family. His father, Ellis, was a pianist and his three brothers, Branford, Delfeayo, and James would all make their mark in jazz. Named after jazz pianist Wynton Kelly, Marsalis received his first trumpet at the age of six from one of his father's fellow musicians.

He progressed quickly and studied all the great trumpet players from the New Orleans tradition, including Buddy Bolden, Freddy Keppard, King Oliver and Louis Armstrong. He was also enchanted with the bop styles of Dizzy Gillespie, Fats Navarro and Clifford Brown. The cool one, Miles Davis, made an impact on Marsalis, as did the great composers. Wynton cut his musical teeth in local marching bands, funk groups and classical orchestras. The broad range of musical experiences would greatly help him later on in his career. His stint in his teens as first trumpet in the New Orleans Civic Orchestra only added to his growing resume.

During his youth his best friend was his brother Branford and they often practiced together. The special bond that they would develop would be revisited when they became professional musicians. They learned from one another, but at the same time they competed against each other, fueling the honing of their respective skills. Both were talented individuals but by the time he was twelve Wynton was consumed by his obsession for music and practiced more than his brother.

By seventeen he had won many awards, but interestingly enough his first love was classical music, not jazz. Aside from his stint with the New Orleans Civic Orchestra, he had also been a member of the New Orleans Philharmonic Symphony. In 1978, he spent the summer months at the Tanglewood Music Festival in Massachusetts, which was a definite turning point in his career. Although he had won many scholarships to a variety of Ivy League schools, instead of opting for college like his older brother Branford had done, Wynton decided to audition for the prestigious Juliard School of Music in New York and was accepted.

Although he enjoyed attending Juliard and loved to be surrounded by students as serious as he was about music, he pondered the current path of his career. Eventually he left the famed conservatory to play in Art Blakey's Jazz Messengers. For the next three years he learned more about music and life from the granddaddy of bebop than he would have in ten years of school. He also had the opportunity to travel the world and make his first recordings.

Although he thoroughly enjoyed working in Blakey's group, it was time for Marsalis to head out on his own. He had built up quite a reputation and had caught the eye of Columbia Records executives who were searching for the next big star in jazz. They found him in Wynton, who began his recording career before his twentieth birthday. In an era where jazz fusion ruled the genre, Marsalis burst upon the scene with a return to traditional sounds.

He had made friends with a number of young musicians throughout his short career, including Terence Blanchard, Charles Fambrough, Jeff "Tain" Watts, Kenny Kirkland, and Marcus Roberts. When it came time to form a band he had no problems recruiting musicians. He asked Kirkland, Watts, Fambrough and his brother Branford to join his new group. All jumped at the chance to record and tour as a quintet.

The album *Wynton Marsalis* was a hit and took the jazz world by storm. A well-publicized tour and subsequent album with Herbie Hancock only enhanced his popularity. The tour to promote his first album was also a great success. The quintet became one of the hottest tickets as they renewed an interest in the acoustic, traditional form that sparked a renaissance throughout the jazz world.

In 1982, he was also voted by the *Downbeat* poll as the best trumpeter in jazz, winning over old masters Dizzy Gillespie and Miles Davis. A rift between Davis and Wynton would start soon thereafter as they traded barbs in the press. Despite the feud, Marsalis was quickly being recognized as a force to be reckoned with. His first album had been nominated for a Grammy, and his second effort, *Think of One,* won for best traditional jazz performance. He also earned one of the coveted awards for best classical performance on *Concerto for Trumpet and Orchestra in E-Flat Major.*

In 1984, he scored two more Grammies, one for his third album, *Hot House Flowers,* and another for best classical performance on a solo album for *Baroque Music for Trumpet.* Although the awards were a personal satisfaction, there was a growing rift between Wynton and his brother Branford.

He had also come full circle in his praise for traditional jazz and his dislike for jazz fusion, avant-garde and pop music. His comments irritated others, but by this time Wynton was powerful enough that he could overcome some controversial statement.

In 1985, he won another Grammy for *Black Codes (From the Underground)* that presented a synthesis of his traditionalist beliefs combined with a strong tinge of experimental and modernist attitude. But above all it swung, reverberating the basic musical message that the great Duke Ellington had said years earlier. Marsalis led the revolution of a back-to-basics jazz that paid homage to the great artists of the past.

His next effort, *J Mood,* also won a Grammy, but it did so without the talents of Kenny Kirkland and Branford. The two had departed to play with Sting, the pop star. The defections hurt Wynton but he continued to roll on and played all over the world. He re-formed his group to include blind pianist Marcus Roberts, bassist Robert Hurst and the loyal Watts on drums. Marsalis would eventually add trombonist Wycliffe Gordon, altoist Wes Anderson, Todd Williams on tenor, bass player Reginald Veal, and drummer Herlin Riley. While Marsalis had been praised for his playing, he was still honing his composition skills and it was this burning passion to never stand still that enabled him to remain a head above his contemporaries.

The band remained intact for multiple concerts and recordings. Eric Reed was added a few years later. Wynton, in an effort to emulate one of his idols, Duke Ellington, wrote specifically for members of his septet. The popularity of his group overshadowed all others in jazz and it eventually brought him to the attention of the powers that ran Jazz at Lincoln Center.

In 1987, he was signed to play at the Lincoln Center, but because of his other commitments with his septet, he was able to play only a couple of concerts where he focused on Duke Ellington's music. In the next couple of years, he performed a few times and with each concert endeared himself even more to the board that ran the famous concert hall series. Eventually, Classical Jazz was turned into Jazz at the Lincoln Center and Wynton became the director.

He continued to win Grammy awards for his albums and was featured on the cover of *Time* magazine in 1990. As well, the Jazz at the Lincoln Center series became a very popular event with lectures, films, concerts and tours all done in order to educate audiences about America's classical music. If all of this wasn't enough, Wynton worked on a radio series called *Making the Music* that further promoted the traditional style he loved so much. He won a Peabody Award for his efforts on the twenty-six series radio show. Later he would add television to his medium conquests with a four-part event titled *Marsalis on Music* that ran on PBS.

He continued his projects, including *Jazz for Young People,* and his role as educator was solidified. The fact that he was always willing to take time from his hectic schedule to teach an aspiring musician a particular passage before or after a concert demonstrated his love of the music. He was passing on the torch like his heroes Duke Ellington, Louis Armstrong, Thelonious Monk and so many others had done. In 1996, he went even further, establishing the Essentially Ellington High School Band Competition and Festival. It became an annual event, providing students with the chance to develop a strong musical career.

In the latter part of the 1990s Marsalis' recorded output gained special recognition and provided a solid collection for jazz fans. His *Blood on the Fields* won a Pulitzer Prize, the first jazz-based work to do so. The Midnight Blues: Standard Time, Vol. 5 was a big seller. *Marsalis plays Monk: Standard Time, Volume 4,* was the young lion's way of paying homage to one of the great pianists of all time. His *Live at the Village Vanguard,* a seven-disc package, only increased his powerful hold on the jazz world. With the release of *The Marciac Suite* and *Goin' Down Home* in 2000, Marsalis only added to his crown as the number one performer in the genre.

As Marsalis continues to record and tour all over the world, he reinforces the idea that jazz is a healthy and vital musical force.

Wynton Marsalis is a young lion. No one in the past twenty years has made as large an impact on the jazz world as the trumpeter, leader, writer, and spokesman from New Orleans. In any assessment of exceptional jazz minds of the first hundred years, his name must certainly be added to the list. His influence has had far reaching effects.

Although he has received accolades for other aspects of his abilities there is the underlying fact that Marsalis is a brilliant trumpeter. Often this fact seems to get overlooked because of his many other accomplishments. He has taken jazz back to the pre-evolutionary bop days with his playing, but has given his music a modern sound to please current listeners. He is a powerful player with an emotional depth that is purely arousing.

Marsalis had many influences, including the musicians that came through the house to jam with his father while Wynton was growing up. His brother Branford was an important cog in his development because of the competition and respect they had for each other. Although they were very critical of one another, another important influence on Wynton was Miles Davis. Other great trumpeters like Dizzy Gillespie, Fats Navarro, Woody Shaw, Louis Armstrong, Clifford Brown, and Don Cherry also made a strong impact on his development.

More than anyone else, Marsalis has revived an interest in jazz in the past twenty years. A tireless worker, he has helped spread the popularity of the music through high schools, all corners of the globe and the prestigious Lincoln Center. Because of the deaths of so many greats since his emergence in 1982—Dizzy Gillespie, Earl Hines, Roy Eldridge, Count Basie, Coleman Hawkins, Benny Goodman, Jo Jones, Ella Fitzgerald, Kenny Clarke, Thelonious Monk, Dexter Gordon, Sarah Vaughan, Miles Davis, Art Blakey, and Tony Williams—Wynton has attempted to fill the void.

As the leader of the contemporary scene, he has also nurtured the careers of many of his peers. He has always been able to spot solid talent. Marcus Roberts, James Carter, Mark Whitefield, Jeff "Tain" Watts have benefited greatly from their time spent with Wynton. He is the nexus from which the entire modern jazz movement has grown.

Although he has faced his fair share of critics and detractors because of his controversial statements, Wynton continues to add to his status. He has established himself as the leading voice in jazz in the past twenty years and remains the single most important name. He is a superstar, the creator of real music in a world where electronic programmed music is so highly regarded. He remains the young lion.

Discography

Hot House Flowers, Columbia 39530.
The Midnight Blues: Standard Time, Vol. 5, Columbia 68921.
Big Train, Columbia 69860.
Black Codes (From the Underground), Columbia 40009.
Blood on the Fields, Columbia 57694.
Crescent City Christmas Card, Columbia 45287.
Immortal Concerts: Jody, Giants of Jazz Recordings 53325.
J Mood, Columbia 40308.
Jump Start & Jazz: Two Ballets by Wynton Marsalis, Columbia 62998.
Levee Low Moan: Soul Gestures ... Vol. 3, Columbia 47975.
Live at Bubba's Jazz Restaurant, Chrisly Records 15013.
Live at the Village Vanguard, Columbia 69876.
Marsalis Plays Monk: Standard Time, Vol. 4, Columbia 67503.
Marsalis Standard Time, Vol. 1, Columbia 40461.
Reeltime, Sony Classical 51239.
Sound of Jazz, Volume 14, Galaxy Sound Of Jazz 388614.
Standard Time, Vol. 2: Intimacy Calling, Columbia 47346.
Standard Time, Vol. 3: The Resolution of Romance, Columbia 46143.
Standard Time, Vol. 6: Mr. Jelly Lord, Columbia 69872.
Sweet Release & Ghost Story, Sony Classical 61690.
The All-American Hero, Master Tone Records 8441.
The Majesty of the Blues, Columbia 45091.
Thick in the South: Soul Gestures ... Vol. 1, Columbia 47977.
Think of One, Columbia 38641.
Uptown Ruler: Soul Gestures ... Vol. 2, Columbia 47976.

Wynton Marsalis, Columbia 37574.
The Marciac Suite, Columbia 69877.
Blue Interlude, Columbia 48729.
Citi Movement (Griot New York), Columbia 53324.
In This House, On This Morning, Columbia 53220.
Selections from the Village Vanguard Box Set, Columbia 62191.
Baroque Music, Columbia 46672.
Baroque Music for Trumpets, CBS 42478.
Carnival, Columbia 421733.
Live at Blues Alley, Columbia 40675.
Standard Time, Vol. 4. Sony B00000J280.
Joe Cool's Blues, Columbia 66880.
In Gabriel's Garden, Columbia 66244.
Fiddler's Tale, Sony B00000JBDR.
At the Octoroon Balls: String Quartet No. 1, Sony B00000JBDU.

JOHN MEDESKI (1965–)

Acid Jazz Grooves

The term contemporary jazz encompasses a diversity that ranges from a radio friendly, gentle instrumental sound to a grittier improvisational, swinging style that reaches back throughout the history of the genre for inspiration. Acid jazz, which gained attention in the late 1960s and 1970s during the jazz fusion era, continues to be a popular strain among a coterie of players. One of the best exponents of the style is John Medeski.

John Medeski was born on June 28, 1965, in Louisville, Kentucky. He moved to Fort Lauderdale, Florida, when an infant and it was there in the Sunshine State that he discovered a love of music. He started piano lessons at the age of five and improved quickly, developing a passion for all the great masters, including Bach, Beethoven, and Debussy. But he also had an ear for popular songs and learned them as well.

Medeski had honed his skills to a fine edge by the time he was ten and was good enough to perform at recitals and competitions, as well as playing with dance and theatre companies. He made his first jazz connection as a teenager and immediately fell under the hypnotic spell of Bud Powell, Cecil Taylor, and Oscar Peterson. He furthered his education by studying Western musical theory with Lee Shaw in high school. He built an encyclopedic knowledge of all styles in his head that would someday serve him well.

Although he had been classically trained, Medeski developed a greater appetite for African American folk music. In order to gain experience,

Medeski was always keen on any jam sessions and played in chamber ensembles, at weddings, and at theater productions. He also began to compose his own material and wrote two musicals. He added to his instrumental range by learning how to play the bassoon.

By his late teens Medeski was wholeheartedly into the jazz scene and began to explore the world of the electric piano. He purchased a Fender Rhodes and decided to form his own band. He called it Emergency and it included Mark Murphy. Medeski temporarily left the band to accept jazz fusion bassist Jaco Pastorius's generous offer to perform on his 1981 Japanese tour. However, because Medeski was only sixteen and his parents insisted he was too young, he was forced to pass on the opportunity—much to his sheer dismay.

But he was not deterred. He won an NEA Award in 1982, and upon his high school graduation followed his musical ambitions by moving to Boston to study with Leonard Shure at the New England Conservatory. Although he had spent much of his past few years pursuing his love of jazz and other styles of popular music, Medeski studied classical at the conservatory, enhancing his already deep reference base.

But he was not restricted to the classical style. He studied other musical avenues in his second year at the New England Conservatory, joining the Third-Stream program. On the side, Medeski jammed with George Russell, Dave Holland and Joe Maneri. One of the main connections he made at the conservatory was with Bob Moses; together they managed to work with passing musicians including tenor saxophonist Dewey Redman. Medeski was conducting a balanced education with emphasis on practical and theory.

When the partnership with Moses was over, Medeski continued searching for the right combination that would lead him to success in the music business. He played with a variety of groups, including the Either/Orchestra, the Ken Schaphorst Big Band, and the Jazz Composers Alliance that included Anthony Davis and Sam Rivers. In the interim, he added the Hammond B-3 organ to his arsenal. For the next two years, he freelanced in New York, playing at such clubs as the Village Gate.

In 1990, while playing gigs in New York, he met Chris Wood, Reggie Workman and Billy Martin. They jammed together and there was a magical feeling in the air. Workman would eventually leave the quartet and the remaining three would launch their career in jazz with the release of their first CD, *Notes from the Underground*.

Billy Martin was born in New York City and boasted a strong musical background. His father was a violinist with both the New York City Opera orchestra and the New York City Ballet, while his mother was a former Radio City Rockette. He began to play drums at an early age and was heavily influenced by African and Brazilian polyrhythms. He worked with Bob Moses and Chuck Mangione before discovering the downtown music scene and it was there that he met Medeski and Wood.

Chris Wood grew up in Colorado and studied bass composition before he entered his teens. He developed quickly and by high school had earned All-State jazz bassist and All-State Orchestra credentials. He studied at the New England Conservatory and counted among his classmates Dave Holland, Bob Moses and Geri Allen. While attending school he also gigged with a number of local acts, including Steve Kuhn, Bob Moses, Joanne Brackeen, George Russell, Randy Weston, the Either/Orchestra, and the Ken Schaphorst Big Band. Later he toured with Marc Ribot's Shrek group, as well as the Ned Rothenberg Double Band, the Jazz Passengers, Elliot Sharp, John Zorn, Jack Walrath, Chunk, Oren Bloedow, and the Black Rock Coalition.

Together Medeski, Martin, and Wood hit a successful formula with their laid-back approach. All were highly improvisational players and that allowed them to let the music flow along at a natural pace. They struck gold early and continued to do so with successive releases: *It's a Jungle in Here*, *Friday Afternoon in the Universe*, *Shack-Man*, *Combustication*, and *Last Chance to Dance Trance*. They covered a variety of material, including the songs of Jimi Hendrix, Miles Davis, and David Fiuczynski, among others.

The three became in a short time the practitioners of the acid jazz movement. An avenue of the genre that has been dismissed by some critics, it has not stopped the trio from establishing themselves as one of the top acts on the circuit. Although they aren't the only exponents of the controversial style, they remain the best it has to offer. They continue to record and perform.

John Medeski is an acid jazz artist. His spacey special effects have reached back to the *Bitches Brew* period of Miles Davis. His ability to give jazz fusion a modern twist had propelled him and his bandmates into instant popularity. The trio is one of the coolest jazz groups on the scene today.

Medeski is a master of the Hammond B-3 organ, drawing from it an incredible wealth of music. He has built on the foundation of those before him, including Jimmy Smith, Jack Bill Doggett, Richard "Groove" Holmes, Brother Jack McDuff, Jimmy McGriff, and Sun Ra. Medeski, like these people, has proven that the organ can play a vital role in jazz. He has been able to wrap his technical wizardry around the pulsating bass of Wood and the rock-hard precision drumming of Martin. Individually they are good, but together they are something special.

Although they are solid practitioners of the style, Medeski, Wood and Martin are not the inventors of acid jazz. The style dates back to the 1960s and 1970s. Such practitioners as trumpeters Donald Byrd and Miles Davis, vibraphonist Roy Ayers, guitarist Grant Green, organist Charles Earland, and saxmen Houston Person and Lou Donaldson all played funky jazz with many of the same elements found in the best work of Medeski, Wood and Martin.

In the 1980s the neo-traditionalists with their unplugged music dominated the jazz scene. However, acid jazz made a comeback in the 1990s, spearheaded by the efforts of Medeski, Martin, and Wood. Other practitioners of the style include Greyboy, Gang Starr and Tribe, Jamiroquai, Incognito, Snowboy, Galliano, the James Taylor Quartet, Brand New Heavies, A Tribe Called Quest, Digable Planets, Count Basic, Night Trains, Mother Earth, Chris Bowden, EM & J, Money Mark, Slide Five, Soul Bossa Trio and the Spiritual Vibes. Although acid jazz is not the favorite style among many critics and a portion of fans, it is a viable sound that appeals to a certain section of listeners.

Medeski, Martin and Wood are a perfect example of today's fragmented jazz scene. In the 1920s, during the Golden Age of jazz, the blues trumpet sound of Louis Armstrong set the tone. In the 1930s and 1940s, the big band and swing sounds ruled the airwaves. In the mid–1940s and 1950s bop took over and would eventually be broken down into cool jazz and hard bop. In the 1960s free jazz and the avant-garde dominated. Later in the decade jazz fusion was all the rage. Since that period there has been an increasing diversity of styles. Instead of one dominant sound there is something for every jazz fan living in the multicultural world.

Acid jazz is an extension of jazz fusion. It incorporates elements of acid rock, drawing inspiration from the exponents of the style: Jimi Hendrix, Jefferson Airplane, the Grateful Dead, The Doors, and other late 1960s rock-blues bands. Of the group, Hendrix was probably the single most important proponent and Medeski, Martin and Wood have cleverly recorded some of his songs, giving their music substance and respectability. They have also explored the acid rock/jazz avenue that Hendrix frequented briefly before his untimely death.

Their fusion of jazz and rock has brought in young fans into the fold, thus enlightening a whole generation to the hundred-plus-year history of the genre. Although their music is something of an acquired taste, once it has been experienced it is difficult to do without it. While they have played with many different groups and all three moonlighted outside of the trio, they have remained together creating finely crafted, marketable acid grooves for appreciative audiences.

Discography

The Dropper, Blue Note Records 22841.
Combustication, Blue Note Records 93011.
Friday Afternoon in the Universe, Gramavision Records 79503.
It's a Jungle in Here, Gramavision Records 79495.
Last Chance to Dance Trance (Perhaps): Best, Gramavision Records 79520.
Notes from the Underground, Accurate Records 5010.
Shack-man, Gramavision Records 79514.
Tonic, Blue Note Records 25271.
Medeski Martin & Wood, BLUEN 5228412.

DIANA KRALL (1965–)

Frim Fram Sauce Blues

The United States is the acknowledged home of the birthplace of jazz and boasts the greatest number of practitioners. However, the contagious music has spread all over the world and many countries have produced outstanding figures. While Canada has never been able to boast a great stable of jazz artists, the handful of musicians to emerge from the Great White North have made their presence felt. In the 1990s, a new voice in Canadian jazz turned everyone's head with her frim fram sauce blues. Her name is Diana Krall.

Diana Krall was born on November 16, 1965, in Nanaimo, British Columbia, into a musical family. Both of her parents were piano players and encouraged her interests. Her father's extensive jazz record collection was available to her and the family often gathered around the piano to sing songs. Krall started to take piano lessons at the tender age of four and by her teens was already paying her dues in abundance.

In her teens she did double duty in the high school jazz band and as a singer in a restaurant not far from her home, playing three times a week. It was here that she gained invaluable performance lessons and learned the kind of effort it would take to make it in the music business. It also gave her ample opportunity to hone her skills. She was a talented singer; her tenacity began to pay off in the early 1980s.

In 1981, she won a scholarship to study at the Berklee College of Music in Boston. She remained at the school for a year and a half, then returned to her native British Columbia. One night while she was working through her ever-increasing repertoire, Ray Brown, the great bassist who had played with Oscar Peterson, spotted her. Brown recognized Krall's special talent and became her mentor of sorts, encouraging her to make Los Angeles her home base, which she did. He suggested that she develop her vocal talents to add a distinct dimension to her advanced piano skills.

After a stint in the City of Angels, Krall relocated to Toronto and stayed there for a brief time before moving to New York. In 1993, she recorded her first effort, *Stepping Out.* Ray Brown, Jeff Hamilton, and John Clayton backed her on the CD. It was a good collection of songs that included "This Can't Be Love," "Straighten Up and Fly Right," "I'm Just a Lucky So and So," "42nd Street," "Frim Fram Sauce," and one of her own compositions, "Jimmie."

The group of songs signaled a powerful new voice in jazz that combined elements of swing and romance with a modern twist. There was freshness to her approach that hadn't been heard in the genre in a long time. She managed to illustrate the past by bringing it into the future. Although there were many young female vocalists on the scene, her confidence, determination and sensuality separated her from the others.

She utilized New York as a home base and played concerts up and down the East Coast with Jeff Hamilton on drums and John Clayton on bass. Although her debut recording had not made her an instant star, it had gained her a few more fans. The Diana Krall express had slowly left the station.

In 1995, she released her second CD, *Only Trust Your Heart.* Once again Ray Brown backed her along with Christian McBride, Lewis Nash and Stanley Turrentine. It was another collection of songs that dealt with the complexities of love in the modern world and the record turned a few heads. Those who heard her knew that she was a major talent and it was only a matter of time before she was recognized as a genuine star. It was on this record that she connected with Tommy LiPuma, who would play a major role in her career rise from this point on.

In 1996, Krall recorded *All for You* and life was never quite the same for her again. A personal dedication to the music of Nat King Cole and his trio, the CD smashed its way to the top ten on Billboard's Traditional Jazz charts and remained there for an incredible year and a half. Russell Malone on guitar, Paul Keller on bass, Benny Green on piano, and Steve Kroon on percussion backed her on the award-winning release. Once again Tommy LiPuma was the producer. His ability to guide her but at the same time to allow her talent to flow unchecked was a tribute to his abilities as a producer. They made a good team.

The awards and adulation fell at her feet. *All for You* earned a spot on the prestigious *New York Times* "Top Ten Adult Pop Albums" for the year 1996. As well, in early 1997 she was nominated for a Grammy award for Best Jazz Vocal Performance. She released *Love Scenes* that same year and the CD eventually went gold in 1999. On *Love Scenes* she returned to a trio format and was backed by Russell Malone on guitar and Christian McBride on bass. The biggest hit on the album was "Peel Me a Grape" and it became her signature song.

In 1998, she received her second consecutive Grammy nomination for Best Jazz Vocal Performance. While the recording side of her career had gained strength, her performance side was also picking up momentum. Around the time of the release of *When I Look in Your Eyes,* she toured North and South America, Asia, Europe, and Australia, delighting audiences around the world with her sultry, definitive jazz voice and enchanting piano skills. A few highlights of the tour occurred at the Hollywood Bowl in Los Angeles and at Massey Hall in Toronto, both of them old stomping grounds for the classy artist. Her billing with legendary singer Tony Bennett was a thrill for the blonde beauty and signaled the passing of the torch from the older generation to the younger one.

The CD *When I Look in Your Eyes* was a logical extension of her previous work. On this effort she teamed up with arranger Johnny Mandel, who provided lush orchestral strings to some of the highlights of the album, including Irving Berlin's "Let's Face the Music," and the Cole Porter tune "I've Got You Under My Skin." The latter song was made famous by Frank Sinatra; he had always been one of Krall's biggest influences. As she had on her other releases, she displayed an uncanny ability to sound very modern, but with connections to the rich history of jazz. It was this knack that separated her from the multitude of female singers on the circuit.

She continues her meteoric rise in the jazz world with her recordings and performances. Perhaps the biggest news in her career has not been a musical one, but her marriage to new wave artist Elvis Costello.

Diana Krall is a jazz treasure. She has taken the jazz world by storm with her strong, hypnotizing voice and equally memorable piano skills. There is something nostalgic about her songs, her performance and her approach that reminds listeners of years gone by, but she has been able to insert a contemporary element in her music that makes it relevant. She has made many contributions to jazz despite the fact that her complete talent has not yet been fully tapped.

She is a double threat. Her voice is like the sweet, clear-throated song of a chirping bird outside one's bedroom window in the splendor of a beautiful spring morning. But there are many dimensions to her vocal talent; she can also sound sultry and sexy, creating soothing music for loving couples after the kids have been put to bed. The many shades of timbres in her voice are the stuff of superstars.

While her piano playing may never garner comparisons to Oscar Peterson, Art Tatum, or Teddy Wilson, Krall is an inventive, economic pianist.

She plays an uncluttered brand of jazz that, combined with her special voice, creates a smooth and seamless attack. Her intelligence on the instrument is a reflection of years of listening to the great jazz pianists and incorporating the latent elements that pleased her the most.

But there is another dimension to her music that must be noted. Although she is a solid composer, a talent that continues to blossom with each new release, she also has a knack for picking the right songs to cover. Her choice of material depends on her ability to take the song down avenues that were previously thought to be impossible. Her treatment of Nat King Cole, George Gershwin, Sinatra, Bennett and other songbooks is impeccable. Like Linda Ronstadt, who covered the right songs on her multi-platinum albums in the 1970s, Krall has done the same throughout her career.

The awards have only begun to trickle in, and Krall picked up her third Grammy, this time for Best Jazz Vocal Performance, at the 2000 ceremonies. She won a Juno award for Best Jazz Vocal Album, also in 2000. In 1998, she won Musician of the Year from the *Jazz Report* and Artist of the Year from the *Jazz Times* Readers Poll. In 1999, she won Female Vocalist of the Year awarded by *Downbeat Jazz*. Perhaps her most triumphant award was the Order of British Columbia in 2000. With her unique talent, there will be many awards in the future.

She is part of contemporary culture, a unique feat in jazz since in the past sixty years the genre has been an acquired taste. People who are not true jazz fans recognize the name and like her music. She has crossover appeal not only in music charts, but among the record buying public.

Diana Krall has reinstated a fire in the jazz world with her incomparable talent, good looks, poise, sophistication and heart. She is of the new generation of singers, but has great respect for all those that came before her and it is this character trait that is perhaps the most admirable. As long as she continues to pour out her brand of easily accessible, first-class frim fram sauce blues, she will remain at the top of the jazz heap.

Discography

All for You (A Dedication to the Nat King Cole Trio), Impulse! 182.
Love Scenes, GRP Records 233.
When I Look in Your Eyes, Impulse! 304.
Only Trust Your Heart, GRP Records 9810.
Stepping Out, Justin Time 50.
Have Yourself a Merry Little Christmas, IMPUL MVCJ-19169.

MARK WHITFIELD (1967–)
The Marksman

The guitar tradition runs through the entire history of jazz from the earliest days in New Orleans to the present. The evolution of its role has greatly changed over the past hundred years. In the beginning the instrument was kept strictly in the rhythm section, but ever since Charlie Christian broke new ground, the guitar has gained more respect. There are many vital six-string slingers in contemporary jazz, including the player known as the marksman. His name is Mark Whitfield.

Mark Whitfield was born in 1967 in Long Island, New York, the youngest of five children. He was exposed to jazz from an early age. He received encouragement from his aunt, who gave him some records and a stack of sheet music. He picked up the guitar when he was around seven years old, but soon became discouraged and decided to take up the acoustic bass, then the alto saxophone.

He returned to the guitar when he saw his idol, George Benson, on a television show. Benson, who had scored many crossover soul-jazz hits in the 1970s, inspired many future guitar players. However, just as Whitfield was finding his musical voice in New York, where he gigged with a bunch of schoolmates in various outfits, his parents uprooted him to Seattle, Washington.

Despite his disappointment at being forced to travel across the country to a strange place where he had to start all over, Whitfield found life grand in the state of Washington. After all, Seattle was the home of the greatest guitar player that ever lived—Jimi Hendrix, and although he was dead people talked about him as if he were still alive. The music scene in the West Coast city was rich in tradition and it didn't take long for Whitfield to settle in, as he became the guitarist in the high school band.

He led a double life, one of a normal student playing guitar in the high school band, and a second one that saw him jam with a variety of the best six-string warriors Seattle had to offer. As a result of these informal workshops, he incorporated chunks of rock, blues, jazz, pop, and soul into his developing style. His diligent practice and performances at local competitions earned him a scholarship to the Berklee College of Music in Boston.

The debate over traditional versus the new thing raged on during his college days, when he was exposed to a number of different ideas and philosophies of how to play guitar. Whitfield declared himself a traditionalist since he cherished Benson, Kenny Burrell, Wes Montgomery, and Grant Green rather than then the current jazz guitar school of thought that favored Pat Metheny and John Scofield. But Whitfield was always open to new ideas. He also loved to jam and while at Berklee he had the opportunity to trade musical ideas with the Marsalis Brothers—James and Delfeayo. It proved to be a very rewarding experience.

Upon his graduation, Whitfield returned to his native New York to become a bona fide jazz guitarist. He worked for a stockbroker to support himself and his new bride. While daydreaming of his future success, he wrote some of the songs that would one day appear on his debut album. On the weekends, he could be found in any number of jazz clubs sitting in with a variety of bands, paying his dues and waiting for his big break.

He managed to land a gig with the Blue Note after-hours band that was comprised of older, more experienced players. He had to mature in a hurry and the method of putting himself in the heat of the battle was perhaps one of the best accelerators for his development. He quickly honed his skills to a much higher level and was accepted by the older professional musicians.

The Blue Note Jam Band also opened the door that would lead to his success: one night George Benson arrived on the scene and was impressed with the young guitar player. Benson, who had many connections in the music business, introduced Whitfield to organist Brother Jack McDuff. Some time later Mark went to work for McDuff and despite a rough start, he began to absorb the important lessons that the elder statesman was willing to teach him.

As well, the friendship between Whitfield and Benson blossomed and they jammed together whenever their busy schedules allowed for it. The vital role that Benson played in Whitfield's developing confidence is crucial, since it enabled the young guitarist to be ready when Warner Bros. came knocking on his door. Tony LiPuma, one of the leading producers of jazz in the past fifteen years, signed Whitfield.

In 1990, *The Marksman* was released and all of the musical ideas that he had been working on since his high school days finally became concrete songs. After his straightforward jazz album, Whitfield was talked about in the same breath as the current giants of jazz guitar—including his hero George Benson, the smooth one, Wes Montgomery, and the electric warrior Larry Coryell. As with practitioners of every other instrument, there exists a brotherhood among guitarists that is a bond stronger than blood.

Despite the promise of his debut recording, Whitfield's second work, *Patrice,* and his third, entitled *Mark Whitfield,* showed him veering off the jazz path. Their experimental nature alienated a lot of hardcore fans who had championed Whitfield as the next great thing in jazz guitar after the splash he made with his initial effort. Despite his flair for experimentation, he was still an enthusiast and had not totally abandoned the genre.

Whitfield returned to his artistic vision of making pure jazz records and his first effort for the Verve label, *True Blue*, welcomed him back to the fold. The personnel on the album included drummer Jeff "Tain" Watts, saxophonist Branford Marsalis, and pianist Kenny Kirkland. The quartet was an all-star jam featuring some of the best young talent on the current scene. The fans he had lost with his two previous recordings returned.

He relocated his family to Baton Rouge, Louisiana, where he hooked up with Alvin Batiste, who headed Southern University's jazz program. It was an experience that turned out to be another important turn in his blossoming career. The rich jazz tradition in the state enhanced Whitfield's status and gave him the incentive to push on to new projects.

While he had returned to making good jazz albums, Whitfield had also shored up the performance side of his career when he appeared with Delfeayo Marsalis at the Crescent City Brewhouse on Decatur Street. On the same gig was trumpet player Nicholas Payton, who would be a vital future figure in Whitfield's story. They later played together on a cruise ship and Payton added his sharp trumpet to Whitfield's *True Blue* sessions. The pair worked together again on Payton's *From This Moment* CD, as well as with soul-jazz organist Jimmy Smith on his CD *Damn!*. They also backed Smith on a few concert dates that officially began Whitfield's soul phase.

Although there had always been a touch of the soul in his style, the New Orleans environment truly brought out this dimension. This new identity could be heard strongly in his next recording, *7th Ave. Stroll*, which paid tribute to his heroes, George Benson and Wes Montgomery. Although it had a definite southern feeling, 7th Ave. Stroll also captured the frenzy and anxiety of living in the Big Apple. All of his personal experiences from his three years in New York could be found scattered throughout the CD's tracks. The juxtaposition of ideas made for some very interesting listening.

Since then, Whitfield has been a notable session man and led a quartet that includes Payton. He remains one of the best and busiest young jazz guitarists in the business. He performs regularly and every new collection of material sheds some light on his many musical dimensions.

Mark Whitfield is a link in the chain. He has carried on the guitar tradition established decades ago and has added his particular chapter to the story. He is one of the finest players on the scene today and though a young man, he has already built up quite a reputation.

There are many elements to his guitar style. Without a doubt, his biggest influence was George Benson and Whitfield has emulated his idol by putting down some funky jazz with a good dose of soul to give it an emotional edge. There is a clean, precise side to his guitar sound that is accessible, much like Benson's approach. While he has borrowed heavily from his mentor, Whitfield does possess his own unique touch. There is urgency in his music, an undercurrent to the laid back image that he projects.

Although he is a leading light in jazz guitar, Whitfield shares the spotlight with a solid group of players, including Dave Stryker, John Hart, John Abercrombie, Ted Dunbar, Pat Martino, John Scofield, Russell Malone, Ronald Shannon Jackson, and Norman Brown. There is an individuality that sets Whitfield apart from the others. Undoubtedly, it is his personal experiences and artistic vision that gives him a slight edge over his contemporaries.

During his short career he has worked with a great number of jazz figures, including Jimmy Smith, Turtle Creek Chorale, Roy Hargrove, D'Angelo, Cyrus Chestnut, Carl Allen, Courtney Pine, Cleo Laine, Ron Carter, Mack Richard, Frederick Moore, Peter Mena, Bill Kotch, Kit Kayton, Gene Hempy, and Martin Guerra. As more artists discovered his vast guitar talents, Whitfield was included on more sessions. He is a dream in the recording studio because of his seemingly effortless crisp, clean guitar lines pumped out with an inimitable touch.

Perhaps his biggest contribution to jazz has been his dedication to the jazz guitar tradition and the expansion of its role. Jefferson Mumford played an acoustic guitar in Buddy Bolden's band and was strictly a rhythm player. Although Lonnie Johnson and Eddie Lang gained the instrument some respect, it was the parallel careers of Django Reinhardt and Charlie Christian that truly brought the guitar into prominence. Every guitarist since then, including Kenny Burrell, Herb Ellis, Barney Kessel, Wes Montgomery, Larry Coryell, John McLaughlin, and George Benson, has expanded the parameters of jazz guitar. Whitfield has carried on like a proud warrior.

Mark Whitfield is a businessman, a family man, and a leader in modern music. He is an example of the new player, college educated, and a city-dweller who has retreated to a quieter environment. He has forged his own personal musical direction and continues to combine straightforward jazz with an element of soul to give his music the necessary grit. He remains the supreme marksman of the guitar.

Discography

Raw, Transparent Music 3.
7th Ave. Stroll, Verve 529 223.
Forever Love, Verve 533 921.
Mark Whitfield, Warner Bros. Records 45210.
Patrice, Warner Bros. Records 26659.
The Marksman, Warner Bros. Records 26321.
True Blue, Verve 523 591.

CHRISTIAN MCBRIDE (1972–)

Freewheeling Bass

The diversity of bass players in the history of jazz has added a special flavor to the music. Ever since the personal exploits of Jimmy Blanton, bassists have stepped forward to take a leading role in the creation and arrangement of every style. Today's bass players have an established standard to live up to. One of the newcomers with his freewheeling bass has not only drawn from the deep well of great players of the past but has added his own dimension. His name is Christian McBride.

Christian McBride was born on May 31, 1972, in Philadelphia, Pennsylvania. His fascination for the bass comes naturally since it is a family trait. His father, Lee Smith, played bass for the Delfonics, Billy Paul, and Mongo Santamaria, among others. His uncle, Howard Cooper, was a member of Sun Ra's cosmic groups. Christian is one of the few current players who can brag of such a diverse and interesting pedigree.

McBride himself first took up the electric bass when he was nine, but two years later switched over to the acoustic model. He studied under a variety of classical instructors including Margie Keefe, Anne Peterson, and Neil Courtney; Courtney associated with the Philadelphia Orchestra. McBride also was interested in jazz, rhythm and blues, and rock and worked with locals like the Landham Brothers, Joe Sudler's Swing Machine and Edgar Bateman.

His facility on the bass was quickly accelerated and in his early teens he hooked up with Wynton Marsalis, the hottest name in jazz circles at the time. They developed a friendship based on their healthy respect for one another's ability and their dedication to traditional jazz. McBride further added to his musical education by attending the School for the Creative and the Performing Arts in his hometown. At the high school, a breeding ground for future musicians, he struck up friendships with members of The Roots, Boyz II Men, organist Joe DeFrancesco, guitarist Kurt Rosenwinkel, singer Amel Latrieux, and Mark Nelson, who would go on to become a member of the Kenneth Edmunds band. It was an impressive list of contacts for someone so young.

A brilliant student among a cast of intelligent individuals, McBride excelled in his studies enough to secure a scholarship with the prestigious Juliard School of Music. That summer while waiting for the fall semester to begin, he padded his resume as a member of the classical-jazz group Free Flight and the Philadelphia Youth Orchestra. The experiences only enhanced his blossoming talent that had turned heads, and they provided him with further encouragement to pursue his goals.

Since he had been involved in music almost his whole life, the lessons at Juliard seemed repetitive, so McBride turned his attention to the many clubs in New York. He easily found work at places like the Village Gate and Bradley's. His studies suffered even more when he became a permanent member of Bobby Watson's group. Although he managed to make it through an entire year of the Juliard program, he realized that his best education existed in on-the-road experiences of band life instead of the stuffiness of the classroom.

He played in Roy Hargrove's band, then joined Freddie Hubbard's group, with which he recorded and toured. His time spent in the outfit was more valuable than ten years of school. He also played in the bands of Benny Golson and Benny Green, developing a reputation as a first class force on the bass and as someone who was easy to work with. His youthful enthusiasm and drive enabled him to take on more than one project at a time.

In 1992, he beamed with pride at the fact that he had been named *Rolling Stone* magazine's Hot Jazz Artist of the Year. Some time later he joined the Special Quartet, which was led by guitarist Pat Metheny and included Billy Higgins and tenor saxophone player Joshua Redman. Like McBride, Redman was a promising young talent. A year later, McBride was touring in Redman's band and also found the time to record his first album as a leader.

The lineup for his first effort, *Gettin' To It*, included Redman, Hargrove, piano player Cyrus Chestnut and drummer Lewis Nash. One of the highlights of the effort was the song "Splanky" that featured talented bass players Milt Hinton and Ray Brown squaring off against McBride in a three-way duel. The appearance of the two famous statesmen signaled the respect that McBride garnered from the older set of jazz musicians.

He played at the Philadelphia Mellon Jazz Festival dedicated to his honor and that of the late saxophonist Lee Morgan. Although he could have stolen the show, he showed his tremendous respect for Morgan and proved once again that he possessed maturity beyond his years. Although he was of the new breed of young players, he revered the older set for their vast accomplishments in the genre.

He composed a long work called "Bluesin'" that he performed with his longtime friend, trumpeter Wynton Marsalis, and the Lincoln Center group. He also toured and recorded with an all-star band that included the legendary Chick Corea. It was a thrill for him to be on a project with another personality from the old guard of jazz.

The mutual respect that the two developed for each other was reflected on McBride's second album as leader, *Number Two Express*. On the work, Corea joined a cast comprised of Kenny Garrett, Gary Bartz, Jack

Dejohnette, Kenny Barron, Mino Cinetu, and Steve Nelson. The highlights of the album included "Miyako," "Jayne," and "A Morning Story," written by Wayne Shorter, Ornette Coleman, and McBride respectively.

A Family Affair, McBride's third solo album, included "Summer Soft," "I'll Write a Song For You," "Open Sesame," "I'm Coming Home," and "Family Affair." All of these songs derived from some of his favorite influences while growing up: Stevie Wonder, Earth, Wind and Fire, Kool and the Gang, the Spinners, and Sly and the Family Stone. Although none of the aforementioned names are considered pure jazz artists, they did have a funky feel for rhythms and melody. The album also featured McBride's own songs "A Dream of You" and "Or So You Thought," with the addition of lyrics. He played electric as well as standup bass on the session.

Around this time, he formed the Christian McBride Band with tenor and soprano sax player Ron Blake, keyboardist Shedrick Mitchell and drummer Rodney Green. They backed him on his next release, *Sci-Fi,* which included songs such as the Police's "Walking on the Moon," Stanley Clarke's "Butterfly Dreams," Steely Dan's "Aja," and Oliver Nelson's "Stolen Moments." The release also contained the originals "Xerxes," "Uhura's Moment Returned," "Via Mwandishi," and "Lullabye for a Ladybug." With each successive release he was creating a strong fan club among fans as well as fellow musicians.

In the past few years McBride has established himself as the number one bass player in jazz, carrying on the tradition of all the past greats. He is now the torchbearer of the legacy and carries the honor with pride. He continues to record and perform in a number of settings with a variety of artists.

Christian McBride is a one of jazz's young turks. He has in just a few short years made a name for himself in the music business, warming everyone who has stood close to his creative fire. His boundless energy is intimidating and his deep talent is truly spectacular. His creative well seems infinite and the future seems very promising.

He is recognized as the best and most explorative bass player in jazz today. Although he has ventured on electric versions, he prefers the acoustic models. He has expanded on the Blanton, Pettiford, Mingus, and Brown axle to create his own unique sound. He plays fat notes with expert control that he can drop like tiny pellets or major bombs. He has broken out of the usual role of the bass player to explore new territory with his highly respected plucked and bowed style.

Although he is acknowledged as a tremendous team player, he is also known for his ability to make the bass a lead weapon. This ability is the desire of every musician who ever picked the instrument and wanted to steal some of the spotlight from others in the group, particularly the front line horn players. McBride has reiterated what Mingus had proven long ago: the bass could be a lead and solo instrument in jazz.

Although his recorded catalog as a leader is limited, he has played on dozens of other sessions. He has backed up such diverse artists as David Sanborn, Kathleen Battle, Diana Krall, Michael Franks, Bobby Hutcherson, D'Angelo, Chick Corea, George Benson, Jimmy Smith, Lee Ritenour, McCoy Tyner, Milt Jackson, and the late, great Betty Carter. One of his more impressive recordings was entitled *Fingerpainting,* a dedication to the music of Herbie Hancock. The trio on the album consisted of trumpeter Nicholas Payton, guitarist Mark Whitfield, and McBride.

He has worked in different mediums. He has given his time as an instructor for the Berklee School of Music as well as the Henry Mancini Institute. He has also taken part in a forum called "Racism in the Performing Arts" and another called "The Influence of Black Performing Arts on Mainstream America." McBride has also been active in cyberspace as host of a weekly series called Jazz Chat for SonicNet.com. Other activities included a role in the movie *Kansas City,* as well as participation on two soundtracks.

He is another of the many practitioners from the very fertile Philadelphia area. He joins Stanley Clarke, Paul Chambers, Clifford Brown, Lee Morgan, McCoy Tyner, Alphonso Johnson, Randy Brecker, Gerry Brown, Joe Beck, Pat Martino, Bobby Timmons, and Philly Joe Jones as modern jazz voices from that city.

Christian McBride is a solid example of the contemporary jazz artist. He has honored the past through the present. Although he is a modernist, he has not forgotten the roots of the music and with his freewheeling bass has proven that the jazz fire lit by Buddy Bolden over a century ago still burns brightly in his very capable, young hands.

Discography

A Family Affair, Verve 557 554.
Gettin' To It, Verve 523 989.
Number Two Express, Verve 529 585.
Sci-Fi, UNIVE UCCV-1001.
The Philadelphia Experiment, Atlantic B00005JXQL.
Vertical Vision, Warner Bros. B000084T3T.

Bibliography

Allen, Daniel. *Bibliography of Discographies, Vol. II: Jazz.* New Providence, N.J.: R.R. Bowker, 1981.

Anderson, Jervis. *Harlem: The Great Black Way, 1900–1950.* Washington, D.C.: New Republic Books, 1980.

Arnaud, Gerald, and Jacques Chesnel. *Masters of Jazz.* New York: Larousse Kingfisher Chambers, 1992.

Baker, Houston A. *Blues, Ideology, and Afro-American Literature: A Vernacular Theory.* Chicago: University of Chicago Press, 1987.

Balliet, Whitney. *American Musicians II: Seventy-One Portraits in Jazz.* New York: Oxford University Press, 1996.

_____. *American Singers: Twenty-Seven Portraits in Song.* New York: Oxford University Press, 1988.

_____. *Improvising: Sixteen Jazz Musicians and Their Art.* New York: Oxford University Press, 1977.

Baraka, Imamu Amiri. *The Music: Reflections on Jazz and Blues.* New York: Morrow, 1987.

Barlow, William. *Looking Up at Down: The Emergence of Blues Culture.* New York: Temple University Press, 1990.

Berendt, Joachime. *The Jazz Book: From Ragtime to Fusion and Beyond.* New York: Lawrence Hill, 1992.

Bernal, Martin. *Black Athena: The Afroasiatic Roots of Classical Civilization.* New Brunswick, N.J.: Rutgers University Press, 1987.

Bernhardt, Clyde E. *I Remember: Eighty Years of Black Entertainment, Big Bands, and the Blues.* Philadelphia: University of Pennsylvania Press, 1986.

Berry, Mary Frances, and John W. Blassingame. *Long Memory: The Black Experience in America.* New York: Oxford University Press, 1982.

Blackstone, Orin. *Index to Jazz: Jazz Recordings 1917–1944.* Westport, Conn.: Greenwood, 1978.

Bradley, Arthur. *Silver Threads.* El Paso, Texas: Aplomb, 1994.

Buerkle, Jack V., and Danny Barker. *Bourbon Street Black: The New Orleans Black Jazzmen.* New York: Oxford University Press, 1973.

Carr, Ian. *Miles Davis: A Critical Biography.* New York: William Morrow, 1982.

Carruth, Hayden. *Sitting In: Selected Writings on Jazz, Blues, and Related Topics.* Iowa City: University of Iowa Press, 1993.

Chambers, Jack. *Miles Davis, 1945–1960.* Toronto: William Morrow, 1983.

_____. *Miles Davis Since 1960.* Toronto: William Morrow, 1985.

_____. *Milestones 1: The Music and Times of Miles Davis.* New York: Beech Tree Books, 1983.

_____. *Milestones 2: The Music and Times of Miles Davis.* New York: Beech Tree Books, 1989.

Charters, Samuel. *The Blues Makers.* New York: Da Capo, 1991.

Cherry, Gwendolyn, Ruby Thomas, and Pauline Willis. *Portraits in Color: The Lives of Colorful Negro Women.* New York: Oageant, 1962.

Cohn, Lawrence, ed. *Nothing but the Blues: The Music and Musicians.* New York: Abbeville, 1993.

Cole, Bill. *Miles Davis: A Musical Biography.* New York: William Morrow, 1974.

Collier, James Lincoln. *Jazz: The American Theme Song.* New York: Oxford University Press, 1993.

Cone, James H. *The Spirituals and the Blues: An Interpretation.* New York: Seabury, 1972.

Cook, Bruce. *Listen to the Blues.* New York: Da Capo, 1995.

Cook, Richard, and Brian Morton. *The Penguin Guide to Jazz on CD, LP, and Cassette.* New York: Penguin, 1992.

Cooper, Sarah, ed. *Girls! Girls! Girls!: Essays on Women and Music.* New York: New York University Press, 1996.

Crowther, Bruce, and Mike Pinfold. *The Jazz Singers: From Ragtime to the New Wave.* New York: Sterling, 1986.

Dahl, Linda. *Stormy Weather: The Music and Lives of a Century of Jazz Women.* New York: Proscenium, 1984.

Davis, Francis. *Outcats: Jazz Composers, Instrumentalists, and Singers.* New York: Oxford University Press, 1995.

Davis, Miles, and Quincy Troupe. *Miles: The Autobiography.* New York: Simon & Schuster, 1990.

Dennison, Sam. *Scandalize My Name: Black Imagery in American Popular Music.* New York: Garland, 1982.

Dicaire, David. *Blues Singers: Biographies of 50 Legendary Artists of the Early 20th Century.* Jefferson, N.C.: McFarland, 1999.

_____. *Jazz Musicians of the Early Years, to 1945.* Jefferson, N.C.: McFarland, 2003.

_____. *More Blues Singers: Biographies of 50 Artists from the Later 20th Century.* Jefferson, N.C.: McFarland, 2002.

Ellison, Mary. *Lyrical Protest: Black Music's Struggle Against Discrimination.* New York: Craeger, 1989.

Erlewine, Michale. *All Music Guide to Jazz: The Best CD's, Albums, and Tapes.* San Francisco, Calif.: Miller Freeman, 1996.

Feather, Leonard. *From Satchmo to Miles.* New York: Da Capo, 1987.

_____. *The Pleasures of Jazz.* New York: Delta Books, 1976.

Finn, Julio. *The Bluesman: The Musical Heritage of Black Men and Women in the Americas.* Northampton, Mass.: Interlink, 1992

Fordham, John. *Jazz.* New York: D. K., 1993.

_____. *Jazz On CD: The Essential Guide.* 3rd ed. North Pomfret, Vt.: Trafalgar Square, 1996.

Friedwald, Will. *America's Greatest Voices: From Bessie Smith to Bebop and Beyond.* New York: Charles Scribner's Sons, 1990.

Garon, Paul. *Blues and Poetic Spirit.* San Francisco: City Lights, 1996.

Giddins, Gary. *Celebrating Bird: The Triumph of Charlie Parker.* New York: William Morrow, 1986.

_____. *Riding on a Blue Note: Jazz and American Pop.* New York: Oxford University Press, 1981.

Gitler, Ira. *Jazz Masters of the 40's.* New York: Macmillan, 1966.

Gleason, Ralph J. *Celebrating the Duke: And Louis, Bessie, Billie, Bird, Carmen, Miles, Dizzy, and Other Heroes.* Boston: Little, Brown, 1975.

Gourse, Leslie. *Louis' Children: American Jazz Singers.* New York: Quill, 1984.

_____. *Swingers and Crooners: The Art of Jazz Singing.* Danbury, Conn.: Franklin Watts, 1997.

Green, Benny. *The Reluctant Art: The Growth of Jazz.* New York: Horizon, 1963.

Gridley, Mark C. *Jazz Styles: History and Analysis.* Englewood Cliffs, N.J.: Prentice-Hall, 1996.

Grimes, Kitty. *Jazz Voices.* New York: Quartet Books, 1983.

Hagar, Andrew G. *Satin Dolls: The Women of Jazz.* New York: Michael Friedman, 1994.

Horricks, Raymond. *Profiles in Jazz: From Sidney Bechet to John Coltrane.* New Brunswick: Transaction, 1991.

Koch, Lawrence O. *Yardbird Suite.* Bowling Green, Ohio: Bowling Green State University Popular Press, 1988.

Larkin, Philip. *All What Jazz: A Record Diary, 1961–1971.* Rev. ed. New York: Faber and Faber, 1985.

Longstreet, Stephen. *Storyville to Harlem: Fifty Years in the Jazz Scene.* New Brunswick, N.J.: Rutgers University Press, 1986.

Lull, James, ed. *Popular Music and Communication.* Newbury Park, Calif.: Sage, 1987.

McRae, Barry. *Miles Davis.* New York: Apollo, 1990.

_____. *Ornette Coleman.* London: Apollo, 1988.

Meadows, Eddie S. *Jazz Reference and Research Materials: A Bibliography.* New York: Garland, 1981.

Palmer, Richard. *Oscar Peterson.* London: Tunbridge Wells, 1984.

Pratt, Ray. *Rhythm and Resistance: Explorations in the Political Uses of Popular Music.* New York: Praeger, 1990.

Reisner, Robert George. *Bird: The Legend of Charlie Parker.* New York: Citadel, 1961.

Roach, Hildred. *Black American Music: Past and Present.* Malabar, Fl.: Krieger, 1992.

Scherman, Tony, and Mark Rowland, eds. *The Jazz Musician.* New York: Saint Martin's, 1994.

Schuller, Gunther. *Early Jazz: Its Roots and Musical Development.* New York: Oxford University Press, 1968.

Shaw, Arnold. *Black Popular Music: From the Spirituals, Minstrels, and Ragtime to Soul, Disco, and Hip-Hop.* New York: Schirmer Books, 1985.

_____. *The Jazz Age.* New York: Oxford University Press, 1987.

_____. *The World of Soul.* New York: Cowles, 1970.

Spaeth, Sigmund. *A History of Popular Music in America.* 12th ed. New York: Random House, 1971.

Spencer, Jon M. **Blues and Evil.** Knoxville: University of Tennessee Press, 1993.

Stearns, Marshall W. *The Story of Jazz.* New York: Oxford University Press, 1970.

Tanner, L.E. *Images of Jazz.* New York: Michael Friedman, 1996.

Tanner, O.W., and Maurice Gerow. *A Study of Jazz.* Dubuque, Iowa: William C. Brown, 1973.

Terkel, Studs. *Giants of Jazz.* New York: Thomas Y. Crowell, 1975

Tirro, Frank. *Jazz: A History.* New York: Norton, 1993.

Travis, Dempsey J. *Autobiography of Black Jazz.* Chicago: Urban Research, 1983.

Ullman, Michael. *Jazz Lives: Portraits in Words and Pictures.* Washington, D.C.: New Republic Books, 1980.

Wilbraham, Roy J. *Jackie McLean: A Discography with Biography.* London: Oxford, 1968.

Wild, David, and Michael Cuscuna. *Ornette Coleman, 1958–1979: A Discography.* Ann Arbor: University of Michigan Press, 1980.

Williams, Martin. *The Art of Jazz: Essays on the Nature and Development of Jazz.* New York: Oxford University Press, 1959.
_____. *Jazz Heritage.* New York: Oxford University Press, 1985.
_____. *The Jazz Tradition.* Rev. ed. New York: Oxford University Press, 1983.
_____. *Where's the Melody? A Listener's Introduction to Jazz.* New York: Da Capo, 1966.
Wilmer, Valerie. *Jazz People.* New York: Da Capo, 1991.

Index

269